Shell Shock Cinema

Mourning the dead. Ellen sits among crosses at the sea (from *Nosferatu*).

Shell Shock Cinema: Weimar Culture and the Wounds of War

Anton Kaes

PRINCETON UNIVERSITY PRESS
Princeton and Oxford

Published by Princeton University Press, 41 William Street, Princeton, New Jersey 08540

In the United Kingdom: Princeton University Press, 6 Oxford Street, Woodstock, Oxfordshire OX20 1TW

Library of Congress Cataloging-in-Publication Data

Kaes, Anton.

Shell shock cinema : Weimar culture and the wounds of war / Anton Kaes.

p. cm.

Includes bibliographical references and index.

ISBN 978-0-691-03136-1 (hardcover : alk. paper) 1. Motion pictures—Germany—History—20th century. 2. World War, 1914-1918—Motion pictures and the war. 3. World War, 1914-1918—Influence. 4. Silent films—Germany—History and criticism. 5. War and motion pictures. 6. Psychic trauma in motion pictures. 7. Culture in motion pictures. I. Title.

PN1993.5.G3K295 2009

833'.909358—dc22 2008053044

British Library Cataloging-in-Publication Data is available

This book has been composed in Minion and Myriad

Designed by Tracy Baldwin

Printed on acid-free paper.

press.princeton.edu

Printed in the United States of America

10 9 8 7 6 5 4 3 2

Contents

Illustrations

All frame enlargements courtesy of Friedrich-Wilhelm-Murnau Foundation Wiesbaden.

Acknowledgments

This book owes most to my students at Berkeley. For almost three decades they have shared my belief that Weimar cinema still speaks to us. Their enthusiasm has inspired my research and their probing questions have sharpened my sense of Weimar's uncanny presence in our time. I also owe thanks to my students in a seminar at Tel Aviv University, whose observations substantially nuanced and expanded my understanding of post-traumatic cinema.

I am indebted to the many interlocutors, often anonymous, at conferences, symposia, workshops, and lectures in various parts of the United States and in Seoul, Beijing, Canberra, Jerusalem, Vienna, London, Cambridge, Amsterdam, and Berlin. Unknowingly they have contributed to the book in its present form. I am grateful to the generous hosts of the various events for inviting me to present my work in progress.

My greatest thanks go to my friend and colleague Eric Rentschler, loyal collaborator for more than thirty years, who has accompanied this book from the beginning. The shape and substance of this project became clearer to me in the course of our many discussions. I also thank Edward Dimendberg, trusted friend and co-editor of our "Weimar and Now" book series, who read the manuscript at a crucial stage and claimed it was finished. Both Rick and Ed are the hidden coauthors of this book, along with Paul Dobryden, my brilliant research assistant, who was instrumental in readying the manuscript for print. Many of my students over the years (most of them colleagues now and some of them Weimar film scholars in their own right) have been involved with the subject of this book in one way or another: Eric Ames, Maya Barzilai, Christian Buss, Steve Choe, Michael Cowan, Melissa Etzler, Sara Hall, Dayton Henderson, June Hwang, Noah Isenberg, Jennifer M. Kapczynski, Kristin Kopp, Barbara Kosta, David Levin, Rick McCormick, Robert Schechtman, Gabriel Trop, Justin Vaccaro, Chad Wellmon, Jennifer Zahrt, and especially David Gramling. There were others, including undergraduate students in my film noir classes, who have challenged my thinking. The book is a product of the many ideas generated in Berkeley's collaborative intellectual environment; nonetheless it goes without saying that all errors and weaknesses are mine alone.

I was privileged to discuss lesser-known Weimar films with colleagues at the bi-annual German Film Institute during the summers of 2004 and 2006 in Ann Arbor. Our spirited exchanges brought the cinema under discussion to life in surprising and compelling ways. I want to thank Johannes von Moltke of the University of Michigan for organizing this exciting forum and the participants of the GFI for their lively contributions.

I am grateful to my friends Nurith Gertz, Roger Hillman, Walter H. Sokel, and David Bathrick, who read the manuscript or parts of it and made excellent suggestions. Other colleagues discussed aspects of the book with me or shared materials: Stefan Andriopoulos, Moritz Bassler, Elisabeth Bronfen, Yun-Young Choi, Jason Crouthamel, Thomas Elsaesser, Michal Friedman, Gerd Gemünden, Michael Geyer, Sander Gilman, Deniz Göktürk, Tom Gunning, Miriam Hansen, Hans-Georg Hofer, Bernd Hüppauf, Martin Jay, Christian Kiening, Gertrud Koch, Niklaus Largier, Paul Lerner, Helmut Lethen, Sandra Meiri, Raya Morag, Yael Munck, Lutz Musner, Judd Ne'eman, Kaja Silverman, Philipp Stiasny, Cornelia Vismann, Joseph Vogl, Wilhelm Vosskamp, Andrew Webber, Jay Winter, and Anat Zanger. Special thanks go to Elaine Tennant for help with the *Nibelungenlied*. I also want to thank my friends at the Deutsche Kinemathek Berlin, who have, as always, been inordinately helpful, especially Gero Gandert, Peter Latta, Hans Helmut Prinzler, Rainer Rother, Christine Seuring, and Werner Sudendorf.

The book could not have been completed without the generous support of several organizations and institutions. First of all, I thank the Alexander von Humboldt Foundation for awarding me the Humboldt Prize, as well as Klaus W. Scherpe and Joseph Vogl for hosting me at the Humboldt University of Berlin. I also extend my thanks to the Mortimer and Raymond Sackler Institute of Advanced Studies (especially Abraham Nitzan and

Ronit Nevo) for inviting me to be a Fellow in Residence at the University of Tel Aviv. I am further grateful to the University of California for granting me the President's Research Fellowship and to Berkeley's Division of Arts and Humanities (especially Dean Janet Broughton and former Dean Ralph Hexter) for their longstanding support.

All illustrations come from original 35mm film copies, and I want to thank Gerhard Ullmann of the Munich Film Museum for making the frame enlargements with his inimitable skill and care. I thank the Friedrich-Wilhelm-Murnau Foundation for granting me permission to reproduce these images. My editors at Princeton University Press, Hanne Winarsky and Mary Murrell before her, deserve the highest praise for their boundless patience and unflagging support. I also thank Mark Bellis for shepherding the book through production with great efficiency and Eva Jaunzems for her passionate copyediting. Although none of the chapters have been published in their present form, the book draws on my previous research on Weimar cinema and culture. Parts of Chapter 2 appeared as "*The Cabinet of Dr. Caligari*: Expressionism and Cinema" in *Masterpieces of Modernist Cinema*, Ted Perry, ed. (Bloomington: Indiana University Press, 2006); portions of Chapter 4 appeared as "Siegfried—A German Film Star Performing the Nation in Lang's *Nibelungen* Film" in *The German Cinema Book*, Tim Bergfelder, Erica Carter, and Deniz Göktürk, eds. (London: British Film Institute, 2002); and parts of Chapter 5 (pursuing a different argument) appeared as "Metropolis: City, Cinema, Modernity" in *Weimar Cinema: An Essential Guide to Classic Films of the Era*, Noah Isenberg, ed. (New York: Columbia University Press, 2009). I thank the respective copyright holders for permission to reprint.

Translations from German are mine unless quoted from a translated source. I checked all published English translations against the original and modified them when necessary. In addition, I compared the English intertitles with the original German for accuracy and connotative range.

I dedicate this book to Christine for bearing with me longer than the Weimar Republic lasted.

Berkeley, California
January 2009

Shell Shock Cinema

Introduction

Very bad form to mention the war.

—Osbert Sitwell, *Out of the Flame*, 1923

"May 9th, 1919. A Friday. Paul Simon returned from the World War." This laconic notation opens Edgar Reitz's 1984 television series *Heimat*, an eleven-part chronicle of German history in the twentieth century.[1] On that Friday in May 1919, Paul, a common soldier, is released from a prisoner-of-war camp and marches home. With the war over, a new life begins for him and for the nation. Or does it?

Striding through the village, Paul pauses a few times: how strange everything looks to the returning soldier! When he finally arrives at his parents' house, relatives and neighbors gather and bombard him with questions, but Paul is unable to respond. "Wasn't it noticeable at the end of the war," remarked Walter Benjamin famously in 1936, "that men who returned from the battlefield had grown silent—not richer, but poorer in communicable experience?"[2]

Paul seems to be caught in another world; his catatonic stare suggests that he is a victim of shell shock. For a brief moment we catch a glimpse of his private hell: a dead comrade comes out of nowhere and stands in front of him, addressing him from beyond the battlefield. Have the dead risen to torment the living? *Heimat* suggests that the ghosts of the fallen soldiers, even though they cannot be seen, coexist with the living. The film juxtaposes two realities: it observes Paul sitting forlorn and delirious in the midst of his family, and it reveals through radical point-of-view shots a subjective, phantasmatic realm that is normally submerged and hidden. The uncanny return of the dead soldier is a function of Paul's traumatic memory and literalizes the power of the past over the present. When the apparition finally vanishes, Paul falls over and faints. He has come home, but the war has come with him. Shell shock has long-term repercussions, not just for the soldier, but also for his family, the community, the state, and the nation.

How do societies cope with the lingering effects of war? How does the shock of humiliating defeat affect a nation's identity? And what part do movies play in making trauma visible? In this book I will argue that the classical cinema of Weimar Germany is haunted by the memory of a war whose traumatic outcome was never officially acknowledged, let alone accepted. Though the Great War was more thoroughly documented in photographs, newsreels, and autobiographies than any previous armed conflict,[3] the painful reality of defeat remained taboo for everyone except left-wing intellectuals and pacifists—the very parties held liable for this devastating outcome. The shocking conclusion to the war and the silence in its wake had disastrous consequences for the first German democracy and its culture.[4] Unspoken and concealed, implied and latent, repressed and disavowed, the experience of trauma became Weimar's historical unconscious. The double wound of war and defeat festered beneath the glittering surface of its anxious modernity. The Nazis exploited that shameful memory and mobilized the nation for another war to avenge the first.

It is fitting that Reitz uses the end of World War I as a point of departure for his account of twentieth-century Germany. Although historians disagree as to whether the Great War was the primal shock (*Urkatastrophe*) of the modern age or the culmination of unbridled industrialization,[5] no one would deny the unprecedented ferocity and destructiveness of the world's first technological war. This eager resolve to engage in unthinking violence is still astonishing today. Machine guns, tactical bombers, submarines, tanks, explosive shells, and poison gas grenades were invented and perfected to systematize mass killing. These weapons inflicted injury and death on millions of combatants and noncombatants alike. Germany ended the war only when its soldiers began to desert and the Kaiser determined that the economic "balance sheet" no longer permitted a continuation of the fighting.[6]

In four years, seventy million people were called to arms, and close to nine million died on the battlefield. Two million German men never returned home. In the Battle of the Somme alone, more than three hundred thousand soldiers killed each other within a few months. These young men were not just soldiers; to those they left behind they were sons, fathers, husbands, fiancés, brothers, relatives, and friends. Many received no proper burial but simply disappeared into the bloody muck of the battlefields. How does the home front deal with carnage on such a scale?[7] Twelve million soldiers came back physically disabled, and untold numbers endured long-term psychological damage.

This book is not about the Great War but rather its tragic aftermath. The term "shell shock," which doctors used to diagnose frontline soldiers suffering nervous breakdowns, provides a metaphor for the invisible though lasting psychological wounds of World War I.[8] Some of the most seminal German movies made in the 1920s found artistic expression for this elusive yet widespread syndrome. Just as shell shock signified a broad array of symptoms, the movies of this shell shock cinema took on a variety of forms. But despite their manifest differences, all of these films found a way to restage the shock of war and defeat without ever showing military combat. They were post-traumatic films, reenacting the trauma in their very narratives and images.

Robert Wiene's *The Cabinet of Dr. Caligari*, Friedrich Wilhelm Murnau's *Nosferatu, a Symphony of Horror*, and Fritz Lang's *Die Nibelungen* and *Metropolis*, all of which are hallmarks of Weimar film culture, represent the most prominent examples of this shell shock cinema.[9] Articulating an indirect, but more poignant understanding of trauma than many traditional war movies, these films translate military aggression and defeat into domestic tableaux of crime and horror. They transform vague feelings of betrayal, sacrifice, and wounded pride into melodrama, myth, or science fiction. They evoke fear of invasion and injury, and exude a sense of paranoia and panic. These films feature pathological serial killers, mad scientists, and naïve young men traumatized by encounters with violence and death. They show protagonists recovering from unspeakable events both real and imagined, and they document distressed communities in a state of shock.

A traumatic event inscribes itself and becomes stored in the body without the mind having any overt awareness of its presence. The trauma returns involuntarily by way of flashbacks, repetition compulsions, and psychosomatic illnesses. Precisely because a traumatic shock eludes conscious understanding, it is not directly accessible to memory or speech; it constitutes a "failure of symbolization."[10] Traumatic experience manifests itself only through its symptoms, and therefore requires that its meaning be constructed retroactively. Three of the four films discussed in this book have narrators who are struggling to reconstruct a traumatic event in the past. These films provide the opportunity to work through that repressed shock from the perspective of the present.

Forced to find a language for extreme psychological states, shell shock films developed aesthetic strategies that pushed the limits of visual representation. In their fragmented story lines and distorted perspectives, their abrupt editing and harsh lighting effects, they mimic shock and violence on the formal level. Shell shock cinema thus contributed to the emergence of a modernist film language that shaped the look of film noir at the end of World War II, and that continues to inspire Hollywood's horror and science fiction movies today.

Unlike the classical war film that uses documentary or staged footage of soldiers in combat, shell shock cinema focuses instead on experiences of loss and grief—experiences that resonate against a background of shared wartime memories. In the early 1920s, the war was a reality so profoundly immediate and pervasive that it did not need to be mentioned by name. The war could remain invisible, but it was present all the same.

Not all films produced between 1918 and 1933 are shell shock films, nor would I claim that the classical Weimar movies considered here are only to be understood as such. These films do gain new and different meanings, however, when read against the backdrop of the war experience and not as precursors to the Third Reich. My project thus seeks to reverse the perspective of Siegfried Kracauer's influential book *From Caligari to Hitler: A Psychological History of the German Film*, published by Princeton University Press in 1947.[11] Traumatized by his forced emigration from Germany in 1933, Kracauer tried to explain to himself and his American readers how the rise of Hitler was possible, even predictable. He hoped to expose, as he put it in the preface to his book, "the deep psychological dispositions predominant in Germany from 1918 to 1933," because they "will have to be reckoned with in the post-

Hitler era."[12] Kracauer also believed that the kind of study he had undertaken could help in the "planning of films . . . which will effectively implement the cultural aims of the United Nations."[13] His book, then, is first and foremost the intervention of a public intellectual in American debates about how to avoid another Hitler. Elucidating Weimar's attraction to fascism was thought to be crucial for the reeducation of the German populace.

Kracauer's use of film as an instrument of sociopolitical analysis was pathbreaking and fully warranted given its immediate postwar context. His method comes at a cost, however, because his persistent "back-shadowing" views history from its catastrophic endpoint, and thus diminishes the contradictory fullness of the discrete historical moment.[14] According to his overarching teleology, all Weimar cinema points forward to fascism. Even a cursory look at the cultural richness of the period after 1918 suggests, however, that Hitler's rise to power was far from inevitable. Considering, in retrospect, the fate of approximately two thousand Jewish and Leftist members of the film industry who had to flee Germany in 1933, one might just as well argue that Weimar films foreshadowed exile and emigration, not Nazism.[15] In order to sustain the master narrative from Caligari to Hitler, Kracauer must downplay not only the diversity of Weimar production but also the aesthetic complexity of individual works. Films are never organic, unified wholes carrying a single message. Rather, they are fractured entities that must be read, like products of the unconscious, by means of their omissions and silences. I am no less interested than Kracauer in explaining why Weimar's modernity ended in the grip of a fascist system; my emphasis, though, is on the ways in which films after 1918 allude to, displace, and relive the experience of war and defeat. For me, Weimar culture is as much post-traumatic as it is pre-fascistic for Kracauer. The Weimar Republic could have ended differently, and films give us glimpses of this alternative history.

The gravity of World War I helped the new medium of film gain respectability and wider acceptance even among the educated class. Newsreels brought moving pictures from the battleground to the home front, making war as well as the nation visible and giving both a narrative dimension. The military defeat in fact spurred German filmmakers to prove that Germany's true identity was to be found in the arts, not on the battlefield. Judging from the polemical pronouncements by Lang and others about Hollywood's lack of *Kultur*, it seems as if the movies continued to wage the war that the military had lost. These filmmakers were eager to transform a denigrated vehicle of mass entertainment into an art form in dialogue with the avant-garde in painting, architecture, and literature of the day, and in open competition with theater and opera. Their artistic ambitions won them respect abroad and, for a brief moment in the early 1920s, even posed a threat to Hollywood's domination.[16]

Still, we must not forget that almost all of Weimar's film output consisted of formulaic genre movies; between 1920 and 1927, an average of five hundred features appeared annually, close to 80 percent of which are no longer available. German studios supported only a small number of artistic endeavors, often at great financial risk. These ambitious films were designed for export as masterworks from Germany and hence were especially motivated to tell stories that were specific to national history.[17] All of the shell shock films under discussion here belong to this group of aesthetically innovative works that have come to form the canon of Weimar cinema. These postwar films of doom and despair became synonymous with expressionist cinema and even with Weimar cinema in general.[18]

A silent film's historical moment—the political, social, and cultural force field within which it was produced, distributed, seen, reviewed, and discussed—is anything but obvious. Many references that were readily understood by contemporary audiences are lost on us today. Although no archive, no matter how immense, will ever allow us to unearth and reconstruct a historical moment in its totality, situating films from the 1920s in their original "habitat" can go a long way toward unlocking and reactivating their symbolic power. This means repositioning films within the cultural production of a time and a place, but also appreciating them as complex appropriations of the world and unique interpretations (not reflections) of historical experience.

The manifest appearance of a film cannot be taken for granted; it is an *event* that needs to be explained—not solely as the expression of an artist's creative sensibility, but also as a social product that reacted to specific concerns and constraints in specific ways.[19] Why, for instance, did a vampire film like *Nosferatu* appear in 1922? What were the questions to which this film was the answer? *Shell Shock Cinema* attempts to study films as entities that arise from and exist in concrete historical moments; that supply aesthetic responses to economic, social, political, ideological, and institutional determinants; and that still resonate with us today. By examining what films implied but did not articulate, by "reading what was never written," we may be able to apprehend the forces that generated a cinema of shell shock.[20]

The War at Home

We could see ourselves that the war made demands not only on the nerves of the soldiers but also on those who had to stay at home.

—Alois Alzheimer, *Der Krieg und die Nerven*, 1915

August 2. Germany declared war on Russia. In the afternoon, swimming lessons.

—Franz Kafka, *Diaries, 1910–1923*

"Can't films be therapeutic?"

—Ari Folman, *Waltz with Bashir,* 2008

1

The Wounded Soldier

There is no such thing as shell shock.

—George C. Scott in *Patton*, 1970

The movie, grainy and silent, begins in the middle. "Groundwater!" flashes on the screen in an intertitle, followed by a view of a young soldier trapped in a collapsed trench. He is buried under a jumble of planks and beams, and gushing water threatens to drown him. A close-up captures his distorted face from above. Like an animal pinned against the wall, he squirms to free himself, his arms flailing. Terrified by the rising groundwater, he screams for help. The camera stares at him, motionless, as if trapped itself. Cut to two soldiers who hack and saw their way through the chaotic wooden structure, struggling, along with a rescue dog, to reach the victim. In a take that seems interminable, the camera's tight frame holds the soldier down, unflinchingly recording his imminent death. Then a sudden cut. Well-dressed men and women enter a sanitarium garden; the camera focuses on a patient, the young soldier, now wearing dark glasses that suggest blindness. We must assume he was rescued at the last minute, but his near-death experience caused a psychic breakdown resulting in the loss of sight—a frequent and unmistakable symptom of shell shock.

According to the film's censorship cards, the soldier was found and saved by the very dog that Ossi, the soldier's fiancée, had given up for military emergency service. The original film apparently had included an exhaustive documentary sequence depicting the ways in which civilian dogs were trained by the Red Cross for service at the front. The dog, named Senta, sits next to her blind master as he dictates to a nurse a letter to his fiancée. Cut to Ossi, played by Ossi Oswalda, a young and attractive star (known as the "German Mary Pickford"), on the home front. Idly lounging on a couch, she seems excited about the arrival of news from the front, which a servant delivers on a platter. The soldier's letter, seen in an intertitle, reads: "Senta has saved my life and almost gave hers. Hopefully I will see you again?" The last sentence, referring to her fiancé's blindness, is deeply ironic. She immediately asks her father if she may "see" him again, and both visit him in the sanitarium. His Seeing Eye dog recognizes Ossi and pulls her along to meet her blind lover. As they embrace, Ossi touches the soldier's eyes, which he tries to cover with his arm. He: "I don't know if I will ever see again, and you want to stay with me?" She, emphatically nodding: "I will guide you—

toward the light." His black glasses glint in the sun; he appears soothed and happy. Cut to a domestic setting, followed by a title: "And a morning of a new vision came." He takes off his glasses, miraculously cured. As the couple opens the window shades, light falls into the room. A final title reads: "With new eyes toward new light." A last image is devoted to a close-up of Senta, the dog who saved our hero's life. The end.

This remarkable ten-minute fragment is all that remains of Georg Jacoby's film *Dem Licht entgegen* (*Toward the Light*). It is the only extant film from World War I that dares to show both the cause and effects of shell shock as a psychosomatic illness. One of the first feature films made for the newly established Universum-Film-Aktiengesellschaft, or Ufa, *Toward the Light* was shot in December 1917.[1] It opened on April 1, 1918, at a time when casualties from the last battles of the war were mounting, and the home front had to cope with thousands of soldiers returning home physically wounded or mentally broken. Because World War I was by and large fought outside of Germany, wounded soldiers became the most visible reminders of the war's devastation. *Toward the Light*'s spatial trajectory—from the trenches to the sanitarium to the living room—illustrated the gradual intrusion of the battlefield into the home front. It also made plain the reward for sacrifice on the home front: by giving up her dog to the war effort, Ossi saved her fiancé's life. Further, because she agreed not to abandon the blinded soldier, she is rewarded with his recovery. The message for the home front was clear: military and civilian lives are inextricably intertwined. If you give to the war effort, you will be amply compensated. Sacrifice pays.

What astonishes in this film is the stylistic contrast between the harsh realism of the trenches and the overdecorated domestic space. As if shot by a different cameraman, the drawn-out agony of the young soldier, trapped and drowning in a collapsed trench, addressed fans of action and adventure pictures. Such films typically showed the hero struggling against the elements and being saved at the last minute. *Toward the Light* maps this genre pattern onto a war scenario, giving the audience a fictional glimpse of what the battlefront was like. The film does not show combat scenes nor does it glorify war; instead it focuses on a war-related, psychosomatic injury and its impact on the home front.

A propaganda film at heart, *Toward the Light* seeks to demonstrate that a woman's selfless loyalty heals the wounds of the broken soldier. The film is specifically directed at women on the home front, who in early 1918 had to face the likely prospect of having husbands and fiancés return from the war crippled or shell-shocked. Men lucky enough to come back at all were often physically or psychologically damaged, powerless, and dependent on the help of others. They returned to wives who had become strong and assertive during their long absence, and who had in many cases been unfaithful. The protagonist's question, "Will you stay with me?" articulates this anxiety. The scene in our film fragment also encapsulates a new power dynamic: while the young man is shell-shocked and childlike, his bride is steadfast and nurturing, assuming the additional roles of mother and nurse.

Coming down to us as a mere remnant of a full-length feature film, like a piece of shrapnel that has accidentally survived, *Toward the Light* is a revealing document. Not only does the film's broken, fragmentary state uncannily reinforce its abrupt stylistic breaks and sudden reversals of fortune; it also dramatically demonstrates the brazen way in which Ufa resignified the life-threatening danger of the battlefield within a propagandistic framework. The film manages to provide a positive, even erotic spin on the crippling illness of shell shock by holding out the hope that with time and affection, even this most mysterious and horrifying psychological wound can be healed.

Although symptoms of shell shock—loss of vision, hearing, and speech; amnesia; paralysis; and sudden violent outbursts—had been reported in earlier wars, the term itself was not coined until about six months into the First World War. In February 1915, an article titled "Contribution to the Study of Shell Shock" appeared in *The Lancet*, the leading British medical journal, in which the military doctor Charles S. Myers described the blindness and memory loss that three frontline soldiers experienced after heavy shelling.[2] Because no physical injury could be found, Myers speculated that the shock caused by bursting shells and exploding grenades brought about yet undetected physical changes (for instance, microscopic lesions) in the brain and spinal cord. Shell shock was understood here as a somatic condition, or basically a wartime variation of what in 1899 the German neurologist Hermann Oppenheim had termed "traumatic neurosis."[3]

According to Oppenheim, traumatic neurosis could be triggered by a sudden physical shock to the central nervous system. Events such as railway collisions, industrial catastrophes, or traffic accidents often set off hysterical or neurasthenic symptoms even in those who had survived the impact otherwise unharmed. Oppenheim himself stood within the nineteenth-century tradition of psychiatry that decreed all mental or nervous diseases to be the

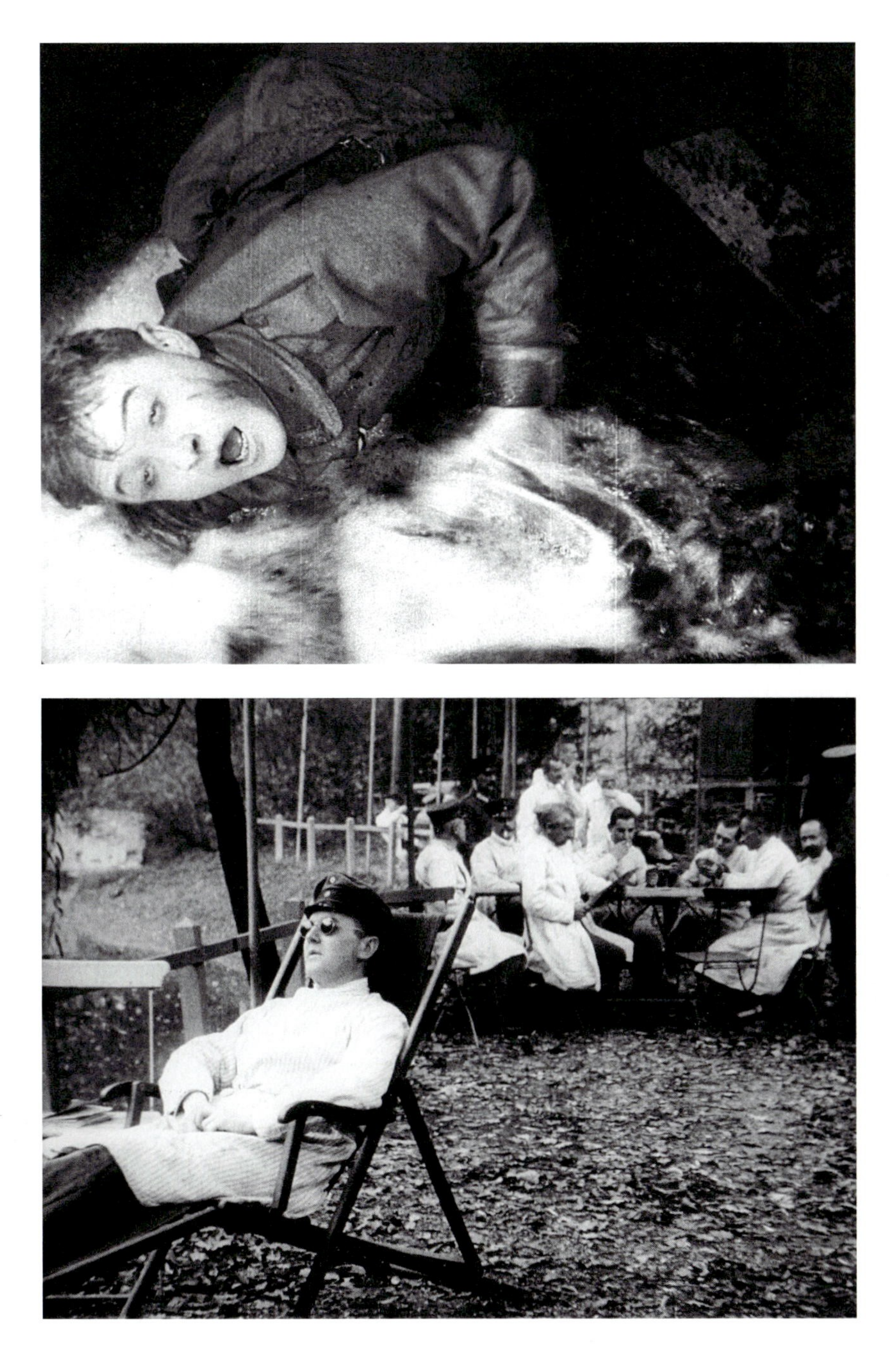

Shell shock victim after he is rescued from a collapsed trench. The trajectory of war—from the trench to the sanatorium—in Georg Jacoby's *Toward the Light*.

result of physical damage to the brain. This somatic theory had come under attack during the 1880s and 1890s, however. Younger neurologists—among them Hippolyte-Marie Bernheim, Pierre Janet, and Sigmund Freud—argued that mental and nervous diseases, including hysteria, neurasthenia, and traumatic neurosis, were not necessarily brain diseases but rather disorders of the *mind*, best treated by mental means—that is, psychotherapy, hypnotism, and psychoanalysis. Hysterical and neurasthenic cases had a wide range of symptoms, including catatonic stupor, shaking, paralysis, blindness, depression, and hallucinations, but no somatic basis for them could be found. The symptoms were present even though no bodily shock to the spinal cord, the peripheral nerves, or the brain itself had occurred. Questions arose: Can there be psychological damage without physical cause? Can bodily symptoms be generated and "willed" by the mind? Was it possible to simulate mental disorder if some advantage could be gained from it?

There were two competing schools in psychiatry at the time of the First World War: one claimed that traumatic neurosis had a physical origin (even though no bodily wounds could yet be detected); the other contended that it was "all in the mind," and thus had more to do with unconscious desire, mass suggestion, and the will to deceive than with physical injury. The debates about traumatic neurosis at the turn of the century gained new urgency in late 1914, after the first major battles had produced an astonishingly high number of mental breakdowns. Soldiers and officers had to be removed from the front and sent to mental institutions for treatment of shell shock. Alois Alzheimer, a professor of neurology and a specialist in memory loss at the University of Breslau, addressed the impact of war on the nervous system in a public lecture in 1915:

> So we see, for example, that soldiers in war lose their speech or hearing or become suddenly deaf-mute simply by being in the vicinity of an exploding grenade. Without being hit by shrapnel or injured in any way, they show signs of paralysis in their legs or in a part of their body, or they experience cramps, totally as a result of the violent shock. In other cases, a so-called cataleptic state develops, a numbed, dream-like state of consciousness, in which the patient appears disoriented about place and time, making all sorts of confused remarks, often tied to the shock experience.[4]

Alzheimer identified other symptoms of this "shock experience," such as somnambulism, sudden unconsciousness, convulsion, tics, and tremors. What he described were typical symptoms of shell shock victims or, as they were called in German, *Kriegszitterer* (war quiverers). The traumatic neurosis of the nineteenth century, associated with railway crashes and industrial accidents, had reemerged on a massive scale as war neurosis.[5]

Traumatic neurosis was the conceptual model used at the beginning of the war when dealing with soldiers suffering mental breakdown. *Kriegsneurose*, or war neurosis, suggests a stronger psychological dimension than is implied in the term shell shock, which emphasizes somatic impact.[6] Shell shock covered a large terrain of psychological and physical illnesses that baffled not only the military but the medical establishment as well. Even the healthiest soldiers on the battlefield could be suddenly stricken by a severe mental breakdown, suffering bodily symptoms that ranged from catatonic stupor to blindness, from shaking to rigor mortis. The number of soldiers turning paranoid, hysterical, and crying uncontrollably was unprecedented. What kind of illness was this?

On the most basic level, shell shock was an unconscious rebellion and bodily reaction to the horror of trench warfare, which on the western front settled into a stalemate as early as the fall of 1914. Weeks of endless waiting in the trenches alternated with suicidal attacks across no-man's-land into the enemy's trench, where soldiers often charged right into the teeth of machine-gun fire. Commanders dispatched entire divisions of men only to see them mowed down in serried rows. The mind-searing mass slaughter of long-range artillery fired by unseen opponents, the bombardment, and the resulting wounds caused long-term "combat fatigue" even among those not suffering from shell shock.

The German military justifiably feared an epidemic of soldiers simulating shell shock symptoms in order to escape the front. It enlisted psychiatrists, who had pledged before all else "to serve our military and our fatherland," to help identify malingerers among war neurotics and return them to the front as quickly as possible.[7] At a 1916 war conference in Munich, the psychiatric establishment decided to reject Oppenheim's view that traumatic (and now war) neurosis must have a physical cause, even if it was undetected and invisible.[8] Instead, it followed Oppenheim's opponents—Robert Gaupp, Max Nonne, Ferdinand Kehrer, and Fritz Kaufmann—who strenuously argued that war neurosis was imagined and willfully induced by morally inferior minds bent on evading military service. These psychiatrists pleaded for the harsh punishment of war neurotics as suspected malingerers. While some doctors treated shell shock by experimenting with hypnosis, strict isolation, and extended hot baths, Kaufmann promoted the use of electroshock (the so-called Kaufmann Cure), applying painful electric currents to scare patients "into health" so that they could return to the front as cured. When diagnosed as deliberate defiance of military duty, war neurosis was suddenly no longer only a medical category; it became a social and political tool, used to repress and regulate behavior that doctors in the service of the military saw as "deviant." For the majority of the psychiatric establishment, the breakdown of a young soldier was considered ample proof of a psychopathological disposition. It is not surprising that war psychiatrists were among the most despised professional classes after the war, and it was clearly provocative to portray the psychiatrist in Robert Wiene's 1920 film *The Cabinet of Dr. Caligari* as a villain who masterminds a string of murders.

Men suffering from shell shock found themselves isolated and estranged from their families at home. Their psychosomatic illness made it hard to resume their place in society. It was up to a propaganda film like *Toward the Light* to suggest ways of reintegrating shell-shocked soldiers into domestic life. Women were called upon to support all men who had been psychologically damaged and physically brutalized by nurturing them back into civilian existence. The sociologist Marianne Weber spoke of the special cultural mission of women:

> How the years of living in foxholes and trenches, in the wet and filth, in ghastly spiritual uniformity, how the experience and commission of unspeakable things have swamped the souls of our male compatriots is difficult to measure. In the struggle for life and death, the form-giving power of civilization is nullified. One can only hope that the millions of men who had to withstand the years of inconceivable hardships have not lost their desire for it.[9]

A film like Jacoby's *Toward the Light* wanted to play a role in the return of these savaged men to civilization. In fact, it stages exactly what Weber suggested: the transition from the mud of the trenches to the feminized domestic space of a living room, from temporary blindness to the bright light of day—with the help of a caring woman. While *Toward the Light* represented war and shell shock in all their cruelty, it also sought to create a forum in which medical (and implicitly political and social) histories could be configured as grand opportunities for the home front to show its gratitude

"I will guide you." Miraculously cured by a woman's love. Adolf Klein and Ossi Oswalda in *Toward the Light*.

to the wounded heroes of the fatherland. The movie industry collaborated with the government and the military in this effort. It was a close (and clandestine) partnership that had begun only a few months earlier, in the fall of 1917, when Ufa was founded.

The Spirit of 1914

Believe us: we shall fight this war to the end as a cultured people for whom the legacy of Goethe, Beethoven, and Kant is as sacred as hearth and land.

—"An Appeal of Ninety-three Artists and Scholars to the Civilized World," October 4, 1914

On August 1, 1914, when the news spread that Germany had declared war on Russia, most of the movie theaters in Berlin canceled their programs and closed early. There was no need for films that day, nor on the days that followed—the action had moved into the streets. History was being made. On August 3 Germany declared war on France, Russia's ally, and on August 4 Germany invaded Belgium. On the same day, Britain declared war on Germany. Soon most of the nations of Europe found themselves drawn into the war. In Berlin, tens of thousands congregated on the broad avenues and plazas, waiting for something to happen in the unusually hot early August days. Newspapers tried to quell the insatiable hunger for news by printing multiple editions each day as well as hourly one-page bulletins with gigantic captions. Shouting "Extra, Extra," street vendors distributed them for free, turning the streets into a giant newsroom buzzing with reports, stories, and rumors. There was no escaping the latest developments. Headlines screamed for attention, small crowds formed spontaneously, and news traveled quickly by word of mouth in the busy streets. The news coursed like blood through the veins of the city. The body politic, united as never before, became mobilized—a unique experience that made both young and old giddy with anticipation and euphoria. As playwright Carl Zuckmayer wrote in his memoir, the declaration of war was greeted as a kind of liberation:

> Liberation from the pettiness and narrowness of middle-class life, from school and cramming, from doubts about the choice of a career, from everything which consciously or unconsciously we

felt to be the stultification of our world—all that we had already revolted against in the *Wandervogel* movement. Now that revolt was no longer limited to weekends and holidays; it was all serious, deadly and sacredly serious; at the same time it was a tremendous, intoxicating adventure. For such excitement we were willing to put up with a little discipline and military drill. We shouted "Freedom!" as we rushed into the straitjacket of the Prussian uniform. It sounds absurd. But at one blow we had become "men," were confronting the unknown, danger, life in the raw. The threat of an early death seemed to us insignificant compared to this. It was in fact a kind of intoxication, a craving for immolation in blood that swept a good deal of the world at that time. . . . We saw the meaning of the war in this inner liberation of the whole nation from its obsolete conventions, in this "breakthrough" into the unknown, into some heroic venture, no matter whom it devoured. This was what fired our enthusiasm.[10]

Tension had been running high for days; the final, official declaration of war came as a relief.

In August 1914, Germany was poised to attack its neighbors under the pretext of defending itself. This paradoxical project required a high volume of ideological confabulation on behalf of the fatherland, and most writers and intellectuals rose to the occasion. Presenting the war as a battle of classical German *Kultur* against the threat of modern Anglo-French-American *Zivilisation*, they spewed forth tirades against "Western" decadence. The patriotic wave swept up even those intellectuals and writers who were known to despise all things political. In fiery articles aglow with nationalist fervor and an unprovoked hatred of Germany's neighbors to the east, west, and north, they emphatically painted Germany as an innocent victim forced into self-defense. In a matter of days, Russia, France, and Britain became mortal enemies. Poems, philosophical essays, and editorials began to spread imaginary and paranoid fantasies of invasion and revenge—fantasies that would live on in many of the plot lines of Weimar cinema.

"I no longer recognize any parties or any denominations; today we are all German brothers and only German brothers," exclaimed the Kaiser in August 1914, suggesting that the war would abolish political and class distinctions.[11] And indeed the enthusiasm for war seemed to do more to unite German society than its political unification in 1871. The number of volunteers was astonishing. In August 1914 alone the German army swelled from roughly 800,000 men to approximately 3 million. In January 1916, there were 4.3 million German soldiers in the field. All classes, from the landed gentry and the educated middle class to workers and farmers, welcomed the declaration of war. Although each particular class had different goals, few objected to the war itself. The war was a wish come true for those who had long complained about the fragmentation, isolation, and alienation of modern industrialized life. The war would simplify things once again. In its enormity, the sheer will to fight a war would eclipse all nuances and subtleties, all discord and strife, as well as the division of labor generated by the process of modernization.

It was the war, in fact, that gave the nation concrete meaning by defining it in unambiguous terms of friend and foe. In war, primordial law rules: life or death, survival or extinction, victory or defeat, us or them. The experience of a collective determination and the awareness of the magnitude of the moment had a rejuvenating effect. Never had the German populace been more energized and inspired. The *Augusterlebnis* meant the life-changing experience of national unity and enthusiasm in the first August days of 1914. It lived on as the "Spirit of 1914," a mythical ideal held up throughout the 1920s but never again attained.[12]

But how was one to express this euphoria? More than a million poems were composed in August 1914 alone—a number that testifies to the unprecedented affective investment of the cultured class in the nation's cause. Even the sixteen-year-old Bertolt Brecht participated in the patriotic frenzy in Augsburg—until, in 1916, he and countless others abruptly changed their tune.[13] Mixing high idealism with aggression, love of the fatherland with contempt for everything un-German, this poetic brushfire was fanned by fear as much as patriotic ardor. Poems such as Ernst Lissauer's "Hassgesang gegen England," known in English as the "Hymn of Hate" (it ended with the lines "We love as one, we hate as one / We have one foe and one alone—England!"), achieved frightening popularity in 1914. Spontaneously and swiftly, poets expressed the shared sense of excitation and self-righteous defensiveness. Journalists and popular philosophers also marshaled their talents in service of the war effort, delivering legitimization and commentary. Novelists and playwrights followed soon after.

What role, then, did the movies play in this unique cultural mobilization? Unlike poetry or journalistic prose, the production of films was an expensive and cumbersome undertaking that made spur-of-the-moment reactions impossible. Creation, distribution, and exhibition required sophisticated technical equipment and extensive facilities. While there were millions of amateur poets and philosophers—every reader was a potential writer—filmmaking was limited to those few professionals hired by film production companies. Thus cinema necessitated a strict separation between production and reception, prohibiting involvement by the audience. While we have thousands of war photographs made by soldiers, film was not for amateurs. The future of the medium itself was in doubt, as the trade journal *Der Kinematograph* acknowledged: "On August 1, the world stood still; it seemed as if everything would sink and disappear."[14]

One of the first decisions of the German government was to ban the importation of films from enemy countries, a measure with unforeseen consequences for the national film industry, which in 1914 was still underdeveloped. In the two years preceding the war, European and American films had dominated the German market while domestic production hovered around a mere 12 percent. Because Germany had an open market, most foreign production companies could do brisk business, opening branch offices in Berlin and elsewhere. Some companies (such as Gaumont and Eclair) even produced films in Germany with German intertitles. Filmmakers and stars from Scandinavia also made movies in Germany—indeed, one of the most celebrated "German" film stars, Asta Nielsen, came from Denmark. Because most of the film companies were inextricably intertwined on various levels of production and distribution, all sorts of evasions were possible after the foreign film ban. The very notion of what constituted a foreign film was far from clear, and hence films from abroad could still be shown after being purchased or distributed by German companies that acted as fronts for foreign distributors. Because the making of any film (unlike the writing of a novel or poem) demanded a large capital investment, the film industry always had its eye on export to recoup the high cost of production; also, requiring little translation, the "universal language" of silent pictures could be understood everywhere. Although the war did not bring the dynamic crossnational traffic to a complete stop, it did initiate a nationalization of the various film industries. It finally forced the German film industry to "think German," to consolidate, and increase its national production, which in contrast to that of France, Italy, Scandinavia, and the United States had been grossly neglected.

Due to its official neutrality, the United States continued to send films to Germany via Scandinavia and initially benefited from the German import ban. In the first two years of the war, American and Danish films were still circulating in German theaters, as were some older French and British films, with their origins obscured or deleted. The market changed again in early 1916 when the Reichskanzler barred imports of dispensable goods, which included film. Only the Danish company Nordisk escaped the ban because it had been heavily financed by German banks and was considered a quasi-German company. When the United States entered the war in April 1917, it lost the German market. As imports dwindled and finally dried up, Germany felt growing pressure to build a national film industry strong enough to compete with the productions of enemy countries. Thus a national cinema was born—not only in the middle of the war but also in the very spirit of (cultural) warfare: German cinema had to be superior to the cinemas of France and the United States. Above all, it had to be "German."

Film and Nation

War is cinema and cinema is war.

—Paul Virilio, *War and Cinema*, 1984

Most foreign films shown in Germany before the war were popular fare—crime serials, Westerns, melodramas, and slapstick comedies—exactly the kind of movies despised and feared by the educated middle class for their corrupting influence on German youth and the national spirit. For the German elite, early cinema's crude images and hectic pace symbolized the decline of culture. By 1913, German cinema was trying to change its image as a fairground attraction into something more respectable. Max Reinhardt, the most famous theater director and impresario of the time, had become interested in moving pictures and had directed a wildly inventive film, *Insel der Seligen* (*Island of the Blessed*, 1913), in which he cast stage actors. Star actors from his company soon appeared in other films as well, raising the level of the medium's acceptance among the educated class. Also in 1913, the respected film director Max Mack succeeded in engaging Albert Bassermann, whom critics called the best actor of his time, for a film titled *Der Andere* (*The Other*), written by the well-known playwright Paul Lindau. Their cooperation produced a film that followed the French *film d'art*, and inaugurated the so-called *Autorenfilm*, or author's film. *Der Andere* foreshadowed a number of motifs of postwar cinema: the split personality of the protagonist, the fascination with extreme psychological states, the uncertainty of moral maxims, and the general threat to the subject's identity—a threat that movie technology had itself produced. Split identity and doubling were also themes in Stellan Rye's *Der Student von Prag* (*The Student of Prague*, 1913), based on a screenplay by Hanns Heinz Ewers. In this film Paul Wegener, another Reinhardt actor, played the role of a student who sells his mirror image only to be confronted and killed in a duel by his own doppelgänger. The neoromantic narrative and special attention to visual effects elevated the film into the realm of art. Despite these valiant efforts to ennoble the technical medium, film theaters were still flooded with Sherlock Holmes serials, melodramas, and adventure flicks.

Shortly before the war, cinema's popular fare had come under heavy criticism by a group of educators, clergy, and self-appointed arbiters in matters of taste and morals—all bent on stopping the "moral decay" and "harmful influence" of the movies, which were fast becoming the public's prime leisure activity. Representatives of this cinema reform movement began their highly publicized campaign in 1912 by making a case for stricter censorship laws against smut (*Schmutz und Schund*). It is not surprising that they took the ban on foreign films in 1914 as a victory for their cause, because for them the war was being fought to defend German high culture against Western civilization. As early as October of that year, Hermann Häfker, the main proponent of the movement, boldly proclaimed:

> So far the war has been the greatest cinema reformer of all. Beyond all else it has accomplished what we had barely dared to dream. It has eliminated the large foreign-rooted business organization representing and guaranteeing the success of trashy movies. This organization miraculously managed to keep alive, week in and week out, in hundreds of thousands of film theaters around the world, the artificial, indeed perverse demand for thousands of worthless meters of film in which the investors, not the movie theaters, have an interest. This organization, which can be traced back to the Pathé model, is broken, and if we have even the slightest understanding of what we want, it shall never return.[15]

Häfker asserted that the war had quickly changed the taste of the masses: everything that was inauthentic, fake, and false had purportedly vanished when confronted with the war's awe-inspiring reality. Yet he admitted that in its present state the commercial film theater was an inappropriate space in which to experience the war's "deepest sorrow and most blessed joy," and he suggested that an outside organization (in addition to the military and the police) should oversee the dignified presentation of war films. No longer merely a resort for thrill seekers and the lower classes, the film theater would become a place where something as grave as the war could be represented and relived. Although the experience would necessarily be vicarious, projected moving images nevertheless could depict the spectacle of war more realistically than any other medium. The war elevated cinema's role as a public institution.

Film theater owners, though, were hard-pressed to make their programs nationalistic and serious. Because at first no footage from the war was available, film theaters showed older films with national themes. For instance, on August 15, 1914, the Monopoly-Distribution Company advertised a "patriotic war program" that consisted of military documentaries made several years before the war: *Überfall auf Schloss Boncourt: Heldentaten eines deutschen Gardeoffiziers, 1870/71* (*The Attack on Castle Boncourt: Heroic Deeds of a German Officer, 1870–71*), *Unsere Marine: Bunte Bilder von der deutschen Flotte* (*Our Navy: Living Pictures of the German Fleet*), and a potpourri of war photographs from previous wars.[16] The ad claimed that this war program had met with broad approval among those who had seen it. Short documentary "war films," which included prewar shots of German soldiers and footage taken far behind the lines in the first weeks of the war, were often added to regular movie fare.

To keep the movie audience up to date, theater owners resorted to projecting slides with the latest news bulletins from the war. These slides, consisting of press releases scribbled on transparent paper and sandwiched between two glass plates, were shown between films, most of which were only one- or two-reelers.[17] According to a report in *Der Kinematograph*, movie houses became spontaneous assembly halls in which a community experienced itself, collectively rejoicing at the latest good news from the front (bad news was censored).

Due to the gravity of the war, most daily movie programs suddenly seemed frivolous. After all, in the eyes of the educated bourgeoisie, the purpose of fighting was to protect German *Kultur* against the *Zivilisation* of Western democracies,[18] and so it was particularly important to take a stand against mass culture and entertainment. Thrills and fun became suspicious, unpatriotic, even un-German. On August 22, 1914, an editorial in *Licht-Bild-Bühne* spoke of the "high cultural mission" that cinema must fulfill at a time when young men were sacrificing their life for the fatherland.[19]

If cinema's entertainment value was under fire, its role as a chronicler of reality was enhanced. Documentary films from the front—soldiers' faces before or after a battle, the devastated landscape, and snapshots of life behind the lines—became as important as fictional stories. The war itself was the adventure—it just needed to be filmed. In contrast to theater's artifice, film's "natural" authenticity was extolled in 1914 as the most fitting expression of the "realness" of the war:

> People find it absurd to allow themselves to be distracted by footlights, by stage make-up, by the affected gestures of prima donnas precisely now at the moment when such violent events are unfolding, when everything is a matter of world history and bitter reality. The theatrical performance seems childish, fake and escapist. . . . The theater has lost its magic. We do not want a dream, we want reality.
>
> The movie theater provides this. Here are the images from Belgium, the smoking rubble of razed villages, the ruins of the Forts Lousin, the cheerful ceremonials of German musicians in Brussels. The dark floor is packed with spectators: they hold their breath; they abandon themselves to their excitement: they are astonished, fearing for their loved ones out in the field. Here is the truth. The cinematic image conjures it up in all of Germany's cities; and in viewing it, each individual takes part in the victories of German weapons, in the efforts of the German men. One thing remains to be noted: Piqued curiosities are not satisfied here. This pleasure has nothing to do with sensation, lasciviousness, or with superficial satisfaction. It is participation which cinema maintains. . . . The cinema has become almost a temple. Unfortunately it had previously been considered an exhibition booth; but here people now partake of emotion, sympathy, and the will to endure.[20]

Because the war lent visible reality itself a new intensity, the mere recording of it seemed more than sufficient. Civilians wanted to experience the war, albeit vicariously. Fake trenches were dug in front of the Reichstag to allow the population to feel what life in them was like.[21] A mixture of curiosity, empathy, and a wish to be part of the war made visitors—including families with children on Sunday outings—stand in line to enter these deep, narrow ditches one by one. To present the trenches as popular entertainment and spectacle was, perhaps unwittingly, a public relations stunt designed to make warfare understandable. The simulation brought the war home and, like the documentaries, involved civilians in an adventure by proxy.

For the first wartime Christmas season, German cinema produced a number of films about the war as it was imagined and experienced on the home front. Films with self-explanatory titles like *German Women, German Loyalty*; *It Should Be the Entire Germany*: *On the Field of Honor*; and *The Fatherland Calls* opened in the late fall of 1914. They told melodramatic stories of crisis in which the war provided the populace with a unique opportunity to prove themselves true German patriots, caring parents or sons, and loyal lovers or friends. Invariably, these films resolved private dilemmas by resignifying them (as in *Toward the Light*) within the public master narrative of wartime national welfare.

In early December 1914, Lunafilm issued one of these short features, Carl Hofer's *Weihnachtsglocken* (*Christmas Bells*), which depicted war as a force that unifies the nation and even transcends social class. The film focuses on Egon Halden, the son of a wealthy landowner, who comes home from the front for Christmas. With him is Hans Herting, a common soldier who has saved Egon's life. Hans falls in love with Egon's sister and would like to marry her, but the glaring class difference makes any union between them unlikely. With the help of Egon, who owes Hans his life, the father finally agrees to the marriage. *Christmas Bells* is a film with a basic message: despite the sacrifices it requires, the war is beneficial for German society because it rewards time-honored virtues such as courage and loyalty, while eliminating class privilege. The film stands out because of its convincingly realistic depiction of the gloom that has spread over even the well-to-do as they wait for their missing son "who is fighting for the fatherland." The mood in the castle lifts only when a telegram arrives announcing an unexpected Christmas furlough for Egon. The film cleverly links the story of Jesus' birth with the story of the war that gave birth to a newly classless society in which the poor soldier marries the daughter of a rich man. These films were not documentaries about combat or battles; instead, they were made to justify the war and the sacrifices it demanded on the home front.

As political propaganda films they differed significantly from those produced by the French, British, or American film industries, which invariably attacked and disparaged their German enemy. On the whole, German film propaganda did not portray the enemy as brutal and bloodthirsty ogres, the way that Germans were depicted abroad. An equivalent to Rupert Julian's 1918 feature film *The Kaiser, the Beast of Berlin*, for instance, would be hard to find in Germany. While faraway nations like the United States and Australia had to mobilize public opinion against the Germans to justify entering the war, Germans went into the war with overwhelming enthusiasm. They saw themselves as righteous defenders of their nation and culture, fighting a war that had been forced upon them. After the first massive losses, the true challenge in Germany was the battle at home. Disconnected from the events on distant battlefronts, the home front needed constant reminders and explanations of the war. Not surprisingly, the movies volunteered to play a large role in this crucial propaganda work. The traditional melodramatic genre with its emphasis on exaggerated national idealism and altruism, on sacrifice and suffering, became the natural vehicle for ideas about the individual's responsibility to the nation in wartime.

The Battle of Images

The war has used up words; they have weakened,
they have deteriorated like motorcar tires.

—Henry James, interview in *The New York Times*, March 21, 1915

Documentaries from the front were supposed to produce semblances of a war experience for civilians at home. In the first two years of fighting, however, the military command—partly for fear of espionage, and partly for disdain of the movies in general—was extremely hesitant to allow cameramen or photographers to shoot "the real thing." The ultimate medium for documenting visible reality could not be used to capture the action on the battlefields, for fear that it might reveal too much.

As early as August 26, 1914, *Der Kinematograph* complained about the lack of film coverage from the front. While illustrated weeklies showed topical photographs from the war, no equivalent newsreels were to be found. In October 1914, the Supreme Command relented and allowed two cameramen representing four film companies to go to the front. Several conditions had to be met: the film companies had to be patriotic and "purely German"; only German cameras and German film stock could be used; the companies had to send reliable representatives to the battlefield; and most importantly, filming was only allowed with the permission of the chief of the army's general staff.[22] It was an impossible task for a few cameramen to cover the entire western front. Because of a rigorous screening and censorship process involving the local police and the military as well as the government, newsreels from the battlefield were slow to reach the movie theaters. Ultimately, Oskar Messter, whose newsreels were known for their reports on current events, natural catastrophes, and train wrecks, was commissioned to make film reports on all war fronts.[23] The "Messter Weeklies" provided short documentaries week after week—a huge industry that processed 4.5 million meters of film in 1916 and 1917 alone. What did they show?

Messter Woche No. 9 of 1915, for example, a newsreel of eight minutes' duration, presents a total of eleven brief vignettes about various aspects of the war away from the battlefield: the arrival of replacement troops, the destruction of houses, soldiers taking a swim behind the front, soldiers waiting two hundred meters behind the trenches, and finally, a parade of U.S. marines in New York. The newsreel is episodic, and often without precise reference to where and when the footage was taken, as if to transmit the atmosphere rather than the specifics of the war. Nevertheless, by dividing the totality of war into discrete segments, the Messter Weeklies gave form to an event that was fundamentally chaotic. War was represented as a complex organizational task, consisting of isolated elements, each with its own function.

The fourth segment, only twenty-five seconds long, is introduced as follows: "A modern battlefield. Threefold trenches, enemy artillery fires in the background. Special shots from our reporter." What we see is a long panning shot of a devastated territory, a scorched landscape completely denuded of trees and plant life. We discern slight elevations of rocky terrain; in the background there appears to be black smoke from artillery fire. It is likely that the censorship office insisted on not specifying the location of the battlefield or the date on which the newsreel was shot. The film simply confronts us with the barrenness of the no-man's-land between the trenches, the eradication of nature, and the absence of human beings, who may be dead or hiding. It is even unclear if the images were made before or after a battle—which itself could not have been filmed live under any circumstances. The sequence is devoid of any kinetic quality and takes on a symbolic dimension; it stands for the desolation of battlefields anywhere.

Because the High Command did not allow any military action to be filmed, the cameras could not show adventure, risk, and action at the front but only the endless waiting and the daily routine: soldiers preparing food, smoking, writing letters, playing cards, or watching movies in a makeshift hut (*Feldkino*). Newsreels from the war soon became so predictable and boring that they drove away the audience. *Bild und Film* wrote at the end of 1914 that "the hopes to see real battles were not fulfilled. There were people who had actually believed the cinematographer could film battles!"[24]

The story goes that an Austrian filmmaker, desperate to capture a moment of drama for the demanding home audience, defied the ban on battle pictures and was quickly arrested by military police. He was told to get out of the line of fire, because the enemy might mistake his highly visible film apparatus for an observation telescope or machine-gun setup and fire on it.[25] Martin Kopp, one of the few cameramen allowed to film at the front, complained in an article: "It's particularly difficult to get scenes from the trenches onto film because the way these trenches are built does not allow cinema to see well. To shoot a direct battle scene is even harder because the cinematographer is of course not informed of a planned attack."[26]

But how can war be shown on film? The spectacle of fighting armies had been a popular subject from the very beginnings of cinema. From the first action pictures of the Boer War in South Africa (1899) and the Boxer Rebellion in China (1900) to the Balkan Wars (1912–13), the lure of clashing armies was irresistible for a medium that laid claim to authenticity and objectivity. D. W. Griffith made *The Battle* in 1911, a one-reeler with staged combat scenes from the American Civil War; *Massacre* (1912), a two-reeler of "Custer's Last Stand"; and *Hearts of the World* (1918), a melodrama (with documentary inserts) commissioned by the British government to rally support for the war against Germany.

German cinema's interest in war also began before 1914. On October 1, 1913, *Der Kinematograph* featured a lengthy article by cameraman Robert Schwobthaler, who reported from the Balkan War front where three hundred thousand soldiers from Greece were fighting. Sixty thousand died in that war, and large parts of Macedonia were destroyed. "As much as possible, we captured this devastation in live pictures," he wrote in 1913, "thus creating a historical document which in its raw truth bears witness to the indescribable destruction and horror of a war."[27] Like his colleagues later in the First World War, he complained that it was nearly impossible to represent the fighting itself because nobody knew when or where a shell might hit. "One only hears the hissing, and once the shell has hit it is too late to set up the camera."[28]

Made at the behest of the king of Greece, Schwobthaler's documentary film *Mit der Kamera in der Schlachtfront: Darstellungen aus dem Griechisch-*

bulgarischen Krieg (*With the Camera at the Battle Front: Images from the Greek-Bulgarian War*) was shown to Kaiser Wilhelm II "at his command." According to an advertisement in *Der Kinematograph* on December 17, 1913, the Kaiser praised these "exceptional moving pictures," which showed for the first time the reality of modern warfare, including "scenes such as the bloody battles between Greeks and Bulgarians; the wasted countryside of Macedonia; starving Greek and Turkish refugees; captured Bulgarians; attacks with bayonets, the impact of shells and shrapnel. Even the dead and wounded in the line of fire were shown, as well as the arrival of the wounded in an ambulance, the moving selfless work of the Red Cross; and the terrible injuries of hundreds of poor soldiers."[29] The advertisement went on to claim that "these pictures were taken at close range in a rain of bullets under risk of death." Another ad declared: "Millions of people will exclaim, 'Down with Arms' after they have seen our Monopol Film *With the Camera at the Battle Front*. . . . [T]he impression of these living pictures on the spectator is such that nobody who has seen these images can ever forget them."[30] This war documentary played in New York on March 1, 1914, drawing five thousand people to a theater that seated only nine hundred. It was again shown during the first weeks in August 1914, in lieu of current footage from the western front.

In *War and Cinema*, Paul Virilio asserted that movie houses became cathedrals of the military state, organizing mass society for war. "The essential capacity of cinema in its huge temples was to shape society by putting order into visual chaos."[31] Moreover, cinema trained the mass audience to live with the potentiality of sudden death. War documentaries in particular had an innate and implicit relationship with death: a soldier captured on film may have been killed the next minute. Although death might not be seen in a war documentary, it always hovered in the air, depending on where the next shell fell.

Already accustomed to adventure films, moviegoers expected war documentaries to be filled with gore and violence. But the very nature of modern technological warfare—its principles of invisibility and deception, its surprise attacks, and inconspicuous weapons like poison gas—made direct and authentic representation of fighting nearly impossible. "A modern battlefield offers the public . . . almost nothing clearly recognizable," stated the editorial writer of *Der Kinematograph* as early as August 26, 1914. "The distances are extremely long, the shooters in the trenches hardly visible, and the whole landscape gives the impression of an almost dead area. Moreover, attack scenes can be shot in the comfort of a prepared studio lot, but not in the proximity of those who are actually fighting."[32] And even if such films could have been shot on location in the trenches, there were still the strict censorship regulations of the general staff. Thus documentary films from the front showed nothing that the audience did not know or expect. *Der Kinematograph* further complained about the lack not only of battle scenes but also of images depicting the private dimensions of the war: the farewells, the preparations of young men about to join the army, and "other small yet gripping scenes characteristic of a society mobilized for war."[33]

The First World War was also difficult to capture on film because much of it took place underground, in rat-infested, muddy trenches, where hundreds of men lay hidden from view, waiting, often for weeks, to attack or be attacked. "To be seen was to be dead"—this slogan epitomizes the aporia for visual media in the first all-out technological war. What is there to show if nothing is visible, if all is hidden or camouflaged? "When they sit full of expectation in front of their hometown screen, the voyeuristic spectators in the movie theaters demand the most 'turbulent scenes' and don't understand that the more static and still films are, the more reality they have in them."[34] Static reality runs counter to the expectations of the movie-going public and counter to the nature of moving pictures. Because no scenes from the decisive battles could be screened, interest in war pictures soon waned.

A Medium for Deception

Viewed as a drama, the war is in some ways disappointing.

—D. W. Griffith, interview in *Photoplay*, March 1918

On August 10, 1916, while the fighting was still on-going, the British premiered a full-length "documentary" film on the Battle of the Somme. Lasting from June to December 1916, this engagement was one of the bloodiest of the entire war. Instead of breaking the deadlock on the western front, it produced a million casualties on both sides. Two British newsreel cameramen from the Committee on War Films were present during the first two weeks of the offensive—an attack by thirteen divisions along an eighteen-mile front that resulted in fifty-seven thousand British casualties. With heavy stationary cameras mounted on tripods and cranked by hand, they captured companies of infantry marching in formation. They caught artillery batteries in action and wounded Germans; they also filmed an actual attack—the infamous over-the-top maneuver in which thousands charged up out of the trenches across no-man's-land into enemy machine-gun fire. This attack was, however, staged behind the front lines and edited into the documentary, as is clear now when studying camera locations, camera angles, and mise-en-scène.[35] Even authentic footage of the battle was shaped by the presence of the camera, of which the soldiers were clearly aware. Although it was the War Office that supplied intertitles and released the film, *The Battle of the Somme* counts as the first cinematographic document of actual fighting on the front, and as such it had an enormous impact. More than sixty minutes long, it was the first time that the British at home saw realistic moving pictures of life and death at the front. Film represented a unique opportunity to enlighten women on the home front about the war so that they could admire the heroism of their fighting men, nurture them back into health, and see meaning in their deaths if they did not return.

Although *The Battle of the Somme* presented the British as victorious, it also suggested—perhaps unintentionally—that there would be no winners in this war. Though the deaths were staged, it was nonetheless the first time that a state-commissioned film showed men getting killed on the battlefield. As the camera follows several soldiers scrambling out of a trench, one of the soldiers slides back down its sloping wall, hit by an invisible bullet. Other soldiers also fall to the ground.

Despite these shocking images of simulated death, the War Office used *The Battle of the Somme* as propaganda to show the British army's resolve against the Germans. The intertitles create a coherent narrative in which the British are supposedly winning, despite the fact that individual scenes appear random and fragmentary, lacking identifiable characters or a linear story line. Here it finally was: a memorable film that changed the way the home front imagined the war.

The Battle of the Somme was widely shown in Great Britain, the Commonwealth, and most of the neutral countries as well, where it had only weak competition from German films. The official in charge of German film propaganda in Scandinavia sent a cable to Berlin complaining about the poor quality of German propaganda films and arguing that viewers were begging for "the most gruesome, sensational scenes of battle, similar to the English Somme film."[36] Even though the fighting scenes were faked, they looked authentic to contemporary viewers. And through editing and the use of intertitles, calculated messages were infused into the film. *The Battle of the Somme* was not shown publicly in Germany, but the German military command studied its effectiveness as propaganda and tried to copy it.

It was not until 1916 that the German government and military even acknowledged the importance of film propaganda abroad. All countries not directly involved in the war were inundated with films from France and Britain asserting their cultural as well as military superiority over Germany. They also presented films that staged atrocities allegedly committed by German soldiers against unarmed Belgian civilians. As early as 1914, the American Life Photo Film Company began producing bogus war documentaries in New Jersey, showing actors in German uniforms brutalizing and killing innocent women and children. Intended to incense the American public and prepare it for eventual entry into the European war, these films introduced images of physical cruelty previously unknown in cinema, and they did so in the name of "documentary truth." War propaganda reproduced the violence of warfare on the home front.

The popular success of British film propaganda in 1916 seemed to have jolted the German High Command into action. It abandoned the arrogant stance that the movies were unfit to serve the national cause. Of course, it was paradoxical to first denigrate the movies as the odious epitome of Western modernity and then to use them as a weapon in the fight against that very same modernity. Nevertheless, cinema, which Oswald Spengler had once placed on the level of "boxing contests, nigger dances, poker, and racing,"[37] soon became the High Command's favorite instrument for shaping public opinion, both at home and abroad. In order to control Germany's image, censorship of films for export was introduced in January 1917.

One important organization founded during this period was Bufa (*Bild und Filmamt*, or the Photography and Film Office). Established by the War Ministry in January 1917, its purpose was to coordinate the various film initiatives and to use the new medium to mobilize the masses.[38] Modeled after the French army's Service Cinématographique, its main tasks were to deliver German films to the western and eastern fronts as well as to foreign countries, and to supervise the import and export of films. Bufa's first public event was the January 16, 1917 premiere of a thirty-minute documentary titled *Bei unseren Helden an der Somme* (*With Our Heroes at the Somme*). The film broke new ground in that it contained realistic shots of battle. It was celebrated in the press as Germany's answer to *The Battle of the Somme*, on which it was obviously modeled. Reviews of the German film emphasized the immediacy with which civilians could now for the first time envision the front. "Words, a hundred times heard, are now pictures. How simple it sounds in a military report: we detonated a mine in the Saint-Pierre-Vaast forest and sprang from a trench. You should see this film. It will give you an idea of how 'simple' it really was: the detonating of the mine and the springing from a trench."[39]

In a particularly enthusiastic review, Hans Brennert tried to convey the exhilaration of war as experienced through the film:

> From the hell of Somme, from the flaming earth of the Saint-Pierre-Vaast forest, heroic German film team operators, at the command of the highest military leadership, have created the greatest cinematic document of this terrible war. Steel helmets on their heads, cameras in hand, they faced direct enemy fire alongside the long transports of storm troops. They attacked the first trenches, experienced the gas attacks, and in spite of fierce enemy fire, poured over the tops of the trenches with the storm troops. They moved from crater to crater, over forest and field, through barbed wire, ditches and wild forest streams, with the minelayers, between the sharp blows of heavy shells and bursting mortars until, aided by the wall of fire from our barrage, they tossed hand grenades at the fleeing enemy.[40]

Like its British predecessor, the German Somme film contained authentic and staged documentary footage side by side, including images of German soldiers enacting an "over-the-top" attack. Judging from camera positions and the undamaged countryside, film historian Rainer Rother has determined that these shots were most likely filmed in a training area behind the front lines.[41] Furthermore, inconsistencies in the type of helmet (the pickle helmet was replaced by a steel helmet around 1916, but the film contains both) reveal that the film spliced together footage from different time periods. *With Our Heroes at the Somme* is an obvious propaganda film made both for audiences abroad and on the home front. It begins with a brief segment titled "How German doctors provide for the wounded enemy," which shows soldiers being lifted into an ambulance. While these images are designed to exhibit the generous side of Germans, other segments blame the destruction of towns on ruthless shelling by the French and British. One intertitle asks the rhetorical question, "Toppled towers and dead debris are asking the world: Who are the barbarians?" The film ends with a long pan across a cemetery where crosses have been hastily stuck in the ground. This surprising scene is introduced with a title card that quotes a popular military song from Germany's victorious liberation war against Napoleon in 1813: "Those who found death in the holy battle are resting in their fatherland even if buried in foreign soil." Such a memento mori was meant to assure the home front that death was meaningful—even on French territory—because it meant ultimate German victory.

The German film, only about a half hour long, was more a critical than a popular success. It ran as a second feature in Berlin's main theaters for three weeks in tandem with such films as Joe May's *Die leere Wasserflasche* (*The Empty Water Bottle*), a "Detective-Adventure-Satiric Drama in Four Acts." *With Our Heroes at the Somme* was neither a commercial nor an aesthetic breakthrough, but it was a turning point in the cinematic representation of the battlefield, heralding the sudden recognition of the medium's propaganda value.

The few reviews that were critical of the German Somme film pointed out the basic contradiction inherent in any war film: the impossibility of filming brutal and senseless violence without making it into an aesthetic object. A perceptive reviewer complained:

> Overall, the film prettifies! Man, who patiently suffers in war, is so small and insignificant in modern battle. The optical lens, an aesthete without feeling, takes distant bits of landscape, composes, and is the architect of wonderful landscapes, seen through a silver cloud. . . . It never looked this way in the eyes of a soldier, and never felt this way in a soldier's heart.[42]

The writer alludes not only to the irreality of the staged documentary but also to the filmmaker's mediation, which mocks the real experience of a soldier. The optical lens is called an "aesthete without feeling"—a brilliant turn of phrase because it highlights the paradoxical nexus of the objective, unfeeling coldness of a technical device with the aesthetic spirit that inheres in framing, selecting, ordering, and depicting (i.e., creatively reproducing) a segment of reality. It is the structuring act of filming itself that simplifies, and thus distorts, war's incoherent jumble of events, noises, smells, spaces, emotions, and memories.

The borders between warfare and daily life were further blurred when cinematographic shooting ranges opened to the public. The moving targets were actually short film loops projected on a screen, thereby offering the shooter, as a popular science magazine proudly proclaimed,"the opportunity to practice shooting animals, airships, automobiles, horse riders, motor boats, etc." Also included were, "for instance, Serbian troops which appear on a mountain top trying to climb down an incline, using every possible cover."[43] Shooting at them had visible results: if the projection screen was penetrated, the film stopped to show the bullet hole as a point of light and register whether the target was hit or not. After a moment's pause, the film moved on. The article assured its readers:

> That this invention represents not only a source of entertainment but that it has importance for the training of soldiers in firing weapons, is demonstrated by the lively interest of the military in this innovation. Already in May of this year a first cinematographic shooting range was dedicated at a training area in Döberitz in the presence of the Kaiser.[44]

A crude prototype of today's video war games, this cinematographic shooting range shows the remarkable interpenetration of military and civilian life. The simulated shooting of Serbian troops for fun also demonstrates how quickly the population had become militarized. War was no longer confined to the front. It had become mass entertainment.

The New Empire

One has to recognize the war underneath the peace.

—Michel Foucault, "From the Light of War to the Birth of History," 1976

Erich Ludendorff, major general and chief manager of the German war effort, had been one of the first to realize that the enemy was fought not only on the battlefield. An avid proponent of propaganda, he had suggested from the beginning of the war that film be utilized to manipulate public opinion. However, it was not until July 4, 1917, after the debacles of Verdun and Somme, that he wrote his famous letter to the Ministry of War, a letter that is today considered the founding document of the Universum-Film-Aktiengesellschaft (Ufa): "The war," he wrote, "has demonstrated the supremacy of image and film as instruments of education and influence. . . . Unfortunately, our enemies have so thoroughly exploited their advantage in this area that we have suffered serious harm as a result."[45] Ludendorff was referring to the propaganda shorts made by the British and French showing German atrocities in Belgium, and of course to the wildly successful British pseudo-documentary *The Battle of the Somme.*

To make up for past errors in underestimating the power of mass media, he strongly suggested embracing the very medium that the Right had maligned as a contemptible symptom of Western modernity. He proposed no less than a radical reversal in policy: consolidating the movie industry with Deutsche Bank funds, placing it secretly under state control, and concealing the deal as a business venture. At Ludendorff's urging, on December 18, 1917, less than a year before the war's end, Ufa was founded as a new umbrella organization financed jointly by the state and private industry. It was designed to oversee both domestic and foreign film propaganda, and to coordinate the activities of the commercial film industry in relation to the war effort. Ufa bought Nordisk for twenty million marks, along with a number of other German film companies (including PAGU, the company that made *Toward the Light* in 1917–18). It is significant that the government wanted to hide its leading role in this venture from the public, so that Ufa's films would not appear to be mere propaganda. From the beginning, in fact, Ufa's mandate had been to improve the quality of films while still serving the interests of the armed forces and big business. The High Command and the imperial government would unite propaganda and high art, in order to express "the German spirit, German economic power, and German science abroad."[46]

After the war, the German government's secret involvement in Ufa was exposed and publicly condemned in the National Assembly. Even though the state had to sell its holdings in the company, the consolidation of the German film industry had produced an unprecedented pool of artistic talent in every department, spanning screenwriting, acting, set and costume design, as well as directing. Fully privatized in 1921 and incorporating Decla-Bioscop, Ufa soon became the largest film enterprise in Europe, and Germany's film production in the 1920s was second only to that of the United States.

Born from the spirit of war, Ufa did everything possible to conceal its origins as a military propaganda tool. War was taboo with Ufa as with other film production companies after 1918. Nevertheless, traces of it can be found in even the most commercial movies of the period. For example, on November 9, 1918, the day the Kaiser abdicated and Germany was declared a republic, movies shown in theaters included *Die Sünden der Väter* (*Sins of the Fathers*), *Der Gattenmörder* (*The Husband's Murderer*), *Verlorene Töchter* (*Lost*

Daughters), and *Im Zeichen der Schuld* (*Under the Sign of Guilt*). As if to mock the *grand récit* of political events, these popular movies unconsciously resignified the political discourse of defeat, deceit, and betrayal into private melodramas that dealt with crime and guilt, lost children, and the sins of the older generation. While at first glance these movies seem undisturbed by the day's chaotic events, they betray a historical unconscious of which neither the filmmaker nor the audience was likely to have been aware.

Shock at the unexpected outcome of the war, which ended with Ludendorff's hasty request for a cease-fire on September 29, 1918, was compounded by a feeling of mutual betrayal: the population felt deceived by the military command, the government, and the media for having been misled about the progress of the war; in turn, Ludendorff and the army claimed that in fact it was the home front that had betrayed the army. The returning soldiers, disillusioned and weary, did not join in the Leftists' struggles against the nationalist press and the government. Bertolt Brecht's *Trommeln in der Nacht* (*Drums in the Night*), written in 1919, features one such soldier, who came back from the front only to find his wife in the arms of another man. Confronted with the choice of joining the Spartacist revolutionaries or reuniting with his wife despite her infidelity, he chooses the latter course. He even rails against revolutionary idealism: "Hahaha. My flesh should rot in the gutter so that your Idea can be victorious? Are you drunk?"[47]

Movie houses overflowed after the war, as did theaters and dance salons. At the movies the masses found safe entertainment, an alternative to the turmoil of the streets, that nevertheless frequently alluded to relevant moral dilemmas or high-risk scenarios. Domestic melodramas expressed the mood of the home front, while adventure serials echoed the treacherous experience of combat. Popular serials named after their lead actresses (such as the Ira Witt, Mia May, or Lu Synd serials) often represented the home front's attempt to renegotiate a set of previously patriarchal gender relations that had been disrupted and discredited by the war. What was expected of women now that the war was over? Was it, as Marianne Weber suggested in 1918, a woman's duty to help the soldier-turned-civilian reacclimate to society? Or could women now maintain and pursue the independence that had been thrust upon them while the men were away?

Many films during the Weimar Republic register and negotiate a crisis in gender relations brought about by a war and military defeat that left two million young men dead and countless more crippled or psychologically damaged. The serials showed no compunction about making their heroines suffer—like soldiers in battle—through all manner of perils, thus restaging again and again in the confined environment of a movie theater the trauma of near-death experience in war. At the same time, the serials offered their female viewers a range of possible strategies for dealing with troubled patriarchal relations. It was not only in adventure and action films but also in melodramas of suffering men and women that the war lived on.

Mental Breakdowns

This war comes from the decadent conditions of the time.
It is the true realization of the status quo.

—Karl Kraus, *Aphorismen*, 1915

Written in 1916, Carl Sternheim's short story *Ulrike* depicts the gradual decline of its eponymous heroine into self-destructive madness. The text, composed in profligate expressionist prose, shows how Ulrike, a young Prussian aristocrat and volunteer nurse at a military hospital, becomes drawn into the war by assimilating herself to the abject position of the crippled soldiers she is attending. Traumatized by her grotesquely disfigured patients, who taunt her sexually, she strips herself of all layers of civilization, mimicking the raw passions that she imagines soldiers experience in their struggle for mere survival. Becoming ever more unhinged by her exposure to her patients' utter misery, she fantasizes about sexual submission and imagines herself living barbarously in an African jungle. Ulrike is presented as an avid moviegoer. In Berlin she visits the cinema "every free hour," drawing succor from films that correspond to her emotional needs:

> Creatures were shown in situations that were barely probable but opened channels to familiar emotions. There were natives in the bush, revengeful Indians on the warpath, jackals in hunting frenzies, but the viewer could always participate in the creatures' violence. God, as it were, remained visible. Not Christ but Jehovah, Mohammed or a fetish that ran things in a higher sense. There was retribution in murder, hunger in robbery, crime before verdict. Music made in the orchestra accompanied these events. Hardened by the fiery gusts of such adventures, Ulrike was able to perform her daily work more easily.[48]

The anonymity of death.
Robert Reinert's *Nerves* links
war and murder.

Overwhelmed by the senselessness of chance and coincidence that caused one soldier to die and allowed another to survive, Ulrike treasures the movies where stories have a measure of justice and logic. The exotic adventure movies also serve as stand-ins for war movies—the conflicts remained the same: good versus evil, friend versus enemy, honor versus cowardice, violence versus peace. The simulated world of the movies, however, soon screens out the real world: "The fire close to the hotel did not interest her because another fire had burned more strikingly in the movies. On the screen a victim overcome by smoke could be rescued through a window, while in reality cries behind the wall of smoke indicated a bad ending."[49] Fueled by the movies, Ulrike's fantasy life of willed abjection takes over and she gives in to her death wish. Cinema is portrayed not as a cause for her descent into insanity but rather as a risky refuge from an unbearable reality caused by war. Whereas Sternheim's *Ulrike* provides a glimpse at the possibility of secondary trauma on the home front, Robert Reinert's rediscovered film *Nerven* (*Nerves*) illustrates how secondary trauma spreads like a contagious disease, ravaging individuals, families, and entire communities.

Nerves encapsulates like no other film the anguish of the turbulent months that saw the end of military action and a subsequent civil war. The film was shot in Munich in the summer of 1919, in the aftermath of a proletarian revolution that failed to overthrow the old social order. It was released in Munich in December 1919, about three months before *The Cabinet of Dr. Caligari* opened. The Berlin premiere of *Nerves* on January 22, 1920, predated *Caligari* by less than five weeks.

Digressive and fragmentary, Reinert's film follows a group of people whose nerves have been shattered by war and revolution; traumatized and racked with guilt, they exist on the edge of madness.[50] The film's own perplexing narrative structure imitates the liminal mental states it portrays, ranging from despondency to suicide, from agitation to delirium, from mental breakdowns to hallucinations of a harmonious life in nature. "In my own nerves I recognize the nerves of the world. The nerves of the world are sick," we read in an intertitle that demonstrates the film's project as a commentary on the collective disposition in 1918–19. The film's title, *Nerves*, also alludes to the Kaiser's contention in 1910 that victory in the "coming war" would be decided by which nation had the strongest nerves. Ascribed later to Paul von Hindenburg, this mantra was well known on the home front, and the film appears to comment on Germany's obvious failure of nerves.

The telepathic power of film editing: a mother sees her son die on the front in Reinert's *Nerves*.

The film begins with a brief prologue that shows a mother reacting to her son's dying on the battlefield. Film editing makes the juxtaposition of home front and battlefront possible. The camera cuts between mother and son, even suggesting an uncanny telepathic relationship between them. The first shot captures a middle-aged woman suddenly leaning forward as if something has caught her attention. The film then cuts to a highly stylized battlefield with bodies strewn around a dead tree stump, smoke rising in the background, a single large wheel from some vehicle looming disconnected in the background. A grenade must have just hit and killed several men. A young soldier, his head bandaged, is carried off, followed by a cut back to the mother peering offscreen. An intertitle stating, "Mother! A thousand miles from the homeland your son is dying," is followed by a close-up of the son gesturing with his raised hands and exclaiming, "Mother!" We then see a close-up of the mother, who similarly throws up her hands in desperation. Cut back to the son who with wildly exaggerated bodily convulsions expires. An intertitle addresses the mother: "Mother! Mother! You feel it a thousand miles from him at the same minute. What is this?" She collapses in a final close-up.

The tantalizing question "What is this?" is answered in a brief sequence of shots that at first glance seems completely disconnected from the war sequence. Preceded by his shadow, a dark-clad man enters the frame, furtively looking at something offscreen. An intertitle exclaiming "Murderer!" appears. The man seems startled. Another intertitle addresses the murderer directly: "You who are not deterred from anything." He suddenly seems to catch a glimpse of his victim, a sleeping woman. He lunges at her and strangles her. To keep the murder abstract, we do not know the identity of the murderer or of the woman, nor can we imagine a motivation for the murder. We see the victim for no more than a split second, and immediately after the crime, the murderer's nervous gaze (underscored by an unsteady camera) fastens on a bird in a cage. "The poor creature," the intertitle states, "it dies without water—it dies." Looking deranged and haunted, he gives the bird water before running away. End of the prologue.

None of these characters will play a major role in the main story, thus making these opening scenes extremely enigmatic. While the mother appears briefly to mourn her second son, who is executed by soldiers, images of the murderer flash up later in one of the character's feverish hallucinations. The murderer sequence, which juxtaposes cold-blooded murder and compassion for a helpless creature, provides an answer to the earlier sequence that portrayed the death of a soldier. The film dares to ask about the meaning of death on the battlefield—"What is this?" the intertitle reads—and dares to equate this death with murder. Still, the murderer who commits the crime without passion, almost mechanically, is also shown as someone who cares about the survival of a bird in a cage. Killing and being killed are two sides of the same coin in war, as is schizoid attention to the needs of an animal immediately after a murder is committed. The prelude's juxtaposition of these two sequences also equates killing on the battlefield with crime on the home front.

The ensuing narrative provides several instances of irrational behavior, self-abjection, and nervous breakdown. The film often takes unexpected turns, compresses cataclysmic events into a few images, and in general tries to invoke a state of "nerves." The cinematographer (Helmar Lerski) experiments with space; frequently the characters come toward the camera or appear uncomfortably close, forcing on the viewer various degrees of hysteria and madness.

The story begins with the recognition of a rupture: Marja, the female protagonist, who in her exaggerated gestures and bodily gyrations prefigures Ellen in *Nosferatu* two years later, stops the preparations for her wedding. "Don't you feel," she asks her mother who holds her gown, "how mysterious currents quiver through the air, how the earth shakes under something unprecedented and monstrous?" She becomes agitated watching a steady stream of revolutionary workers marching by her house—ostensibly a staged scene, but of documentary value because it refers to the organized workers' revolt which took place in Munich while the film was being shot.

Marja's question also addresses the heightened sense of anxiety and nervous apprehension in the wake of the war. Her brother, an industrialist, is shown as a shell shock victim who has "lost his nerves." He trembles and is haunted by bad dreams, flashbacks, and "overexcited nerves" that make him imagine things (for instance, the rape of his sister). Strangely enough, the film shows what he hallucinates as real occurrence, thereby deliberately disorienting the viewer. The film also depicts the collapse of the brother's factory in a huge cloud of smoke, and we begin to suspect that this may also be a figment of a fever dream. He consults a psychiatrist, who gives the following diagnosis when asked about the causes of his nervous disorder: "The continuing civilization, the struggle for existence, the fear and horror of the war, the sins of the parents."

While it is true that debates about nerves and nervousness emerged in the late nineteenth century and were invariably linked to discussions about the psychological consequences of industrialization, the issue of "strong nerves" achieved new relevance during and after the war. Seen from this angle, war and revolution were symptoms of a larger malaise: a collective neurasthenia in response to belated but frenzied modernization and urbanization. The discourse on nerves also allowed the filmmaker to create a nexus between the battlefield and the home front. The very fact that a film in 1919 represented a case study of a civilian suffering from *imagined* guilt, specifically the guilt of having killed someone, proves that symptoms of shell shock are not confined to soldiers alone. As in Sternheim's *Ulrike*, the home front is shown to be susceptible to secondary trauma resulting not only from caring for traumatized soldiers (so-called compassion fatigue) but also from identifying with the fate of others, be it real or imagined. *Nerves* stages the precise traumatic implications of empathy: the industrialist "sees" his sister's imaginary rape because the camera actually shows it. The film, then, suggests that it, too, could render things merely imagined real and that those imagined realities could have a traumatizing effect. Many writers and critics at the time remarked on the psychological edginess of postwar society, oscillating between excitation and exhaustion of nerves.[51] *Nerves*, writes a reviewer in July 19, 1919, presented the "incendiary fuel," created by war and misery, as a "nervous epidemic that has gripped mankind and has driven it to actions and guilt."[52] In contrast to Jacoby's propaganda film *Toward the Light*, which focuses on the private fate of a shell-shocked soldier—from his near-death in the trenches to his recovery—Reinert's film dramatizes the extent to which the toxic effects of war and defeat have infected an entire culture. War and revolution are portrayed as events that have disturbed the natural, cosmological order, such that human beings seem no longer in charge of their own lives. Buffeted by malevolent historical forces, they struggle to understand what is happening to them. Since films tell stories, these forces frequently appear embodied as evil doctors, bloodthirsty vampires, or powerful industrialists. But more often than not, the viewer shares the traumatic helplessness of the victim.

By the end of the war, German filmmakers realized that a truthful and realistic depiction of technological warfare was not possible; no film could convey the experience with full authenticity. Although the war at first initiated a new interest in documentary film, the result was disappointment, followed by a return to the fantastic streak in German cinema that had its auspicious beginning in Stellan Rye's *The Student of Prague* (1913), which itself builds on the romantic tradition. Sharpened by the war's assault on sight and sound, postwar films addressed questions of perception. They focused on the medium-specific difficulty of distinguishing between the record of visible reality and the subjective vision that necessarily distorts it. Stories about deception, delusion, and madness abounded, and narratives became intricate affairs that interlaced memory and hallucination. In defiant opposition to the staged realism of war pictures, some films foreswore realism altogether, breaking up coherent story lines and ignoring the pictorial conventions of realist art to make visible the war's destructive force. Viewed in this light, Wiene's *The Cabinet of Dr. Caligari* may be the ultimate film about war.

Tales from the Asylum

When Reisiger was picked up and brought to Corps headquarters, he announced that he considered the war the greatest of all crimes. He was therefore put under arrest and confined in a lunatic asylum.

—Edlef Köppen, *Heeresbericht*, 1930

Madness is rare with individuals—but with groups, parties, peoples, and times it seems to be the rule.

—Franz Jung, *Spandau Diary*, 1915

We had never before been confronted by such a quantity of male hysteria.

—Otto Binswanger, "Die Kriegshysterie," 1922

War Neurotics

Psychotherapy in all its forms has come into its own in shell–shock.

—E. E. Southard, *Shell-Shock and Other Neuropsychiatric Problems*, 1919

On February 25, 1920, a day before Robert Wiene's *The Cabinet of Dr. Caligari* opened in Berlin film theaters, Dr. Sigmund Freud delivered a written memorandum on the electric shock treatment of war neurotics to a Viennese courthouse.[1] Freud had been asked to serve as an expert witness in a much-publicized malpractice suit in which a patient, a common soldier by the name of Walter Kauders, accused his psychiatrist of torture, including solitary confinement in a padded cell and treatment with electric currents. He also charged his doctor with misdiagnosing him as a malingerer who had allegedly simulated his symptoms to avoid being sent back to the front. Kauders had sustained shell shock in August 1914, when a grenade exploded in a trench nearby. He had lain unconscious for hours. Even though no external injury was discovered, he subsequently experienced various motor disturbances and a crippling headache. He was first diagnosed as variously suffering from neurasthenia, traumatic hysteria, and traumatic neurosis—all terms designating what had become known during the war as shell shock.[2]

After three years of unsuccessful treatment, Kauders was referred to Dr. Julius Wagner-Jauregg, a respected professor of psychiatry at the University of Vienna and director of an insane asylum that specialized in war neurosis. Here Kauders was treated, he claimed, as a malingerer and punished with electroshock for his failure to recover. It was well known that during the war mental clinics used electric shock therapy to shorten treatment and frighten suspected simulators out of their supposedly imagined psychological illnesses. The inflicted pain was designed to make malingering undesirable.[3]

Accusations against the medical profession had become widespread after the war. The malpractice suit against Wagner-Jauregg followed Kauders's publication of his war diary in *Der freie Soldat* (*The Free Soldier*), a weekly paper of the Social Democratic Party. On December 11, 1918, the paper had blamed the medical profession for collaborating with the army to return shell-shocked soldiers to the front. "Electrical power currents were passed through the bodies of . . . war neurotics, causing them such excruciating pain that many died during treatment, but most of them escaped the torture by taking flight from the hospital—without, of course, having been cured."[4] The paper claimed to have documentation that more than one patient had committed suicide in Wagner-Jauregg's clinic. The newspaper stopped short of accusing the doctor of murder, but implied that the whole psychiatric establishment, encouraged by the military, had gone mad in punishing suspected malingers. There was a general distrust of all soldiers suffering from shell shock and other nervous disorders, and in this atmosphere of doubt and deception, most war psychiatrists were more concerned with exposing alleged simulation than with diagnosing or curing psychological illness. All this was done, wrote *Der freie Soldat*, "so that the Moloch of militarism will not have to miss one human sacrifice!"[5]

In contrast to the psychiatric establishment, Freud did not see war neurosis as an expression of cowardice or moral weakness. His psychoanalytic theory viewed it instead as a mostly unconscious reaction on the part of the body for the purpose of self-preservation. Freud was less suspicious than Wagner-Jauregg of war neurotics, believing that though there were some bluffers and malingerers, they were a minority among those hospitalized. According to Freud's testimony,

> [t]he immediate cause of all war neuroses was an unconscious inclination in the soldier to withdraw from the demands, dangerous or outrageous to his feelings, made upon him by active service. Fear of losing his own life, opposition to the command to kill other people, rebellion against the ruthless suppression of his own personality by his superiors—these were the most important affective sources on which the inclination to escape from war was nourished.
>
> A soldier in whom these affective motives were very powerful and clearly conscious would, if he was a healthy man, have been obliged to desert or pretend to be ill. Only the smallest proportion of war neurotics, however, were malingerers; the emotional impulses which rebelled in them against active service and drove them into illness were operative in them without becoming conscious to them. They remained unconscious because other motives, such as ambition, self-esteem, patriotism, the habit of obedience and the example of others, were to start with more powerful until, on some appropriate occasion, they were overwhelmed by the other, unconsciously operating motives.[6]

It was most convenient, of course, to treat a soldier's mental illness as a secret desire to withdraw and then mark him a malingerer. "Just as he had fled from the war into illness," Freud averred in 1920, "means were now adopted which compelled him to flee back from illness into health, that is to say, into fitness for active service. For this purpose painful electrical treatment was employed, and with success."[7] Because electric shock treatment did not last long, many army doctors, who were torn themselves, as Freud put it, between "the claims of humanity" and the "demands of a national war," increased the strength of the electric current "in order to deprive war neurotics of the advantage they gained from their illness."[8] The fact has never been contradicted, wrote Freud, "that in German hospitals there were deaths at that time during treatment and suicides as a result of it."[9]

Concluding his testimony, Freud boldly asserted that the psychoanalytic method introduced by him had, by the end of the war, replaced the electroshock method. He described plans to set up centers for the strictly psychoanalytic treatment of war neuroses, with full knowledge that "with this considerate, laborious and tedious kind of treatment, it was impossible to count on the quickest restoration of these patients to fitness for service."[10] But these plans were never implemented because the war ended, and "with the war the war neurotics, too, disappeared—a final but impressive proof of the psychical causation of their illness."[11] Even though Freud set psychoanalysis in stark contrast to the cruel war psychiatry represented by Wagner-Jauregg, he never openly condemned his colleague, who, not surprisingly, was cleared of all charges in his trial.

The protagonists in this court trial—the powerful director of an insane asylum who may be crazy or evil, and a shell-shocked patient who may be hallucinating—are also central characters in Wiene's feature film, *The Cabinet of Dr. Caligari.* Like the trial, Wiene's story centers around a doctor and a patient in a mental institution. Both also bring into focus the postwar atmosphere of distrust, deception, and paranoia. Trial and film may be seen as public events that addressed the same questions in 1920: Was war psychiatry criminal? Is it the straitjacket and padded cell or psychoanalysis that cures? Who is mad: the doctor or the patient, or both? The exposure of Dr. Wagner-Jauregg as a torturer and the unmasking of Dr. Caligari as a murderer in Wiene's film are part of a larger postwar reckoning with those forces that had participated in and prolonged the madness of war.

Recovering the Past

Not knowing something essential makes you more involved.

—Michael Ondaatje, *Divisadero*, 2007

The Cabinet of Dr. Caligari begins with the classical scenario of someone telling a story.[12] Visibly tormented by traumatic memories, a young man, Francis, begins his talking cure: "I will tell you." His face parched white and sickly looking, he addresses an older man who sits next to him on a bench at the far left side of the frame, while staring at a space beyond the camera. Dead branches hang down in front of them, partly obscuring the image. The scene might be read as a psychoanalytic session in which the patient reveals to his doctor a traumatic experience that is part lived and part imagined. It is a story told from a subjective point of view: It is I who will tell you. Even at first viewing we might feel slightly uncertain, given the setting, whether this narrating "I" can be trusted.

As Francis tries to recover his past, his companion (and fellow patient) assumes the role of listener, mimicking the viewer's position as the addressee of the tale. The practice of remembering as telling and listening is further dramatized by the editing. The film crosscuts three times between the narrator, the story he tells, and the listener; and this halting rhythm gives a sense of Francis's reluctance, his uncertainty of how best to recount the past. The abrupt cuts jolt us into an early awareness that the film will present not a coherent, linear story but rather a jumble of memory fragments fabricated by an agitated, ostensibly troubled narrator, who seems to be the victim of a traumatic experience that he is forced to retell and relive over and over again.

The film's storyline is Francis's own "film." Ernst Simmel, a prominent war psychiatrist close to Freud and a pioneer in treating shell shock victims with psychoanalysis, believed that the forgotten or repressed memory of a trauma could be recovered through hypnosis, which he likened to running a film. By means of hypnosis, an experience can be repeated. "The 'film' is made to roll once again; the patient dreams the whole thing one more time, the sensitized subconscious releases the affect, which in turn discharges in an adequate emotional expression, and the patient is cured."[13] The process Simmel describes mirrors the film's trajectory: the retelling of the story ends in the doctor's pronouncement in the last scene of the film that "at last I understand the nature of his madness (mania, or *Manie* in the original Ger-

"I will tell you." Francis and Jane cope with the murder of their friend in Robert Wiene's *The Cabinet of Dr. Caligari.*

man, A.K.). He thinks I am that mystic Caligari. Now I see how he can be brought back to sanity again." The film itself thus doubles as a psychoanalytic session for Francis: as if under hypnosis, the film of his traumatic memory is "made to roll once again."

Freud elaborated his theory of trauma in the shadow of the Great War. Written between March 1919 and July 1920 (overlapping with the production and run of *Caligari*), his treatise *Beyond the Pleasure Principle* conceptualized trauma as a violent rupture that breaks the protective shield normally insulating a subject from excessive excitation. Culturally constructed and negotiated, this psychological shield regulates and guards the flow of stimuli across the boundaries of the self. Trauma occurs if a sudden shock (an explosion of a shell, for instance, or the expectation of imminent death) cannot be integrated into one's conscious personality. Freud noted in 1920:

> An external trauma is bound to provoke a disturbance on a large scale in the functioning of the organism's energy and to set in motion every possible defense measure. At the same time, the pleasure principle is for the moment put out of action. There is no longer any possibility of preventing the mental apparatus from being flooded with large amounts of stimulus, and another problem arises instead—the problem of mastering the amounts of stimulus which have broken in and of binding them, in the psychical sense, so that they can then be disposed of.[14]

Trauma appears here as the result of an unexpected attack on a psyche unable to cope with it. Simmel, who had successfully treated shell shock victims with hypnosis, had similarly argued in his treatise, *Kriegs-Neurosen und "Psychisches Trauma"* (*War Neuroses and Psychic Trauma*): "Whatever in a person's experience is too powerful or horrible for his conscious mind to grasp and work through, filters down to the unconscious levels of his psyche. There it lies like a mine, waiting to explode the entire psychic structure. And only the self-protective mechanism . . . prevents a permanent disturbance of the psychic balance."[15]

It is primarily in dreams that neurotics revisit their trauma. "These dreams," wrote Freud, "are endeavoring to master the stimulus retrospectively, by developing the anxiety whose omission was the cause of the traumatic neurosis."[16] Like dreams, films work through trauma by restaging it. Horror films in particular, with their shock effects and near-death encounters, might be seen as attempts to thicken the stimulus shield; they allow the viewer to take part in the experience of the traumatic event, but from a distance, vicariously and safely. Repetition compulsion associated with unacknowledged and repressed trauma may explain the popularity of horror films in Germany after the Great War.

"How long do I have to live?" This was the central question for every soldier in the trenches; for every wife and mother on the home front, it was how long does he have to live? The mere question, asked in a film of 1920, recalled the war's most traumatic presentiment. Alan, Francis's friend, rushes forward to pose this question to Cesare, Dr. Caligari's somnambulist medium and fairground clairvoyant. "How long do I have to live?" As Alan nervously awaits the answer, Francis gazes at him with a puzzled look. By crosscutting, the camera shows close-ups of Cesare's menacing visage, grotesquely made up in the manner of a death mask with black rings around his eyes, and Alan's fervent, pleading face. An abrupt close-up of Cesare underscores his shocking answer: "Until tomorrow's dawn." Alan, seen in a high angle shot, is taken aback, contorting his face, uncertain whether to cry or laugh at the somnambulist's prophecy. He stumbles backward, shaking, unstable on his feet. He knows that he has stared death in the eye—and indeed shortly afterward we see the shadow of Cesare repeatedly stabbing Alan in his bed.

As predicted, the murder happens at dawn, a time of day that had a special meaning during wartime. It was usually then that soldiers were ordered to storm out of their trenches across no-man's-land into the enemy's deadly machine-gun fire. Even before 1920, this tactic, which sacrificed tens of thousands of men, was perceived as de facto murder. In retelling Alan's murder, Francis relives the shock of his friend's untimely death at dawn—a suggestive allusion to the deaths of the dawn offensives, when soldiers often saw comrades near them killed in an instant. Who murderered his friend? Francis's pursuit of this question structures the film's main narrative.

Death in *The Cabinet of Caligari* is configured as murder, not as fate. In contrast, Fritz Lang's *Der müde Tod (Destiny,* or literally, The Weary Death), which opened in October 1921, is a melancholic ballad, a "German Folksong" (the film's original subtitle) about the fatefulness of sudden death of a loved one. Death emerges embodied as an uncanny stranger, snatching a young man away from his devoted fiancée. The film tells the story of the young woman's attempt to win back her lover from the realm of the dead. In three visionary episodes set in Arabia, China, and Renaissance Italy,

Destiny demonstrates the universality of love and the inevitability of death. Only after the woman resigns herself to accepting death can she be reunited with her lover. Whereas *The Cabinet of Dr. Caligari* is an aggressive diatribe against the murderous practices of war psychiatry, *Destiny* works through the trauma of loss by implying that the acknowledgment of death brings redemption. *Caligari* lacks *Destiny*'s humanistic dimension; it stands closer to Dada's nihilistic attacks on the establishment, its anarchic breach of aesthetic and moral conventions, and its delight in shock and confusion.

Caligari's intertwined stories are told in flashbacks, the ideal narrative trope for conveying the recovery and enactment of traumatic memory.[17] A popular device in film noir, the flashback juxtaposes two moments in time; past and present are separate, but at the same time the past inserts itself into the present as memory. Flashbacks also subjectivize history by filtering it through the consciousness of a narrator. The master narrative—Francis's psychoanalytic talking cure—situates his own story in relation to that of Dr. Caligari. Caligari's story, in turn, is also told in flashbacks, resulting in a Chinese box effect. In addition, Francis projects his own relationship to Dr. Caligari onto Cesare, another patient in the asylum, who (according to Francis) had become the object of Caligari's experimentation with hypnosis.

The various life histories of Francis, Cesare, and Dr. Caligari are presented in brief flashback scenes with radical shifts in place and time. The film stages the recovery of repressed traumatic memory, which works by association, sudden reversals, and the shock of recognition. At the very end of the film, as the two men get up from the bench, they enter—shock and surprise?—an insane asylum. The camera lingers on the sign "Irrenanstalt (mental institution)," as they go into the courtyard of the clinic. The end of Francis's talking cure session signals the end of the flashback; the split between Francis as narrator and as protagonist in his own story is over. When Francis sees Dr. Caligari, he attacks him (physical attacks on psychiatrists by traumatized war neurotics were not uncommon at the war's end), screaming "You all believe I am mad. That is not true. It is the Director who is mad."

After a struggle, Francis is subdued, put into a straitjacket, and transported to a cell, which is the very cell that (we suddenly realize) Caligari had occupied in Francis's imagination. We understand now that the film's story was told by an unreliable, even deluded narrator whose memory cannot differentiate between fiction and reality, projection and observation.

Who is to tell whether Francis is victim or perpetrator, detective or mental patient?

Caligari's historical unconscious—what it does not speak aloud—is the memory of a traumatic experience. The film itself serves as a flashback to an event that has hardly passed, inviting the audience to recover the memory, however discomfiting. The film's disregard for temporal linearity and illusionism further unsettles the viewer, affording no clear delineation between past and present, fantasy and real occurrence, dream and delusion.[18] Who is the monster in our midst? At its core a detective story, the film conceals as it reveals, deceives as it uncovers, represses as it remembers.

If the enigma at the center of this film is the true identity of the mysterious Dr. Caligari, the riddle is never solved. Even after the film ends, the viewer cannot decide who Caligari is: a fairground charlatan, the director of an insane asylum, a crazy scientist, a murderous psychiatrist? The proliferation of his roles runs parallel to other doppelgänger effects that similarly confound the viewer's understanding: just as Caligari doubles as doctor and charlatan, so does Francis as detective and patient, and Cesare as murderer and life-size dummy. Once it is shown that the narrator himself is crazy, the roles seem suddenly reversed: the doctor becomes the benevolent psychoanalyst who, in Simmel's words, is able to release his patient "from the fetters of his unconscious mind and thus is in a position to guide the neurotic into health and save him."[19]

Like Jekyll and Hyde, Caligari oscillates between two types of psychiatry operative in World War I: the traditional model (practiced by Max Nonne, Fritz Kaufmann, and Wagner-Jauregg) that became sadistic and even murderous because of unchecked authority, and the newer psychoanalytical model (practiced by Simmel and others influenced by Freud) that wanted to cure the patient by slowly uncovering the cause of his trauma. Francis's "film" consists of a recovered traumatic memory that has played tricks on his mind: in his "mania" he unmasks Caligari as a charlatan and murderous mastermind, exposes the doctor's hubristic scientific ambitions, and in an act of transference projects his own madness onto his doctor.

The film's flashback structure and its unexpected ending call into question naïve notions about narrative linearity and historical truth. In developing its story—the recovery of one man's traumatic memory—the film at the same time gives expression to the doubts, suspicions, and uncertainties that a traumatized nation experienced in confronting its painful history.

Phantoms and Freaks

From its beginnings in the late nineteenth century, film delighted in shocking audiences with its ghostlike projections. Reduced to the play of shadows and light, even the familiar could be made uncanny and frightening. The camera rejected traditional time-space relations, reconstructing the world in a fantastic but also threatening way. Plots revolved around violent confrontations with criminals, foreigners, and other mysterious figures who threatened safe and comfortable communities. Films produced nightmares, frequently dealing with the dark, repressed side of a rigidly regulated society. In the safety of cinema's fictional space, the spectator was free to taste fear, albeit in the form of danger that was simulated: controlled and controllable. Although aware of the film's illusory status, the audience often felt torn between contradictory reactions to the images. Fascinated yet shocked, frightened yet unable to avert its eyes, it could vicariously experience quasi-traumatic events from a distance.

The cryptic first sentence in *The Cabinet of Dr. Caligari*, "Es gibt Geister . . . überall sind sie um uns her" (There are ghosts . . . they are all around us), spoken by the older man in the first scene, points to the spooky and uncanny reality of the film medium itself. *Geister* in German also means "phantoms," "apparitions," or "specters." The allusion to *Geister* places the film in a pre-cinematic tradition dating back to ghost shows and phantasmagorias, in which spirits were made to rise from the dead in a dark room—spectacles produced by the optical illusions of a magic lantern. "One knew ghosts did not exist," writes Terry Castle, "yet one saw them anyway, without knowing precisely how."[20] As precursors to filmmakers, illusionists invented apparitions and supernatural effects to frighten audiences for entertainment. Although most of the phantasmagoria shows pretended to give a scientific explanation for their technologically created apparitions, they nonetheless produced moments of simulated madness in which the supernatural intruded into the rational world. Such, of course, is cinema, and Weimar cinema in particular.

Because ghosts and phantoms refer to the spirit world, to the world of the recently deceased, they took on a special resonance at the end of a war that saw millions killed. "There are ghosts all around us," the old man says. "They have driven me from home and hearth, from wife and child." These remarks also allude to the fear that the dead exert power over the living, that in fact they have come to take revenge and have forced him to be dis-placed, making him *ver-rückt,* and causing insanity. What we only guessed in the first scene becomes clear toward the end: both men are in fact patients in a mental institution.

The first scene also adds another unsettling motif: the ghostly apparition of a woman, who seems to trigger memories in Francis. Dressed in a flowing white gown that marks her as a patient in the mental clinic, she walks by the two men as if in a trance. An intrusion from another world and a flash from the repressed past, Jane, as we learn later in the film, embodies the trauma surrounding the premature death of Alan, a mutual friend of her and Francis. "Robbers, burglars, and ghosts," writes Freud in his *Interpretation of Dreams*, "of whom some people feel frightened before going to bed, and who sometimes pursue their victims after they are asleep, all originate from one and the same class of infantile reminiscence. . . . Analyses of some of these anxiety-dreams have made it possible for me to identify these nocturnal visitors more precisely. In every case the robbers stood for the sleeper's father, whereas the ghosts corresponded to female figures in white nightgowns."[21] Reminiscent of Victorian paintings of weightless women in white, the young woman, her eyes gazing upward, gestures as if she were parting an imaginary curtain, but nothing is revealed. Her zombie-like appearance, which may well be a hallucination of the narrator's, stands in the tradition of Gothic fiction that combines horror and romance with the desire to communicate some traumatic experience. Wiene encodes the war experience as a Gothic horror tale that begins with an invocation of the supernatural ("*Geister* are all around us . . ."), the uncanny image of a female ghost, and the eerie setting of two distressed men telling each other stories about traumatic events in their past. This first scene (part of the allegedly "realistic" frame) indicates that the film will make no claims to realism.

Early cinema often featured a narrator who, standing next to the screen, introduced the film's characters and highlighted things the audience might otherwise overlook. Invoking this tradition, Wiene's film introduces its protagonist, Dr. Caligari, by having Francis identify him ("He"), as an iris closes in on an old man dressed like a nineteenth-century bourgeois in top hat and cape. The iris, focusing on his face, creates a close-up effect, forcing us to see what the narrator sees.

Throughout the film, Wiene uses iris-in and iris-out masking devices, deliberately deploying earlier cinematic conventions to achieve the subjective focus and restricted view implied by first-person narration. By watching the image through a circular or rhomboid opening, the viewer is forced to consider the frame as well as what is seen within it. The visuals of the film thereby reinforce the narrative structure that consciously employs subjectivized perspectives, partial awarenesses, and the circumscribed, angst-ridden maneuvering of viewpoints. The frequent use of the iris also produces a claustrophobic peephole effect that allows us to glimpse only what the storyteller wants us to see; the rest remains literally in the dark. Reminiscent of the camera obscura, the iris both illuminates and obscures, highlighting the extreme artificiality of cinematic representation. In addition, in this film about madness and crime, the iris takes on yet another level of meaning: it places the viewer in the role of a warden who peeps through a hole in the door to observe the patient or prisoner in his cell.

We first encounter Caligari as he enters a carnivalesque scene: an organ-grinder and his dancing monkey, a merry-go-round, and dwarves with tall pointed hats, all set against crudely hand-painted scenery that recalls Luna Park, a popular place of amusement in 1920s Berlin. This is the fairground where Dr. Caligari (in his doppelgänger role as sideshow entrepreneur, hypnotist, and charlatan) presents his freak show featuring Cesare, a somnambulist and psychic, who he claims has been asleep for twenty-three years. Cesare stands motionless in an upright coffin, suspended in a state between death and life, a state that resonates with stories returning soldiers told of their near-death experiences. The show takes place in a small, primitive tent—the cabinet of the film's title. The audience is seated on benches in front of the stage, as if in a movie theater.

Like a magician, Caligari toys with the anticipation of his audience, endlessly delaying the revelation of his attraction.[22] After assuming the role of a barker in front of his tent, he heightens the tension by slowly opening the coffin, first one door, and then the other. Time seems to stand still, the story has come to a halt; and like the audience sitting in Caligari's cabinet, we breathlessly await what secrets the coffin may contain. Early silent cinema reveled in astonishing its audience with a succession of tricks. It was a "cinema of attraction" in which each scene, each episode built tension and then released it.[23] Caligari's public display of Cesare is just such an attraction, functioning like a film within a film. His roles as mad doctor, fairground hypnotist, and magician echo that of a film director who commands his actors to perform for the camera. Caligari's act of creation consists in the transformation of his medium from sleep to wakefulness, from stasis to movement, from quasi-death to life—a highly suggestive metamorphosis that echoes early film exhibition practice. As Tom Gunning remarks,

> [i]t is too infrequently pointed out that in the earliest Lumière projections the films were initially presented as frozen unmoving images, projections of still photographs. Then, flaunting a mastery of visual showmanship, the projector began cranking and the image moved. Or as Gorky described it, . . . suddenly a strange flicker passes through the screen and the picture stirs to life. . . . This coup de théâtre, the sudden transformation from still to moving illusion, startled audiences and displayed the novelty and fascination of the cinématographe.[24]

As Caligari brings life to the catatonic Cesare with the touch of his wand, so does the film projector bring life to still pictures—twenty-four (or eighteen in silent film) per second. For many, this was the real magic, even after twenty-three years of cinema, which coincidentally is also the number of years that Cesare allegedly slept before Caligari awakened him.[25] Is Cesare a medium in more ways than one? Or does the film suggest that its radical innovations will rouse the new medium from its slumber?

Caligari's hypnotism sideshow was part of a postwar resurgence of fringe science and the occult within popular entertainment. On August 6, 1919, a full-page ad in *Der Kinematograph*, the German film industry's premier trade paper, announced a newly available act: "Minx, the Man with the Black Mask—Telepathic novelty that forces a randomly chosen person to do an experiment the audience thought up, and that without any hypnosis and suggestion." Minx, the '"man with the black mask," foreshadowed Cesare, the telepathic man in black in *The Cabinet of Dr. Caligari*, which opened about six months later. In the September 12, 1920 issue of *Der Kinematograph*, about half a year after *Caligari*, we find an advertisement for the Minx and Medy Duo, who toured movie theaters with their show titled "In the Grip of Hypnosis." Minx was billed as the "famous hypnotiseur and master clairvoyant," with Medy as his "lovely and enchanting dream artist." The program consisted of the four segments: Telepathy and Thought Transference; Solutions of a Crime; Hypnosis-Somnambulism with Medy (advertised as "a riddle for science and the best hypnotic phenomenon"); and finally Mass Hypnosis.[26] Caligari's own show is not much different: it features hypnosis, somnambulism, and a clairvoyant medium (who in the film is male). Even "mass hypnosis" is a veiled reference to the effects of a cinematic cabinet such as Thomas Edison's Black Maria Studio, where the first film projection took place in 1893. Wiene's film literalizes the mass-cultural link between cinema and hypnosis.[27]

Hypnotism enjoyed a questionable reputation in 1920. While Freud, afraid of the charge of charlatanism, had been critical of Jean-Martin Charcot's use of the technique, war psychiatry had revived it as a treatment for shell-shocked soldiers. Ernst Simmel and Sándor Ferenczi, for example, were ardent advocates.[28] However, as the need to quickly cure traumatized soldiers receded, hypnosis was again taken up by entertainers, charlatans, and self-appointed psychodoctors. Newly validated by medical research, it was part and parcel of a rapidly growing interest in the occult, telepathy, and spiritism.

By 1919, the use of hypnosis and the occult in popular entertainment had become so widespread that the Berlin police chief commissioned a report on the legal and public health questions this raised. Interestingly, the author of the report was none other than Albert von Schrenck-Notzing, the period's foremost specialist on the occult, who had since 1888 published numerous tomes on hypnosis and parapsychology.[29] His report was delivered in November 1919 and published in the *Archiv für Kriminologie* in 1920. In his report, Schrenck-Notzing stated that the phenomenal success of self-styled psychologists, clairvoyants, and psychics had two explanations: the "mass psychosis of the war and the revolution," and the desire of a public destabilized by "war, depression, economic decline, and perturbations of the revolution for mysterious and uncanny sensations."[30]

Stage shows and illustrated lectures featuring hypnosis existed in a twilight zone between scholarly-scientific pursuit and downright charlatanism. Paralysis, sleepwalking, and somnolent trance were artificially (and more often than not deceptively) produced, in virtual mockery of the shell-shock cases of just two years prior. Schrenck-Notzing's report gives numerous examples of clashes between itinerant showmen and local authorities. Like Caligari, these entrepreneurs needed a written license from the towns in which they appeared, but often they violated the rules by illegally hypnotizing members of the audience, which demanded cheap thrills for its money. Erik Jan Hanussen, Herbert Krause, Max Liechtenstein, Lo Kittay, and Leo Erichson were some of the most famous psychics who through techniques of "suggestion" (without resorting to hypnosis) managed to make members

Trauma as entertainment:
Alan is told he will die
at dawn tomorrow.

of their audiences do things against their will, even inducing motor paralysis, speech impediments, delusions, and mood changes. Most of their shows were billed as educational experiments, in much the same pseudoscientific spirit as Dr. Caligari's exhibition of his somnambulist.[31]

When Caligari announced that Cesare had been sleeping for twenty-three years, audiences understood that he has been under hypnosis. "In persons disposed toward hysteria, difficult awakening happens after deep hypnosis, followed by loss of language, paralysis, and hallucinations."[32] What is dangerous, according to Schrenck-Notzing, is that the public psychic picks victims from the audience at random, regardless of whether they are "heart patients, hysterical epileptic[s], war neurotics, or other individuals with a pathological disposition."[33] War neurotics are included in this list of those who should not be exposed to the shock and surprise tactics of psychics and hypnotists precisely because their hysterical disposition made them most susceptible to harmful influence. Because shows featuring nonmedical hypnosis had become so fashionable by 1920, Schrenck-Notzing recommended that hypnosis, while a blessing in principle, needed to be banned in public places. Caligari's show would have fallen under this ban, had it not occurred in a movie.

The Cabinet of Dr. Caligari's return to the suspect pleasures of hypnosis and the occult points to another film-historical subtext. The movie's fairground scenes with their crude sensationalism and transgressive subtext are strongly reminiscent of the early *Wanderkino*, a type of tent cinema. In the decade following the first public film exhibition by the brothers Skladanowsky in Berlin's Wintergarten in December 1895, it was customary for entrepreneurs in the emergent movie business to take their films from town to town, displaying them at fairgrounds as part of variety and freak shows. Fixed movie theaters in city centers did not exist in Germany before 1907 (1902 in the United States). The one-reelers featured in *Wanderkino* programs were raw and lurid, capitalizing on the sheer visual pleasures of movement and action. *Caligari* alludes to this earlier phase of cinema by making Caligari the owner of a "cabinet," a traveling show with a small stage and benches. In one shot of the film, the camera places us in one of the seats. We look at the stage, where we see Caligari, the hypnotist, gesturing wildly with his magic wand at his hypnotized subject.

So that he might exhibit Cesare, his *Schaustück* (literally his "object to look at"), Caligari must apply for a local permit at the town hall, exactly as if he were a *Wanderkino* entrepreneur. During the early years of cinema, communities strongly controlled what was exhibited; traveling directors had to gain official approval, a process that we actually witness in the movie. As Caligari enters the town hall, he is told that the town secretary is in a bad mood. Perched on a cartoonishly tall stool, the clerk looks down on Caligari (his power further emphasized by a low-angle shot from Caligari's perspective) and admonishes him twice to wait. After a while, Caligari approaches the clerk:

"I want to apply for a permit to show my exhibit at the fair."
"What sort of an exhibit is it?"
"A somnambulist."

The secretary looks bemused, and after referring Caligari to a colleague, climbs down from his chair and walks out. The scene bristles with antagonism between the anarchic spirit of the fair and the tight-lipped arrogance of the bureaucracy that oversees the town's entertainment. Knowing that the fairground was a potential site of subversive and anti-authoritarian energy, towns were apprehensive of the many transients, tricksters, and movie entrepreneurs who traveled from fair to fair. Caligari glowers on the margin of the frame, visibly fuming with frustration at the paradoxical requirement that he obtain a permit for his suspicious activities. Is it surprising, then, that the bad-tempered town clerk in charge of issuing the permits becomes Caligari's first murder victim? The crime dramatizes the clash between the world of the carnival and the world of law and order. By murdering the supercilious clerk, Caligari signals resistance against the authorities who decree what is allowed in popular entertainment and what is not.

More than any other country, Germany had resisted the seductive allure of cinema as mass entertainment. Classical education had produced a cultured middle class that saw Germany as a *Kulturnation* and associated national identity with high culture. The plebeian origins of the movies and their supposedly pernicious influence on women and the young long kept the medium under governmental control. Thus, to murder the very bureaucrat who issues the permit for Caligari's show was, even in 1920, a provocation. To kill off the guardian of discipline and order at the very beginning of the film was indeed downright rebellious, a self-conscious act of defiance that asserted cinema's dangerous and transgressive potential.

The filmmaker as hypnotist, sideshow entrepreneur, and psychiatrist: Caligari lays out a panorama of the conflicting roles film artists assumed in the early years of cinema. His hypnotizing gaze controls his medium and his audience, recreating the trance state of film viewing itself, and situating cinema at the juncture of science, magic, and trickery.

From Dr. Charcot to Dr. Caligari

Madmen are made here.

—André Breton, *Nadja*, 1928

As in a nightmare, Dr. Caligari appears everywhere, shifting shapes and identities. He is at once fairground entrepreneur and impostor, scientist (testing the effects of hypnosis) and madman, psychiatrist and charlatan. Tellingly, he is modeled after the foremost psychiatrist of the time, Jean-Martin Charcot (1835–1893), the director of the premier Parisian insane asylum, the Salpêtrière hospital. Caligari's countenance and hairstyle, his professorial habitus and top hat, bear an uncanny resemblance to descriptions and caricatures of Charcot. Freud, who had studied under Charcot in 1885–86, described the psychiatrist, shortly after their first meeting, in a letter to his fiancée on October 21, 1885, "a tall man of fifty-eight, wearing a top hat, with dark, strangely soft eyes . . . long wisps of hair stuck behind his ears, clean shaven, very expressive features with full protruding lips."[34]

Charcot was best known for the public lectures in which he displayed and diagnosed his hysteric patients in a five-hundred-seat amphitheater. These public exhibitions attracted the entire Paris intelligentsia, including Henri Bergson, Sarah Bernhardt, Émile Durkheim, Guy de Maupassant, and in the winter of 1885–86, Freud. Conducted in a circus-like setting, these famous Tuesday lectures helped make hysteria known to the wider public, and established the role of the psychiatrist as both scientist and entertainer. There was a widespread (and not unwarranted) suspicion that some of Charcot's patients actually simulated their symptoms, at the very least exaggerating their reactions to please and entertain the doctors as well as the audience members (who had, after all, come to witness acts of hysteria). It was also likely that the patients learned to simulate hysteria by imitating other patients. Maybe the patients were merely actors, and Charcot merely the director of their show?

Some critics took issue with this theatrical exhibition of mentally ill patients—Bernheim, for instance, called Charcot's work "hystericulture"—and denigrated him as a showman and quack.[35] Brilliant psychiatrist or clever charlatan? Or both? This ambivalence in Dr. Charcot's role finds its exact echo in the fictive figure of Dr. Caligari, whose ambivalent role in the film as psychiatrist and/or charlatan leaves the spectator forever guessing.

Fascinated with documenting the symptoms of the hysterics first by means of sketches and later photographs, Charcot created an archive of images representing madness that has had an indelible influence on theatrical and cinematic reflections of mental illness and hysteria ever since. A photography studio was installed in the asylum, and once a year, *Iconographie photographique de la Salpêtrière*, founded in 1876, published a record of hysterical symptoms that circulated throughout the world. The invention of film only helped broaden the archive of the insane. In a 1909 treatise titled *Die Kinematographie im Dienste der Neurologie und Psychiatrie* (*Cinematography in the Service of Neurology and Psychiatry*), the German psychiatrist Hans Hennes pleaded for the wider use of film in the recording and diagnosis of mental patients' behavior. He foresaw the creation of a cinematographic archive that would fix mad behavior on film forever and make it available for serious study. (Exhibiting patients, who often behaved in unexpected ways, to live audiences was deemed too unreliable for teaching purposes.[36]) Expressionist poetry, too, saw affinities between early silent film (with its discontinuous movement, lack of speech, and abrupt juxtapositions) and the disjointed world of the insane.[37]

In the asylum courtyard shown at the end of *Caligari*, various characters enact the by then well-known attributes of hysteria: extreme agitation and exaggerated gesticulation, contortions, convulsions, languor, delirium, and stupor—the full range of symptoms recorded in Charcot's iconography of hysteria and madness. The acrobatic behavior and theatrical posing of Charcot's patients presaged the jerky motions and convulsions of acting in early silent film. It is difficult to tell in *The Cabinet of Dr. Caligari* (as it is in the photos from the Salpêtrière) whether there is method in the madness. Are these characters hysterics, or do they pose as hysterics with their stylized contortions and grimaces? This question is further complicated by the fact that in the movie everyone is an actor; the viewer is faced with the referential paradox of actors embodying figures who are obviously acting—that is, faking the traits of madmen. *Caligari* explores the affinity of "hystericulture" to cinematic representation, against the background of a war that produced a large number of victims of hysteria and split personality disorders. *Caligari*'s setting may well be the sideshow, but its poignant subtext is the experience of war neurosis.

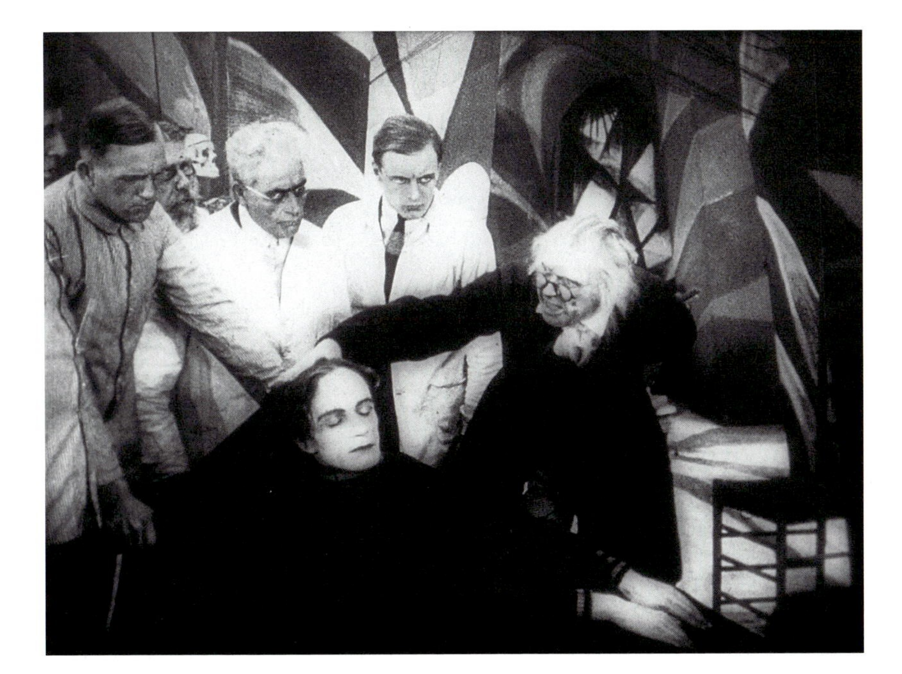

Cesare in the thrall of the mad doctor; Francis fights back. Doctors and patients in *The Cabinet of Dr. Caligari*.

Cesare, Dr. Caligari's patient and fairground freak, is shown in a flashback as a young man with symptoms reminiscent of shell shock. He is brought into the psychiatrist's office, pallid and catatonic, reclining in a wheelchair. He might have been case number 365, as recorded in a 1919 medical collection called *Shell-Shock and Other Neuropsychiatric Problems Presented in 589 Case Histories from the War Literature, 1914–1918*:

> A man, aged 22, was brought to the Saint Nicolas Hospital in a sort of coma. He lay on the bed, eyes closed as if asleep, insensible to excitation, unresponsive. Flies crawled on him with impunity. He did not blink. His arms when raised fell back inert. Corneal reflex was absent on the left side, diminished on the right. Knee-jerks and skin reflexes were normal.
>
> The next day he had to be fed and cared for like a child. Lifted from bed, he stood on the ground with flexed legs in a kind of crouch. It seemed as if he was about to fall, but he did not. . . . If taken by the hand, he would walk quickly without falling but with his feet dragging, and even holding back with a certain amount of force. His walk suggested that of a somnambulist.[38]

A typical symptom in soldiers who had been buried alive by the explosion of a shell, somnambulism becomes Dr. Caligari's obsession, as we find out in an explanatory flashback. Francis and three doctors, looking for incriminating evidence in Caligari's office, discover a book whose title page reads "Somnambulism. A Compendium of the University of Uppsala, published in the year of 1726." They remark that somnambulism had been the doctor's area of expertise and read on—only to be confronted with the film's very story. Shown again in insert, printed in black-letter type, it reads:

> The Cabinet of Dr. Caligari.
>
> In the year 1703, a mystic by the name of Dr. Caligari, together with a somnambulist called Cesare, used to frequent the fairgrounds . . . and for months he kept town after town in a state of panic by a series of murders, all of them perpetrated in similar circumstances . . . for he caused a somnambulist, whom he had entirely subjected to his will, to carry out his fantastic plans. By means of a puppet figure, modeled in the exact likeness of Cesare, which he laid in the chest when Cesare was away, Dr. Caligari was able to allay any suspicion that might fall on the somnambulist.[39]

They also find his diary, which they read with great eagerness. The film once again shows the relevant passages on a title card: "March 12th. At last—at last! Today I have been notified of the case of a somnambulist. . . . Now I shall be able to prove whether a somnambulist can be compelled to do things of which he knows nothing, things he would never do himself and would abhor doing—whether it is true that in a trance one can be driven to murder."[40]

The desire for scientific "proof" of this kind dates back to nineteenth-century debates and experiments that involved hypnotism, crime, and the question of hypnotic control and power. Charcot himself had believed that his manipulative power over the hypnotized subject was without limits:

> I have observed some very curious facts about [the workings] of suggestion during . . . *grand hypnotisme*. I have at my clinic particularly sensitive patients who have provided the material for some extremely interesting experiments. . . . In effect, once plunged into sleep, the brain of the subject may be considered absolutely blank and incapable of any will of its own. The hypnotist can then . . . imprint on it sensations and pictures as well as generate the will to perform any act. These sensations, pictures, and this will are photographically reproduced . . . without modifications.[41]

Do subjects in fact obey commands that they cannot remember after they wake up? Is a somnambulist responsible for his deeds?[42] These are precisely the questions that Dr. Caligari seeks to answer upon admitting Cesare to his insane asylum. It is significant that he induces Cesare to murder again and again—an uncanny echo of the organized mass murder demanded by people in power during the war. But it is also important to note that Cesare is able to disobey his master when he refrains from killing Jane. This disobedience seems to cost him his life. After he abandons her, he falls to his death amid the stark, leafless trees. The film does not take a firm stance with regard to questions about freedom of the will under hypnosis.

A week before *Caligari*'s premiere, posters appeared all over Berlin, advertising the film with a command that was as eerie as it was mysterious. Depicting a spiral that suggested hypnotic power, the posters carried the message: "Du musst Caligari werden" (You must become Caligari). No mention was made of the film's title; there was simply the demand that passersby assume Caligari's identity. The exhortation to become someone else resonated in the postwar years, when many Germans found themselves in a state of denial and disavowal about their identity. You must become a stranger to yourself, the poster exclaimed; you must fall under Caligari's spell—in the cabinet of the movie theater. The mesmerizing power of film allows for a temporary double identity. By identifying with the protagonist, one splits one's personality and could indeed become Caligari.

The splitting of identity was also a central concern in contemporary debates about shell shock and war neurosis. In his contribution to the symposium on psychoanalysis and war neuroses at the Fifth International Psychoanalytical Congress in Budapest in September 1918, Ernst Simmel wrote:

> The war neurosis, like the peace neurosis, is the expression of a splitting of the personality. The conditions for such a splitting are brought about by the consistent narrowing of the personality complex as a result of the compulsory discipline and above all by the psychic and physical exhaustion of one or more years of war. The soldier severely burdened with undischarged mental material is compelled to meet abnormally heavy demands. An accident or a disastrous event then causes the obstructed personality to break down.[43]

Freud also explained war neurosis as a result of an unresolvable mental conflict that splits the ego:

> The conflict is between the old ego of peacetime and the new war-ego of the soldier, and it becomes acute as soon as the peace-ego is faced with the danger of being killed through the risky undertakings of his newly-formed parasitic double. Or as one might put it, the old ego protects itself from the danger to life by flight into the traumatic neurosis, thus defending itself against the new ego which it recognizes as threatening its life.[44]

The somatic symptoms of war neurosis are, according to Freud, a defense mechanism that appears primarily among conscripted soldiers of the national army, less among professional soldiers or mercenaries. As the new warrior ego threatens the peacetime ego and one's physical existence, a split occurs in the patient's conscious personality. In Freud's view the difference between war neuroses and other traumatic neuroses derived from the fear of this internal enemy, the threat of a coercive inner voice that overwhelms the old ego: You must become someone else. You must become Caligari.

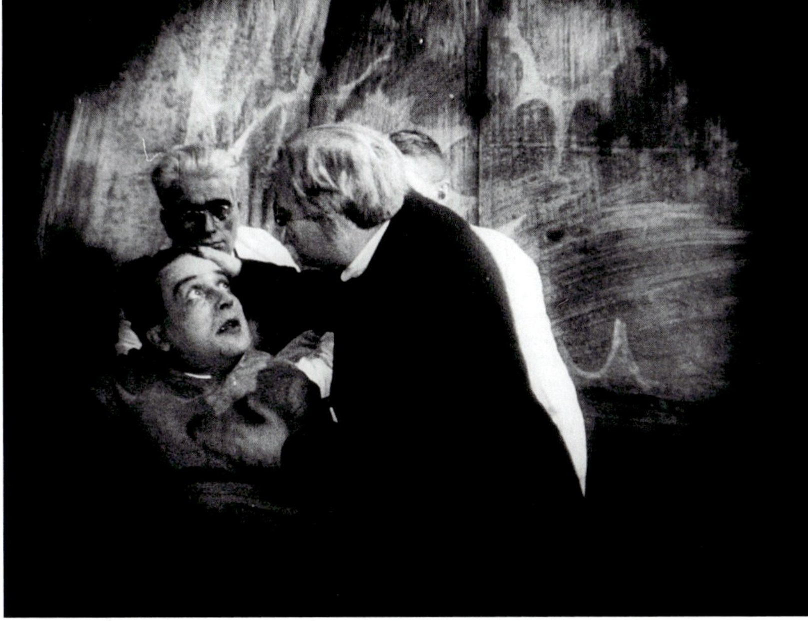

"You must become Caligari."
The transference of madness
from doctor to patient.

The poster slogan, "Du musst Caligari werden," reappears in the film fully encoded as a turning point in the narrative. In a flashback we read the tale of the historical Caligari, the fairground charlatan. Is this not exactly the story we have been watching? We suddenly realize that our Dr. Caligari may actually be a double of the historical Dr. Caligari, an eighteenth-century charlatan and scientist who conducted psychosomatic experiments with a hypnotized victim that ended in murder and mayhem. In a further flashback we see Caligari becoming extremely agitated as he learns about these experiments. He jumps up, lifts the book high above his head, stares at it, and exclaims, "I must know everything. . . . I must penetrate into his innermost secrets. . . . I myself must become Caligari." He staggers out of the frame, while the camera lingers on his desk, cluttered with books.

Overcome by the power of his reaction, Caligari, at that point still a psychiatrist, begins hallucinating. Against the night sky, scattered letters appear, the letters form words, and the words form a sentence: "Du musst Caligari werden." Caligari attempts to shield himself from the threatening command, the letters disappear, he freezes with fear, and immediately the sentence "Du musst Caligari werden" appears again and again, spreading across the frame, encircling him. In an innovative technical trick, the letters penetrate the image; the psychic breakdown of the psychiatrist is signified by one sign system assaulting and invading the other. Writing as a competing and "older" representational form threatens the integrity and exclusivity of the visual.

The writing in the sky forces Caligari to *see* the voices in this hallucinatory scene. (Later in sound film a voice-over would give expression to inner thoughts.) Are these written words perhaps signs of an unconscious and unspeakable wish to escape the present? In an early paper on aphasia, Freud described such an experience:

> I remember having twice been in danger in my life, and each time the awareness of the danger occurred to me quite suddenly. On both occasions I felt "this was the end," and while otherwise my inner language proceeded with only indistinct sound images and slight lip movements, in these situations of danger I heard the words as if somebody was shouting them into my ear, and at the same time I saw them as if they were printed on a piece of paper floating in the air.[45]

Madness as Resistance

He is gone... Remember him. Have pity. Be friendly. You all have contributed to his death. All of you sitting there.

—Hugo Ball, Funeral speech for Hans Leybold, killed in battle, 1915

During the war, the insane asylum became a sanctuary for young men who refused to go to the front, as well as for those who had returned with symptoms of shell shock. The writer Oskar Maria Graf, who was committed to an asylum for one and a half years after refusing to obey orders, recounts the following conversation with his doctor:

> "You see, I am a human being, like you. . . . My job is to cure you as quickly as possible, nothing more," said the doctor, mildly and almost pleadingly. Suddenly I bent over toward his face, making him flinch slightly and I shouted, ever more loudly, "You are the biggest criminal! You only cure people so that there are more people to kill. . . . The generals, the emperors, all the military commanders, they act as they have been trained to act, but YOU—you learned something different and allow yourself to be used for the most scandalous of deeds. You bring those flogged to death back to life so that they can murder again, so that they can mangle again. . . . You are a pimp, you are a whore!"
>
> The doctor then leapt up in alarm and he grabbed me, shaking me, "Calm down, Graf. You are critically ill." He was at a loss himself and stuttered. But I was never silent. I had also stood up and I bawled him out. An immeasurable rage had taken hold of me. . . .
>
> "You are going to a sanitarium," said the doctor flatly, and the guards surrounded me. I calmed down somewhat. Everyone parted, embarrassed. Many looked at me as though I were a ghost or a devil. We left the clinic and walked through a park. Suddenly there appeared an arch curving upwards. Above it was written in large letters, "Royal Prussian Regional Insane Asylum Görden."[46]

Simulating madness became a political issue during the war, because it was a means of dodging military service. It was difficult to determine who among the patients in the asylum was merely feigning the condition. There was simply no foolproof way to distinguish true victims from clever *Simu-*

lanten (as malingerers were called in German), who were determined to sit out the war in a mental ward. Some doctors such as Wagner-Jauregg believed that only the threat of severe punishment would discourage potential pretenders. Artist George Grosz was conscripted in January 1917, but suffered a nervous breakdown only a month later. From the sanitarium he wrote a friend:

> My nerves broke down, this time before I could even get near the front and see rotting corpses and barbed wire. . . You work on, polish, build yourself up for years—and suddenly it's all over, you can't adapt and adjust any more to the way the particular powers that be want you to be—you never will be able to. . . . Nerves, down to the tiniest fiber, nausea, revolt—pathological, maybe—anyway, a total breakdown, even in the face of omnipotent regulations.[47]

Nonetheless, Grosz's doctors did not believe he had a nervous condition and pronounced him fit for service at the front. When he was ordered out of bed by a medical student, Grosz attacked him (as Francis attacks Caligari at the end of the film) and in turn was beaten by other patients. This experience, explained Grosz, "burned an indelible scar in my brain—the way those normal everyday fellows beat me up, and the fun they had doing it."[48] After this incident in May 1917, Grosz was discharged as unfit for service. In countless drawings and paintings, he took revenge: one painting originating from 1916–17 shows a skeleton with gold-rimmed glasses (a clue that Grosz is referring to himself), and it is this skeleton that the doctor declares "KV" (*kriegsverwendungsfähig*), or ready for the front. Brecht also used this motif in his sarcastic ballad, "Legende vom toten Soldat*en*" ("Legend of the Dead Soldier"), written in 1918.

Looking back at the war years, Carl von Ossietzky, a respected pacifist and the editor of the leftist review *Die Weltbühne*, declared in the preface to Wilhelm Lamszus's book *Das Irrenhaus: Visionen vom Krieg* (*The Insane Asylum: Visions of War*, 1919):

> The insane asylum, usually a separate realm itself, carefully sanctioned off from the city of rational people, was our present, our gruesome present. We were indeed all possessed. It was by chance that it broke out wildly in one and not in another. We know that each and every day madness prevailed in medical exams, that perfectly healthy fellows were suddenly writhing on the floor in hysterical convul-

sions. We know how these creatures were crouching in the hospital train, sunken-eyed, bent over, their jaws flapping, unable to bring a bit of bread to their mouths for shaking.[49]

Lamszus himself reiterated the parallels between war and insanity: "We were drawn into this war as into an insane asylum, and we were mentally ill, even before the first bullet was fired. . . . Even as I outwardly displayed composure before the horrible events, it felt to me as though the world had become an insane asylum."[50]

Throughout the period of the Weimar Republic, autobiographies and confessions of war resisters and war neurotics appeared, recounting how soldiers rebelled against the war by feigning madness, and how they used madhouses as hiding places in which to avoid the real madness of the front. Ernst Toller, in his 1933 autobiography *Eine Jugend in Deutschland* (*I Was a German),* distinguished between two types of sick men: "The harmless ones lay in barred and bolted rooms and were called lunatics, while the dangerous ones proved that hunger was good for a nation and founded societies dedicated to the downfall of Britain. The dangerous were allowed to lock up the harmless."[51] True revolutionaries, noted Dada poet Hugo Ball in 1916, were more likely to be found in an insane asylum than in the "mechanized" literature and politics of his day. "The primeval strata, untouched and unreached by logic and by the social apparatus, emerge in the unconsciously infantile and in madness, when the barriers are down; that is a world with its own laws and its own form."[52]

Dada embraced and glorified this world of madness in poems, performances, and exhibitions in Zürich and, after 1917, in Berlin. Exponents of a young avant-garde determined to offend and shock the public, the Dadaists managed to capture the limelight with their sarcastic critique of the war as well as of the humanistic impulses of expressionist art. *The Cabinet of Dr. Caligari,* which opened only a few months before the First International Dada Fair in Berlin, was no less mordant in its denigration of war psychiatry than the drawings of a George Grosz. Caligari's freak show displayed an obviously sick person who had been brought to the psychiatrist's office in a wheelchair with symptoms of shell shock. This public exhibition of a patient from a mental institution is as shocking as the effigy of a uniformed soldier with a pig's head that was suspended from a ceiling at the Dada Fair.[53] In 1920, the offensive Dada exhibition and the outrageous film illuminated each other.

The scriptwriters of *The Cabinet of Dr. Caligari*, Hans Janowitz and Carl Mayer, shared the antimilitaristic attitude of the postwar period. Janowitz was a volunteer in the Austrian army but soon turned against the slaughter, particularly after his brother was killed in battle. He reputedly wrote antiwar poems in a notebook, which (according to his later testimony) once prevented a piece of shrapnel from entering his body: "My strongest words against war and its perfidious madness were destroyed by bullets, but they were the means of saving the life of the writer."[54] This anecdote may be apocryphal, but Janowitz's pacifism after the war was real. In 1918, he met Mayer, who had been called up in October of that year to serve in the Austrian army. According to Janowitz's report, Mayer had a contentious encounter with a military psychiatrist who did not find his symptoms of mental illness credible (and they were indeed simulated). After only one day in the army, he was proclaimed unfit for service. At the end of 1918, Janowitz and Mayer, the pacifist and the malingerer, began to collaborate on a film script that, in Janowitz's words, drew on various sources: the case of a mysterious murder in an amusement park, and a variety show about a "machine man" and a fortune-teller. But it was the antiwar sentiment of the immediate postwar years, refracted through their own experience of the war's madness, that fueled their intricate narrative.

On April 19, 1919, Janowitz and Mayer sold their screenplay, titled "Das Cabinett des Dr. Calligari[*sic*]," to Erich Pommer, who would become Weimar Germany's most creative and adventurous producer. At the time, Pommer was director of Decla, a small film production company that would later merge with Ufa. The film was shot between December 1919 and January 1920. The time period in which *Caligari* was conceived, produced, and shown—between late 1918 and early 1920—was one of most traumatic periods of German history. The country suffered a devastating military defeat, an unsuccessful and bloody workers' revolution, a humiliating peace treaty, loss of land and power, and worst of all, the sudden realization that two million German soldiers might have died in vain. Because all attempts at attaching sense to these cataclysmic events failed, only one explanatory model remained: to declare the war and its aftermath a period of collective madness.

The Cabinet of Dr. Caligari articulated this diffuse sense of insanity and hysteria, but also the desperate need to find the meaning for all the suffering. Its sudden narrative turns and "duping" of the audience (the narrator turns out to be mad); its hallucinations, projections, and doppelgänger effects; its commercial appeal as a crime and detective story as well as its avant-garde aesthetics have made *The Cabinet of Dr. Caligari* an emblematic product of the early Weimar Republic. It does not show the war itself, but the conditions under which it functions.

The Hitler Connection

I'm continually worried about the slight degree of power man has over his fellows.

—Bertolt Brecht, *Diary*, September 25, 1920

A number of conflicting stories have circulated about the origin of *The Cabinet of Dr. Caligari.* In an unpublished manuscript about the film's genesis, Janowitz claimed that the story was meant to be a revolutionary tale directed against the authority and tyrannical power personified by Caligari. Yet this intention was neutralized, so Janowitz's story goes, by the addition of a narrative frame that declared the accusations against Caligari to be the imaginings of a madman. This account also appears in Siegfried Kracauer's 1947 history of Weimar cinema, tellingly titled *From Caligari to Hitler: A Psychological History of the German Film.* For Kracauer, *The Cabinet of Dr. Caligari* was meant to unmask and repudiate a madman who incites people to kill against their will; he sees Caligari as a harbinger of evil to come, a symbol of unlimited power wielded over subordinates, and hence as a presentiment of Hitler and the Nazis. Kracauer writes:

> This horror tale in the spirit of E.T.A. Hoffmann was an outspoken revolutionary story. In it, as Janowitz indicates, he and Carl Mayer half-intentionally stigmatized the omnipotence of a state authority manifesting itself in universal conscription and declarations of war. The German war government seemed to the authors the prototype of such voracious authority. Subjects of the Austro-Hungarian monarchy, they were in a better position than most citizens of the Reich to penetrate the fatal tendencies inherent in the German system. The character of Caligari embodies these tendencies; he stands for an unlimited authority that idolizes power as such, and to satisfy its lust for domination, ruthlessly violates all human rights and values. Functioning as a mere instrument, Cesare is not so much a guilty murderer as Caligari's innocent victim. This is how the authors themselves understood him.[55]

With the tacit understanding that a film's meaning arises from the unambiguous expression of authorial intent, Kracauer then castigates director Wiene for adding the frame in which Francis, the narrator, is himself shown as mad:

> The original story was an account of real horrors; Wiene's version transforms that account into a chimera concocted and narrated by the mentally deranged Francis. . . . Janowitz and Mayer knew why they raged against the framing story: it perverted, if not reversed, their intrinsic intentions. While the original story exposed the madness inherent in authority, Wiene's Caligari glorified authority and convicted its antagonist of madness. A revolutionary film was thus turned into a conformist one—following the much-used pattern of declaring some normal but troublesome individual insane and sending him to a lunatic asylum.[56]

It is Wiene's purported encasing of the "initial film" in a subjective frame story that in Kracauer's view makes the film "conformist" in a way that no longer exposes Caligari as a tyrant.

Kracauer's reading of Caligari as a despot figures within a larger discourse about the German national character—a matter of major concern at the end of the Second World War to both the German exile community (Kracauer had fled to Paris in 1933 and to New York in 1941) and the U.S. State Department. What was to be done with a vanquished Germany? Were the Germans by nature authoritarian? Could they be reeducated as democracy-loving citizens? Numerous books and articles addressed these questions. "Can Germany be cured?" was the title of a conference held in New York in 1945. *Time* magazine reported that many intellectuals who attended the conference had doubts that Germans would ever shed their autocratic attitude and despotic conduct.[57] An innate German authoritarianism, many commentators believed, explained the nation's turn to fascism. In order to reeducate its defeated enemy, the United States would first need to understand the collective German psyche.

Enter Kracauer. Struggling to make ends meet as a writer in exile and seeking institutional funding, he hoped to demonstrate that his work on Weimar cinema could play a role in the American attempt to comprehend the German catastrophe. After all Kracauer had been the most prolific and influential film critic of German film throughout the 1920s.

Although he wrote an outline for his book on the German cinema as early as 1942, he recognized the study's uncanny relevance for the political debates about the future destiny of Germany. In 1947, in the preface to *From Caligari to Hitler*, he observes:

> It is my contention that through an analysis of the German films deep psychological dispositions predominant in Germany from 1918 to 1933 can be exposed—dispositions which influenced the course of events during that time and which will have to be reckoned with in the post-Hitler era. I have reason to believe that the use made here of films as a medium of research can profitably be extended to studies of current mass behavior in the United States and elsewhere. I also believe that studies of this kind may help in the planning of film—not to mention other media of communication—which will effectively implement the cultural aims of the United Nations.[58]

Kracauer's interest in German psychological dispositions (especially the authoritarianism that he considered to be ubiquitous in Weimar cinema) calls to mind the exiled Frankfurt School's research on the *Authoritarian Personality*, an empirical study launched in 1945 in collaboration with social scientists at the University of California, Berkeley, to grasp the emergence and impact of fascism and anti-Semitism.[59] Kracauer knew of this inquiry into collective traits and may have seen *From Caligari to Hitler* as a contribution to this larger project.

In addition, Kracauer's claim that the frame narrative in *The Cabinet of Dr. Caligari* had been tacked on, has been subsequently undermined by the discovery of the original screenplay. Contrary to Janowitz and Kracauer's assertion, the script, from its inception, contained a narrative frame, albeit one that sets the uncanny happenings in relief.[60] The frame depicts an evening of entertainment interrupted by wandering gypsies, who trigger Francis's memory. In the film both the frame and the story are equally eerie, causing the viewer to doubt that there is an external point of reference from which the action can be judged.

Rather than suggesting that the ending negates the ostensibly revolutionary impulse of a story that leaves Caligari straitjacketed in a cell, we should instead highlight the unreliability of the narration and the ambiguity over who is insane and who is simulating. This reading of the film surely resonates with contemporaneous debates in the psychiatric establishment over wartime madness. Who could tell for sure if mental patients were not in fact faking their psychosomatic symptoms? In addition, we must realize that deception is innate to film. Cinema, of course, as a medium involves acts of deceit, simulation, and pretending. *The Cabinet of Dr. Caligari* gives expression to a deep ambivalence within the art form and the culture from which it arose about the ways in which cinema presents itself. Both the tangled narrative and the fragmented visual style underscore this ambivalence, complicating and destabilizing meaning, and marking the film as thoroughly modernist.

According to Kracauer's assertion, Caligari foreshadowed Hitler—a teleological claim made ex post facto and marred by political and aesthetic reductionism. Might there perhaps be another, less deterministic way to relate the fictional Caligari to the politics of Weimar?

Two days before the premiere of *The Cabinet of Dr. Caligari*, on January 24, 1920, Adolf Hitler gave his first major speech in a Munich beer hall. It was the first public meeting of the German Workers' Party (later renamed as the National Socialist German Workers' Party). What do Hitler's speech and Wiene's film have in common?

Like so many other soldiers, Hitler was himself a victim of shell shock. After being struck and blinded during one of the last battles of the war, a British poison gas attack in Flanders on October 15, 1918, he was admitted to a hospital in Pasewalk, a town near Berlin. His blindness was diagnosed by Edmund Forster as "psychopathic hysteria."[61] Forster, a professor of psychiatry at the University of Berlin, was no more tolerant of alleged malingerers and fakers than Vienna's Wagner-Jauregg. One of his assistants recalled that Forster "took hysteria to be mostly humbug and treated hysterics accordingly: he would shout at them that they ought to be ashamed before real sufferers."[62] In a 1922 article, "Hysterical Reaction and Simulation," Forster claimed:

> War hysterics would produce every imaginable symptom from fear of the front, are admitted by inexpert doctors to hospitals in the rear or even back home, and then use their special technique to lay first claim to supplies meant for the war wounded. At the same time they would speak with indignation about slackers and tell those who would listen that they could not understand how cowards should exist at such a moment. If only they themselves were well, they would eagerly report for any duty, however dangerous.[63]

Although Hitler's blindness was unquestionably caused by the poison gas attack, the tremors and visions that he suffered while hospitalized made him look like a war neurotic. On hearing about the revolution in Berlin in November 1918, he reportedly had a seizure that restored his eyesight, and this "miracle" gave him the resolve to enter politics. On November 19, 1918, after four weeks in the hospital, he was proclaimed to be cured and released.

An early biographical sketch of Hitler states in 1923:

> The nurse holds the twitching, feverish soldier of the betrayed army in her arms. . . . And a miracle comes to pass. He who was consecrated to eternal night, who had suffered through his Golgotha in this hour, spiritual and bodily crucifixion, pitiless death as on the cross, with senses keen, one of the lowliest out of the mighty host of broken heroes—he becomes seeing! The spasms of his features subside. And in an ecstasy peculiar to the dying seer, new light fills his dead eyes, new radiance, new life![64]

In *Mein Kampf*, Hitler describes the blackout as an epiphany: "While everything began to go black again before my eyes, stumbling, I groped my way back to the dormitory, threw myself on my cot and buried my burning head in the covers and pillows."[65] He weeps but then pulls himself together, adopting the unforgiving attitude of his psychiatrist vis-à-vis war neurotics: "When, under the impact of the shock of fear of becoming blind forever, I was about to despair for a moment, the voice of Conscience thundered at me: Miserable wretch, you want to cry while thousands are a hundred times worse off than you; then I bore my fate apathetically and silently."[66]

Other patients remembered Hitler during his stay in the Pasewalk clinic as "nervously deranged, disturbed. . . . He heard 'voices' and the voices called upon him to become Germany's deliverer."[67] According to his psychiatrist, it was sheer will that would triumph over the war neurotic's body and mind. Leni Riefenstahl's Nazi propaganda film *Triumph of the Will* would later feature Hitler as a God descending from heaven to redeem the German nation.

Very soon after his miraculous recovery and release from the hospital, Hitler joined the newly founded German Workers' Party. In January 1920, as stated, at the organization's first public meeting in the Munich Hofbräuhaus before two thousand listeners, he pleaded for the exclusion, if not yet the extermination, of "foreign elements" from the German populace. The fourth point of his twenty-five-point program stipulated that only Germans with German blood could be citizens; hence Jews were excluded. He also translated anti-capitalist into anti-Semitic sentiments and vowed to reinstate Germany's former glory. Perhaps in order to compensate for his own status as an outsider (an uneducated common soldier from a small Austrian town who did not possess German citizenship), he dedicated himself to the homogenization of what he called the Aryan race, praising all efforts to eliminate everything that was not pure in it. Hitler's program issued from an atmosphere of suspicion and mistrust and it sought to heighten the paranoia, inciting a collective fear of unseen enemies that threatened to attack the body politic.

Germans of many classes and stations, whose nation had experienced crushing defeats both on the battlefield and during peace negotiations, were susceptible to this fearmongering. Especially affected was the German middle class, which felt a deep loss of security after the war. A suspicion of having been deceived and betrayed, both politically and economically, expressed itself in xenophobic discourse. In the beginning of the film, Caligari is portrayed as an evil stranger who wreaks havoc on the small town of Holstenwall. Although his origins are not revealed, he is presented as an itinerant who must obtain a permit for his fairground show. Both the film and the platform of the National Socialists could be viewed, then, as commentaries on the mistrust and paranoia that characterized the early years of the Weimar Republic. However, in contrast to the Nazis who constructed "outsiders" (i.e., non-Aryan Others) as the cause of Germany's problems, the film seems instead to point inward. At the end of his journey, Francis indeed discovers the monster—but the monster from outside turns out to have been inside all along. The evil stranger is no other than the respected director of the local mental ward. In the tradition of the classical detective story, the encounter with the Other turns into a discovery of oneself. More subtly than Grosz or Otto Dix, who at that time obsessively depicted the German professional class as hypocritical war profiteers, the film suggests that psychiatry managed to hide its murderous nationalist intentions and scientific charlatanism behind the façade of professorial respectability.

Shattered Space

Time and space died yesterday.

—Filippo Tommaso Marinetti, *The Manifesto of Futurism*, 1909

On September 14, 1914, about one and a half years before he was killed in the battle of Verdun, the expressionist painter Franz Marc wrote to his wife from the trenches:

> The war will not make a naturalist out of me,—on the contrary: so strongly do I feel the spirit that hovers behind the battles, behind each bullet, that the realistic, the materialistic, disappears completely. Battles, wounds, movements have such a mystical, unreal effect, as though they meant something quite different from what their names signify; everything just stays coded in an awful silence—or my ears are deaf, deafened by noise, in order even now to sound out the true languages of these things. It is unbelievable that there were times in which war was represented by painting campfires, burning villages, galloping horsemen, falling horses, and patrol-riders and the like.[68]

The modern war challenged older forms of representation. A realism that implied a familiarity with and affirmation of one's surroundings could not capture the eerie and alienating desolation of the battlefield, the anonymous mass killing, the permanent threat of poison gas, machine guns, and bombs. Technological warfare had destroyed the natural landscape and turned entire regions into no-man's-land. The battlefields looked empty, with soldiers hiding in their dugouts and all movement restricted for fear of exposure. Stripped of all contingencies and ambiguities in the life-and-death situation of the front, the world, radically reduced to its bare essentials, had become more abstract. The war demanded a new aesthetics.

The Cabinet of Dr. Caligari is neither a war film nor an antiwar film, but its very form produces the aesthetic rupture that, according to Marc, was an inescapable consequence of the war. Different from all naturalistic depictions of "life in the trenches," from staged battles and all-too-harmonious depictions of life behind the front, *Caligari* is relentless in rejecting any semblance of realism. The film refuses to adhere to the standards of cinematic representation that were fully in place by 1920. Its anti-mimetic stance is political: all too often realism had been misused to disseminate false images for war propaganda. Films had to be simple and realistic to be effective in political campaigns against Germany's enemies. *Caligari*'s radical otherness—its tortuous story line, its distorted visuals, its disturbing ending—implies a critique of both the artistic naïveté of earlier films and the deceptive purposes to which they had been put. As Dada destroyed the syntax and semantics of what it considered the language of war, domination, and oppression, so did *Caligari* destroy conventions in the visual realm. It mocked perspective, undermined realistic expectations, decomposed and shattered forms, shapes, and lines. Barren and abstract, *Caligari* is shorn of naturalistic detail; it is an artificial, eerie, and silent witness to a mortified world that is at once elemental and liminal.

A studio production through and through, the film presents an unreal, visibly constructed world without open spaces or roads; cars or horses are unimaginable in these "streets." With high walls leaning inward everywhere, the sets seem to envelope the figures as they move through warped paths that resemble ditches more than streets or sidewalks.

The overall effect of this extremely compact scenery is the kind of claustrophobia that soldiers reportedly experienced while hunkered down in their self-dug trenches. The walls of dirt and mud and the wooden beams that reinforced them tilted precariously like the walls in *Caligari*, seeming to close in on the soldiers who had to live in them for months at a time. In fact, a trench system functioned much like a small, cramped town with pathways zigzagging in different directions; primitive painted signs for orientation; and sloping, low-ceilinged sleeping quarters burrowed into the earthen walls.[69]

The feeling of constriction in the film is further enhanced by the camera. It rarely takes long-distance views and pans only once; it never tracks, thus avoiding shots that might imply freedom of movement. Instead, the camera alternates between medium shots (to advance the story) and abrupt close-ups (to create a shock effect). Because the action is filmed on a studio set—the facsimile of the set in the Cinémathèque Française shows how extraordinarily small it actually was—the camera is not free to roam. The film's dynamic thus derives less from a moving camera than from strong editing that underscores *Caligari*'s narrative of manipulation, control, and shock.

It was the war, claimed Wiene in his 1922 essay "Expressionismus im Film" that deprived German cinema of the ability to move about.[70] Wiene argued that in normal times cinema has the entirety of the natural world—sky, earth, and water—as a film set at its disposal. The war, however, "which

The spaces of trauma: deep shadows and denuded landscapes in *The Cabinet of Dr. Caligari*.

is still continuing even without weapons," restricted such freedom. Filmmakers had to resort to simulated sets and relinquish any mimetic resolve. For Wiene the question became one of exploring the realm of the unreal, the spiritual, and the emotional. The flatness of the image, the stylized starkness of black and white, and the distorted artificiality of the sets created a fantastic tale in the tradition of E.T.A. Hoffmann.

Film space becomes constricted by harsh lighting that produces deep shadows cutting across a scene or splitting a face. Because the set designers and gaffers at the small Decla studio did not have access to the latest electric searchlights developed for military purposes (only the large film studios were beneficiaries of the new war technology), they tried to enhance their lighting effects by crudely painting shadows on the walls and floors. The set and lighting design show *Caligari*'s affinity to the expressionist theater, which had experienced its heyday between 1917 and 1920. Widely discussed productions—for instance, Max Reinhardt's staging of Reinhard Johannes Sorge's *Der Bettler* (*The Beggar*) in 1917, and Leopold Jessner's productions of Friedrich Schiller's *Wilhelm Tell* in 1919 and Toller's *Die Wandlung* (*The Transformation*) in 1920—became known for their deliberately nonrepresentational style, radical abstraction, and stylized acting.

Similarly, *Caligari*'s scenery looks unabashedly theatrical and nonrealistic. Its houses with skewed windows and crooked doors are uninhabitable, and the dead trees have a painted look. And yet in their artificial state they interact with the characters, giving added force to their inexpressible turmoil. For Gilles Deleuze, "[t]he non-organic life of things, a frightful life, which is oblivious to the wisdom and limits of the organism, is the first principle of Expressionism. . . . From this point of view natural substances and artificial creations, candelabras and trees, turbine and sun are no longer any different. A wall, which is alive, is dreadful; but utensils, furniture, houses and their roofs also lean, crowd around, lie in wait, or pounce. Shadows of houses pursue the man running along the street."[71] In silent film, speech, desires, and anxieties must find expression in mute signs that signify what cannot be put in words. The protagonists' restless inner world animates their surroundings; they encounter their environment like a repressed and haunting double.

Ludwig Kirchner, a shell-shock victim himself, painted streets and carnivals that share with *Caligari*'s sets a jagged angularity and two-dimensionality that deconstructs central perspective with its illusion of depth, the visual principle that had governed artistic representation since the Renaissance.

Reviewers at the time criticized *Caligari*'s simplistic association of nonnaturalistic style with insanity: "If you are mad, you see the world in expressionist terms," or alternatively, "if you are an expressionist, you are most likely mad."[72] The National Socialists later capitalized on this association of expressionism and mental illness in their 1937 Degenerate Art Exhibition, denigrating all avant-garde art as the work of madmen.

In his magisterial book *The Production of Space*, Henri Lefebvre states:

> Around 1910 a certain space was shattered. It was the space of common sense, of knowledge, of social practice, of political power, a space hitherto enshrined in everyday discourse, just as in abstract thought, as the environment of and channel for communications. . . . Euclidean and perspectivist space have disappeared as systems of reference, along with other former "commonplaces" such as the town, history, paternity, the tonal system in music, traditional morality, and so forth. This was a truly crucial moment.[73]

At this "truly crucial moment," film emerged as a cultural medium worthy of serious attention. It may well be that this new art form both echoed and contributed to Lefebvre's "shattering of space." No medium made spatial disjuncture and the proliferation of conflicting perspectives easier. None was better suited to recreate the disorienting visual experience of the war. Breaking with the principle of spatial continuity pioneered by Griffith, *Caligari* was one of the first films to exploit cinema's revolutionary potential.

"I very well remember," writes Gertrude Stein in her book on Pablo Picasso, "at the beginning of the war, being with Picasso on the Boulevard Raspail when the first camouflaged truck passed. It was night, we had heard of camouflage but had not yet seen it, and Picasso, amazed, looked at it, and then cried out, yes it is we who made it, that is Cubism."[74] What Picasso saw were structural affinities between Cubism and camouflage: a decomposition of forms and shapes, a deformation of objects and their reconfiguration in artistic space, a leveling of foreground and background, an interpenetration of objects and space. In their paintings Picasso and Georges Braque also employed conflicting multiple perspectives, geometrized forms, and the insertion of numbers, letters, advertisements, and other prosaic objects. Looking carefully at the sets of *Caligari*, one is struck by their affinity with Cubism and camouflage. Intensifying a tale of deception and concealment, simulation and disguise, the painted sets have a camouflage effect in which foreground and background mesh, and objects blend into their surroundings. Like Cubist paintings, *Caligari*'s sets disregard empirical reality for the sake of a purely artistic reality; they break down forms, reduce depth, and even incorporate numbers, paragraphs, and other unrecognizable scrawls and graffiti.

All spaces are equal on canvas, said the Cubists—and the sets of *Caligari* demonstrate this. There is, however, a strange tension between the film's radically two-dimensional Cubist sets and the living actors traversing the painterly surfaces in what is clearly three-dimensional space. Reduced to two dimensions, the characters themselves, like soldiers in camouflage, blend into the scenery, reminding the viewer once again of the war as the film's silence that speaks.

The Cabinet of Dr. Caligari marks a bold beginning in Weimar's engagement with the trauma of the war. Participating in the contemporaneous debates about military psychiatry, shell shock, and malingering, the film is concerned with recording and saving a memory of the war experience that must not be lost—precisely because it runs counter to the official orthodoxy with its intent to harmonize and heroicize the conflict. In the spirit of Grosz, Dix, and the Berlin Dadaists who painted a scathing portrait of the German professional class in 1919–20, *Caligari* offers an equally aggressive and grotesque image of bureaucracy and the medical establishment. Using motifs borrowed from Gothic fiction, it also rejects traditional cinematic realism by adopting a form that mimics the physical and mental wasteland left behind by the first technological war. By extending the concept of shell shock to the cinematic medium itself, and thereby exploding its visual grammar and narrative syntax, *Caligari* preserves the liminal experience of the front more authentically than any naturalistic depiction of war and its human consequences. If *The Cabinet of Dr. Caligari* encodes the war without pity and humanist appeal as a psychiatrist's horror cabinet, Friedrich Wilhelm Murnau's 1922 film *Nosferatu* tells a different story of mass death, sacrifice, and redemption.

The Return of the Undead

Away with you, I am the ghost. I am dead, they buried me.
—Kragler in Bertolt Brecht, *Drums in the Night*, 1922

I must clear up once and for all a fundamental error: that we dead are somehow dead. We are full of protest and energy. Who wants to die?
—Alexander Kluge, *Die Patriotin*, 1980

Dying is nothing. You have to know how to disappear.
—Jean Baudrillard, *Cool Memories*, 1990

The Lost Generation

The old men should be shipped off to war. They can kill one another if they want, they shouldn't rob youth of its blood, which is a vicious act against the future of society.

—Gershom Scholem, *Lamentation of Youth: Diaries*, 1913–19

"Generation of 1914—close your eyes and a host of images leaps to mind: of students packing off to war with flowers in their rifles and patriotic songs on their lips, too young, too innocent to suspect what bloody rites of passage awaited them."[1] Thus begins Robert Wohl's influential study of the generation of 1914, the "lost generation" born between 1880 and 1900 whose life was doomed by the Great War. Wohl traces the fate of this young European generation whose suffering and sacrifice have been recorded in autobiographical literature as well as novels, poems, plays—and, I would like to suggest, at least one film: Friedrich Wilhelm Murnau's *Nosferatu, eine Symphonie des Grauens* (*Nosferatu, a Symphony of Horror*), which opened in March 1922. The film tells the story of Hutter, a naïve young man who is sent east by his elders (like the generation of 1914 was sent to the eastern front), only to return traumatized by "bloody rites of passage." His encounter with Nosferatu, the vampire, allegorizes his encounter with death.

It is revealing that the film takes recourse to vampire lore to narrate the war experience: for Murnau, the vampire's need for blood and his ruthless victimization of innocence connotes the nature of war. In *Nosferatu*, Hutter's story parallels that of a soldier from the lost generation, while his equally traumatized wife, Ellen, embodies the home front living in fear and gripped by a death wish. The film shows how the young man's initial decision to go east on a business venture is like a disease that infects not only him but also his wife and the whole community. Count Orlok, Nosferatu's double (whose name is evocative of *oorlog*, the Dutch word for "war"), invades the town and brings mass death with him. The killing does not stop until a young woman sacrifices herself for the community. A lost generation indeed.

Nosferatu begins with title cards that mimic handwritten diary entries by an anonymous author (identified by three crosses):

> Account of the mass death in Wisborg in the year 1838, by +++

> I have thought long about the beginning and the end of the mass death in my hometown of Wisborg. Here is its history: there lived in Wisborg Hutter and his young wife Ellen.[2]

As in *The Cabinet of Dr. Caligari*, *Nosferatu*'s story is set in the past, but here the exact date is noted, lending an air of precision and historical objectivity that is lacking in the earlier film. *Nosferatu* does not rely on a character's flashback but on a written account by an unidentified survivor whose comments periodically (no less than thirteen times in the course of the film) interrupt the flow of the story. Ostensibly perturbed, the chronicler and diarist reflects on the origins and consequences of "the mass dying" (*das grosse Sterben*). In the tradition of romantic storytelling, a sympathetic but unsophisticated narrator tells a supernatural tale, mediating between the fantastic world of fiction and the rational world of the audience, and thus providing a measure of normalcy against which the bizarre fictional characters and events are thrown into relief. The diary entries distance us from the monstrous tale, as if its shock can be tempered by a rational account. Moreover, the uncanny event of mass death is verified by the authority of the written word, set in opposition to the instability of moving images.

The first image of the film, an aerial shot of a small town with a steeple at its center, establishes the narrator's detached perspective. An old-fashioned iris closes and opens to a medium shot of the young protagonist Hutter, who rearranges his collar in front of a wall mirror, his face doubled. He appears self-absorbed and puerile. We soon see him in a long shot in an open field plucking flowers. Hiding the bouquet behind his back, he playfully returns to the room where his wife, Ellen, knits. He acts like a child as they embrace and kiss on the cheeks. His innocence is betrayed by her reaction. Her expression turns somber and she asks, "Why did you kill them, these beautiful flowers?" The word "kill" introduces the theme of violence against nature, against living things, a premonition of events to come. Hutter soothes her, but it is clear that he has no clue of what she means. This brief encounter leads to another mysterious scene: as Hutter walks briskly down a cobblestoned lane he runs into a distinguished-looking older man, Professor Bulwer (as we learn later), seemingly an acquaintance. They shake hands, and the title card reads: "Not so hasty, young friend. Nobody escapes his fate." The professor's odd warning and bemused expression betray knowledge unavailable to our young hero. The old man seems to know

"Why did you kill the flowers?"
Sacrifice and death
in F.W. Murnau's *Nosferatu*.

what awaits Hutter. Could he be part of a conspiracy against him? The encounter takes on a sinister note when we recall that it was the older generation that sent its innocent youth to meet their fate on the battlefield.

Nosferatu's third scene further highlights Hutter's naïveté. His employer, a gnomelike old wizard, is introduced in an intertitle: "There was also a real estate agent Knock who was the subject of many a rumor. All that was certain was that he paid his people well." Knock reads a letter (shown in a close-up) filled with a jumble of astrological signs, letters in Hebrew, miniature swastikas, and Stars of David. He summons Hutter and proposes that he travel to a certain Count Orlok in Transylvania to sell a house in Wisborg. (Count Orlok turns out to be the vampire called Nosferatu.[3]) "You could earn good money," Knock says, prodding young Hutter to embark on the journey, though "it will cost some efforts, a bit of sweat and perhaps . . . a little blood." While Hutter tries to find Transylvania on the map, tracing the road to Eastern Europe with his finger, it is made clear that Knock's intentions are evil. "Travel fast," Knock admonishes him, "travel well, young friend, to the land of ghosts (*Gespenster*)." (The opening scene of *The Cabinet of Dr. Caligari* similarly invoked malevolent "ghosts.") Knock shakes Hutter's hand with such a frenzied laugh that Hutter, who at first joins in, suddenly becomes frightened. Again he has no notion of what is at stake.

When Hutter takes leave of Ellen, she is overcome with foreboding, in stark contrast to his own childlike enthusiasm. He runs back and forth, while the untouched bed—a reminder of their marital status—remains clearly in view. He is undeterred by her sadness. A title explains that Hutter has placed his worried wife in the custody of a friend and his sister. He rushes away, but the camera suddenly cuts from a long shot to a close-up of Ellen, who cries out for him. She rushes down the stairs after him and gives him another embrace. As he leaves, she breaks down. He mounts a waiting horse and rides off. This drawn-out farewell is reminiscent of classical cinematic leave-taking scenes, which took on new resonance during the war. A naïve young man leaves behind the secure and feminized world of domesticity in order to experience a radically different realm in which he will confront death. What *Nosferatu* stresses, however, is that it is the older generation that sends this innocent young man into harm's way. Murnau emphasizes Hutter's youthful eagerness and incomprehension—traits he shares with Wohl's young generation of 1914, "too young, too innocent to suspect what bloody rites of passage await them."[4]

Murnau himself was deeply conscious of the human cost of war. A young actor in Max Reinhardt's theater, he was drafted in 1914 at the age of twenty-six, fought on the western front, and was soon promoted to the rank of officer. After surviving the battle of Verdun, he was sent to Galicia and Latvia on the eastern front. He joined the German Air Force in 1916 and served as a radio operator.[5] In December 1917, after making an emergency landing in Switzerland, he was interned as a prisoner of war until the fighting ceased. His closest friend and lover from his bohemian days in Berlin, the young poet Hans Ehrenbaum-Degele, volunteered to join the army but was not as lucky as Murnau. He was twenty-five when he was killed on the eastern front in the first year of the war. An editor of the modernist journal *Das neue Pathos*, Ehrenbaum-Degele had introduced Murnau to expressionist painters and poets, including Franz Marc and Else Lasker-Schüler. The premature death of his friend shocked Murnau profoundly. One of the poems that Ehrenbaum sent him from the front ends with the following stanza:

Dig your grave deeper, soldier!
Perhaps one day peace will be born
To the sound of bells
From one tower to another;
And everything will shine again.[6]

The poem's author finds solace in the belief that the sacrifice of his life may contribute to the moral progress of humanity. It is a religiously tinged sentiment common for its time and reminiscent of a best-selling short autobiographical work, *Wanderer zwischen zwei Welten: Ein Kriegserlebnis* (*Wanderer between Two Worlds: A War Experience*), written by another young soldier of the lost generation, Walter Flex. His book memorialized a friend who was one of the many idealistic, innocent, "pure" youths who fell in battle in 1914. A volunteer himself, Flex was killed on the eastern front in 1917. Posthumously published and hugely popular, *Wanderer* attributed meaning to the war by figuring it as a transcendent and mystical encounter with life on the edge of death.[7] Numerous descriptions of nature and the elements were meant to naturalize the soldiers' untimely end on the battlefield. According to this argument, dying for a higher cause was a blessing because it put an end to egotism and materialism. By drawing an analogy to the passion and sacrifice of Christ, the lost generation found a deeper spiritual, even heroic significance in their premature deaths.

Murnau's relationship to his fallen friend was so intimate that he moved in with the Ehrenbaum family after the war and became a substitute son, thus facing the loss daily. It may have been the trauma of his friend's death that led Murnau to revisit the scenario of a young man eagerly departing for a long journey. Although Hutter is not killed, his passage into the realm of death cuts his youth short; afterward he appears traumatized, only a shadow of his former self. His fate alludes to that of tens of thousands of romantic and idealistic young German men who rushed into combat, flushed with blind enthusiasm despite admonitions and warnings.[8]

The film depicts Hutter's journey as the zealous excursion of an unprepared young man into a death zone, beyond the bounds of civilization. While in the film's first half Hutter travels east to meet Count Orlok, in the second half the vampire travels west, bringing death and pestilence. At the close of the film, Hutter is stricken with symptoms of shell shock and impotence; his wife is dead, as is most of the town's population. What started out as a wild and exhilarating adventure ends in catastrophe: *das grosse Sterben*, dying on a mass scale. The film's narrative reiterates the trajectory of a war in which millions eagerly set off only to return in despair, if they returned at all.

Mass Death

Nosferatu's pseudo-documentary style elicits a surge of associations in the spectator. Its first title card refers to the fictional town of Wisborg, an allusion to the (still well-preserved) northern German port city of Wismar, in which Murnau did some of the location shooting. The year 1838 is mentioned as the date of the mass death, vaguely referencing the cholera outbreak in Germany in the 1830s that killed hundreds of thousands in Europe (including such figures as Georg Wilhelm Friedrich Hegel and Carl von Clausewitz). Cholera returned periodically in the nineteenth century, claiming an estimated one million victims in Europe alone. Even after Robert Koch discovered the cholera bacillus in 1883, an epidemic broke out in Hamburg again in 1892, killing ten thousand.[9]

While tuberculosis and other diseases claimed even more victims, the psychological impact of cholera was unprecedented because death often occurred within a few hours of the first signs of illness. According to William McNeill,

[t]he speed with which cholera killed was profoundly alarming, since perfectly healthy people could never feel safe from sudden death when the infection was anywhere near. In addition, the symptoms were peculiarly horrible: radical dehydration meant that a victim shrank into a wizened caricature of his former self within a few hours, while ruptured capillaries discolored the skin, turning it black and blue. The effect was to make mortality uniquely visible: patterns of bodily decay were exacerbated and accelerated, as in a time-lapse motion picture, to remind all who saw it of death's ugly horror and utter inevitability.[10]

The disease was understood as a return of the infamous bubonic plague, or Black Death, which in fourteenth-century Europe killed close to half the population in just four years. Toward the end of the war, from March 1918 to June 1920, a global influenza pandemic (the so-called Spanish flu) hit Europe, killing twice as many people as had died during the war. The disease spread just as the plague had centuries before, aggravated by poor diet, poverty, and a sharp decline in sanitation caused by the war. It affected the front lines and the home front equally. The epidemic, according to Alfred Crosby, "had a worse effect on the fighting qualities of an army than death itself. The dead were dead, and that was that: they were no longer assets, but neither were they debits. But flu took good men and made them into delirious staggering debits whose care required the diversion of healthy men from important tasks."[11] Arriving on the heels of defeat and starvation, the epidemic produced striking images of the frightful contagiousness and transmissibility of death. Murnau shows a city official marking large crosses on door after door with chalk, to indicate that everyone in the house has died and the building is abandoned. We also see a long procession of pallbearers, carrying coffins along a cobbled street out of the town to the cemetery, a scene that Ellen watches from her window and that strengthens her resolve to end the misery by sacrificing herself.

"Why doest thou scourge mankind with war, plague, and famine?" Satan is asked in Murnau's film version of *Faust*, released in 1926. The nexus of war, plague, and famine—three of the Four Horsemen of the Apocalypse—left indelible marks in popular memory, scars that persisted throughout the 1920s. In *Nosferatu*, the epidemic is a visually potent substitute for the experience of death in the First World War; it is a mask that at once expresses

The overwhelming
presence of death
in Murnau's *Nosferatu*.

and represses the traumatic experience of mass killing. Representations of previous plagues provided a language with which Murnau could symbolize the "Great Death" of the recent war.

The numbers of those who died in battle were staggering. The October 1914 Battle of Langemarck, the war's first major battle, saw three thousand young men mowed down by experienced British riflemen.[12] These were for the most part high school and university students—many belonged to the Wandervogel, a prewar youth movement; all were volunteers with romantic ideas of war and patriotism. They were reported to have sung "Deutschland, Deutschland über alles" as they were sent into machine-gun fire. The myth of Langemarck, which the Nazis were to exploit in World War II, was built on a forceful premise: fallen heroes had sacrificed their young lives for the fatherland. "The bloom of German youths," wrote nationalist author Werner Beumelburg in 1929, "proved themselves to be experts in the art of attacking and dying."[13]

The Battle of Verdun lasted ten months, from February to December 1916. Of the approximately 2.5 million German and French soldiers who took part, approximately 350,000 were killed, an average of 6,000 men per day. About 770,000 were wounded. The Battle of the Somme lasted five months, from July to November 1916. It involved four million soldiers along a thirty-mile front between Amiens and Péronne. More than a million men died or were wounded—two hundred thousand casualties each month.[14] The Battle of Passchendaele (Third Ypres) lasted a little more than three months (July 31 to November 10, 1917). The casualties amounted to over half a million. Ninety thousand British and Australian bodies were never identified; forty-two thousand bodies were never recovered because they had been blown to bits or had drowned in the bottomless mud after four days of incessant rain. "The battlefield is really nothing but one vast cemetery," wrote a young German soldier in a letter home.[15] Not one of these three major battles produced any significant military gains on either side.

According to official figures published in 1934, an estimated two million Germans died of the 13.25 million called up for military service.[16] Almost half of these men were twenty-five or younger when they were killed, and almost a third were married. The total number of women widowed by the war was around six hundred thousand (two-thirds of them were still receiving pensions in 1930), and over a million children were left fatherless. Here we indeed witness a "grosses Sterben," the large-scale death that the film's opening title card invokes.

Reflections on death abounded "in these days of monstrously accelerated dying," as Rainer Maria Rilke wrote in a letter on October 4, 1914, only two months after the war's outbreak.[17] Freud, in his 1915 essay, "Thoughts for the Times on War and Death," speaks of a "disturbance that has taken place in the attitude which we have hitherto adopted towards death."[18] The war, which confronted the living with the long-suppressed reality of violent death, "strips us," writes Freud, "of the later accretions of civilization, and lays bare the primal man in each of us. It compels us once more to be heroes who cannot believe in their own death; it stamps strangers as enemies, whose death is to be brought about or desired; it tells us to disregard the death of those we love."[19] Freud ends his essay with an admonishment:

> But war cannot be abolished; so long as the conditions of existence among the nations are so different and their mutual repulsion so violent, there are bound to be wars. The question then arises: Is it not we who must give in, who should adapt ourselves to war? Should we not confess that in our civilized attitude towards death we are once again living psychologically beyond our means, and should we not rather turn back and recognize the truth? Would it not be better to give death the place in reality and in our thoughts which is its due, and to give a little more prominence to the unconscious attitude towards death which we have hitherto so carefully suppressed?[20]

Murnau's film about mass dying answers Freud's exhortation to confront death openly as it lets us vicariously and safely experience what has been deemed unimaginable: one's own death. Freud is fully aware of the price of denying death in modern civilization: "Life is impoverished, it loses in interest, when the highest stake in the game of living, life itself, may not be risked."[21] Life without the danger of death becomes, in his words, "flat, superficial, and inconsequential, and boring. Thus we are torn: while we crave security for ourselves and our loved ones and forego many things simply because they are too dangerous, we are secretly fascinated by what we have suppressed: adventure, risk, death."[22] Fiction, Freud goes on to say, has long acted as a substitute for adventure, risk, and life-threatening dangers:

> It is an inevitable result of all this that we should seek in the world of fiction, in literature and in the theatre compensation for what has been lost in life. There we still find people who know how to die—

> who, indeed, even manage to kill someone else. There alone too the condition can be fulfilled which makes it possible for us to reconcile ourselves with death: namely, that behind all the vicissitudes of life we should still be able to preserve a life intact. For it is really too sad that in life it should be as it is in chess, where one false move may force us to resign the game, but with the difference that we can start no second game, no return-match. In the realm of fiction we find the plurality of lives which we need. We die with the hero with whom we have identified ourselves; yet we survive him, and are ready to die again just as safely with another hero.[23]

Freud offers a theory of the status and function of fiction in a modern age characterized by increased security, monotony, and predictability, an age in which death is banned and risk is seen as something to avoid. It is fiction—literature, and even more so the cinema—that provides thrills, and allows a confrontation with death and dying. The war, however, according to Freud, changed this fictionalization of death:

> It is evident that the war is bound to sweep away this conventional treatment of death. Death will no longer be denied; we are forced to believe in it. People really die; and no longer one by one, but many, often tens of thousands, in a single day. And death is no longer a chance event. To be sure, it still seems a matter of chance whether a bullet hits this man or that; but a second bullet may well hit the survivor; and the accumulation of deaths puts an end to the impression of chance. Life has, indeed, become interesting again; it has recovered its full content.[24]

In this disturbing passage, Freud captures the double nature of danger and risk as it pertained to the millions who went to war in August 1914. No longer dependent on simulations in literature and film, they were to experience death in reality.

Dracula Revisited

Murnau's *Nosferatu* is a film about mass death and self-sacrifice. It works through the experience of the war at a time when German society had just begun to mourn its dead and commemorate their sacrifice. It is also the story of an undead vampire who sucks blood from the living. Even though the film's narrative draws heavily on Irish writer Bram Stoker's popular vampire novel *Dracula*, it is very much a German film of the postwar period. It was the first and last film of the production company Prana-Film, founded by businessman Enrico Dieckmann along with set designer and spiritist Albin Grau in January 1921. Prana-Film (*prana* meaning "life force" in spiritualist lingo) wanted to create an artistic film in the tradition of *The Cabinet of Dr. Caligari*, and certain narrative tropes from that film reappear in *Nosferatu*: the invasion of a life-threatening stranger, the desperate and ultimately hopeless fight against him, and the embrace of the insane and supernatural underscored by the set design. Grau stated: "The terror of the war is gone from the eyes of the people, but something remains, namely the longing to understand, if only subconsciously, what lies behind the horrific events, what roared like a cosmic vampire."[25] In 1921, Grau hired Henrik Galeen, author of the Golem films of 1915 and 1920, to write the screenplay for *Nosferatu*, a loose adaptation of Stoker's 1897 novel that was translated into German in 1908.

Stoker's *Dracula* stands in a long tradition of vampire stories from high romanticism: John Polidori's *The Vampyre*, the first English-language vampire story, was published in 1819, one year after Mary Shelley's *Frankenstein*. Polidori's tale depicts an aristocrat who seduces young women in order to drink their blood. The figure of the cruel ruler who does not die a normal death mixes fantastic elements with folkloric accounts of a certain Vlad, nicknamed "the Impaler," a fifteenth-century count from Romania known for impaling his enemies. Stoker's *Dracula* modernized the story: true to the scientific spirit of the late nineteenth century, the vampire's antagonist is the philosopher and scientist Van Helsing. Stoker's novel depicted the triumph of science and common sense over occultism and repressed desire.

What attracted *Nosferatu*'s screenwriter to Stoker's novel is not known. Henrik Galeen, born in Berlin in 1881, had been a member of Reinhardt's theater before he coauthored (with Paul Wegener) the screenplay for the 1915 version of *Der Golem*, now lost. As with *Nosferatu*, he drew his material from folklore—in this case, a legend about the creation of an artificial being who was both a murderous monster and the protector of the embattled Jewish ghetto in Prague. In 1920, Galeen directed a film (also lost) titled *Judith Trachtenberg: Die Tragödie einer Jüdin* (*Judith Trachtenberg: The Tragedy of a Jewess*). He also cowrote with Wegener the screenplay for *Der Golem, wie er in die Welt kam* (*The Golem, How He Came into the World*, 1920), wrote the script for Paul Leni's *Wachsfigurenkabinett* (*Waxworks*, 1923), and in 1926 directed a remake of the original 1913 *The Student of Prague*, yet another film based on an old folktale of the uncanny. In his adaptation of *Dracula*, Galeen changed the setting from 1890s Britain to northern Germany in the 1830s; he also eliminated or combined various minor characters, changed the names of the protagonists, and altered the story line to avoid having to pay copyright fees.[26]

In the film, Jonathan Harker becomes Hutter; Mina becomes Hutter's wife, Ellen; Van Helsing becomes Professor Bulwer; Dr. Seward becomes Dr. Siewers; and the real estate dealer Knock is a composite of a real estate agent named Peter Hawkins and Renfield, an inmate at the lunatic asylum.

A closer comparison, though, reveals more substantial differences between Stoker's novel and Murnau's film. Both contain a significant double movement: first, a young man travels from the west to the mysterious and dangerous east where the vampire resides. Then, in a sort of "reverse colonization," the vampire travels from the east to the west—with deadly consequences. But whereas the novel ends with the triumph of science and manly courage (the vampire is killed by Van Helsing's men), Murnau's film ends with a woman's lethal self-sacrifice for the survival of the community. She is not seduced or raped but takes her cue from the Book of Vampires, which states, "No other deliverance is possible, but that an innocent maiden maketh the vampire heed not the first crowe of the cock by giving willingly of her bloode." The film shows her reading this passage twice.

Stoker's vampire is seen as an invader who must be destroyed, while Murnau's Nosferatu goes completely unchallenged by Hutter and the entire town's population; in fact, he is never even visible to the townspeople. A mere phantom, he does not interact with anyone, and his presence is not acknowledged, except by Ellen. Is Nosferatu a figment of the woman's imagination triggered by her reading? Echoing the experience of many women left alone on the home front, she is shown as desirous, vulnerable, and susceptible to infidelity. She also embodies an unconscious death wish characteristic of those who stayed behind while their betrothed died in the trenches.

Stoker's novel ends happily with marriage triumphant over the vampire's debauchery. In the novel's epilogue we hear that Mina and Jonathan Harker have had a son, signaling the return of normalcy. Murnau's film, on the other hand, ends on a mournful note. The last scene shows Ellen on her deathbed (also the site of her transgression), where she is held in the arms of her husband. The camera jumps to a long shot framing the couple and bringing into view the scientist Bulwer, a resigned expression on his face. Murnau's narrative culminates in a woman's self-sacrifice and the utter impotence of the male characters.

The novel is centered around the conflict between Dracula and Van Helsing, allegorizing the struggle between untamed nature and rational civilization, between menacing yet mesmerizing forces of sexual, cultural, and ethnic otherness and the safe but dull reign of Victorian domesticity. The monster embodies transgression; it represents the return of the repressed in horrific form. Murnau's *Nosferatu* has an altogether different agenda. The film abbreviates the cast of characters: no female vampires inhabit the castle, and the number of Nosferatu's victims is reduced. All but eliminated from the film is the figure of Lucy, Mina's sexual counterpart, who after turning into a vampire herself, is killed with a stake. While *Dracula*'s Van Helsing is an imposing figure capable of reviving dying brides and killing monsters, *Nosferatu*'s Professor Bulwer seems a caricature of the insulated academic, inscrutable to those around him. The sexual rapaciousness of the Victorian monster is present but de-emphasized, as is the scientific didacticism of the narrative's protagonist, in favor of an exploration of death, sexual anxiety, and sacrifice. While in Stoker's novel everyone lives happily ever after (no less than three marriages are celebrated at the end of *Dracula),* Murnau's film ends with the death of Ellen.

To this day, Murnau's vampire figure conjures up a host of associations. The "vampire film" has become a genre whose iconography and narrative tropes still draw on *Nosferatu*, the first moving picture to feature a vampire. Is the undead a reminder of death, a phantom of the unconscious, or a corpse roaming the earth to take revenge on the living? Even though these contradictory connotations compete with each other, one overriding meaning is undeniable: the vampire represents an ultimate otherness that must be eliminated.

First of all, the vampire in Murnau's film personifies a state between life and death, a liminal state that was all too familiar to soldiers in the trenches. Eric Leed describes the structure of the war experience:

> In war death lost the perfect, abstract clarity that it normally enjoyed as the brief moment between life and not-life. It ceased to be an abstraction and became a term defining the growing distance from

which the combatant viewed his home. It described the sense of total isolation from "the external world," a sense that is most intensified in the experience of living burial. In general, death began to define the range of events that removed the front soldier further and further from the values, sensory certainties, and hierarchies of status that had once rendered his experience unambiguous and his "self" identifiable.[27]

When reading *Nosferatu* historically, yet another parallel emerges. In the mass killing of World War I, tens of thousands of war dead were never properly buried and mourned. Corpses were strewn over the battlefields or dumped into mass graves; the trenches themselves often served as graves where soldiers were buried alive after a shell explosion. Hence, there was a widespread fear that the ghosts of unburied soldiers would roam the earth in search of a final resting place. A large spiritist and occultist movement sprang up in Germany in the immediate postwar years because it held out the promise of contact with the spirits of relatives killed in battle.

The fear of ghosts is deeply rooted in myth, folklore, and primitive religions, with ritual burial functioning to protect the living from the vengeance of the spirits of the deceased. In his study *Vampires, Burial, and Death*, Paul Barber states: "There are such creatures everywhere in the world, it seems, in a variety of disparate cultures: dead people who, having died before their time not only refuse to remain dead but return to bring death to their friends and neighbors."[28] Because, according to these myths, the ghosts of soldiers who died before their time frequently appeared on the battlefields, corpses of military personnel were at times maimed to prevent the dead from walking. Burial and mourning rites therefore began not as acts of respect for the deceased, but rather as acts of self-defense. Barber explains: "The dead may bring us death. To prevent this we must lay them to rest properly, propitiate them, and, when all else fails, kill them a second time."[29]

When Nosferatu (in the guise of Count Orlok) is first mentioned in the film, Hutter turns to the map on the wall to find his location. He runs his finger across it until it comes to rest on the Balkans, the southeastern part of Europe, the place where a single shot by a Serbian nationalist triggered a war that brought mass death and destruction over Germany and the world. Identifying a concrete geographic site where the phantom resides has an ironic tinge, considering the imaginary nature of the vampire. Indeed, the film is rendered only the more striking because its uncanny narrative unfolds within the stylistic conventions of documentary filmmaking. It presents a new and surprisingly effective mixture of ethnographic *Kulturfilm* and phantasmagoria, oscillating between the material and the immaterial. To posit the existence of a mythical count in faraway Eastern Europe is a conceit that blends the fantasy of a classical fairy tale with the concreteness of a travel film.

Much of *Nosferatu* was shot in Dolné Kúbin, a town in Slovakia, where Murnau and his team stayed. They used the nearby Oravsky Podzámok fortress as the setting for Orlok's castle[30] and recruited peasants from the surrounding villages as extras. Location shooting and a cast of natives lent authenticity to the implausible and bizarre story. Before Hutter enters the vampire's realm, he stops at an inn where peasants flinch and recoil at the mere mention of Count Orlok. Acting with studied simplicity, they warn Hutter against meeting with the Count and leave the *Book of Vampires* next to his bed. Once again, the film uses writing as a counterpoint to the visual: Hutter begins reading the book "Of Vampyres, Terrible Phantomes and the Seven Deadly Sins," but scorns it. With a laugh, he casts it aside, but not before the spectator (now a reader as well) gets a lesson in vampire lore: "From the seed of Belial," the intertitle explains, "sprang the Vampyre Nosferatu, who liveth and feedeth on human bloode. This unholy creature liveth in sinister caves, tombes and coffins which are filled with cursed dirt from the fields of the Black Death."

The next morning, as Hutter approaches "the other side," his coachman refuses to proceed beyond a certain point. Hutter continues his journey on foot. After crossing a bridge he is met by a carriage with Count Orlok/Nosferatu as its coachman. To indicate Hutter's (and our own) entry into another realm, the film stock briefly turns into negative print: trees and road appear in spectral white, while the coach remains black (Murnau had it wrapped in white linen). This uncanny effect of reverse printing suggests to the viewer a realm that is normally invisible, like the negative on which a photographic print is based. The film thus literalizes Freud's analogy between the unconscious and photography: "A photographic picture begins as a negative and only becomes a picture after being formed into a positive. Not every negative, however, necessarily becomes a positive; nor is it necessary that every unconscious mental process should turn into a conscious one."[31] In this way, the negative sequence—the film's hidden unconscious side—suggests that Hutter enters an invisible realm that is also the realm of film technology itself.[32] Murnau uses time-lapse and stop-motion animation to render a fast yet jerking movement through space. Shots of the

Nosferatu's territory
of the unreal: trauma
as phantasmagoria.

coach hurtling through the woods are intercut with close-ups of Hutter's distraught expression as he realizes that he is rapidly losing control over his fate. His experience of speed, violent jolts, and disorientation mimics early train rides, which sometimes resulted in trauma-inducing accidents.[33] The transition from civilization to Nosferatu's realm of death is created by the medium itself: the vampire requires the language of cinema inasmuch as his otherness is only figurable in visual terms, through cinematic technology. Negative printing, staccato stop-motion, and rapid editing are devices without an equivalent in any other art. More than just a manifestation of the unconscious, Nosferatu is a phantom created by film technology, but in this he is no less real than other figures on celluloid.

The physiognomy of Count Orlok as Nosferatu is replete with animal features: besides rodent-like fangs and ears like those of a bat, he has long claws (nails grow even after death), a beaklike nose, and hollowed-out eyes. He wears a long black coat and tight pants that give the impression of skeletal limbs tightly wrapped in funereal clothes. Max Schreck, an established theater actor at age forty-three, performed Nosferatu in a manner that inspired later embodiments.[34] Unlike Count Dracula (as immortalized by Bela Lugosi), Count Orlok is devoid of suave and seductive charm; his strangeness is unrelenting, preventing the viewer from identifying with him.

The film sets up a clear visual contrast between Hutter's Wisborg and Nosferatu's fortress: the vast horizontal and vertical expanses of a castle in the mountains, protected from intruders by a series of huge portals, stands in radical contrast to the small northern German town. An air of authenticity and uncompromising presence surrounds the strange count within his castle. While Hutter's body language expresses a combination of nervous eagerness and apprehension, the count's solicitous demeanor displays the formality of an Eastern European aristocracy that has outlived its social function. The camera plays the role of an ethnographer studying the whimsical count in his habitat. The horror lies in the clash of incompatible figures: the young and naïve clerk against the vampire in the guise of an ancient patrician untouched by the triviality of the modern world.

Nosferatu resides in a realm of eternal values (symbolized by his love for blood), not in the erratic sphere of commerce—a difference that was bound to fascinate an audience whose values were rapidly shifting at a time of unprecedented inflation. In a world that seemed fragmented into a multitude of contradictory histories, memories, experiences, languages, and cultures, the radical otherness epitomized by Nosferatu had an uncanny attraction.

Lying beyond the bounds of European civil society, nature itself—the majestic waterfall, thick forests, dark clouds, a pack of howling wolves—becomes part of *Nosferatu*'s mise-en-scène. The camera periodically cuts away to capture images of wild animals, embodiments of the primordial.

The tension between different symbolic regimes is first played out in Nosferatu's realm, demarcated as non-western if not otherworldly, beyond the human entirely. About halfway through the film the monster leaves the periphery to invade the center. The colonized subject visits the colonizer, bringing pestilence and death with him and wreaking havoc at the very heart of civilization. What underlies every horror film—namely, the return of the repressed in misshapen form—is staged here with terrifying precision: the unacknowledged dead return to haunt the living.

In one of the film's scariest scenes, Hutter is tempted to explore Nosferatu's habitat in the basement of the castle. Approaching a rough-hewn coffin, he suddenly faces the vampire staring at him from between two planks of the coffin, his huge animal fangs dominating the picture. He is half buried in dirt, an image reminiscent of Otto Dix's 1924 etchings of decomposing dead soldiers peering out from muddy trenches with open eyes.[35] Being buried alive, which was one of the most frequent precipitants of shell shock, evokes the eerie ambivalence of a state between life and death. Hermann Broch's 1930 novel *Die Schlafwandler* (*The Sleepwalkers*) featured a soldier buried by the nearby explosion of a grenade:

> When Gödicke, a bricklayer in the Landwehr, was unearthed from the ruins of his trench, his mouth, gaping as if for a scream, was filled with earth. His face was a blackish blue and he had no discernible heartbeat. Had not the two ambulance men who found him made a bet about his survival he would simply have been re-buried immediately.[36]

Nosferatu uses images of shell shock throughout. The images are not bound exclusively to one character, but it is Hutter who displays most clearly symptoms of the shell-shocked soldier. One scene makes this abundantly clear: after Hutter has hurt himself escaping from Nosferatu's castle, he is delivered to a hospital. This scene is followed by an aerial shot of a raft full of coffins going downstream; we know from previous scenes that one of the coffins contains the vampire. Cut back to Hutter, sick in bed, a doctor and a nurse by his side. He is asleep but suddenly awakes as if startled by a night-

Distant dangers:

Ellen senses death,

Hutter sees coffins.

mare; he lifts himself up and with outstretched arms cries out, "Coffins . . . I see coffins." The feverish vision distorts his face. Doctor and nurse hold him back and force him down on the bed. What might at first seem to be the hallucination of a shell-shocked patient is actually "true" because we see through crosscuts that coffins are indeed on their way to Wisborg. The film validates what appears to be a subjective vision of horror.

Nosferatu's coffins end up in the belly of a ship; he himself, a spindly elongated body, is sleeping in one of them. He is surrounded by rats and even resembles them with his rat-like teeth. As one of the sailors hacks open one of the coffins, a swarm of rats escapes, biting him. Before long, the entire crew is killed. As in Wilhelm Hauff's 1824 romantic fairy tale *Die Geschichte vom Gespensterschiff* (*The Tale of the Ghost Ship*), the ship then sails onward, with its crew dead and an invisible undead at the helm. There are also allusions to the phantom ship of Richard Wagner's "Flying Dutchman," the 1843 opera in which a ghost, the undead captain, seeks to be released from his state and redeemed through the love of a woman. When Nosferatu's plague-ridden ghost ship lands, the deceased are carried to the city hall and laid out like victims of a major disaster. While the clerks try to make sense of the ship's log, Nosferatu, a coffin under his arm, steals away. Here again we see why the film is so unsettling: it alternates between realistic semi-documentary sequences (such as the bureaucratic registering of the dead sailors) and utterly fantastic fever dreams. Within one shot, the imagined figure of Nosferatu scampers through "real" cobblestoned streets, crosses a canal in a boat, and then fades into the walls of a building. Like a phantom, the figure simply vanishes. Is there another reality behind the one we see? The film teases us with occasional glimpses at this hidden world of the undead. *Nosferatu* gives expression to a realm that only film can show.

A Community under Siege

The film stages the vampire's movement from periphery to center as an invasion propelled forward by nature at its most inexorable: strong winds fill the sails of Nosferatu's ghost ship, which seems to steer itself. In contrast to the studio space in which *The Cabinet of Dr. Caligari* was shot, the ship appears on the high seas: we see a phantom boat in a real setting. Shot from a low angle with a fixed camera, the ship invades the frame and fills it, underscoring the vampire's inescapable assault.

The crew of the ship does not know that Nosferatu is deep below, stowed among the ship's cargo. To the audience, however, he is shown sleeping in a coffin filled with earth and teeming with rats. This frightening shot, which associates the vampire with filth and vermin, clearly contradicts the previously aristocratic image of the count; both images, however, connote strangeness, otherness, and above all, a latent, incomprehensible danger approaching from the East. In Stoker's novel, Dracula had likewise personified the fear of an "invasion" by immigrants from the East. Seen as carriers of disease and strange customs, they stood for a fantasized Other—primitive, dirty, and dangerous—that threatened to infect the refined West.

In 1922, however, the image of sleeping in rat-infested dirt had an added connotation drawn from the trench experience: during the war, millions of soldiers were forced to live with rats and unburied corpses for months at a time. Trapped like animals in the ditches they had themselves dug, soldiers referred to themselves as vermin, moles, and rats. "In what way have we sinned," wrote a student from the trenches, "that we should be treated worse than animals? Hunted from place to place, cold, filthy, and in rags . . . in the end we are destroyed like vermin."[37] *Nosferatu* focuses on rats, even using close-ups, to a greater extent than Stoker's *Dracula*, in which they are chased away by dogs. Sharing their habit of sleeping in dirt, Nosferatu is likened to rats, which in the nineteenth century had also become symbols of transgression, disturbing divisions between high and low, pure and contaminated, civilization and its repressed.[38]

Despite the construction of sewer systems as well as improvements in hygiene and public health, the immense population of rats could not be eliminated. Demonized as an Other insidiously emerging from sewers, slums, and fetid darkness, rats were simultaneously objects of horror and fascination. The fact that soldiers in the trenches lived in close proximity to this despised animal made a mockery of their high ideals.

The rat was a perfect symbol in a film that violates taboos by unsettling clear demarcations between life and death, ideals and reality, mystery and repulsion. Since the Middle Ages, rats were also prominent in anti-Semitic imagery. In caricatures and illustrations Jews were associated with rats as carriers of infectious diseases. Fritz Hippler's Nazi propaganda film *Der ewige Jude* (*The Eternal Jew*, 1940), one of the most rabid anti-Semitic productions of Joseph Goebbels's Ministry of Propaganda, cuts between images of Eastern Jews and rats to symbolize the spread of the "Jewish Plague."

The origin of the vampire in *Nosferatu* is clearly established by specific references to Transylvania, a territory located in the Austro-Hungarian Empire. In 1916, Transylvania was invaded by Romania, resulting in a mass migration of the Jewish population, a migration that brought thousands of Eastern Jews to Berlin. Large numbers of Jews from Russia and Poland fleeing pogroms, civil war, and epidemics also settled in the city, swelling the number of *Ostjuden* (Eastern Jews) to roughly forty-five thousand. The immigrants from the east were accused of undermining the völkisch ideal of ethnic purity and cultural homogeneity.

Of all the people that the war swept into Berlin, the Eastern Jews were the least integrated; they spoke Yiddish and maintained their own synagogues, schools, eating places, and newspapers. Congregating in the Scheunenviertel, an impoverished area next to bustling, modern Alexanderplatz, they appeared as archaic relics of a past age, embodiments of anti-modernity. Their dress was medieval and they adhered rigidly to ancient religious laws and customs. They were objects of extraordinary attention not only for nationalist circles for whom the Eastern Jews symbolized *Überfremdung* (a sense of being overrun by foreigners), but also for the assimilated western Jews, who kept as much distance from them as possible. Most of these latter had suppressed their religious identity and were fully integrated into German society. To them, the Eastern Jews seemed like strangers in the house, uncanny doppelgängers from a world of primitivism, magic, and the occult. "The Jews brought the Middle Ages along," Alfred Döblin wrote in his *Reise in Polen* (*Journey to Poland,* 1924), "they have their Torah, a single book, but it is accompanied, namelessly, by magic and by faith in witchcraft."[39] Döblin describes his experience with Eastern Jews as an eerie encounter with his double, who personified what he had repressed: otherness, abject poverty, adherence to old customs, and a belief in what he thought was the occult.[40]

In the immediate postwar years, most of the five hundred thousand Jews living in Germany (less than one percent of the German population in 1922) still felt that they belonged to German society. They were assimilated and active (despite restrictions) in political, social, and cultural affairs. Nevertheless Jews were used as scapegoats by the right-wing press and by large portions of the population, which blamed them for the disastrous outcome of the war. Although the majority of westernized Jews held positions that allowed them to disregard the rising anti-Semitism, the new wave of accusations became increasingly intimidating.

Already at the beginning of the war it had been rumored that Jews were malingerers and war profiteers, deliberately sabotaging the German military and mocking German patriotism. In October 1916, the German High Command and the Prussian war minister commissioned a *Judenzählung*, or Jewish census, in order to obtain statistical evidence that Jews were in fact disproportionately shirking military duty. Even though the census outcome (tellingly not published until after the war) demonstrated that such rumors were false, the damage had been done and the "Jewish problem" was once more on the table. The very taking of the census insinuated that German Jews were first and foremost *Jews* who had to be excluded because they threatened the German nation. Anti-Semitism grew worse in 1920 when a fabricated document outlining a worldwide Jewish conspiracy, the infamous *Protocols of the Elders of Zion*, was published in German translation. The text described how Jews planned to undermine and control European societies. Over a hundred thousand copies quickly went into circulation. In June 1922, Walter Rathenau, the Jewish German foreign minister, was murdered by two right-wing former military officers, who claimed that Rathenau was one of the elders of Zion.

Predictably, the trauma of defeat was displaced onto an already stigmatized group. A prevailing fiction, the so-called *Dolchstoßlegende*, the "stab-in-the-back myth," blamed Germany's military defeat on the Jews. Although close to one hundred thousand German Jews had served in the army (12% as volunteers) and twelve thousand of them died in battle, it was alleged that Jews betrayed the German army by opposition both in the field and on the home front. Generals Ludendorff and von Hindenburg declared that the German army would have been victorious if the home front had not been brainwashed by the "Jewish press." An unending stream of anti-Semitic brochures and other sub-literary works (speeches, songs, newspaper editorials, etc.) began to appear at the end of the war, all purporting to "set the record straight" and identify the party responsible for Germany's shame. The title of a brochure from 1919 sums up the debate: "The Contribution of Jewry to Germany's Collapse."[41]

Is the vampire myth yet another anti-Semitic fantasy? The most odious and persistent stereotype, dating back to the Middle Ages, has indeed been the notion of the Jew as "parasite," a vampire invading a body and feeding off it. Nineteenth-century thinkers, obsessed with questions of nationalism and race, employed elaborate pseudoscientific scholarship to prove not only the racial inferiority of Jews but also their danger to "host" countries. From biology to theology, scholars in every field attributed vampiric qualities to the Jews. There were a few variations: the "Jew" as an archetypal stranger and outsider; a capitalist who drinks the blood of the working class; and a "foreign element" that infects and kills the national body. Artur Dinter's novel *Die Sünde wider das Blut* (*The Sin Against Blood*) deals with the horrific price of miscegenation between a German woman and a Jewish man. It appeared in January 1919, together with Houston Stewart Chamberlain's deeply anti-Semitic pamphlet *Rasse und Nation* (Race and Nation), and a slew of other anti-Semitic flyers and brochures, which often displayed caricatured Eastern Jews with features not unlike those of Nosferatu.[42] Dinter assembled and recycled every anti-Semitic cliché from over the centuries: "If the German people do not succeed," he wrote, "to throw off and exterminate the Jewish vampire which it nursed with its heart's blood . . . then it will die in the not-too-distant future."[43] In 1925, Hitler used the same metaphor of Jews as parasites and vampires in *Mein Kampf*: "After the death of the victim the death of the vampire will come sooner or later."[44]

Orlok has a double in the figure of Knock, a real estate agent and the local contact of the vampire. An eccentric figure in the tradition of E.T.A. Hoffmann, Knock communicates with Nosferatu by means of mysterious letters and telepathy as the two set a trap for poor Hutter. Catching flies to suck their blood, and distorting his face with wild grins and grimaces, he acts like a comic, lower-class copy of his master. The film shows Knock as demented, more a victim than a perpetrator. After the plague has killed the population, an intertitle explains: "Shaken through and through by fear, the town was looking for a victim; it was Knock." The film draws attention to mechanisms of fear, the assignment of blame, and victimhood. Women gossip about him (foreshadowing a misogynist scenario repeated in Murnau's 1924 *The Last Laugh*), accusing Knock of strangling his guard; the men pursue him in a comical chase (anticipating the chase of the monster in James Whale's 1932 film version of *Frankenstein*). They drive Knock out of the village, but are fooled by him when they mistake a scarecrow for their scapegoat. The camera shows this chase in extreme angles: in an aerial shot emphasizing the narrow lanes, and in an extreme long shot that adds irony to the crowd's blind rage. The chase in fact takes on a comedic quality that undermines possible associations with persecution and pogrom in favor of slapstick.

Knock is played by Alexander Granach, a famous stage performer who met Murnau while both were actors in Max Reinhardt's theater school, as early as 1909. Born Jessaya Granach in the East Galician town of Werbowitz, Poland, Granach became best known for his portrayal of Shylock, a role with which he fully identified. He ends his autobiography, written in U.S. exile, with a long description of Reinhardt's famous production of *The Merchant of Venice* at Berlin's Grosses Schauspielhaus in 1920: "For twelve years I had been absorbed in Shylock, and still I could not wholly understand him. I compared him with my father, I compared him with Shimshale from Milnitz, but could find no great resemblance."[45] Granach's struggle with the figure of Shylock was a struggle with his own identity as an Eastern Jew living in Germany. His encounter with the director of Reinhardt's theater school illustrates this: "I was particularly obnoxious to him. I still spoke with a foreign accent. And he imitated me, ridiculed me. If he had not been a Jew himself, I should have supposed that he was an anti-Semite. He was really a Jewish anti-Semite."[46] By the time he played Knock in *Nosferatu*, Granach was known as the most famous Jewish actor in Berlin, clearly not afraid of performing anti-Semitic clichés in order to parody and deconstruct them.

But even Nosferatu, whose physiognomy, habitus, and mode of being are incarnations of extreme otherness, is capable of human longing and desire. More reminiscent of the disfigured Phantom of the Opera than a monster, toward the end he becomes the object of a strange allure and, for Ellen, sexual attraction. Seeing the vampire powerless vis-à-vis Ellen, we even begin to sympathize with him. And Knock's obsession with blood—from his very first remark "it will cost you some blood" to the ominous "blood is life" (said as he sucks blood from a fly)—might even be seen as an ironic reference to Dinter's bestseller, *The Sin against Blood,* which by 1922 had sold two hundred thousand copies.[47]

Hysteria on the Home Front

I am working away as hard as I can to get dead as soon as possible.

—Alice James, letter to William James, 1890

"There doesn't seem to be anything that historians haven't said about hysteria," writes Mark Micale in his overview of the "female malady."[48] Indeed the notion of a hysterical affliction dates back to antiquity (Freud reminds his readers that *hysteria* is derived from the Greek word for "uterus."[49]) A source of perennial fascination—perhaps because of the way in which it seems to conflate clinical and imaginary symptoms—hysteria fired the imagination of psychiatrists, artists, and writers with special urgency in the late nineteenth and early twentieth centuries. While some viewed the hysteric as a disturbed woman subject to delusions, others have associated hysteria with "woman's capacity for amazing and empowering self-transformations."[50] Elisabeth Bronfen relates the condition to the Victorian notion of femininity: "Neither fulfilling nor rejecting the norm, the hysteric's slight but crucial exaggeration of ideal nineteenth-century femininity undermined these norms in that her fits violated any sense of refinement while her incapacitating physical symptoms made her so helpless as to parody the delicacy and softness she was meant to incorporate."[51]

Murnau constructs the character of Ellen as a prototypical female hysteric of the period. Her corporeal symptoms are highly coded but readily recognizable as signs of hysteria: histrionic gestures and convulsions, heightened suggestibility, the acting out of hypnosis-induced desires, a sense of isolation and irrelevance, a proclivity toward semiconscious states, extremes of excitement and lassitude, and nocturnal somnambulism and hallucinations. Her bodily contortions and gyrations strongly recall the pictures of hysterics recorded and published by the photo studio in Charcot's Salpêtrière starting in 1875.

We are introduced to Ellen as she plays with a cat on the windowsill, using a toy ball on a string that is suggestive of a hypnotist's pendulum. Although introduced in a playful manner—the cat tries to stop the ball's repetitive swings back and forth—the activity suggests from the start Ellen's susceptibility to hypnotic states, a theme that is played out later in the film. She is often shown sitting in front of an open window, embodying (in the tradition of romantic painting) boundless longing and desire. Hutter's departure reduces her to a state of anxious waiting. In one scene, remarkable for its innovative crosscutting, Nosferatu is seen approaching Hutter, while Ellen, surrounded by her doctor and family, lifts herself from her sickbed. As Nosferatu's shadow creeps over his sleeping victim, ready to sink his teeth into Hutter's neck, Ellen, now sitting up with hands outstretched, calls out "Hutter!" Nosferatu, startled, lifts his head as if in response to her cry, and, pulled by some unknown force, slowly withdraws. Ellen falls back onto her bed. Her telepathic identification with Hutter saves him, suggesting a close affinity between battlefront and home front in the traumatic encounter with death. If hysteria is the failure to overcome trauma, then Ellen's hysteria is based on a secondary trauma that afflicted the home front. There are signs from the beginning: her empathy with the "murdered" flowers and, in the parting scene, her prescient sensitivity to Hutter's suffering.

The town doctor diagnoses her as suffering from "harmless blood congestion," a mysterious illness that makes her sleepwalk and hallucinate. It seems as if Nosferatu has entered her mind as Hutter's malevolent double. An intertitle in the voice of the narrator provides a more accurate explanation: "The doctor described Ellen's anxiety to me as some sort of unknown illness. But I know that on that night her soul heard the call of the bird of the dead (*Totenvogel*). And Nosferatu was already lifting his wings." Her fear that Hutter will lose his life produces her hysterical symptoms. The home front, in the person of Ellen, is shown as vulnerable to suggestion; she is just as susceptible to a failure of nerves as her absent husband.

"What is the meaning of hysterical identification?" asks Freud in *The Interpretation of Dreams*:

> Identification is a highly important factor in the mechanism of hysterical symptoms. It enables patients to express in their symptoms not only their own experiences but also those of a large number of other people; it enables them, as it were, to suffer on behalf of a whole crowd of people and to act all the parts in a play single-handed. I shall be told that this is not more than the familiar hysterical imitation, the capacity of hysterics to imitate any symptoms in other people that may have struck their attention—sympathy, as it were, intensified to the point of reproduction.[52]

Because no organic lesions or injuries were associated with hysteria, its symptoms were often treated as if they were products of suggestion or even simulation (as in cases of war neuroses). Following Charcot, who pioneered scientific research into hysterical neurosis, Freud considered symptoms of hysteria somatic manifestations of unconscious fantasies. In 1911, he admitted "the difficulty of distinguishing unconscious fantasies from memories which have become unconscious," particularly since the unconscious itself "equates reality of thought with external actuality and wishes with their fulfillment."[53] Ellen's sleepwalking is the most extreme symptom of her subconscious wish to join her husband at the front. The camera observes her, dressed in white, as she rises from her bed in the middle of the night, leaves the room, and walks with outstretched arms on top of a narrow balustrade.

A friend in an adjacent room, who hears a noise, rushes to keep her from falling. Like the somnambulist Cesare in *The Cabinet of Dr. Caligari*, Ellen occupies a state between waking and sleeping, life and death.

In *Nosferatu*, fantasy and reality are indistinguishable. Is the vampire a hallucinated effect of Ellen's imagination? No one else seems to notice, let alone pursue, Nosferatu once he has landed; he may well be the phantom of a hysterical fantasy. The ontological status of film, as a semi-hypnotic medium, calls into question the boundary between conscious and unconscious states. It can blend desires and deeds, emphasize states of dream, trance, madness, and possession. Even before the vampire arrived, Ellen was seen sleepwalking, dressed in a white nightgown, resembling a ghost. In another scene, she sits alone in the dunes staring at the sea, waiting for her husband's return. The editing, however, betrays her unconscious desire for the vampire by cutting to his imposing ship, as it battles the waves.

To achieve the hallucinatory tone of the film's second half, Murnau borrows from the aesthetics of the German romantic artist Caspar David Friedrich, who painted his most famous works in the period in which the film is set.[54] His paintings show vast empty spaces ("The Monk at the Sea" or "Rise of the Moon at the Sea") or objects far away ("Two Men Contemplating the Moon"), observed by lonely human figures in moments of immobility. Friedrich's gaze is also Murnau's: ineffable, sublime nature produces in the viewer a shuddering pleasure tinged with anticipation and fear. On the beach Ellen is surrounded by crosses; they designate graves of sailors, but in this painterly setting they also connote the presence of death. Death is not visible but it is felt. A cut to the vessel that brings the undead vampire, first seen from a distance but then filling the frame, imbues the image with her intense death wish.

Ellen seems possessed by the phantom of Nosferatu just as the young bride Leah'le is possessed by the dybbuk in S. An-ski's Yiddish play *The Dybbuk or Between Two Worlds*. Published in 1914 and translated by Arno Nadel into German in 1921 under the title *Der Dybbuk: Dramatische Legende in vier Akten* (*The Dybbuk: Dramatic Legend in Four Acts*) and again by Rosa Nossig in 1922 under the title *Zwischen zwei Welten: Der Dybbuk* (*Between Two Worlds: The Dybbuk*), the play was widely read and performed across Europe.[55] In 1921, the Vilna Jewish Theater Group brought it to Berlin, where it was enthusiastically received by critics, even if a passionate fan like Döblin admitted to not having understood every word of the Yiddish.[56] A dybbuk in Kabbalah and Jewish mythology is the wandering, malevolent ghost of a dead person who enters the body of a living person. In *Nosferatu*, Ellen is from the very beginning haunted by the unseen presence of the "bird of death." Her black clothes resemble those of Nosferatu, and her mental state hovers "between two worlds." Her sleepwalking and even more her telepathic communication with the undead show that she is controlled by an external force. Is she possessed by the dybbuk, who stands in for the ghosts of the soldiers who died before their time? Does she sacrifice herself in order to exorcise the evil spirit?

Tormented by the phantom dybbuk who has taken hold of her, Ellen is shown to be the unwitting heir of a shameful and disavowed national history. The refusal to acknowledge defeat causes repressed truth to reappear in a grotesquely misshapen form. In Nicolas Abraham's words, the dead do not return, but their unfinished business is unconsciously handed over to the living, even to future generations. The phantoms of the dead remain active, demanding a reaction to their suffering, even demanding that the living share their death.[57] It is as if the dead, who have died too young and in too great numbers, feel that they have not received either the full life or the dignified death to which they are entitled, and out of envy and frustration they will not leave the living to enjoy peace. In this sense, Ellen acts out the fate of millions of soldiers who went to their deaths in the prime of their youth.

In the thrall of the vampire, both Ellen and Hutter are mere shadows of their former selves: Hutter, once bitten by the vampire, hovers listlessly between conscious and unconscious states. Nosferatu now speaks through the medium of their bodies, having trapped them in the twilight state between life and death that he himself occupies. Her gesticulations as she faces Nosferatu articulate the silent struggle between her conscious wish for self-preservation and an unconscious, erotically tinged death drive.

The home front was often ambivalent about the sudden return of a soldier believed to be dead. Several literary and dramatic works as well as films deal with this theme of conflicted welcoming, in which the returning soldier is greeted as if he had risen from the grave to seek revenge. *Hintertreppe* (*Backstairs*, 1921), written by Carl Mayer and directed by Leopold Jessner and Paul Leni, features a young kitchen maid who desperately waits for mail from her absent fiancé. A crippled mailman, who is in love with her, sees her plight and delivers letters that are allegedly from her fiancé, but are in fact written by him to endear himself to her. She discovers the deceit but, assuming that her fiancé has been killed, is moved enough to accept the mailman's proposal of marriage. Soon after, however, the lost fiancé returns, explaining that he has been in a hospital after an "accident." The film does not specify the nature of this accident, but it did not have to: in 1921 a long absence and severe injury alluded to the war. Her new fiancé feels betrayed and out of jealousy kills his rival with an ax. When the woman realizes that her first fiancé has been killed, she commits suicide by jumping from the roof. *Backstairs*, a "chamber play film" (*Kammerspielfilm*) in the tradition of an Ibsen play, does not mention the war once, but leaves no doubt about the underlying conflict: the soldier's unexpected return. Brecht's play *Drums in the Night* (1922) also depicts a soldier's return as a traumatic event, but Brecht resolves the conflict unheroically. Faced with his wife's infidelity, the protagonist decides to forgive her and vows to resume his former life. In *Nosferatu* we encounter a different version of the return-of-the-soldier scenario: Hutter returns but his vampire double, the embodiment of his traumatic experience, comes with him, entering Ellen's domestic sphere and competing with Hutter.

Abel Gance's 1919 film *J'accuse* (like *Nosferatu*, the story of a woman caught between two men) or Lang's *Destiny* conjure up the fallen as walking ghosts among the living—visible only to those on the home front who possess special sensibilities. In Gance's film, it is the poet who observes a band of dead and fatally wounded soldiers marching as diaphanous ghosts (an effect achieved by double exposure and superimposition), as if visible reality had suddenly been penetrated by interlopers from the afterlife. In *Destiny*, it is the woman (not unlike Ellen in *Nosferatu*) who sees a ghostly procession of the living dead as she tries to enter the space of death, visualized as an impenetrable wall so high it fills the entire frame. Horror film and melodrama are here tightly interwoven. The fear of the return of the dead—think of George Romero's 1968 low-budget classic *Night of the Living Dead*—has become a staple of horror films ever since.

In 1921, as *Nosferatu* was being shot, expressionist playwright Ernst Toller, in prison for his participation in the German Revolution of 1918–19, was writing *Der deutsche Hinkemann* (*The German Hinkemann*). The play deals with a soldier, Hinkemann, who returns from the front disabled; he is not only missing a leg, but castrated as well. Hinkemann accepts a job as a freak at a fairground, playing a human vampire: he bites the throats of living animals and drinks their blood. During his absence on the front, his wife had succumbed to the advances of one of his friends, but she decides to stay with Hinkemann when she realizes the magnitude of his sacrifice. Meanwhile, his friend brags about his affair with Hinkemann's wife and ridicules his war wounds. Hinkemann suffers a mental breakdown, proclaiming in a crazed dance that Priapus is now God. When Hinkemann's wife tries to apologize for her adultery, he rejects her. The play ends with her suicide. Although Toller's play draws on Georg Büchner's nineteenth-century play *Woyzeck*, the contemporary audience recognized its radical postwar agenda: exposing in literal terms the symbolic impotence of the German male who lost the war. Not surprisingly, the play's premiere on September 19, 1923 was interrupted by nationalist provocateurs, and the ensemble received death threats. The court did not punish the perpetrators however, arguing that Toller had insulted the nationalists' love for their fatherland.

Toller's play, then, makes explicit one of the submerged themes of Murnau's *Nosferatu*: a pervasive anxiety about the status of masculinity and male sexual power in the wake of the war. The battle between nations was brought home and lived on as a war between the sexes. What Toller's play and Murnau's film have in common is a basic melodramatic premise: tempted and seduced by the more potent rival, the wife betrays her "dismembered" husband and kills herself out of guilt.

The sexual subtext of Hutter's wife giving herself to the vampire also refers to the experience of soldiers who returned home sexually dysfunctional. In his 1920 book *Impotence in the Male*, Wilhelm Stekel, an Austrian physician and follower of Freud, wrote:

> Not among the least damages which the World War has caused are to be counted the enormous dissemination of venereal diseases and the derangement of sexual life in the male, which I could demonstrate with innumerable examples. Within recent years, I have been astonished, in particular, by the increase of impotency among participants of the war. Almost every consultation hour brought one or more ex-soldiers who had become impotent while in the field. The picture was almost monotonously similar. They were mostly

married men who had longed for a wife and child and who could hardly await the hour of meeting them again. To their horror, they were impotent upon the first intimacy with their wives—it usually concerned married men. This war-impotency either subsided rapidly or became permanently established; and, as a result of autosuggestion, developed into a fear of impotence, whose pernicious effect is already familiar to us.[58]

Stekel estimated the number of men who became impotent because of their experiences in the war "at hundreds of thousands without being guilty of exaggeration."[59] The war, fought to resurrect and recapture ideals of masculinity and heroism, had instead pushed male agency further into crisis. After encountering Nosferatu at a life-threatening moment, Hutter appears shell-shocked and disoriented. He returns from his mission effeminate, weak, and impotent, spending his time languishing in an easy chair. He is dozing when Ellen is overcome with desire for the vampire whom she sees waiting at an open window opposite hers. She glances at the sleeping Hutter and shrugs her shoulders—a gesture that demonstrates both bafflement and frustration at his stupor and lassitude. She is visibly torn between the two men: the impotent and shell-shocked Hutter and the vampire who gazes at her in full libidinous anticipation. After a last exasperated look at Hutter, Ellen throws the window wide open and prostrates herself on the bed, awaiting the vampire's arrival.

The Allure of the Occult

In his essay on the uncanny, which appeared a year after the war's end, Freud emphasizes that the return of the dead is the most striking of all its instances:

> There is scarcely any other matter upon which our thoughts and feelings have changed so little since the very earliest times, and in which discarded forms have been so completely preserved under a thin disguise, as our relation to death . . . . Since almost all of us still think as savages do on this topic, it is no matter for surprise that the primitive fear of the dead is still so strong within us and always ready to come to the surface on any provocation. Most likely our fear still

implies the old belief that the dead man becomes the enemy of his survivor and seeks to carry him off to share his new life with him. Considering our unchanged attitude towards death, we might rather enquire what has become of the repression, which is the necessary condition of a primitive feeling recurring in the shape of something uncanny. But repression is there, too. All supposedly educated people have ceased to believe officially that the dead can become visible as spirits, and have made any such appearances dependent on improbable and remote conditions; their emotional attitude towards their dead, moreover, once a highly ambiguous and ambivalent one, has been toned down in the higher strata of the mind into an unambiguous feeling of piety.[60]

A traditionally complex relationship to death and dying, which consisted simultaneously of denial and deference, rejection and obeisance, fear and awe, entered a crisis phase after the war, when millions of young men did not return home. Hundreds of thousands of husbands, fathers, and brothers died in the trenches. Often their relatives did not know when or how their loved ones lost their lives. Not surprisingly, many grief-stricken widows and mothers tried to establish contact with the dead with the help of clairvoyants and psychics. Freud observed with slight astonishment in 1919: "In our great cities, placards announce lectures that undertake to tell us how to get into touch with the souls of the departed; and it cannot be denied that not a few of the most able and penetrating minds among our men of science have come to the conclusion, especially towards the close of their own lives, that a contact of this kind is not impossible."[61]

A huge wave of occultism swept over Germany and Europe after the war. Even an established writer like Thomas Mann attended séances organized by Albert von Schrenck-Notzing in December 1922 and January 1923, which he described in his essay "Occult Experiences." Spiritualism, as promoted by Madame Blavatzky and her circle since the late nineteenth century, gained new adherents and religious sects flourished. The occult even cropped up in matter-of-fact chronicles from the front. Ernst Jünger tellingly begins his diary of a shock troop commander with the following passage:

Our first day of the war was not to pass without making a very decisive impression on us. We were sitting over breakfast in the school where we were quartered. Suddenly there was a series of dull concussions, and all the soldiers rushed out of the houses towards the entrance of the village. We followed suit, not really knowing why. Again there was a curious fluttering and whooshing sound over our heads, followed by a sudden, violent explosion. I was amazed at the way the men around me seemed to cower while running at full pelt, as though under some frightful threat.

Immediately afterwards, groups of dark figures emerged onto the empty village street, carrying black bundles on canvas stretchers or fireman's lifts of folded hands. I stared, with a queasy feeling of unreality, at a blood-spattered form with a strangely contorted leg hanging loosely down, wailing "Help! Help!" as if sudden death still had him by the throat. He was carried into a building with a Red Cross flag draped over the doorway. What was that about? The war had shown its claws and stripped off its mask of coziness. It was all so strange, so impersonal. We had barely begun to think about the enemy, that mysterious, treacherous being somewhere. This event, so far beyond anything we had experienced, made such a powerful impression on us that it was difficult to understand what had happened. It was like a ghostly manifestation in broad daylight.[62]

An acute sense of powerlessness in the face of technological weaponry led to superstition as well as belief in ritual, magic, and omens. If one survived, it was not on account of courage or cleverness but only coincidence (or fate or luck). "In war no one is master of his fate . . . He can only say 'Thy will be done.'"[63] The home front had to believe that supernatural forces were at work in the world, and that life was dependent on the will and greater plan of God.

Because the war was beyond comprehension (Who is responsible for it? Will I be alive tomorrow?), it produced passivity, confusion, and resignation. It was widely believed, as Eric Leed reports, "that the roaring chaos of the barrage effected a kind of hypnotic condition that shattered any rational pattern of cause and effect, allowing, even demanding, magical reversals. This state was often described in terms of a loss of coherence and the disappearance of any sense of temporal sequence. It created the setting for irrational thoughts and unbidden associations."[64] The contradiction between modern industrialized war and the irrational, illogical, and fantastic within it (Jünger's "ghostly manifestation in broad daylight") was glaring: technology brought with it a total loss of individual control over life and death, resulting in a regression to archaic forms of thinking that were less linear and logical than associative and evocative.

Nosferatu's formal structure is informed by such chaotic correspondences: using crosscutting, the film establishes unanticipated links between characters; Nosferatu at various times appears as the uncanny double of Hutter, Knock, and Ellen. The screen is no longer just a window but a mirror that destabilizes identities by doubling, even tripling them. The constant endeavor to insinuate correspondences also creates a spatial complexity that undermines the linear progression of the story line.

The film's very first title card underlines the tension between presence and absence, thereby complicating representation: "Nosferatu. Doesn't this name sound like the very midnight call of Death? Speak it not aloud, or life's pictures will turn to shadows, and nightmares (*spukhafte Träume* or "phantomlike dreams" in literal translation) will rise up to feed on your blood."

The rhetorical question and the warning not to name what should remain hidden invoke an image of Nosferatu as an harbinger of death who dwells in the subconscious: the vampire's manifestations are "shadows" and "phantomlike dreams"—properties associated with film as well as occultism. The very warning results in a paradox: as the danger of naming is spelled out, the phantom is named. And what ensues is exactly what the warning foretold: the film turns "life's pictures" into shadows and summons ghosts in dreams that drown the viewer. The film itself doubles the unspoken, unspeakable vampiric thoughts of death; it gives them a body in the form of a monster. This textual tease (it is here but cannot be revealed) foreshadows Ellen's irresistible temptation to read the *Book of Vampires*, which is expressly forbidden to her. She hesitates and wavers, but as she furtively glances at the book, she commits an act of transgression: by opening it she literally opens herself to be possessed by the vampire. The film displaces its own hypnotic effect onto an earlier medium—the printed page. As in occultism, forbidden knowledge is associated with secret writings.

It has often been reported that soldiers who lived in the trenches for weeks at a time experienced an eerie state between life and death that made them susceptible to superstition and the occult. The extremely restricted vision in the trenches gave rise to hallucinations and apparitions.[65] How can silent film articulate these liminal experiences? How can it show what cannot be seen? How can it bring the immaterial and phantasmagorical into representation? Film itself, based on the interplay between light and shadow, has a precarious status: its elusive materiality (it comes to life only thanks to electric currents and a complex apparatus) is most radically demonstrated by its conscious use of shadows. As E. H. Gombrich argued in his study of the shadow in Western art,

> Shadows are part of our environment but they . . . are fugitive and changeable. . . . shadows are not part of the real world. We cannot touch them or grasp them. . . . It was believed by the ancient Greeks that when we take leave of the real world, we survive only as shades among shades.[66]

Adelbert von Chamisso's fictional character Peter Schlemihl sells his shadow to the devil but soon realizes that because he no longer casts a shadow, he has lost his place in the real world. It was in the German cinema of the postwar period that shadows again asserted an independent existence, exemplifying the degree to which the solidity of the self had been shattered and the unconscious had seized power. For instance, Artur Robison's *Schatten. Eine nächtliche Halluzination* (*Warning Shadows: A Nocturnal Hallucination*, 1923), presents the shadow world as a treacherous second reality in which jealousy, deceit, and revenge can be acted out. Like *Nosferatu*, *Warning Shadows* was shot by Fritz Arno Wagner, one of the most innovative cinematographers of the 1920s, and designed by Albin Grau. Both films are self-reflexive commentaries on the power of projection, revealing how shadows play tricks on perception and blur boundaries.

Seen in this way, the medium of film continues the tradition of phantasmagoria, or ghost shows, that began in Europe toward the end of the eighteenth century. After various experiments in summoning spirits through magic lanterns and lighting effects, Etienne Robertson, a Belgian inventor, scholar of optics, and stage magician, presented what he called the first "phantasmagoria" in Paris around 1800. Audiovisual performances that conjured up gothic images of skeletons, skulls, and spirits, phantasmagoria shows used optical illusions as well as sound effects and eerie music to frighten the audience. In an atmosphere of smoke and mirrors along with complete darkness, audiences believed they saw ghosts of the recently deceased. In London as well, Paul Philidor opened a phantasmagoria production featuring performances that attempted to represent what was invisible, physically impossible, or merely imaginary. His shadow images brought the dead to life, animated inanimate matter, and summoned supernatural forces. "Phantasmagoria" has since then also become a metaphor for psychic processes having to do with hallucination and delirium.[67]

"Yesterday I was in the kingdom of shadows," wrote Maxim Gorky about his first visit to a movie house in 1895. "If only you knew how strange it felt. There were no sounds and no colors. . . . This is not life but the shadow of life, and this is not movement but the soundless shadow of movement."[68] The narrative of *Nosferatu* unfolds by posing fundamental questions of cinematic representation. For Murnau, film is "not life but the shadow of life," just as it was for Gorky. Film is, one might say, a phantom that "shadows," spectralizes, and "ghosts" our real lives. Nosferatu, a purely cinematic creature (with no life outside the movies), rules in the kingdom of shadows, which is none other than the kingdom of film. As he approaches Ellen's bedroom, he is lit from below by footlights that elongate and enlarge his shadow; it looms larger and larger until it fills the entire frame. The figure that throws the shadow is invisible, thus literalizing Nosferatu's phantomic existence.[69]

Since the mid-nineteenth century, the spiritualist movement used photography to "capture" ghosts of the recently deceased.[70] So-called "spirit photographs" showed dead family members hovering above or standing behind a living person who was being photographed. It was alleged that the sensitivity of the photographic emulsion was greater than that of the human eye and could pick up phenomena that the unaided human eye could not. But in fact spirit photographers used optical illusion, double exposure, superimposition, and manipulation of negatives to represent the ghost. Not surprisingly, they were popular again after World War I, when they promised to include images of a recently fallen son or father in family pictures.

Film as a ghost show was found to possess a magic dimension deriving from film technology itself. The new medium could indeed make visible what no human eye had perceived before. In *Nosferatu*, extreme close-ups of a Venus flytrap and of a translucent polyp gave viewers perspectives that were not possible for the naked eye. They recognized what they saw, but it appeared unreal, not because it was imagined, but because it was all too real—and yet unfamiliar. Documentary nature films made by Ufa's scientific film division were shown publicly, and a film like *Der Wasserfloh* (*The Water Flea*, 1921) made use of the microscope to show tiny crustaceans magnified a hundred times.[71] Murnau included scenes of scientific observation to blur the boundaries between science and the uncanny—the very essence of filmmaking from its beginnings. Images of carnivorous plants that trap and devour their prey also functioned on a thematic level, establishing vampirism as a common occurrence in a Darwinian universe. A "Paracelsian," as he is called in the film, Professor Bulwer sees nature as the common denominator between body and world.[72]

The vampire in Murnau's film—a spirit whose body is rendered immaterial and phantomic qua film—moves about town without being seen by anyone except the camera. There is a scene in which Nosferatu, instead of entering a building through the door, dissolves into thin air. He simply becomes transparent, implying that he is both substantial and insubstantial, both visible and invisible. The film uses its technology (stop-motion and double exposure) to foreground the immateriality of phantoms. It is film (like photography eighty years earlier) that was able to give life to the ghosts of the dead.

Rather than corroborating material reality, many films of the Weimar Republic complicate easy appropriation. At the end of his essay on the uncanny, Freud draws a categorical distinction between "the uncanny that we experience and the uncanny that we merely picture or read about," between, in other words, the realm of art and that of the everyday.[73] But the distinction is hard to maintain, as Freud himself admits. As spectators we have an aesthetic experience no matter whether we see an invented or true story, some artist's imaginary happening or a representation of the "world of common reality. . . . We react to his inventions as we would have reacted to real experiences."[74] This makes film the perfect medium for the experience of the uncanny: How is one to distinguish between reality and hallucination, since "reality" itself is, after all, part of the fictional universe created by the very act of filming? If it is true, as Freud says, that "an uncanny effect is often and easily produced when the distinction between imagination and reality is effaced, as when something that we have hitherto regarded as imaginary appears before us in reality, or when a symbol takes over the full functions of the thing it symbolizes,"[75] then film itself becomes an instance of the uncanny. In a horror film like *Nosferatu*, the symbolic function of film language expresses this rupture when hallucinations suddenly appear embodied. What is real? What is hallucinated? Film qua film—that is, its technological capacity for lifelike representation—is the ultimate double, an uncanny experience in itself to which we submit ourselves.

The Work of Mourning

I couldn't see that it mattered to myself or anyone else if I caught and even died from one of my patients' dire diseases, when so many beautiful bodies of young men were rotting in the mud of France and the pine forests of Italy.

—Vera Brittain, *Testament of Youth*, 1933

Mass death called for mass mourning. Film's reception in the public space of a movie theater could foster a sense of collective mourning. It could revisit sites of trauma and reanimate the dead, who existed in a nether zone between death and life. Freud claimed in 1917: "Mourning is regularly the reaction to the loss of a loved person or to the loss of some abstraction which has taken the place of one, such as fatherland, liberty, an ideal, and so on."[76] The difference between mourning as a natural reaction and melancholia as a pathological response is that the latter is accompanied by apparent damage to the ego, a drop in self-esteem. In Freud's view, the melancholic directs reproaches and grief that are related to the loss of a loved one onto the self. The newly detached libido produces identification with the mourned object, the loss of which corresponds to a loss in the ego. Melancholia might thus be equated with failed mourning, a denial of loss, and an unyielding identification with the lost object.

Ellen (rather than the scientist, as in Stoker's novel) becomes the focus of Murnau's film. She stages her death, drawing the viewer to her narrative, fulfilling her operatic desire to sacrifice her life for the town and become a martyr for civilization. The deaths of Ellen and Nosferatu end the film, which had promised an account of the Great Death. Is Ellen's fate an allegory of the home front that exorcises the evil shadow of the undead? Or are the undead an allegory of the war's enduring power to haunt the living?

The final shot of the film, lasting little more than a second, is of Nosferatu's castle in ruins. The still picture brilliantly summarizes the film's meditation on death, mourning, and memory. Occupying a state between past and future, the ruin is an overdetermined and paradoxical site. Its state of decay and decomposition bears traces of what once was, while showing temporality at work. Suspended in time, ruins have long been objects of fascination and curiosity, contemplation and reverence. Nosferatu's castle (as seen in an extreme low-angle shot at the beginning of the film) was an imposing, phallic-looking emblem of power, but when the vampire expires,

Drawn to the occult:
the phantom of the text
in Murnau's *Nosferatu*.

it is reduced to an overgrown pile of stone. "What has led the building upward is human will," wrote Georg Simmel in his 1911 essay on ruins, "what gives it its present appearance is the brute, downward-dragging, corroding, crumbling power of nature."[77] This power of nature has overcome the human spirit—a fitting coda to a film about the relationship between nature, death, and remembrance. The experience of war is thereby elevated to a higher form of existence that does not shrink from "giving death its due," as Freud put it in 1916. It naturalizes Germany's defeat in a universal framework of life and death.

In an instant, the film's story has become history. The ruin is what remains, as a relic and reminder of a mythological past long gone. "A kind of camera obscura of memory," writes Philippe Hamon, "the ruin is responsible for giving meaning to the 'as is' of history, for the ruin provokes the pure effect of memory (according to Flaubert's *Dictionnaire des idées reçues*, the ruin 'induces reverie') and can therefore send the visitor back to the image of his impending death."[78] Like any other fragmented object, the ruin asks for completion—demanding, provoking, and spurring the spectator's imagination. Half overgrown by vegetation, the ruin serves as a reminder of the vanity of human intrusion. Nature inexorably retakes its stolen territory, thereby covering over and shrouding the past. The sheer progress of time dissolves history into the long *durée* of the natural landscape. The battlefields of Ypres, Verdun, or the Somme would be forgotten, covered by grassy fields, if it were not for war memorials, literature, and film.

Nosferatu, then, ends with the demise of Nosferatu's Reich. It is the film itself that has recorded and remembered the story. By replaying it again and again, film acts as an enduring memorial of a time swiftly engulfed by forgetting. The film endows the site with a mythical narrative that imparts coherence and meaning to the events that transpired there. The spectators who saw *Nosferatu* in 1922 participated in the production of memory after the war: in seeing the film unfold, they were able to recapitulate and reassess their own experiences of the war and its consequences.

The premiere of *Nosferatu* was part of a stage show that began with a spoken prologue (like Johann Wolfgang von Goethe's *Faust*), followed by a dance interlude. After the screening of the film, a much-publicized "Party of Nosferatu" took place—a dance for invited guests, many of them in Biedermeier costumes with frock coats and gowns. The next day some newspapers reported more elaborately on the social event, attended by luminaries such as Ernst Lubitsch and lasting into the morning hours, than they did on the film. The *Film-Echo* commented with irony that those who craved more of the "ghastly" vampire were given more goose bumps at the ball, forgetting over jazz and Shimmy "creepiness, occultism, and vampirism as well as closing time."[79] Does the film's project—the remembrance of mass death—not conflict with the wild abandonment of dancing? Is the film's paranoia about a global pandemic and the threat of invasion not cause for alarm instead of a pretext for carousing? In 1922, not a single critic saw a contradiction. Both the film's morbidity and the frenetic dance fever were reactions to multiple realities that coexisted in postwar Germany. To give oneself up to the hypnotic effects of a horror film was not so different from losing oneself in mass entertainment. Film dealt with death and trauma, but it also was "just a movie," part of a hectic leisure culture trying to forget the war.[80]

Nosferatu was still playing in theaters when the first part of Fritz Lang's two-part film *Dr. Mabuse, der Spieler* (*Dr. Mabuse, the Gambler*) opened in April 1922. Touted as a "realistic picture of the times," *Dr. Mabuse* commented on the social and cultural turmoil of the immediate postwar years. At first glance vastly different, the two films share a number of commonalities. In both, hypnotism and the occult are used to convey a pervasive sense of manipulation and powerlessness. As in *Nosferatu*, predator fantasies articulate the vague fears (stemming from the war) of a traumatized community under siege, except that in *Dr. Mabuse* the threat comes more explicitly from inside. Both films explore phenomena that transgress the boundary of psychological realism, making use of effects specific to the film medium. Both feature telepathy, spiritualism, and dialogue with the dead—*Dr. Mabuse* even features a classical séance—to suggest the abandonment of rational thought. Both *Nosferatu* and *Dr. Mabuse* propose that ruthless but invisible forces are at work, thus obscuring the concrete causes and effects of the lost war. And both films reveal a shell-shocked society in search of an enemy who can be blamed for the defeat.

Lang's two-part film *Die Nibelungen* (1924) seems to tell another story—or does it? The clinically unhinged figures of the immediate postwar cinema may have been replaced by heroic characters from the Middle Ages, but their maniacal obsession with loyalty and honor to the point of self-destruction is no less disturbing. Like *Nosferatu*, Lang's *Nibelungen* is consumed with recovering a traumatic past.

Myth, Murder, and Revenge

He kept falling asleep, waking to images that for a half a minute he could make no sense of at all—a close-up of a face? A forest? The scales of the Dragon? A battle-scene?

—Thomas Pynchon, *Gravity's Rainbow*, 1974

What rivers of blood have already flowed, what nameless sorrow has come over the countless innocents whose houses have been burnt and pillaged! I am often overcome by dread when I think of this and I feel I should take responsibility for this horror: and yet, I could not have acted otherwise than I did.

—Helmuth von Moltke, *Erinnerungen*, September 1, 1914

Myth is catastrophe in permanence.

—Theodor W. Adorno, *Wagner's Relevance for Today*, 1963

The National Project

Germany, as always limping loyally behind,
according to its idiotic Nibelungen code of honor.
—Werner Scholem, letter to Gershom Scholem, September 8, 1914

In December 1916, the German Kaiser offered the nation an unusual Christmas present: he dedicated the Berlin Reichstag building to "the German people." Workers mounted massive bronze letters atop the classical columns below the frieze that read: *Dem deutschen Volke* (To the German People). This unusual dedication had been part of architect Paul Wallot's original plan for the Reichstag's opening in 1894. The Kaiser, however, objected to the phrasing's implied democratic message and delayed the installation. Finally, at the end of 1916, he agreed to the symbolic gesture as a way to thank the German people for their sacrifices during the bloodiest year of the war.[1] The year 1916 had indeed been an ill-fated one: close to half a million young Germans had died on the battlefields of Verdun and the Somme and no end was in sight. *To the German People* assumed multiple meanings during the 1920s, as the Reichstag itself became a contested site in the struggle between democratic and antidemocratic forces. The Left saw the dedication as an admonishment to elected officials to devote themselves to the service of the German people, whereas the Right emphasized the word "Volk"—an untranslatable term that referred to a racially based community. Whatever the meaning of *Volk*, the very act of dedicating the Reichstag (both the building and the parliament) to the German People was unprecedented.

Was Fritz Lang inspired by the Reichstag's grandiose inscription "Dem deutschen Volke" when he prefaced his epic film *Die Nibelungen* with the words "Dem deutschen Volke zu eigen" (Given to the German People)?[2] A title card with big Gothic letters evokes not only the dedication on top of the Reichstag but also the intent behind it: uniting a large number of people around the idea of a shared gift was meant to affirm and even construct a community in desperate times. Mimicking the Kaiser's wartime gesture, Lang and his coauthor (and wife) Thea von Harbou offered their film adaptation of the Nibelungen myth as a gift to the "German *Volk*," artfully overlooking the difference between a national community and a movie audience. The desired and implied spectatorship for Lang's film was no doubt the German *Volk* in its entirety. Like the Reichstag dedication, the film's inscription also solicited the public's gratitude for the gift received. Although the film's dedication may itself have been part of a marketing strategy, the first title card makes clear that Lang did not see his *Nibelungen* as mere entertainment. The film intended to offer the German people an *aide memoire*, reminding them of a heroic past that had been lost in the war. The entire campaign surrounding the film's release, masterfully orchestrated by Lang, von Harbou, and Ufa, underscored this national project.

When *Siegfried*, the first part of Lang's long-anticipated *Nibelungen*, opened on February 14, 1924, it was more than a cultural event. It was brazenly political. German society was still traumatized by its military defeat, the failed revolution, numerous political assassinations, widely reported serial killings, and (most recently) by the humiliation of the Ruhr crisis.

In January 1923, in reaction to Germany's failure to pay reparations, one hundred thousand French and Belgian troops occupied the Ruhr area, thus further demoralizing Germany and arousing nationalist sentiments. There were work stoppages, sabotage, and even street battles in which hundreds of people died. Passive resistance by about two million workers cut into the national budget. The government responded by printing more money, which in turn accelerated the hyperinflation of fall 1923. After the dollar reached the equivalent of over several trillion marks and postage stamps cost fifty million, a new currency was introduced on November 15, 1923. The strikes were called off in September 1923, precipitating a prolonged governmental crisis. Hitler's Beer Hall Putsch in Munich was staged on November 8, 1923. The French did not withdraw their troops until August 1925.

The *Nibelungen* film's production paralleled the Ruhr crisis, so that by the time of *Siegfried*'s premiere, French troops were still stationed in Germany's most vital industrial area. Responding to these aftershocks of the war, Lang offered a radical shift in perspective, making a film that would turn viewers' attention away from the nation's baleful recent history toward eternal values enshrined in myth. By these means Lang hoped not only to relativize the severity of the nation's losses but to transcend them. *Nibelungen* would revive Germany's founding myth, which was imbued with epic themes—loyalty, high ideals, heroism in defeat—that resonated with the historical events of the past decade. Lang and von Harbou reinterpreted the war and the Nibelungen saga in terms of each other. The political and cultural stakes seemed higher than in any previous German film.

Newspapers had written for weeks about the film adaptation of the "German Iliad," whose production had consumed two full years. It was marketed as the most expensive European film ever made (before *Metropolis* topped it two years later). A sixty-member symphony orchestra played an original score by Gottfried Huppertz, emulating the leitmotif structure of Richard Wagner's cycle *Der Ring des Nibelungen* of the 1870s. German cinema, after its long denigration as disreputable, frivolous, commercial mass entertainment, found itself now at the pinnacle of high culture. Lang's *Nibelungen* even competed with Jürgen Fehling's celebrated six-hour theater production of Friedrich Hebbel's trilogy *Die Nibelungen*, which opened in April 1924, the same month as the *Nibelungen* film's second part. Film no longer shied away from vying with dramatic theater, which Germans (following Hegel) have traditionally considered to be the highest form of culture.

Lang and von Harbou used the undisputed cultural capital of the *Nibelungenlied* to raise the artistic profile of the new medium. They built on a special brand of German auteurist cinema exemplified by Wegener's *The Student of Prague* (1913) and Lang's own *Destiny* (1921)—films that had set themselves apart from the mass entertainment movies that thrived in Germany (as everywhere else). While popular cinema had developed a transnational stock of narrative and visual tropes, high art cinema tended to draw on ethnic folktales, literary works, and historical legends. National epics such as Griffith's *The Birth of a Nation* (1915) and Gance's *Napoleon* (1928) illustrate that the nexus of artistic aspiration and national founding myth was not confined to Germany.

When Lang and his wife decided to adapt the Nibelungen saga, they added their film to a long lineage of dramatic and literary adaptations of this classical German epic. After its rediscovery in the middle of the eighteenth century, the Nibelungen saga became a popular source of inspiration for literature, theater, opera, and the arts. Hebbel's two-part play *Die Nibelungen* (1860) and, of course, Wagner's four-part opera cycle *Der Ring des Nibelungen* (1876) were the most famous products of the national myth. But the saga's popularity rose again, sharply, during World War I and its aftermath. In 1924, it would have been nearly impossible to find a German who was not familiar with both the story and the character of Siegfried.[3] A youthful nation when compared to Great Britain or France, Germany identified itself with the young and idealistic hero. Siegfried was Germany. Germany was Siegfried.[4]

The Nibelungen was mandatory reading in schools and a favorite subject for illustrated children's books. Lang in fact took his major design concept from

Carl Otto Czeschka's illustrated Nibelungen edition published for children in 1909.[5] His film was meant to have as broad an appeal as possible. Von Harbou, who had played Kriemhild as a young girl in a school production of Hebbel's *Nibelungen*, also published a prose version of the saga, *Das Nibelungenbuch*, which appeared as a "tie-in" in 1924 with illustrations from the film.[6]

Billed as a *Monumentalfilm*, *Siegfried*'s premiere resembled that of an opera, complete with orchestra, curtain, and a long ovation at the end of the film. The director, screenwriter, and actors appeared on stage to take bows and receive flowers. At a banquet afterward, Chancellor Gustav Stresemann expressed the hope that the film would unite the German people and build a bridge to other nations. Stresemann's speech (published in the next day's papers) underlined the *Nibelungen*'s serious political and ethical mission. His words echoed a chorus of voices that had preceded the film's premiere and predetermined its reception.

Lang himself, a Viennese who had become a German citizen only in 1924, openly confessed his trepidation about making the German epic into a movie, fearing that he might be accused of trivializing what he repeatedly called the "sacred national epos" of his new fatherland.[7] On the day of the film's premiere, as if to underscore the gravity of the undertaking, Lang and von Harbou laid a wreath at the grave of Frederick the Great in Potsdam. More than simply a public relations stunt, this act of remembrance affirmed a cultural nationalism that saw a continuum from the *Nibelungenlied* to Frederick the Great to Wagner and finally, so they hoped, to the film adaptation.[8] The film's goal, according to von Harbou, was to instill in the "great, exhausted and overworked German people" a desire for a collective identity based on national myth.[9] Following Wagner's wish to reconstitute a lost national community with his Ring cycle, Lang's *Nibelungen* promised a renewed sense of German identity and dignity at a moment of crisis.

Posing for Germany

If our neighbors want it no other way, if our neighbors do not grant us peace, then I hope to God that our good German sword will see us through to victory in these difficult battles.

—Kaiser Wilhelm II, speech to the German people, August 1, 1914

A painted rainbow arches over a primordial mountain range, linking heaven and earth, gods and mortals. *Siegfried* begins with this still image, setting the stage for a story that is not of this world. A long shot of gigantic tree trunks, dwarfing the few Neanderthal men visible in the distance, reinforces the impression that we have entered a realm of legends and fairy tales. Cut to a medium close-up of a hairy, apelike creature pushing bellows to fan flames for a smithy. These three shots—the mythical rainbow, the primal forest, and the primitive, dark-skinned, barely human creature—prepare us for the first glimpse of the film's hero, who stands in stark relief against these surroundings. Bathed in dazzling white light, Siegfried poses in a moment frozen in time, ethereal and majestic, resembling a youthful Apollo.

Shot from a low angle that makes him look like a sculpture, the image is indeed reminiscent of classical monuments, foreshadowing conscious efforts by the Nazis to appropriate classical art. Only ten years later, Arnold Breker, the most prominent Nazi sculptor, would produce a series of public statues of oversized naked bodies posing similarly with sword or torch in hand. Paul Richter, as Siegfried, does not act here in the conventional sense; he *poses* for the camera, displaying his naked torso and looking down his bare muscular arms to his sword, which is initially outside the frame. His eyes are directed at his extended arms, his slightly angled face a study in self-absorbed concentration, his limbs hard and rigid with a tension reminiscent of bodybuilding poses. He is framed in the center against a uniformly black background, his body set off by strong backlighting. The act of posing is underscored by the camera's cut to an onlooker, the dwarf Mime, Siegfried's mythical guardian and teacher, who provides the intended reaction of awe and wonderment. Siegfried is presented as the bodily foil to Mime: tall versus stunted, erect versus crouching, groomed and taut versus unkempt and slovenly, a blond Aryan superman versus a debased and abject dark Other. Mime, played by Georg John, acts as the primitive, reduced to watching the shining hero with a mixture of jealousy and dread. The camera cuts back and forth between them; they do not share the same frame. In an unexpected, unsettling cut the camera switches to a position slightly behind Siegfried, capturing his back—a subtle foreshadowing of his only vulnerable spot, as we will later discover.

The motionless posing is followed by vigorous activity. With exaggerated vehemence, Siegfried begins to forge his sword. He is surrounded by heavy billows of smoke, his form starkly sculpted by strong overhead, back, and side lighting. The smoke, an old theatrical effect often employed in productions of Wagner's *Ring*, adds to the magical quality of this hero of unknown origins, half god, half human, outside of time and space, heedless of danger and eager for battle. Smoke also gives the light a palpable presence, making

Life and death of a German hero.
Paul Richter and Margarethe Schön
in Fritz Lang's *Nibelungen*.

it visible and alive. The lighting alone valorizes the unique and special character of the hero, adding a radiant glow to his physique, highlighting the texture of his naked, marble-like skin, and lending the translucent image a sense of depth. It seems even to illuminate the onlooker.

As in all films dealing with history and myth, the *Nibelungen* had to make use of widely known pictorial conventions. By 1924, a century of Siegfrieds existed in paintings and book illustrations as well as on stage. In order to be recognizable as the hero, Richter had to model his appearance and habitus after previous portrayals of Siegfried. In this sense, he did not act so much as "enact" prior representations; he inhabits the images that were already known before he donned the role. This led a contemporary critic to speculate: "I do not know whether Fritz Lang had thought of filming the immortal national epic of the Germans before he met Paul Richter. It would be reasonable to think that only the acquaintance with this young actor who was to offer such a perfect incarnation of young Siegfried gave him the idea."[10]

Richter's pale skin and blond mane of hair also invoke the period's racial preoccupations, pointing to ideals associated with the Aryan race and its supposed superiority. Whiteness assumed special significance in 1923 when opposition to the military occupation of the Rhineland articulated itself in openly racist terms against French troops, most of whom came from France's African colonies. The government did not curb the wild tales and lies disseminated in posters, flyers, and brochures. For nationalists it was already an insult to the German psyche to have to face black soldiers, and their fear of widespread intermarriage became positively hysterical. Imagining "mulattoes" in the Rhineland, the homeland of Siegfried, was to nationalists nothing less than *Schwarze Schmach* (black disgrace).[11]

The exaggerated blondness of Siegfried's hair was a semiotic marker of pure Germanness in 1923–24. His blond hair was so dear to von Harbou that she waxed poetic even in the screenplay: "His hair, of the lightest blond and flowing like a golden stream, is brushed backwards from the forehead. He has the habit of tossing it back with wild vigor when it falls, fair and fine as it is, onto his forehead."[12] In addition to special lighting effects, a chemical was applied to make Richter's hair shimmer, enhancing its dazzling blondness. Camera angles, framing, and montage further articulate the power of the white hero over the dark-skinned *Untermensch* Mime, described in the screenplay as resembling a "gorilla with depraved face and bristly hair." In stark contrast, Siegfried appears as the ultimate symbol of what ten years later would be exalted as the Aryan German.

In his 1924 book *Der sichtbare Mensch oder die Kultur des Films* (*Visible Man or the Culture of Film*), Béla Balázs argued that cinema would promote the domination of the white race. Cinema, he claimed in a troubling passage, emanated from Europe and the United States, and it would spread the white man's ideals of beauty across the globe.[13] The whiteness of Siegfried's skin is enhanced by his white clothes and further intensified by the snow-white horse on which he rides away from his underlit habitat: a white knight in search of adventure and love, doing battle against the treacherous darkness that surrounds him.

Whiteness possesses a range of connotations that all play into the image of our hero: untouched purity, virtue, innocence, chastity, and finally death.[14] For as the film shows (and the German viewer already knows) Siegfried is marked for death from the beginning. Lang stages scenes that are in a sense already familiar—hence the preponderance of posing. Action in this film is condensed into pregnant moments of great visual power in which time seems to stand still.

Richter's half-naked torso also conjures up a rush of associations relating the iconic mythical figure to the cultural moment of 1924. Being unfettered by clothes signaled freedom and innocence, but also a position untouched by class and status consciousness. His unclothed body puts him in visual contrast with the courtly Burgundians who wear formal attire that displays rank and wealth, but also hides secrets. In physical terms, Siegfried has less in common with the refined courtiers of Burgundy than with Tarzan, the emblem of natural man, who appeared on screen as early as 1918 and had become widely popular in the Weimar Republic. In 1924, four volumes of William Rice Burrough's serial novel about Tarzan's adventures were published in German translation, prompting the conservative critic Otto Koischwitz to complain about a veritable "Tarzan epidemic."[15] Siegfried's natural state as the noble savage, guileless and impetuous, who sets out to get his Kriemhild (as Tarzan gets his Jane) makes him appear ignorant of, and hence vulnerable to, the treacherous world of civilization.

The position of the actor's sculpted torso and the pose he strikes in the very first shot also draw on the iconography of Weimar's flourishing *Körperkultur*, or "body culture." Promoting health, beauty, and strength, the movement recalls both the prewar *Lebensreform* movement and the training of bodies in the military. In 1924, the very year that *Siegfried* opened, a former high-ranking officer Hans Surén published a small illustrated book on bodybuilding titled *Der Mensch und die Sonne* (*Man and the Sun*).[16] Enjoying a phenomenal success including numerous editions throughout the 1920s, it was later seamlessly absorbed into the Nazi ideology of fitness. (In his 1936 edition, Surén added the subtitle "Arisch-olympischer Geist," or Aryan-Olympian Spirit.) Surén's book contains, in addition to a stylistically overwrought hymn to sunlight and instructions for nude swimming and gymnastics, a large number of pictures of men and women, most of them half or fully nude, in various poses reminiscent of Siegfried's. In his preface, Surén reminds the nation of the importance of physical strength: no strong bodies, no strong nation. Surén's emphasis on the patriotic dimension of gymnastics had itself a long history, dating back to Friedrich Ludwig Jahn's belief in the early nineteenth century that only well-trained bodies would be capable of defending the nation.[17] Gymnastics produced self-control, discipline, and submission. Friedrich Nietzsche's glorification of the heroic body as an antidote to decadence and degeneration, to civilization and cultural nihilism, was also widely known at the time. In 1924, the well-toned body of the actor who played Siegfried carried connotations of a strong and youthful national body. Lang's film anchored national identity in the body of Siegfried.

The emphasis on the strong masculine body also compensated for the war-torn bodies on display in the streets of the republic. Eight million men returned from the war wounded. Ernst Friedrich's controversial illustrated book, written in four languages and titled *Krieg dem Kriege* (*War against War*), which contained shocking photographs of dead and severely mutilated soldiers, was also published in 1924, the year *Nibelungen* premiered. Lang's stress on the strong and beautiful body in *Siegfried* provided a defiant response to Friedrich's grisly, disfigured warriors.

Only a year after the *Nibelungen* film, Ufa promoted a full-length documentary on German body culture, *Wege zur Kraft und Schönheit* (*Ways to Strength and Beauty*). This popular *Kulturfilm* also linked physical beauty and prowess to the regeneration of the community. Twelve years later, Leni Riefenstahl would perfect the analogy between the athlete's body and the national body in her two-part film *Olympia*. Body culture, in short, had become a realm in which patriotism could be openly displayed at a time when the nation was no longer allowed to express itself in military form. The first part of Lang's *Nibelungen* film partakes of this discourse in its focus on Siegfried's physical agility and grace.

Moreover, the film begins with Siegfried forging a weapon: a sword more accurate and more powerful than any before. The vigorous creation of this sword alludes to the German fantasy of developing a *Wunderwaffe* (or "miracle weapon," as it would be called in World War II) that would guarantee victory in battle. The film underscores the phantasmagoric quality of this ultimate weapon in a trick sequence when a bird's feather tumbling through the air falls on the sword and is cut into two halves. The precision of the sword is paralleled by the precision of the camera that miraculously captures this feat in slow-motion. This obtrusive shot, which invokes an earlier cinema of attractions eager to show off its tricks, stops the action for a moment and diverts attention from the actors. It none-too-subtly suggests that for Lang, the actors are part of a larger design and subordinated to his whim. In fact, throughout the film the narrative is driven less by characters as agents than by the filmmaker's juxtaposition of scenes. There are two crosscuts to Siegfried in this scene: in one his face is filled with worry and anguish, in the other with youthful laughter after the sword has passed the test. In both, Richter's gestures are exaggerated in an acting style that unapologetically derives from the pictorial school of acting. This style, as Ben Brewster and Lea Jacobs have shown, was guided by studying statues and paintings as well as copying poses from the other arts.[18] Given the heavy weight of the iconographic tradition that Lang's *Nibelungen* had to carry, it is not surprising that most of the acting in the film is pictorial, although there are also scenes—for instance, those between Siegfried and Brunhilde—that oscillate between pictorial posing and a more modern style that relies on small restrained gestures and subtle facial expressions.

The Will to Form

Monumentality has the effect that big wars, revolutions of peoples, foundations of state have: it is liberating, summarizing, and creating fate, ordering after a long disorder.

—Arthur Moeller van den Bruck, *Der Preussische Stil*, 1916

Like *The Cabinet of Dr. Caligari*'s "I will tell you," or *Nosferatu*'s "Here is their story," Lang's *Nibelungen* consistently foregrounds the act of narrating. Unlike *Nosferatu*, however, *Nibelungen* shows its storyteller, the bard Volker, playing a medieval fiddle and singing the legend. "Then Volker sang thusly, the fiddle sounded," the intertitle states. The *Nibelungen* film thereby emphasizes the narrative's theatricality and artificiality, features further underscored by its division into cantos that give a preview of the action (for example, "How Siegfried slew the dragon") and conclude with the intertitle "Thus ends the canto." This device of separating the film's narrative into discrete parts also highlights the strong authorial hand that controls what we see. The summaries that introduce each canto diminish suspense and direct the viewer's gaze away from the action, drawing it instead toward style. A few years later, Brecht would use this same episodic technique for didactic purposes in his early Epic Theater. In *Nibelungen*, it serves as an orderly narrative edifice that underscores Lang's deliberate artificiality and stylization.

The *Nibelungen* was filmed entirely at the Neubabelsberg studios. Even the outdoor scenes were indoor creations of concrete trees and artificial castles. The film sought to evoke German art from the Gothic period to art nouveau, including literal references to architecture, painting, and book illustration.[19] For instance, a scene of Siegfried riding through a German forest that appears to be illuminated from within recalls not only Arnold Böcklin's painting *Das Schweigen im Walde* (*Silence in the Forest*), but also the thirteenth-century statue of the *Bamberger Horseman*, a favorite image pictured in just about every school text of the period. Wearing neither coat nor helmet, Siegfried appears free and uninhibited, his whiteness contrasting starkly with the gigantic mythical forest—a forest that Lang once compared to a Gothic cathedral.[20]

In opposition to this mythical realm, Lang created the highly stylized and symmetrical world of the Burgundians. They are introduced by means of a church procession that is filmed from a respectful distance; the camera is permitted only to peek between the sentries in the foreground. The ritual quality of this scene suggests inapproachability, power, compulsion, and controlled aggression. Here, the "will to style," which had become the hallmark of German art at the turn of the century, predominates. Lang's self-proclaimed desire was to create a specifically German film style that would differentiate itself above all from Hollywood's commercial fare. In his vision, this German style was predicated on strict form and a stylization that would breathe life into the inanimate world.

Lang's search for a national artistic style was part of an ongoing discourse that began with an 1890 pamphlet titled *Rembrandt als Erzieher* (*Rembrandt as Educator*), which generated renewed interest in the postwar years. Its author, Julius Langbehn, pleaded for a high German style that would draw on

The religiosity of form:

Siegfried's light extinguished.

folk tradition and myth and embody what he termed the "masculine nature of the Germans."[21] Similarly, Franz Servaes's programmatic essay from 1905, tellingly titled "Der Wille zum Stil" ("The Will to Style"), argued against impressionism's sophistication and psychologization, advocating instead a strictly formal neoclassicism.[22] This art-historical argument was carried further by Wilhelm Worringer's 1909 treatise *Abstraktion und Einfühlung* (*Abstraction and Empathy*), by the architectural school that called itself the "Gläserne Kette" (Crystal Chain), and finally by Lang's cinematic style.[23]

Lang acknowledged this lineage when he speculated that "if the *Nibelungen* film was to become a new form for the old epic, it would be necessary to find a style that would illuminate the idea of the work like a crystal."[24] The choice of the word "crystal" shows Lang's indebtedness to contemporary discussions surrounding the model of utopian architecture.[25] The crystal was a figure of fascination because it was an absolutely symmetrical and regular natural form. For the design of his *Nibelungen*, Lang, who had studied under the Jugendstil artist Julius Diez in Munich, also borrowed heavily from the Vienna Secession movement. Geometric patterns cover costumes as well as wall hangings, jewelry, and furnishings, and thus often blur the distinction between figure and background as they share the same ornamental decor. In this way, the human, too, is subjugated to the "will to style."[26]

Lang's film melded the ornamental style with the collectivist production ethics of the Weimar Bauhaus. In 1924, he spoke of the medieval stonemasons' guild, or *Bauhütte*, as a precursor for the harmonious collaboration of arts and crafts in the *Nibelungen* film. This idea echoed Walter Gropius's programmatic statement on the Bauhaus from 1919.[27] The *Nibelungen* film, according to Lang, distinguished itself from Hollywood because of the national spirit that inheres in German cinema. He compared this spirit with the worshipful attitude of the master masons who created Gothic cathedrals and even called for the re-establishment of such artists' communities.[28] In the footsteps of Wagner, Lang seemed to yearn for an aesthetic healing of the torn body politic, and his programmatic statements about the *Nibelungen* project never failed to emphasize the film's regenerative power for Germany. However, what his *Nibelungen* film shows beneath its formalized structure is a community on the road to self-destruction.

For Lang, Siegfried's prehistoric, mythical world stands in opposition to the civilized, Christian world of the Burgundians. But Lang is eager to show that the courtly façade of civilization conceals archaic drives, a lust for power, jealousy, and murderous rage. The innocent and unsuspecting Siegfried is unprepared for the intrigues and deceptions of the court, and so it is not surprising that he is betrayed and killed.

The Fallen Hero

In the great vicinity of death, of blood, and of soil,
the mind takes on harder features and darker colors.
—Ernst Jünger, *Der Arbeiter*, 1932

"We were at our wits' end!" recalls Paul von Hindenburg, field marshal and Chief of the General Staff, in his "political testament" of 1919: "Just as Siegfried fell to the treacherous spear of terrible Hagen, so did our exhausted front lines collapse. They tried in vain to draw new life from the dried-up wellspring of the home front."[29] Both von Hindenburg and Ludendorff had invoked the Nibelungen myth in early 1917 when they established the so-called Siegfried Line on the battlefield between Arras and Reims. After being defeated by the French, the German army successfully retreated to this line because it was heavily fortified and, like Siegfried, supposedly invulnerable. Naming it after the hero of the German epic was also meant to inspire confidence and keep alive the idea of what was widely propagated as a *Sieg-Frieden,* a pun on the name Siegfried, meaning peace (Friede) through victory (Sieg).

When in summer 1918 Ludendorff again retreated to the Siegfried Line, the defense did not hold, and few weeks later the German army was in total disarray. But defeat did not keep Ludendorff from once again exploiting the Nibelungen saga, now by linking the murder of Siegfried to the military defeat. He blamed the outcome of the war on a betrayal. Just like Siegfried, Germany had been betrayed and "stabbed in the back" by a home front that did not sufficiently support the fighting army. (The fact that Siegfried was killed by a spear, not stabbed with a knife, was overlooked.) The so-called stab-in-the-back legend was heavily promoted toward the end of the war by both the government and the Supreme High Command, which had in fact misled the public about the true state of military progress for years. Even in 1924, these mythically tinged lies lived on. In the first volume of Hitler's *Mein Kampf,* which appeared only a year after the *Nibelungen* opened, Siegfried stands metaphorically for the defeated troops. The noncombatants on the home front are figured as having "agitated against and subverted our victory for so long that finally the fighting Siegfried succumbed as a result of the treacherous stab in the back."[30]

There is visual evidence as well that links Siegfried to the heroic self-image of wartime Germany. In early 1918, a short film promoting war bonds appeared under the title *Jung Siegfried*. Julius Pinschewer, a pioneer of advertising films in the first decades of German cinema, created a series of shorts in which the government appealed to Germans' patriotism to help finance the war. Like Lang's 1924 *Siegfried*, which is more than two hours long, this brief, two-minute film shows the hero naked above the waist forging a sword. Later he gesticulates with it in front of a dragon made of cardboard. Although shot without any atmospheric backdrop, the visuals are stunningly close to Lang's opening scenes. The first title cards read: "With German blows he created a sword . . . with which he killed the dragon." As in Lang's dragon-slaying scene, Siegfried appears among trees, approaching the dragon from the right. Pinschewer's film ends with the following appeal: "Germany of today, be worthy of your ancestors, sharpen once more your cutting sword! Buy War Bonds (*Zeichne die Kriegsanleihe*)!" Distributed at no cost to theater owners to be shown before the main feature, the film allegorizes Siegfried to promote not only bonds but also the idea of a combat-ready national body, set to destroy the enemy just as Siegfried vanquished the dragon.

The postwar popularity of the Nibelungen saga suggests that Lang's film was part of a widespread discourse that sought to work through the traumatic experience of war and national defeat. The violent death of millions of young men, the clear military loss, and the ensuing political and social chaos were events that the film could not but restage. Both parts of the *Nibelungen* feature numerous warlike deployments and excursions into foreign territories: Siegfried's march into Worms, the Burgundians' arrival in Iceland, Kriemhild's move to King Attila's country, and the Burgundians' visit there. Lang's film raises questions of power and submission, and discusses ideas of utmost importance in time of war: loyalty and courage as well as betrayal, treason, and murder.

Siegfried's valiant fight with the gigantic flame-breathing dragon, which was animated by sixteen crew members inside, alludes to the cliché of a small army beating a superior enemy against all odds. It also casts Siegfried as a thoughtless aggressor who attacks the dragon without provocation. Laying eyes on the fabled beast, he lifts his sword high in the familiar pose of the famous monument of Hermann, the legendary German leader who defeated the Romans at the Battle of the Teutoburg Forest.[31] Siegfried kills the dragon after piercing one of his eyes, shown in a terrifying close-up that anticipates Luis Buñuel's shot of a razor slicing an eye in *Un chien andalou* (1929). Siegfried then bathes in the dragon's blood, which will make his body invincible, transforming him into an indestructible fighting machine—the ultimate dream of the military. But not quite. A leaf falls between his shoulder blades as he soaks his skin with blood, leaving him with one vulnerable spot. The mythical magic cap that makes Siegfried invisible is depicted in the film as a net thrown over his head, hinting at camouflage techniques used at the front. Representing invisibility was of course a special challenge for Lang and his inventive crew, cinematographers Carl Hoffmann and Günther Rittau, set designers Otto Hunte, Karl Vollbrecht, and Erich Kettelhut, and special effects photographer Eugen Schüfftan. Double exposure and stop-motion produced either ghostlike doubles (as in scenes where Siegfried assumes the identity of Gunther) or disappearance as soon as the camouflage net is put on. Walther Ruttmann, famous for his abstract film studies (such as his 1921 avant-garde short *Opus 1*), was commissioned to produce an experimental film sequence illustrating Kriemhild's dream, in which black falcons attack a white falcon. His short abstract film was inserted into the narrative as a foreshadowing of Hagen's murder of Siegfried. The fairy-tale quality of the *Nibelungen* freed Lang and his collaborators from pressures of verisimilitude, giving them free rein for innovative experiments with film language. The choice of an episodic structure encouraged visual magic and virtuosity as if to say: "Watch what cinema can do!" It was a triumph of visual pleasure over narrative economy, and it gave the *Nibelungen* a richness that justified its claim to be a cinematic gift to the German people.[32]

The *Nibelungen* deals with the war by re-envisioning it as the ultimate national myth. Although this myth is at best highly ambivalent—the tale of a nation destined for catastrophe—it did not deter Germans from embracing it. The first part of Lang's film ends with the death of Siegfried and its traumatic effect on Kriemhild. It is an eerie night scene, in which a curtain rustles, a dog barks, and a procession of men carrying Siegfried's corpse comes to the door. As Kriemhild lays eyes on her dead husband, the music abruptly stops to dramatize her shock. It is the only silent moment in the entire film. As she bends over to stroke his hair, Kriemhild has a vision: a flashback to the moment of her greatest happiness with Siegfried. They sit under a tree in full bloom that swiftly morphs into a skull. This striking trick photography connotes fate at work, a recognition that death was already present behind the beautiful façade.

Like a fallen soldier, Siegfried is laid out on his funeral bier. A film still depicting this scene—the dead warrior with Kriemhild at his side—circulated as a picture postcard at the time. Was this tableau the equivalent of a monument in memory of the young men who died in the war? Britain erected a tomb of the Unknown Warrior at Westminster Abbey in November 1920 to honor the unidentified dead of the war. On November 11, 1920, Armistice Day, France memorialized its fallen with the Tomb of the Unknown Soldier beneath the Arc de Triomphe. Germany did not have a national memorial for its war dead until ten years later.[33] For many Germans there was only the image of the dead Siegfried to symbolize the Fatherland's "unknown soldier." Although no *national* war memorial was possible in the war's immediate aftermath (so divided over its memory was the nation), most cities, towns, and even villages did build monuments to honor their fallen native sons. If memorials are, as Reinhart Koselleck suggests, a kind of "talisman for the identity of the survivors,"[34] then the *Nibelungen* fulfilled that function very well. In Lang's film, Siegfried's corpse is on display for a substantial amount of film time, allowing the viewer to reflect on the meaning of his death for those he left behind. An unsuspecting victim of a courtly plot, a youthful martyr, or an emblem of Germany betrayed, Siegfried offered Germans various options for identification.

Siegfried's significance was not limited to Germany. Austria also used the hero to make sense of a senseless war. In 1916, the Viennese sculptor Josef Müllner planned a monumental war memorial: a huge sculpture of Siegfried's corpse lying in a sarcophagus. For financial reasons, only the head of the sculpture could be completed during the war. According to a contemporary report, the idea that Siegfried would memorialize the fallen soldiers

> affected [the artist] to such a degree, that, when it became clear that the execution of the entire monument was unattainable, he felt compelled to free himself from it. The master reached for his chisel and, by extracting the primary from the secondary aspects, created the powerful bust of Siegfried more or less purely from feeling. This distillation realized the essence of the entire monument: the absorption of Germany's spiritual heroism in temporary stasis.[35]

In the early 1920s, when members of the right-extremist, openly anti-Semitic German-National Student Association at the University of Vienna wanted to honor their fallen comrades, they remembered this award-winning sculpture of Siegfried's head and placed it in the entrance hall of the university. At the unveiling on November 9, 1923, a representative of the German-National Student Association held a eulogy that declared:

> It is our duty to give meaning and value to the heroic deaths of our brothers. Millions of our national comrades have come under foreign domination. In the north and in the south, in the east and in the west, pieces of our national body have been ripped away and the poisoned dagger of the West endeavors to advance ever further into the heart of our Reich, which up until now has preserved its unity. . . . It is our duty to rescue the German soul from destruction and to heal it. . . . We have erected a monument to honor our dead, to serve as our signpost. Their courage and strength were as hard as this stone, and ours should once again become so. With this we confer upon them the motto "Honor, Freedom, Fatherland."[36]

The goals articulated here in 1923—the conferral of meaning, the communication of eternal values, and the promise of guidance in the years ahead—resemble those in Lang's *Nibelungen*. Both the sculpture and the film transform death into a monumental and sacred event, something akin to the passion of Christ. Siegfried appears as a martyr bearing the promise of redemption. The laid-out body is the site of mourning, contemplation, and memory; it is the place where identification with the dead can take place. In the *Nibelungen* film, the individual spectator's political convictions were crucial to the interpretation of Siegfried's corpse: Siegfried could be read as either a victim or a threat, either a catalyst for mourning or an incitement to revenge, a theme taken up in the film's second half. Entwined with liturgical and cult-religious traditions, Kriemhild's oath of revenge at the sight Siegfried's body had an appeal in 1924 that extended beyond the *völkisch* segments of the population. As in Baroque tragedies, about which Walter Benjamin wrote around this time, the body of the fallen hero became an allegory for the national body and the fatherland, which in the eyes of many Germans had also been martyred. As a now fully legitimate art form, film was assigned the task of regenerating the destroyed national body, reanimating it by cinematic means. In contrast to his later film *Metropolis*, though, Lang rejected a utopian conclusion for the *Nibelungen* film. Siegfried's death does not lead to rebirth and salvation but rather to a resolve for revenge that ends in apocalyptic conflagration.

From mythic duel in *Siegfried*
to trench warfare
in *Kriemhild's Revenge*.

Lang's film contributed to the National Socialists' store of collective imagery. Part 1 of the *Nibelungen* was re-released in 1933 with a new title: *Siegfrieds Tod* (*Siegfried's Death*). Now a sound film accompanied by excerpts from Richard Wagner, this version was shortened to focus exclusively on the theme of national identity. While Lang was on his way into exile, Reichsminister Goebbels declared in a letter to national and National Socialist organizations: "This immortal heroic song was born of the German spirit, whose roots absorbed its great strengths from the sacred depths of the German national character and German nature. . . . Today more than ever, in this time of national rebirth, this film belongs to the people, *Siegfried's Death* is the German experience."[37]

Excursus: Lang in World War I

Every film shoot is a condensed big-battle day.

—Fritz Lang, "Working Community in the Cinema," 1924

Like many other young men in their mid-twenties, Lang enlisted voluntarily into the Austrian army in January 1915. In short succession he was promoted to corporal, cadet, platoon leader, sergeant, and finally lieutenant. A member of the Fourth Army, Tenth Corps, Thirteenth Territorial Field Artillery Division, he was in combat in Slovenia from October 1915 onward, spending New Year's Eve 1915–16 in a "reconnaissance shelter in the trenches," as he noted in his recently discovered "War Journal 1915."[38] Lang received several recommendations and decorations for bravery in reconnaissance work. He ventured "into hostile territory, even though Russian artillery was keeping up lively fire in the immediate vicinity," and returned "with a sketch which allowed his battalion to effectively target what had been until then completely unknown Russian positions."[39] Another recommendation for a medal in June 1915 stated: "He withstood twelve hours under heavy fire, and sent exemplary reports which were decisive in stopping a strong opponent from making progress. In this battle, Sergeant Lang received a shoulder injury."[40] Eventually his division lost the battle; Lang's heroism made no difference.

After his second injury on June 25, 1916—a shrapnel splinter entered his eye—he was sent home to Vienna to recover. While convalescing, Lang enrolled at the Vienna Academy of Fine Arts and took on small acting roles. In April 1918, he appeared in a theater production, playing a wounded soldier.

It was on this occasion that he met producer Erich Pommer, who would later engage him as a writer for Decla, his Berlin production company. On June 22, 1918, Lang requested a discharge from the army on account of health problems, which included a heart condition and rheumatism contracted during combat as well as "my nervous ailment" (*mein Nervenleiden*), which was a common euphemism for shell shock. This was a medical condition that had temporarily exempted him from service before.[41] Although we do not know how severe his shell shock was, he was aware of the war-related nervous disorder and used it to justify his request. On June 30, 1918, Lang was officially relieved from active duty "on the grounds that he is unfit for active troop service, only for home duties."[42]

Although Lang never depicted World War I explicitly, his German films are filled with characters who suffer from various kinds and degrees of "nervous disorders," from *Destiny* (1920) and *Dr. Mabuse* (1922) to *M* (1931) and *The Testament of Dr. Mabuse* (1933). Some contain scenarios involving warlike combat (the end of *Dr. Mabuse*), others visual and narrative motifs that address the life-and-death experience of war. Indeed, death pervades Lang's work. In one of his earliest screenplays, a melodrama titled *Hilde Warren und der Tod* (*Hilde Warren and Death*, 1917), Death appears personified, making a pact with a woman who hangs on to life, only to give in to him at the end. "I am the one who relieves sorrow," says Death, "who beds weary heads on pillows, and opens the door to freedom." Written in 1916 and directed by Joe May the following year, this film foreshadows Lang's 1921 artistic breakthrough, *Der müde Tod: Ein deutsches Volkslied in 6 Versen* (*Destiny*, or in literal translation, The Weary Death: A German Folk Song in 6 Verses). In an allegory of the war's ravishing effects on the home front, Death abducts a young man from the side of a young woman. Weary of his task, Death looks on as the woman sacrifices herself to be reunited with her dead fiancé.[43]

Lang's *Nibelungen* is different. Instead of accepting mortality as inherent in the human condition as in *Destiny*, Kriemhild challenges the inevitability of Siegfried's death, pointing her finger at the murderer and vowing revenge. She does not mourn Siegfried but is instead gripped by melancholia. While the first part of the *Nibelungen* culminates in the death of the young and innocent Siegfried, the second part depicts a full-fledged war to avenge his killing. This war exposes the repressed violence that underlies the highly stylized chivalry of the Burgundian court. It is a war at Attila's castle that only ends when all the protagonists (except Attila) have perished.

The Sacred Battle

All great wars are religious wars.

—Werner Sombart, *Merchants and Heroes*, 1915

In the fall of 1914, the Eugen Diederichs Verlag published a small-format anthology of war poetry, *Der heilige Krieg: Gedichte aus dem Beginn des Kampfes* (*The Holy War: Poems from the Beginning of Battle*). It is the first volume of the *Feldpostbücherei* (field-post library) that in the tradition of Johann Gottlieb Fichte and Paul de Lagarde sought a "new German Idealism with a popular and religious foundation."[44] The afterword, which is dated September 1914 and signed by a certain R. Buchwald, claims that the book embodies the "German spirit" of the first few weeks of the Great War. The passionate enthusiasm of the mobilized nation found expression in poems about love of the fatherland, just as the German wars of liberation from Napoleon produced the patriotic poetry of 1813. In the 1914 poetry collection, famous poets are placed next to unknown ones, but all of their poems share a conventional form and a religious vocabulary replete with blood, honor, and sacrifice. Among the themes are celebrations of familiar nineteenth-century ideals—freedom, victory, and homeland—as well as new motifs that justify the conflict as a holy war of Germanic chivalric values against the forces of Western modernity and materialism. Several poems name France and Britain as archenemies of Germany, personifying exactly what Germany is not. Ernst Lissauer's infamous poem "Hassgesang gegen England" (Hymn of Hate against England) proclaims that seventy million Germans have only one enemy, England, and it will be hated even beyond any future peace. The poem ends with a tenfold repetition of the word "hatred." Even well-established writers like Richard Dehmel, Waldemar Bonsels, Ludwig Alexander Schröder, Isolde Kurz, and Gerhart Hauptmann express their exultation that fate has chosen Germany to lead this fight against industrial modernity. Their poetry calls forth apocalyptic images of earth and heaven, clouds and storms, floods and fires. In 1914, Germany in their view was taking preemptive revenge against a "world of enemies" for having violated and killed the spiritual ideals of the German nation. The war was a holy war fought for German virtues and values, a war whose ultimate logic demanded the sacrifice of one's own life for higher ideals.

This is the semantic and ideological field that the second part of Lang's *Nibelungen* film inhabits. *Kriemhilds Rache* (*Kriemhild's Revenge*) opened on

April 26, 1924, about ten weeks after the premiere of *Siegfried*. Although it received less public attention at the time (and still does in the critical literature), it was not a sequel but rather an integral part of the *Nibelungen* project inasmuch as it illustrated Kriemhild's prophecy at the end of *Siegfried*: "You will not escape my revenge, Hagen Tronje." The story revolves around Kriemhild's diabolical plan to use her marriage to Etzel (known to us as Attila the Hun) to kill Hagen and thus avenge the murder of Siegfried, her first husband. After bearing Attila a son, she invites her brothers from Burgundy for a visit, and Hagen, as planned, accompanies them. She asks Attila to kill Hagen, but he refuses. Rüdiger, an emissary of Attila, had sworn to Kriemhild that she would be revenged if harm were to befall her at Attila's court. When Kriemhild reminds him of his pledge, Rüdiger finds himself faced with two mutually exclusive loyalties: his oath to Kriemhild, and his pledge to the Burgundians. This is only one of several dramatic double binds in the film.

More than the first part, which concentrated on the story of Siegfried, *Kriemhild's Revenge* presents a tangled web of conflicting allegiances and loyalties spun around the figure of Hagen, clearly now the central figure. Although Hagen killed Siegfried out of loyalty to Gunther and sunk the Nibelungen treasure to deprive Kriemhild of power, he is now repeatedly referred to as the "loyal Hagen." When Kriemhild demands that her brother Gunther punish Hagen for Siegfried's murder, Gunther replies: "He kept his pledge, I keep mine. That is my last word." Their loyalty to Hagen is such that the Burgundians (also referred to as "the Nibelungs") would rather die than betray him. The camera underscores the finality of Gunther's pronouncement by dramatic lighting and a low-angle shot that elevates the warrior into a monument of the unwavering "German soul."

These frequent references to loyalty and vassalage, to fealty and subordination, have strong resonances with the First World War, in which alliances and treaties played a decisive role. Not only was Germany bound to Austria; France and Russia had formed an alliance, and Britain could not remain neutral once Germany declared war on France. The German invasion of Belgium and Luxembourg was a further provocation to Britain because the 1839 Treaty of London guaranteed Belgium's neutrality. (German Chancellor Theobald von Bethmann-Hollweg famously dismissed the treaty as a "mere scrap of paper.") When Austria fought against the Serbs and their ally Russia, Germany came to its aid, promising Austria undying loyalty, the so-called *Nibelungentreue* ("Nibelungen loyalty"). Although in the first few months of the war all the European governments adopted the rhetoric of honor and allegiance, no country was more vociferous than Germany in pronouncing loyalty as the ultimate virtue.

The concept of Nibelungen loyalty dates back to the German chancellor Prince Bernhard von Bülow, who in a 1909 speech before the Reichstag characterized Germany's close relationship with Austria-Hungary as one of unquestioned loyalty, like the loyalty that bound the Nibelungen. Enemies, however, referred to Germany as Austria's vassal, thereby resignifying loyalty as slavery and submission—a conflict frequently alluded to in the *Nibelungen* film, especially in the struggle between Kriemhild and Brunhild. Germans were mocked as voluntarily subjecting themselves to Austria in the name of a medieval code of honor that had its roots in feudalism. The distinction between loyalty and vassalage became a sensitive issue in debates about the war. For instance, a 1912 book by General Friedrich von Bernhardi, *Unsere Zukunft: Ein Mahnwort an das deutsche Volk* (*Our Future: a Word of Warning to the German People*), which proposed a German military attack on Britain, was translated into English in 1914 under the completely different, inflammatory title *Britain as Germany's Vassal*. This title was a provocation designed to arouse Britain to prevent such a fate.[45] While the German author had aimed to awaken his fatherland to the inevitability of war with Britain, the title of the English translation alluded to Britain's alleged subservience to Germany and was meant to mobilize the British for battle. Questions of subordination and power determined the political landscape of alliances, coalitions, treaties, pledges, promises, and oaths. The virtues of loyalty and friendship were extolled, while the possibility of betrayal was always present.

Lang's *Nibelungen* recast the war in the terms of a medieval honor code, and argued that Germans lost the fight precisely because they upheld archaic notions of loyalty not shared by others. In 1917, Werner Jansen dedicated his "Nibelungen novel," titled *Das Buch Treue* (The Book of Loyalty), to the memory of young fallen Germans because it was the *Nibelungenlied* that had inspired "their heroism and their loyalty."[46] He claimed in his introduction that even a hundred years earlier in 1815, copies of the *Nibelungenlied* had accompanied young German soldiers on their way to battle Napoleon at Waterloo.

Germans contrasted their idealistic loyalty to that of the British, who were, they said, "by nature" egotistical, money-oriented, opportunistic, cunning, and deceitful. Contemporaries also likened the loyalty between Prussia and Austria-Hungary to that between Hagen and Volker: with the former representing the proud, grim, and heavily armed Prussia, and the latter the sanguine Austria-Hungary, always game for a song. The new compound

Nibelungentreue (Nibelungen loyalty) meant nothing less than loyalty to the point of death. Gustav Roethe, a professor of medieval literature, expressed it as follows in 1915: "What a delicious heritage of German greatness is this loyalty! It stands for a whole man's unconditional engagement that does not hesitate, does not doubt, does not vacillate, but persists to the last, even if the world should go to pieces because of it."[47] This loyalty, as exemplified in the Nibelungen epic, is more powerful than survival, and (at least according to Roethe) German loyalty was worth the price of total destruction.

Lang's film relentlessly pursues this line of thinking in its portrait of Hagen, King Gunther's powerful vassal. Hagen kills Siegfried out of loyalty to the king and then accompanies the Burgundians on their visit to Kriemhild, knowing that she will not rest until Siegfried's murder is avenged. Kriemhild's brothers are loyal to Hagen and protect him from her wrath. At the very end, Hagen offers to give himself up and thus spare Gunther, his king, from dying an ignominious death by fire and smoke. Gunther asks the surviving Burgundians if they want to be saved by delivering up Hagen. They shake their heads violently and their gestures betray revulsion at the very thought of being disloyal. Gunther sums up: "Loyalty that hasn't been broken by iron, will not melt in fire either, Hagen Tronje." After that pronouncement the sword speaks: the remaining Burgundians are killed, Gunther is beheaded, and Kriemhild strikes down Hagen before she herself expires.

The stylized violence in *Kriemhild's Revenge* is cast in medieval terms of heroism, chivalry, and sacrifice. In the extended battle scenes, we do not see tanks and machine guns but rather arrows and swords. The Burgundians are knights in shining armor with ornamented shields, but the viewer observes that they are as mortal as any infantryman in the trenches. There are in fact several sequences that anticipate the realistically staged battle scenes of later war films. In one scene, soldiers run through a trench filled with groundwater for dramatic effect. At least one critic, Herbert Jhering, criticized the prolonged battle scenes because he believed that they would damage the film abroad: ". . . [these] are not fighting scenes in any arbitrary film, but fighting scenes in a film that is dedicated to the German people, to its soul, and to its character."[48]

Lang produces a racially tinged image of the Great War by pitting the aristocratic, fully dressed Burgundians in a hopeless battle against the hordes of stooped, half-naked soldiers in Attila's army. Unlike the "civilized" Burgundian warriors, they carry no shields or helmets; they sit on trees, swarm around, and clamber up walls. They are portrayed as *Untermenschen*, living in caves, huts, and tents, soiled with mud and dirt. They are servile, childish, and disorderly in their fighting. Attila himself, the ruler of the Huns, is a visibly exoticized non-Western despot, who lives in a palace with puddles on its dirt floor.

Lang however inverts the clash between the two cultures—the refined Burgundians from the Rhine, and the nomadic martial tribe whose cruelty was legendary. It is in fact Attila who insists on protecting his guests, because the law of the steppe demands hospitality. Lang molds the king of the Huns so strongly against type that even Attila's own soldiers mock his lack of fighting spirit after his marriage to Kriemhild. He is feminized (especially in contrast to the masculinized Kriemhild) and beside himself with joy over the birth of his son. His childlike innocence in the tradition of the noble savage and his fluid body movements provide a stark contrast to the stiffness of the Burgundians and the rigid honor code that forces them to fight to the last man. Only after Hagen slays his only child does Attila declare war and thus become a tool in Kriemhild's plan for revenge. Ironically, Attila, the barbarian, brings a measure of humanity to this desert, where killing is shown to be primal. He does not seem to comprehend the degree of hatred that drives the hostility between the relatives. Far from civilization and law, the Burgundians devastate each other in front of the king of the Huns, exceeding by far the Huns' purported ferocity. Attila remains the only survivor in the final bloodbath.

It is remarkable how consistently World War I propaganda pictured the fighting as a crusade in which armored knights swing mythical swords to cut down their enemies. A poster for the seventh war bond in 1917, for instance, shows a crusader holding up a shield that has been pierced by half a dozen arrows. His arm, encased in metal armor, holds a sword, while his head is covered with a modern helmet. The medieval subtext of a holy war ennobled, in the spirit of the time, both the warrior and the war.

The End of Violence

Violence appears where power is in jeopardy, but left to its own course it ends in power's disappearance.

—Hannah Arendt, *On Violence*, 1969

In the sixth canto, Dietrich von Bern looks down from a tower to the fighting below: the dwarflike men from Attila's army dash about with bows and arrows, battling the formally dressed and outnumbered Burgundians, who fight with long swords and ornate shields, their stance upright, stiff, and stoic. "Too unequal is the battle," he declares. "None of the Nibelungs will see the next dawn."[49] Dietrich von Bern's prediction of certain defeat sets off a number of exchanges and negotiations in the film that grow increasingly pathological. "Blood cries out for blood (*Blut schreit nach Blut*)" is repeated by two different characters in this and the next canto, evoking biblical associations with Genesis 4:10 where God speaks to Cain: Your brother's blood "cries out to me from the ground" and Ezekiel 24:8: "to take vengeance I have put her blood on the bare rock."

The fallen are staged in ways that bring to mind images of those who died in the trenches. The film honors them repeatedly by lingering on them for a few seconds, as if to memorialize their loss. In one shot, the Nibelungs are seen mourning their dead; a line of soldiers stands in silhouette covered by their shields. These moments of stillness are interspersed with hectic battle scenes, shot from low angles to increase the confusion and destroy the order and hierarchy of the *Nibelungen*'s first part. It appears as if the formal constraints and repression of courtly life have shattered. The aggression that lurked behind the civilized façade could no longer be contained; it burst forth into open violence and the chaos of battle. The fight pits the aristocratic Nibelungs against Attila's half-naked hordes, but the film shows that both are dying, regardless of birth and rank. These battle scenes, which are the closest Lang ever came to making a war film, are intercut with close-ups of Kriemhild witnessing the bloodbath. Lang's composition isolates her: she stands alone and motionless, dressed in white against a black background that is replaced, at the very end, by a devastated, scorched landscape. The determination with which she exacts revenge is visible in her statue-like immobility: in some long close-ups of her face only her eyes move; they are wide open in horror or half closed with brutal resolve. After she orders her men to burn down the palace where the Nibelungs have taken refuge, one of her adjutants tells her: "You are not human, Kriemhild." To which she replies: "I died when Siegfried died," repeating her statement from the beginning of *Kriemhild's Revenge*.

When it becomes clear that the Nibelungs are not willing to give up Hagen, she summons Rüdiger, who had sworn an oath to protect her, and demands from him Hagen's execution. He replies that in order to carry out her command he must betray her brothers, who protect Hagen. She again reminds Rüdiger of the oath he made to her. Unblinking, she stretches her hand across the frame, visually obliterating him. A quick flashback depicting

The price of loyalty:
a father kills his son-in-law
in the *Nibelungen*.

the wedding ceremony of Rüdiger's young son-in-law Giselher, one of the likely victims of Kriemhild's plot, does not move her. Kriemhild's gesture is accompanied by her declaration: "Blood cries out for blood, Herr Rüdiger!" The crosscutting shows that the film's narrator in his function as a balladeer is in full command of space and time, free to switch between different locations and to interrupt the present with flashbacks to earlier scenes. The function of the editing here is not to involve the viewer in the psychology of the characters but rather to illustrate, objectively, that self-destruction is the inevitable result of their actions. The epic structure, following the principle of montage (instead of a linear progression), blocks empathy and makes critical distance possible.

In the seventh and last canto, the film cuts to the Burgundians inside the palace. A knock at the gate is heard and Rüdiger is announced. Giselher, overjoyed, exclaims: "He brings us peace!" This echoes the constant hope for peace during the last years of the war, when the casualties mounted and the High Command promised military victory one day and diplomacy the next. Giselher: "What do you bring us, Father?" Cut to an extreme close-up of Rüdiger's face, framed by a helmet. His mouth twitching like Cesare's in *Caligari*, he answers: "*Den Tod* (death)!" Cut away to an extreme long shot of Kriemhild standing on the highest point of the castle. It is a shot that comments on the logic of the narrative by removing us from the perspective of any single character, one that catapults us out of the ongoing story and affords us a larger view. Once again, the camera undercuts our emotional involvement in what will inevitably follow.

It is the analytical talent of Lang's filmmaking that makes shots like this so poignant. His narration not only tells the story but also comments on it. Here Kriemhild personifies death, and her motionless presence implies that fate, driven by notions of honor and revenge, is irreversible. As Rüdiger approaches his son-in-law and brothers, the film cuts back to Volker pleading with Attila to stop the men from killing each other. Attila repeats Krimhield's demand to have Hagen, the murderer of his baby son, delivered to her—an act that would require the Burgundians to betray Hagen. Volker recoils in horror at this thought and declares: "You don't know the German soul, Herr Attila." No further reaction. The camera instead cuts back to Rüdiger, looking now like the angel of death. He says to Gunther: "The oath to which Kriemhild holds me is older than the oath between you and me." He insists that Gunther not force him to break his oath to Kriemhild (and thus violate his honor) but to fight him instead. He challenges Hagen, and as Hagen draws his sword, young Giselher intervenes and is struck down by his own father-in-law.

In contrast to *Siegfried, Kriemhild's Revenge* portrays Hagen in a remarkably positive light. The sympathies in the film's first part were with Siegfried; they shift decisively to his murderer in the second part. While Siegfried embodied the impetuous and idealistic Germany, Hagen represents loyalty, the fighting spirit, realpolitik, and statesmanship. As the audience's sympathies for Kriemhild decline the more her revenge becomes irrational, Hagen gains respect for selflessly battling for the survival of the Burgundians. The film thereby registers the shifting view of Hagen in Nibelungen scholarship, if not in public opinion. In 1924, Arnold Bergmann, a revolutionary nationalist, published a book on the national importance of the Nibelungen saga in which he called Siegfried "shallow," accusing him not only of recklessness and materialism but also of "frivolity and coarse manners."[50] According to Bergmann, Hagen had no choice but to kill Siegfried, the traitor and young fool, because he was a "permanent danger to the Burgundian people and the state."[51] In contrast, Hagen was the man of strong will, a loyal hero and old warrior who fought to his last breath. After the war, an embattled Germany identified more readily with the politically cunning Hagen than with Siegfried, and the film reflects precisely this shift in the nation's understanding of itself. Hagen also embodies a different concept of state power: it is no longer to be gained through naïve idealism, but rather by the ruthless pursuit of political goals even at the cost of murder.

For the nationalist right wing, both the Nibelungen saga and the film provided an artistic roadmap for Weimar's culture of assassinations and unchecked power politics. The shocking assassination of foreign minister Walther Rathenau for "betraying" Germany through his support of the Versailles Treaty occurred in June 1922, around the time when the *Nibelungen* went into production. In the same year, Emil Julius Gumbel published a book, *Vier Jahre politischer Mord* (*Four Years of Political Murder*), in which he documented 354 political murders by the Right and 22 by the Left. He castigated the right-wing courts for their lenient sentences in the case of nationalist perpetrators. For instance, the confessed assassin of Bavarian minister Kurt Eisner, killed for his leftist politics on February 21, 1919, was released early in 1924 because his motives were declared "noble."

For the nationalists, Lang's film furnished the heroic apocalypse that was missing at the war's end. The German army was not epically defeated in one last fiery battle; instead General Ludendorff suddenly called for a cease-fire on September 29, 1918, while the German armies were still deep in enemy territory. Although he changed his mind shortly afterwards, the war was over, the government had collapsed, and German soldiers were marching home. The Kaiser unheroically slipped across the Dutch-Belgian border, and Ludendorff fled to Sweden.

This unexpected and anticlimactic end, however, allowed German politicians (from the nationalists to the social democrats) to herald the army as "unbeaten on the battlefield." Programmatic denial of military defeat (previous defeats during the war had either been kept from the public or downplayed by German war propaganda) also gave rise to conspiracy theories as to who was to blame for the sudden loss. If it was not the army, the military commanders, or the government, then it must have been betrayal on the home front, especially by opponents of the war. There were in fact voices that had urged staging one final offensive to preserve Germany's military honor. Admiral Adolf von Trotha argued in October 1918: "If the fleet fights an honorable battle, even one leading to its own destruction, a new German fleet will be born of it, so long as our people do not fail entirely as a nation."[52] To his radical nationalist way of thinking even suicide would provide more dignified closure than a Götterdämmerung that did *not* happen. A final battle would, for example, have made possible a narrative in which annihilation was followed by rebirth.

There also was no "*levée en masse*," or mass uprising, to defend the nation.[53] Instead, most of the old elites were back in control in 1919, and as far as the Right was concerned, the nationalist revolution did not occur *precisely* because the unheroic outcome of the war did not lend itself to a founding myth. In millenarian terms, there had been no operatic conflagration from which new life could be born. Lang's *Nibelungen* film did not have the power to provide this founding myth, but it did deliver a battle to end all battles.

In the film, it is Hagen who provokes the fiery end. As he approaches Kriemhild (and the camera), he mocks her: "Rejoice in your revenge, Kriemhild. Dead are your young brothers. Dead are Rüdiger and his men." And with an angry gesture he hurls his shield toward her in the sand. "Hagen Tronje still lives who has killed your husband." The camera cuts to Kriemhild, framing her in a long shot as seen from Hagen's point of view. She appears suddenly small and isolated. “Throw fire in the palace,” she demands, and Attila’s soldiers, who emerge from the darkness, shoot burning arrows into the hall. The camera records this spectacle against a night sky. Lang apparently was unconcerned that Kriemhild’s figure throws a long afternoon shadow during this “night.” For him it was the contrast that counted, the stark effect of flames against darkness—indeed, Wagner’s Götterdämmerung transposed into black and white. Lang had publicized the shooting of this scene in the press; huge sets were burnt in real time in front of hundreds of onlookers.

The film moves from the Burgundians inside the hall, slowly dying in the fire and smoke, to Kriemhild and Attila outside. Atilla appears increasingly unhinged, dancing at the news of the firestorm, while Kriemhild stands unmoved. As Attila joins her, he declares: “Have my gratitude. Even if we could never be one in love, we become one in hatred.” Kriemhild: “Never, King Attila, was my heart so filled with love as now.” Cut to a long shot of the building, now in full blaze. Volker, the narrator of the saga, is shown playing chords on his instrument. “Look! Volker tunes his *Fiedel* for the last song.” Cut to Kriemhild, who is told: “I call it a shame and dishonor that you want to destroy those whom you could not conquer by weapons, by fiery distress, defenseless.” The camera cuts to the burning building and once again to Volker. “Do you hear Volker playing?” she answers.

Attila behind her starts to dance, moving his body rhythmically to the music that seems to be emanating from the burning castle. Just as irrationally, a young Nibelung with outstretched arms says: “Oh, I wish we were at the cold, green Rhine.” The fire blazes and the entire wall crumbles, embers fly through the air, and the men are engulfed in flames. Kriemhild smiles: “Do you hear? Herr Volker sings.” Attila, now completely crazed, shouts: “An End. An End!” Impulsive as ever, he wants to kill Hagen with his bare hands, but is rebuffed. The camera cuts to a close-up of Kriemhild’s face, which increasingly displays signs of emotional disturbance. She is given Siegfried’s sword and she embraces it slowly, while the Siegfried leitmotif is heard.

The camera remains outside the closed gate of the burning building; we can only guess what is going on inside. After an interminable wait, when the suspense has become unbearable, the gate slowly opens, and Hagen and Gunther emerge from the smoke. Hagen again stands face-to-face with Kriemhild, who says: “I cannot go home to my dead Siegfried before all injustice is redeemed. Here is the sword. Where is the treasure?” Hagen: “I gave an oath not to betray it as long as one of my Kings lives.” She orders Gunther’s head cut off; a soldier lifts it up in the air. Hagen laughs crazily,

A fiery retelling of cold-blooded murder.
The mad minstrel and the face of revenge
in the *Nibelungen*.

crying out that now only God and he know the location of the treasure, and God will not be more silent than he. Betrayed once again, Kriemhild grips the sword and cuts down Hagen; a jolt passes through her body; she closes her eyes and clutches her breast.

Her final gesture: she takes a folded cloth and opens it, revealing blood-soaked soil from the forest where Siegfried was killed. "Now, earth, drink yourself to the full," she demands. Her words are symbol-laden, a call to the union of blood with soil that will later play such a prominent role in Nazi racist ideology. She opens her eyes wide and falls back, but Attila catches her and lays her on the ground. "Take her home to Siegfried, her dead husband. She never belonged to anyone else." In a final static shot the camera captures Attila kneeling behind Kriemhild, echoing the final scene in the film's first part, where Kriemhild knelt behind Siegfried.

There are signs that Lang critiques the unremitting single-mindedness with which Kriemhild followed through on her revenge. Both the Nibelungs and Attila comment disparagingly on her actions. Her zombielike appearance may be another clue; it recalls that of a dead person who exists only to haunt the living. Finally, at the end, there is the irony of her pointless demand for the treasure, which spoils the purity of her grief for Siegfried. All support an ambivalent reading of the film, not as a postwar nationalist revenge fantasy, but instead as a reminder of the high price exacted by archaic codes of honor and loyalty.

And yet, *Kriemhild's Revenge* sheds new light on the war even as the film tries to incorporate it into German myth. While *Siegfried* mobilized the propaganda lie that the German army was undefeated and an innocent victim of betrayal (the stab-in-the-back legend), *Kriemhild's Revenge* turned Germany's role as victim into that of an avenger, only to see itself victimized once more by its fixation on revenge. The two parts thus address two divergent responses to the war: the glorification of the fallen soldier as hero, and the hesitant realization of the self-destructive potential of revenge. Lang's *Nibelungen* gives mythic expression to the difficulty faced by the German people after the First World War. How were they to assimilate the war experience? Was it possible to fashion a coherent narrative of violence and defeat in which the death of a soldier was something other than senseless?[54]

Despite technological advances in warfare, the ideology harnessed to defend the killing stemmed from medieval myth. Appeals to loyalty and honor during the war—and many books and articles invoked these traits as exclusive characteristics of the German people—have such abstract absoluteness that they become suspect. The "heroism" required to fight to the bitter end is indistinguishable from a death wish. Kriemhild, who at first represents the grieving home front, actively joins the battle in order to exact revenge. It has become a total war, without discrimination between civilians and warriors, entailing the annihilation of all.[55]

Lang again toys with this apocalyptic worldview in *Metropolis*, only to pull back and suggest a conciliatory ending. The *Nibelungen* shows the willing self-destruction of a civilized society, while *Metropolis* invokes the idea of a battle against modernity itself. The *Nibelungen* comments on the war trauma by probing the relationship between ritualized wartime diplomacy and barbaric killing. *Metropolis* in contrast pursues another, more radical path of understanding the war. It seeks to lay bare the deeper roots of the first technological war and offer a critique of the very conditions that made the war possible in the first place. Although Nibelungen is set in the past and Metropolis in the future, both deal very much with the present.

The Industrial Battlefield

To repeat, if this war means anything, it means a revolt against modern civilization. If the modern commercial-capitalist-machine production is right, then why, in the name of common sense, should we crush Germany, which bids fair to be the machine nation, par excellence, of the world?

—G. R. Sterling Taylor, *The Psychology of the Great War*, 1915

Every great epoch deserves the kind and form of the wars which occur in it. The bourgeois-capitalist epoch of modern Europe deserves exactly this war.

—Max Scheler, *War and Reconstruction*, 1916

The longer the War lasts, the more it becomes a war of the masses.

—Friedrich Naumann, *Kriegsgedanken zur Welt- und Seelengeschichte*, 1917

Violence was legimitized by the creation of the New Man.

—Alain Badiou, *The Century*, 2007

Rise of the Machines

Desire is irrelevant. I am a machine.

—*Terminator 3: Rise of the Machines*, 2003

What caused the war? From the beginning of the conflict numerous theories sought to interpret the first technological war within larger philosophical frameworks.[1] Conservative cultural critics in particular had little doubt that large-scale bloodshed was the inescapable result of Germany's accelerated industrialization in the late nineteenth and early twentieth century. Modernity and modernization, which had unsettled the very identity of Germany as a "nation of culture" (*Kulturnation*), soon became embattled concepts. Expressionist painters (starting in 1905) as well as poets and dramatists (beginning in 1911) used modernist techniques to oppose modernity. Discontent and anxiety about the increasing dominance of instrumental reason were widespread in Germany, and brought about countermodern movements, such as the nudist life reformers of Monte Verità or the Nordic-mystical Thule Society. For intellectuals, artists, and in fact for most Germans, the war promised to obliterate in one stroke the kind of materialist thinking that they passionately believed was threatening the innermost core of Germanness.

In *Metropolis*, Lang focuses on the forces of industrial modernity that made this deadly technological war seemingly inevitable. While there have always been wars, World War I was the first that employed advanced technology and instrumental rationality to magnify its killing power. The war became a war machine. *Metropolis* argues that the reification and abstraction characteristic of modern mass production result in apocalyptic destruction. Lang thus places the origin *and* legacy of the war entirely in the machine-controlled industrial zone. In this way the wounds of war were only consequences of the larger malaise of modernity. Lang reconfigures the trauma of the lost war as a desperate revolt of German idealism against the onslaught of the industrial age. Drawing on the Bible, he works through the past by projecting it into the future (*Metropolis* was one of the first science fiction films, and remains perhaps the most influential). Lang rethinks the war in terms of its biblical as well as futuristic dimensions. As the film traces the *underlying* causes of the shocks of modernity, it likewise makes manifest the deep roots of our own present anxieties about technology run amock. Modernity's basic conditions have not changed since *Metropolis*, which may explain the film's enduring appeal and popularity.

Is Fritz Lang the Oswald Spengler of cinema? Does *Metropolis* not echo the ambitious project of Spengler's famous diatribe against Western modernity, provocatively called *Der Untergang des Abendlandes* (*The Decline of the West*)?[2] Published in 1918 (coinciding with the collapse of the German, Russian, and Ottoman empires), the book provided a historical explanation for the advent of a machine-dominated world, the endpoint of which was to be an industrialized global war. Spengler saw World War I as the outcome of the rule of the machine and the emergence of the masses. His thousand-page book (published in two volumes) parallels Lang's film in its scope, which reaches from Babylon to the present, and in its ambitious claim to explain world history. Lang and von Harbou may have never read *The Decline of the West*, but the book's ideas circulated so widely in the aftermath of the lost war that it was impossible to ignore them. Because Spengler's best-selling book delivered an interpretation of Germany's (and other empires') traumatic downfall, it was in high demand. Lang's film not only shows industrial production as a continuation of war—the workers are portrayed as an army of anonymous soldiers—but like Spengler's book it also tries to explain what made the first technological war possible.

Spengler crowned *The Decline of the West*, whose second volume appeared in 1922, with a final chapter simply titled "The Machine." A summary of his reflections on the danger of the doomed mechanical age, this last chapter of his magisterial work can be understood as a blueprint for Lang's *Metropolis*. In "The Machine," Spengler extols the Faustian passion that strives to overcome nature by the invention of machines:

> The intoxicated soul wills to fly above space and time. An ineffable longing tempts him to indefinable horizons. Man would free himself from the earth, rise into the infinite, leave the bonds of the body and circle in the universe of space among the stars . . . hence comes the ambition to break all records and beat all dimensions, to build giant halls for giant machines, vast ships and bridge-spans, buildings that deliriously scrape the clouds, fabulous forces pressed together to a focus to obey the hand of a child, stamping and quivering and droning works of steel and glass in which tiny man moves as unlimited monarch and, at the least, feels nature as beneath him.[3]

For Spengler, however, this unparalleled triumph exacts a price. Faustian man has become "the slave of his creation." All tradition has been subordinated to progress, and the entrepreneur no less than the factory worker is

The machine as fuming god.

Worker-soldiers

in Fritz Lang's *Metropolis*.

forced into obedience. "Both become slaves, and not masters, of the machine that now for the first time develops its devilish and occult power."[4] Spengler anticipates Lang's critique in *Metropolis* when he insists: "The center of this artificial and complicated realm of the Machine is the organizer and manager. The mind, not the hand, holds it together."[5] *Metropolis* calls exactly this separation between mind and hand into question, proposing a solution that appears as a motto between the credits and the title sequence, and is repeated at the very end of the film: "The mediator between head and hand must be the heart." It is the narrative's ultimate resolve to find this mediator. After much danger and destruction, the last scene in *Metropolis* brings the quest to a successful conclusion: Freder, the industrialist's warmhearted and idealistic son, mediates between head and hand—that is, between his father, the master of Metropolis, and the foreman who represents the anonymous mass of laboring worker-soldiers.

The film begins with streaks of light forming the word "Metropolis," spelled out in art deco letters that suggest a union of technology and design. This title, brightly illuminated, gives way to a fast-moving montage in which a mountainous cityscape morphs into close-ups of moving engine parts. Applying compositional principles derived from the abstract film style pioneered by Viktor Eggeling, Hans Richter, and Walther Ruttmann in the early and mid-1920s, Lang uses form and movement, light and shadow, to convey the dynamics of the big city, literalizing its machine-like precision and unquestioning automatism. Over a low-angle panorama shot of skyscrapers we see superimposed close-ups of three pistons moving up and down. Their shafts and triangular tops invert the shape of the pyramidal buildings, and underscore the sublime affinity, on a formal level, between skyscrapers and engine parts. Three horizontal streaks of light shoot across the screen, adding another emphatically abstract layer to the composition and reminding the viewer that this film is not a reflection of some visible reality but rather a self-sufficient product of cinematography and editing.

A highly unusual establishing shot, this opening montage fetishizes both machines and dynamic motion. No human agency is visible and there is no indication of what the machines do or what they produce; we see only mechanical components moving by themselves. The style here has affinities to the postexpressionist art movement known as *Neue Sachlichkeit*, or New Objectivity, whose embrace of machines and mundane objects was a reaction against expressionist subjectivism. The close-ups of gears and pistons in

Metropolis resemble those of New Objectivity photographers such as Albert Renger-Patzsch, whose precise pictures of gleaming machine parts highlighted their beauty.[6]

By projecting a machine over the cityscape, the film visualizes in its first few seconds the city's clocklike mechanical functioning, its exactness and never-flagging energy. But precisely because the montage equates the city with a perfectly functioning system of interlocking cogwheels, it also hints at the catastrophic potential of even the smallest malfunction. The pressure of time and the insistence on precision are further insinuated by a sudden cut to a huge ten-hour clock, yet another impersonal machine, one that synchronizes movement and signals the imminent start of a new ten-hour shift. A siren's blast, visualized as a vertical burst of white steam, signals not only the start of the new shift but also the beginning of the film's narrative—a narrative that may be seen as one long, digressive, yet urgent response to what the montage sequence posits: the domination of the machine.

Spengler's key figure in machine-dominated modernity is the engineer, "the priest of the machine . . . the machine's master and destiny."[7] Echoing the sentiments of Goethe's *Faust*, Spengler reasons that "if engineers were one day no longer interested in perfecting machines, the industry must flicker out in spite of all that managerial energy and the workers can do."[8] Spengler fantasizes that in future generations, engineers might find the "soul's health more important than all the power of the world, and the very elite of intellectuals that is now concerned with the machine comes to be overpowered by a growing sense of its Satanism . . . then nothing can hinder the end of this grand drama that has been a play of intellects, with hands as mere auxiliaries."[9] Again Spengler refers to the split between intellect and hand, between engineer and working class—a split that also informs the central conflict in *Metropolis*. He wants engineers to overcome the machine by their own volition, simply by recognizing that the machine is "satanic." Following Spengler in imagining the end of the "age of the engineer," Lang offers a more dramatic solution. His engineer, Rotwang, marked as a Faustian scientist in the tradition of Rabbi Loew in Paul Wegener's 1920 film *The Golem*, is simply eliminated: after a brief struggle with Freder on the roof of a Gothic church, he falls to his death. The engineer, the third pillar in Spengler's machine world alongside the entrepreneur and the factory worker, is replaced by Freder, the designated mediator and "heart" between the "head" of the manager and the "hand" of the worker.

Unlike Spengler's philosophical invective, Lang's contribution to Weimar's debate on modernity is a fictional work whose rich aesthetic "surplus value" has produced an ideological ambiguity that has engaged interpreters for the last eighty years.[10] On the most obvious narrative level, *Metropolis* is an account of the young generation's rebellion against the cynicism of its elders, who have usurped technology for their own oppressive purposes. The story begins with Freder, privileged offspring of capitalist Fredersen, cavorting with women in the luxurious gardens above the city. He falls in love with Maria, a worker's daughter who had trespassed into the realm of the rich accompanied by a group of scruffy children. "These are your brothers," she says to Freder, before she is ushered out of the exclusive garden. This encounter between two separate spheres sets the story in motion: Freder is intrigued by the girl and wants to find her. The film ends this story line by suggesting that love conquers class, the mechanisms of exploitation, and even the power of the machines that have taken control. The stranglehold of the machines (and their inventor) seems to have been broken.

Lang's film translates Spengler's philosophical analysis into images and stories, myths and allegories, but he sees not only the destructive potential of the machine but also its beauty and metallic elegance. This ideological ambivalence may stem from Lang's collaboration with his novelist wife, von Harbou, who wrote the screenplay and was known for her socially conservative views.[11] But what would *Metropolis* be without this tension? Looking back in the 1960s, Lang famously quipped: "The main thesis was Mrs. Lang's, but I am at least fifty percent responsible because I made the film. You cannot make a socially-conscious picture in which you say that the intermediary between the hand and the brain is the heart—I mean that's a fairy tale—definitely. But I was very interested in machines."[12]

The modernist cult of machines in which *Metropolis* participates was not new in the 1920s. The Italian futurists had embraced technology with a vengeance. Attacking bourgeois values in art and ideology, Filippo Tommaso Marinetti wrote as early as 1911: "Hence we must prepare for the imminent, inevitable identification of man with motor. We must admit that we look for the creation of a nonhuman type in whom moral suffering, goodness of heart, affection, and love, those sole corrosive poisons of inexhaustible vital energy, will be abolished."[13] Machines for the futurists meant modernity, vitalism, and tireless energy; their mechanical nature challenged not only the culture of fatigue, but also humanist values and the classical arts founded upon those values.[14] The futurists later embraced war and its technological weaponry—machine guns, rolling tanks, exploding bombs, and poisoned gas—that were designed to kill more people in less time.

The machine's deadly force inspired awe. Jünger wrote in 1922: "The battle of machines is so astounding that human beings often completely disappear before them. The battle expresses itself as a gigantic, dead mechanism and spreads an icy, impersonal wave of destruction over the land that resembles a crater landscape on a dead planet."[15] In an earlier article, tellingly written for a weekly military paper, Jünger predicted that technology would play an even bigger part in future battles because the goal would be to concentrate the most power in the smallest space: "One man with a machine gun has firepower equivalent to that of a platoon; a tank studded with machine guns and canons can replace a battalion."[16] Killing became industrialized; the war machine rationalized mass slaughter.[17]

Like Lang, Jünger also aestheticized the killing machines: "Ours is the first generation to begin to reconcile itself with the machine and to see in it not only the useful but the beautiful as well."[18] Jünger was referring to the generation of 1914, which experienced the new symbiosis of humans and machines in the trenches. The front generation, he declared, was one that "builds machines and for whom machines are not dead iron but rather an organ of power, which it dominates with cold reason and blood. The front generation gives the world a new face."[19] For Jünger, it was the machine that decided the outcome of the war:

> The battle is a frightful competition of industries and victory is the success of the competitor that managed to work faster and more ruthlessly. Here the era from which we come shows its cards. The domination of the machine over men, of the servant over the master, becomes apparent, and a deep discord, which already in peacetime began to shake the economic and social order, emerges in a deadly fashion. Here the style of a materialistic generation is uncovered and technology celebrates a bloody triumph. Here a debt is being paid which seemed old and forgotten.[20]

Lang's film is fully aware of the machine's "bloody triumph." An elaboration of Spengler and Jünger's reflections on the machine and its relation to warfare, *Metropolis* contributed to postwar discussions that tried to make sense of the terrifying nexus between technological war and industrial modernity.

The images that follow the opening montage expand upon the interplay of moving machine parts. We see battalions of workers marching in lockstep like walking robots. In rows of six, all dressed alike in black uniforms and caps, they shuffle along mechanically, heads bowed, as if operated by remote control. They approach a huge iron gate with bars reminiscent of a prison and wait to be transported deep into the bowels of the city. One group leaves its shift as the other arrives. The marching workers also strongly suggest marching soldiers—an early hint at the link made later between industrial labor and industrialized war.

Moloch War

Technology is our fate, our truth.

—Don DeLillo, *In the Ruins of the Future*, December 2001

In 1923, Henry Ford's popular (and noxiously anti-Semitic) autobiography *My Life and Work* appeared in German translation, only one year after it was published in the United States.[21] In a chapter titled "The Terror of the Machine," he writes: "I have not been able to discover that repetitive labor injures a man in any way. . . . I have been told by parlor experts that repetitive labor is soul– as well as body-destroying, but that has not been the result of our investigations."[22] On the contrary, even if offered another activity, most workers, says Ford, would prefer to stay and keep doing the same work over and over again. Taking this principle to the extreme for the sake of mass production, Ford further notes that the different jobs required to produce his cars could be organized into tidy categories:

> . . . there were 7,882 different jobs in the factory. Of these, 949 were classified as heavy work requiring strong, able-bodied, and practically physically perfect men; 3,338 required men of ordinary physical development and strength. The remaining 3,595 jobs were disclosed as requiring no physical exertion and could be performed by the slightest, weakest sort of men. In fact, most of them could be satisfactorily filled by women or older children. The lightest jobs were again classified to discover how many of them required the use of full faculties, and we found that 670 could be filled by legless men, 2,637 by one-legged men, 2 by armless men, 715 by one-armed men, and 10 by blind men.[23]

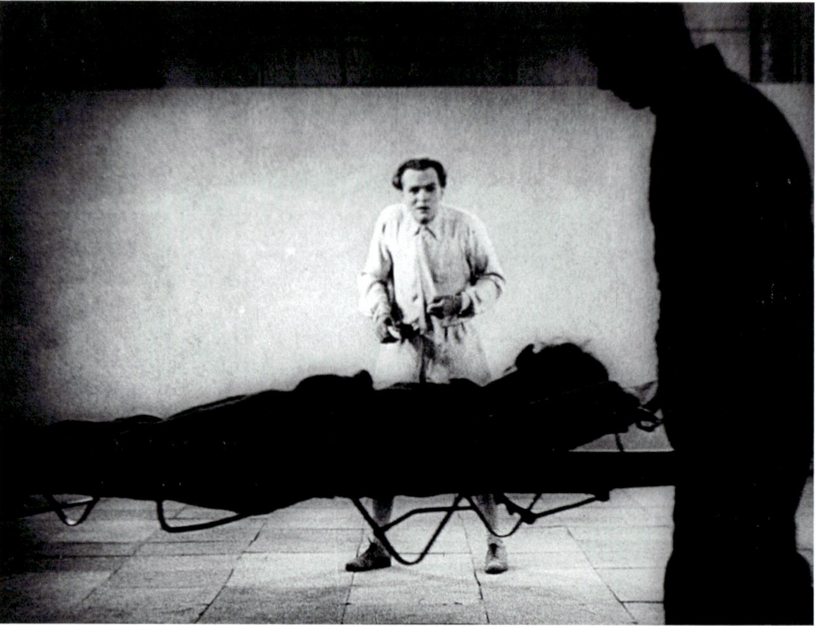

Workers on the industrial battlefield.

Ford takes special pride in employing tuberculosis sufferers, who, he suggests, should be mainly employed outdoors. Apparently anticipating the accusation that he instrumentalized his workers like expendable machine parts, he concludes by emphasizing that it is *not* true that "men are mere machines."[24] The results of "Fordism" speak for themselves: the time it took to assemble a car dropped from fourteen hours in 1912 to ninety-three minutes in 1914 (after the assembly line was installed); by 1925, after further refinements, a new car rolled off the assembly line every ten seconds.

As a commentary on the consequences of instrumental reason, *Metropolis* was part of Germany's response to Fordism.[25] The film took its place in the widespread discussion of the mid-1920s over industrialization and rationalization—exactly those features of radical Western modernity that, according to government propaganda, had motivated Germany's participation in the war. If the war was fought to defend "old-fashioned" German values against the "technological spirit" of Western modernity, then the war seemed lost for good. *Metropolis* betrays the same ambivalence found in the general discourse on modernity at the time. The film resolves the issue in two story lines. First, it shows that workers who rebel against the regime of the machine face certain defeat, because the fight is for them tantamount to self-destruction. The machines are indeed the source of the workers' subordination and repression, but they are the source of their livelihood as well. The other story line involves the rebellion of a young idealistic son, Freder, against his father, Fredersen, whose physique was modeled after the frontispiece portrait in Henry Ford's autobiography. While the father stands for the "heartless industrialist" of Fordism, the son functions as the impulsive, oedipal stock figure from expressionist theater who hopes to transform humankind.[26] Motivated by his love for Maria, the girl from the working class, Freder challenges the entire system on which, of course, his own status is founded, only to reconcile with his father and the repressive system at the end.

The first step in Freder's rebellious journey is to discover the "real world." He is like a sheltered, naïve young man who signs up for duty on the front, hungry for adventure, but is shocked by the terror of the machine guns. Searching for Maria in the workers' quarters, Freder wanders into the machine hall for the first time. An extreme long shot from above shows him dwarfed by the enormous space, confused and insignificant. Dressed in white, he is lost amid the turbines that swirl overhead and the black-clad workers who stand in front of panels, moving their bodies rhythmically from left to right, operating identical machines. Their motions are mechanical and abstracted; we never know what purpose they or their machines serve. Placed symmetrically to the left and right of the central machine, the workers' exaggerated movements are carefully choreographed, recalling Oskar Schlemmer's *Triadic Ballet,* an experimental abstract dance piece performed at the Bauhaus in 1922.

This image of the workers' symbiosis with their machines seems to spring straight from the pages of Karl Marx's *Capital*, in which he famously describes the "industrial battle" of alienated factory work:

> Every sense organ is injured by the artificially high temperatures, by the dust-laden atmosphere, by the deafening noise, not to mention the danger to life and limb among machines which are so closely crowded together, a danger which, with the regularity of the seasons, produces its list of those killed and wounded in the industrial battle.[27]

One gigantic machine occupies the center of the frame. White steam shoots into the air from all directions. Lang depicts the "satanic machine" (Spengler) as a gigantic beast that breathes fire and steam, compared to which the workers appear as mere insects. The camera cuts to a close-up of a worker trying to attend to a panel consisting of many instruments: dials, levers, and pulleys, and in the center a pressure gauge, whose quicksilver is rising rapidly. Warning lights start flashing; close-ups show the worker's frightened face and his hands grasping at a shut-off valve. A cut back to the inexorably climbing pressure gauge is followed by an extreme overhead shot that captures the worker's utter desperation, his hand groping toward the camera as he loses his grip on the lever. Cut back to the gauge that keeps rising toward a mark that must not be crossed. From afar, in a long shot, Freder watches helplessly as the gauge exceeds its limit and, as feared, the machine explodes, emitting large clouds of white smoke. It is as though a shell had detonated: the force of the blast lifts one worker up in the air, and other workers are thrown down from the top of the gigantic machine. Freder runs toward them but is hurled back, blinded by the flash of light. The editing quickens, crosscutting between the scene of devastation and reaction shots of Freder, who can barely get up from the ground. He looks up and sees, behind billows of smoke, the machine transmogrified into a monster with a wide-gaping orifice and two eyes—a hallucination that an animated intertitle calls "Moloch." The letters of this word converge from the corners of the frame and have a more painterly look than the other, mostly narrative intertitles. The viewer understands that Freder, paralyzed by his near-death encounter, is experiencing a mind-altering vision similar to those reported by shell-shock victims.

Lang appropriated the features of the fearsome man-eating god Moloch from *Cabiria*, the famous 1914 Italian film epic, and superimposes them onto the machine.[28] The sudden metamorphosis from futuristic technology to ancient myth lays bare the underlying ideology of *Metropolis*. Freder's vision boldly translates an Old Testament legend where children are sacrificed to a demon god into a comment on the way in which humans are sacrificed to the gods of technology and war. In his delirium, Freder sees battalions of workers being fed alive to Moloch.

The image of the war as a monster in need of constant human fodder can also be found in the autobiographical literature of the time. For instance, the prominent violinist Fritz Kreisler reported of his trench experience: "These grotesque piles of human bodies seemed like a monstrous sacrificial offering immolated on the altar of some fiendishly cruel, antique deity."[29] In the film the first group of half-naked, uniformly shaven men are still dragged up the stairs, clearly against their will, before they are pushed into Moloch's gaping maw, but the battalions that follow them no longer show resistance. These are the same workers who in the film's first scene marched in lockstep from one shift to the next. Now they move like robots toward their extinction. The film speaks loudly here of the terrifying automatism with which workers accept their fate.

As Freder's hands reach out to end this vision, the image in this point-of-view shot blurs and undulates for a split second, marking the return to "reality" immediately after the blast. Workers carry dead or wounded comrades down the stairs, while new workers replace the victims of the explosion. This is the world of machines in which there is no pause for mourning. The camera, however, cuts to Freder and introduces a dimension of grief and remembrance. In a beautifully composed shot we see him far in the background, his hand clutched over his heart, watching a procession of mourners pass by in silhouette. It is an image reminiscent of the war: the wounded walking with the help of others, the dead carried on stretchers. One casualty turns his face to Freder, who rushes forward to intervene, but it is too late.

This scene evokes Benjamin's famous remarks in "The Storyteller" about the changes that the war had wrought: "A generation that had gone to school on a horse-drawn streetcars now stood under the open sky in a landscape

Moments of shock.
Gustav Fröhlich and
Brigitte Helm in *Metropolis*.

where nothing remained unchanged but the clouds and, beneath those clouds, in a force field of destructive torrents and explosions, the tiny, fragile human body."[30] For Benjamin (as for Jünger), industrialized warfare was powerful shorthand for the shocks of urban modernity.[31] Rotwang's creation of a mechanical robot as the "worker of the future" later in *Metropolis* is a response to the vulnerability of Benjamin's "tiny, fragile human body" shown here.

The explosion is the first traumatic shock Freder experiences as he enters the war zone of industrial production, and much of the coming narrative follows from it. We see this scene through his eyes: as a novice, he is faced with unpreventable catastrophe and near-death. His father responds coldly to his son's fiery account of this traumatic experience: "Accidents happen." If industrial production is a giant machine (with workers as expendable parts, just like the soldiers on the front), losses and disasters are no reason for despair. The point of a machine is precisely that it cannot feel.

Lang's America

America is the original version of modernity. We are the dubbed or subtitled version.

—Jean Baudrillard, *America*, 1989

From October to December 1924, Lang embarked on his first trip to the United States. Accompanied by producer Erich Pommer and architect Erich Mendelsohn, he visited New York and Los Angeles to promote the American opening of his *Nibelungen*.[32] The German film industry's daily paper *Film-Kurier* published his reflections, "What I Saw in America. New York–Los Angeles," shortly after his return. "Where is the film," Lang asks, that deals with "one of those Babels of stone that call themselves American cities?" And he continues, waxing lyrical:

> The mere sight of New York at night should suffice to make this beacon of beauty the center of a movie. Flashes of lightning, rotating in red, blue and brilliant white, in between screaming greens, plunging into a black void, only to be immediately reborn, at once, to experience the play of colors! Streets that are shafts full of light, full of spinning, whirling, revolving light that is like an acknowledgment of joyful life. And above all this, sky-high above the cars and

the elevated railroads, towers emerge in blue and gold, in white and crimson, torn from nocturnal darkness by searchlights. Neon signs rise ever higher, up to the stars, outshining them in light and splendor, existing in ever new variation.[33]

Although the screenplay for *Metropolis* was finished in June 1924, more than three months before his trip to America, his unrestrained enthusiasm for New York's sublime verticality and limitless energy influenced the look of his fictional Metropolis: it was to be the mother of all cities (according to its Greek roots "metro" and "polis"), but it was also his paean to New York as the essential modern city of the 1920s.

Weimar Germany's embrace of American modernity was a way of forgetting its traumatic past. The loss of the war and the collapse of the Wilhelmine Empire brought a sudden end to an idealistic value system and culture rooted in the courtly aristocracy of eighteenth-century German classicism. With humanistic values completely discredited by the nihilistic mass destruction of the war, Germany could offer little resistance to the onslaught of American popular culture. The flow of mass entertainment from the United States into the big cities of Germany in the immediate postwar years was unstoppable, ranging from the Shimmy and Charleston dance crazes in the early 1920s to concert tours by Paul Whiteman's jazz band in 1926, from Chaplin and Buster Keaton slapstick movies to revues with Josephine Baker and new spectator sports such as boxing. *Amerikanismus* (Americanism), so it seemed, had invaded every corner of urban postwar culture. Wrigley's Spearmint Gum even opened its own German production plant in Frankfurt in 1925. Emulating New York, Berlin became known as the most American city in Europe; writers like Brecht and Lion Feuchtwanger freely used anglicisms and American idioms in their writings. In a 1923 article, ironically titled "Book Review," Hans Siemsen boldly admitted that instead of reviewing some books as he was supposed to, he would rather review popular new records with titles like "California, Here I Come," Negro spirituals, and American folk songs.

The infatuation with the United States allowed the German avant-garde to demonstrate its rejection of Germany's military past and its disillusionment with the old European values that had proved so powerless against the war. Americanism was supposed to inaugurate a culture free of history, tradition, and specifically the trauma of the lost war. It promised an end of German didacticism and artistic elitism. The vitality of American popular culture inspired German intellectuals who were tired of the German tragic sense of life and the traditional concept of *Kultur*. American culture (deemed democratic because it was accessible to everyone) thus loosened Germany's grip on its own cultural and national identity—with devastating results in the backlash under Hitler's reclaimed nationalism. Aided by the Dawes Plan of 1924, which ended the galloping inflation by using U.S. capital to help pay war reparations, Germany also discovered the lure of a modern consumerist lifestyle patterned on the U.S. model. Compared to the exotic splendor of the United States, Germany seemed, as Brecht wrote in his diary already in 1920, downright "boring."[34] In this idealized "America" technology and modernity seemed to go hand in hand with a new urban culture that had forsworn militarism in favor of consumerism.

By the mid-1920s, the term Americanism had come to signify two related phenomena in Germany: the scientific management of labor and exploitative industrial mass production, on the one hand; and the lure of commercial mass culture, on the other. These attitudes prevailed throughout the Weimar Republic, and both inscribed themselves in *Metropolis*. In 1928, when asked by the avant-garde journal *Transition* about the influence of the United States in Europe, German poet Gottfried Benn answered (in English): "[The American] influence is enormous. . . . The entire young German literature since 1918 is working under the slogan of tempo, jazz, and cinema. . . . The influence of Americanism is so enormous, because it is analogous in certain tendencies with other currents that formed today's young German: Marxism and Communism, the purely animalistic social doctrine, whose common attacks are directed against the individualistic and the metaphysical being."[35] Benn particularly objected to "the purely utilitarian mass production and the collective plan," concluding his invective, not surprisingly, by saying: "Personally, I am against Americanism." In Benn's view, Americanism had conspired with Communism to promote collectivism and crass materialism against the German ideals of individualism and idealism—a polemical juxtaposition that also informs Lang's *Metropolis*.

Most generally, Americanism meant the encroachment of industrial rationality and cost-effectiveness into all areas, including *Kultur* which (at least in Germany) had always been defined as antithetical to the world of commerce: culture and the masses were mutually exclusive. "Mass culture" sounded like an oxymoron in a nation that proudly proclaimed itself a *Kul-*

turnation. Adolf Halfeld, a conservative cultural critic, states this unmistakably on the cover of his provocative book *Amerika und der Amerikanismus*, published in 1927: "Indebted to tradition, the culture of Europe, in particular of Germany, is threatened by America with its concentration on materialism and the mechanization of life. Rationalization in the American example triumphs, even if it kills the human side in mankind."[36] Still, more was at stake in debates about Americanism than the cultural anxiety of the German middle class vis-à-vis American culture; arguments for and against the United States articulated and implied views on national identity, modernity, and the future of *Kultur* in the machine age that followed the war.

Metropolis, shot between May 1925 and July 1926, oscillates between the positive and negative poles of Weimar's discourse on Americanism. Visually it is modeled on America's urban modernity, while in terms of narrative and ideology it opposes it, even revisiting the ideological fault lines of the war that distinguished between German idealistic humanism and "Western" materialism. This distinction was the battle cry that unified the nation in 1914—and a wide range of intellectuals, from Robert Musil to Stefan George, from Max Weber to Thomas Mann, had made powerful arguments for a scenario in which Germany's idealism fought for its survival against the agents of a commercialized and crass "modernity."[37]

The most "Americanist" images in *Metropolis* are cityscapes dominated by gigantic skyscrapers, the ultimate symbols of America's progress and modernity. Imitating New York and Chicago, Berlin experienced what was called a skyscraper mania in the early 1920s.[38] A competition among architects for a skyscraper, or *Turmhaus*, at Bahnhof Friedrichstrasse in 1921 produced 114 submissions by German architects, including such luminaries as Mies van der Rohe, Hans Scharoun, and Hans Poelzig. Many of these architects were unemployed due to the economic consequences of the war and therefore free to conjure up fantastic buildings that could *not* be built—except as models and movie sets.[39] Nothing concrete came of this competition; there was neither the money for such a building in 1921 nor the technology to give it the foundations it would need. (Berlin is built on sand, not granite like Manhattan.) But the publicity was tremendous. Pictures of the prize-winning entries were published in all the papers, and a cartoon linked the cry for skyscrapers (*Der Schrei nach dem Turmhaus*) to the Tower of Babel to indicate the compulsive nature of this desire to build higher and higher. Erich Kettelhut's drawings for the *Metropolis* sets—especially the design for the office building, called the New Tower of Babel—might be seen as a late entry in the Turmhaus competition and a sly commentary on the power of movies to build skyscrapers when the construction industry could not.

Emboldened by his visit to Hollywood, Lang also seemed eager to take on blockbuster Hollywood productions that had begun to make inroads in Germany. Epic films from the U.S.—costly historical spectacles with gigantic orientalist architecture and transnational appeal—were becoming popular in Germany at the time: Douglas Fairbanks's lavish, four-hour extravaganza *The Thief of Bagdad* and Cecil B. DeMille's *The Ten Commandments* both opened in Berlin in 1925 with much fanfare. Lang emulates these monumental American films, even staging some shots in his Tower-of-Babel scene in the manner of *The Ten Commandments*, which he had seen during his visit to the United States. He certainly wanted to compete with them in grandeur and budget, even though his goals were decidedly different. In a 1926 essay titled "The Future of the Feature Film in Germany," he contrasts the Hollywood style with his own:

> Germany has never had, and never will have, the gigantic human and financial reserves of the American film industry at its disposal. To its good fortune. For that is exactly what forces us to compensate a purely material imbalance through an intellectual superiority. . . . The Americans have still not understood how to use their magnificent equipment to elevate the miracle of photography into the realm of the spirit; that means for example, that the concepts of light and shade are not to be made mere transporters of mood but factors that contribute to plot. I recently had the opportunity of showing an American technician a few scenes from *Metropolis*, in which the beam of an electric flashlight illuminated the pursuit of a young girl through the catacombs of Metropolis. This beam of light pierced the hunted creature like the sharp claws on an animal, refused to release her from its grasp. Drove her unremittingly forward to the point of utter panic. It brought the amiable American to a naïve confession, "We can't do that!" Of course they could. But the idea never occurs to them. For them, the thing remains without essence, unanimated, soulless.[40]

Lang here draws on the old adage according to which Germans have privileged access to spirit and soul, in contrast to other "soulless" Western nations. Lang even invokes arguments that recall the prowar position of 1914, when Germany saw itself on the defense against the onslaught of the allegedly shallow Western materialism of Britain and France. Now, in the mid-1920s, a shift of characters had occurred: the United States, the undisputed winner of the war, replaced France and Britain, both of which were exhausted from their fight against Germany. *Metropolis* thus replayed the ideological battles that accompanied and were used to legitimize the war, with one final irony. The fight for spiritual superiority was so expensive that it brought Ufa to the brink of bankruptcy. It needed two large and solvent U.S. film companies, Paramount and Metro-Goldwyn-Mayer, to distribute Lang's film in 1927. The credits identify the production company with the three-part acronym "Parufamet": Ufa is in the center, but propped up on each side by Hollywood.

The Hunger for Religion

Expressionism . . . belongs very essentially to the war and is not its consequence but the spiritual symptom of the same crisis whose worldly symptom is the war.

—Friedrich Gundolf, "Stefan George und der Expressionismus," 1920

In 1918, Kracauer noticed that a new religiosity had crept into the expressionist movement—a religiosity that, in his view, spoke of intense longing for a world of vitality, creativity, and vision.[41] Kracauer's lengthy cultural analysis (only posthumously published), titled "On Expressionism: Nature and Meaning of a Contemporary Movement," predates any of the films discussed here, but it raises questions that Weimar cinema tried to answer only a few years later. Expressionism for Kracauer was the outcry of those who felt enslaved by modernity's instrumental reason. Realism, with its attention to detail, tacitly affirmed a stifling reality, while expressionism challenged the status quo by breaking with conventional practices of representation in the arts. The expressionists' passion for innovation invigorated cultural production before, during, and after the war, which itself was symptomatic of a desire for change. Their demand for a radical reversal of humankind's direction did not allow for nuance and individual differentiation—hence the tendency of expressionist art toward abstraction, typification, and stylization.

More a cultural than an aesthetic movement, expressionism according to Kracauer articulated a vitalist reaction against urban modernity, rationality, and the administered life. Seen from this perspective, the unprecedented enthusiasm for war in 1914 was one massive expressionist gesture. It was meant to throw off the shackles of modernity and "reboot" a program that appeared to have crashed. Even Kracauer, twenty-five years old at the time, had tried twice to enlist as a volunteer in 1914, but was rejected both times for medical reasons. Although expressionists soon turned against the war, the totalizing, apocalyptical attitude that hoped to completely remake the world still informed *Metropolis*. The utopia of a transformed world promised to reestablish a community that in their view was destroyed by industrialization and the economic-rationalist mind-set.

Metropolis echoes expressionism's plea for the restoration of humanistic values. Their own skeptical attitude vis-à-vis expressionism notwithstanding, in *Metropolis* Lang and von Harbou do not shy away from employing narrative and visual tropes from expressionist theater to articulate dissatisfaction with modernity.[42] Theatrical models included Georg Kaiser's *Gas*, a set of three plays that depict a son's failed rebellion against his billionaire father. The trilogy, consisting of *Die Koralle* (*The Coral*, 1917), *Gas–Erster Teil* (*Gas–Part 1*, 1919), and *Gas–Zweiter Teil* (*Gas–Part 2*, 1920), ends with an apocalyptic explosion that annihilates all life.[43] Written in highly stylized language, these plays deal with the destructive nature of industry and make a utopian plea for a return to a premodern state. Reviewers saw Kaiser's abstract stagings of the battle against instrumental rationality as a gloss on the industrial war. Lang's silent film pursues the same goal, although he translates the exalted expressionist language into striking images that need no words.

Another much-discussed play of the early Weimar Republic, Toller's *Die Maschinenstürmer* (*The Machine Wreckers*, 1922), foreshadowed a further narrative strand of *Metropolis*. Based on Gerhard Hauptmann's naturalist play *Die Weber* (*The Weavers*, 1888), Toller dramatized the Luddite revolt in 1830s Britain, another failed instance of the proletariat's rebellion against machines. Its stark expressionist staging by Karl-Heinz Martin in 1922 was one of the most discussed theater productions of its day, in part because its premiere—six days after the assassination of Walther Rathenau—took place in a highly volatile political atmosphere. A gigantic machine, underscoring the desperate dependency of the working class on the very forces it wants to destroy, dominated the stage. The workers appeared as a highly stylized chorus, speaking in one voice before they explode in rage. Lang's choreography of the masses in *Metropolis* follows the conventions of the expressionist theater of his time.

For Kracauer, the ultimate goal of the expressionists' project was the creation of a cultural community that would undo the modern individual's alienation, fragmentation, and isolation. He admitted as early as 1918, however, that it was less than clear what "this empire of individuals who are living an inner-directed life should look like. One only feels and knows that it ought to be. The yearning for it manifests itself in the longing for a new monumental art and the hunger for a new religiosity, a powerful belief that still lacks certain content and form."[44] *Metropolis*'s proclaimed utopian humanism was an answer to the rapidly increasing pace of modernity in Germany after the war. Yet the film's religious inflection and strained monumentalism also suggested the perceived impossibility of such an enterprise in an advanced capitalist society.

This "hunger for a new religiosity" was also a response to the spiritual crisis that followed the lost war. Although less urgent by the mid-1920s, Lang makes use of it in often astonishingly direct ways, both in the film's Christian iconography (for instance, in a scene in which Freder, hitched to the hands of a huge clock, assumes the role of Jesus on the cross, calling out for his father), and in the narrative's appropriation of the Bible's first and last books—the Book of Genesis and the Book of Revelation. Lang's most spectacular biblical set piece introduces the legend of the Tower of Babel as a moral tale directed against discord and rebellion. The scene, really a film within a film, condenses the message of the entire epic into a three-minute parable.

The Tower of Babel sequence takes place in a secret cave far below the futurist world of the city of Metropolis. An earlier intertitle had referred to two-thousand-year-old catacombs, the underground hiding place of early Christians. The Christian framework is underscored by large crosses that surround the virginal figure of Maria, who preaches to the workers. The world below the imagined city is dark and womblike, as if carved out of the soil, a site where revolutionary desire is imbued with mythical and occult meanings. The clandestine assembly hall is shown as a space of regression as well as revolt—a space where workers stand in rows to watch the spectacle and a setup resembling an early working-class cinema. Our first view

Architectural fantasy
and material catastrophe
in *Metropolis*.

of the scene is through a peephole from high above—the equivalent of a projection booth from which to observe the gathering. We see Rotwang and Frederson secretly watching Maria and the workers from this opening. As is frequently the case in Lang's films, the observed do not know that they are being watched.

The workers' eyes are fixed on Maria as she recounts the legend of the Tower of Babel. A short film presents in tableau-like chapters the conception, building, and destruction of the world's first skyscraper. The narrative is set off from the rest of the film by streaks of light shooting from all four corners of the screen, as if Lang wanted to put this film within a film in quotation marks. The last scene shows an emblematic ruin with an inscription at the top. Not unlike a Baroque *Trauerspiel*, the film's allegory carries a didactic message—in this case, both for the working class (Do not revolt!) and its masters (Do not exploit!). The heart, Maria claims, has to mediate between head and hands if a community is to function properly. The workers look skeptical. Later they are manipulated into a self-destructive revolt, clearly (and ironically) showing that they did not learn their lesson.

What, then, is the function of the Tower of Babel sequence? The legend of course goes back to the Old Testament. Genesis 11:1–9 tells of the descendants of Noah who decided to build a city "to make a name for themselves" and to erect in it a tower whose top would reach heaven. But the Lord frowned on the hubris of this project and confounded their languages so that they could no longer understand each other, and thus could not finish the tower. "Therefore it is called Babel," Genesis states, "for there the Lord made the languages of all the world babble. And from there the Lord scattered them over all the earth." This biblical legend is itself a retrospective moral tale and tendentious reminder of the power of an omnipotent monotheistic deity to punish human hubris. It has engendered a rich pictorial and exegetical tradition, ranging from Pieter Brueghel's 1563 painting to Vladimir Tatlin's 1919 plan for a 1,300 feet high tower ("Monument to the Third International") and Jacques Derrida's 1985 ruminations about translation in *Des Tours de Babel*. Centered on mankind's desire to exceed human measure, the Tower of Babel ultimately reveals the impossibility of realizing this desire. It is a story of undeterred progress and secular modernity halted by divine intervention. Oscillating between myth and fact, between architectural fantasy and archaeological reality, the Tower of Babel is not only the oldest visionary building but also an enduring symbol of a modernity gone awry. It is not a coincidence that some commentators linked the destruction of the Twin Towers of the World Trade Center with that of the Tower of Babel; nor is it surprising that Daniel Libeskind in his statement for the proposed Freedom Tower for the New York World Trade Center placed himself in the tradition of visionary architects who see the skyscraper as the "spiritual peak" of a city.[45] *Metropolis*'s largest building is tellingly called "The New Tower of Babel."

Lang began work on *Metropolis* at a time of a renewed interest in the ruined city of Babylon. Guided by the reports of Herodotus, the German archaeologist Robert Koldewey had excavated Babylon under the aegis of the German Orient-Gesellschaft between 1899 and 1917. Koldewey's 1913 book on the discovery of Babylon and the Tower of Babel was republished on the occasion of his death in 1925.[46] On November 9, 1925, an article in *Film-Kurier* on the shooting of the Tower of Babel scene drew a direct parallel between these two cities, Metropolis and Babylon:

> Metropolis epitomizes the city that destroys itself. The film creates the tragedy of our times, which consists of technology becoming the master of man . . . There once was a time when a culture perished of a similar illness. It was the time of the decline of the Babylonian culture, which is symbolized by the legend of the Tower of Babel. The people perished because they no longer understood each other.[47]

Lang's imagined futurist architecture echoes that of the ancient city: the high-tech *Metropolis* quotes the biblical Babylon, charged, in Walter Benjamin's phrase, "by the presence of the now."[48]

The "Babylonian" look was fashionable in silent cinema, especially in epic spectacles such as Griffith's 1916 *Intolerance*. It afforded the new art form gravitas and grandeur. (The oldest surviving movie theater in the center of Berlin is called Babylon; it opened in 1927, the same year as *Metropolis*.) Theorists of early film saw correspondences between the most ancient form of civilization and the newest medium by comparing filmic signs with hieroglyphs.[49] Films set in the pharaonic past seemed to suggest a death-defying eternal present. The Tower of Babel, not unlike the pyramids and the sphinx, represented primal architectural scenes outside of time and space. Orientalist film architecture also imposed a sense of scale against which humankind seemed insignificant.

Nevertheless, Lang's proletarian mass successfully topples the leader and brings down the tower itself. In a low-angle shot Lang stages the workers such that they rush upward and rapidly fill the frame. The shocking image of the destructive power of the masses is an undisguised reference to the proletarian uprisings of 1918–19 in Berlin and Munich, where the workers asserted themselves. Mobilized masses also recall Russian revolutionary cinema, which had become popular in Germany in the mid-1920s. Sergei Eisenstein's *Battleship Potemkin* opened in 1926 (shortly before *Metropolis*) after a much-publicized censorship battle, and was followed by dozens of revolutionary films from Russia. However, unlike Eisenstein's individualized workers, Lang's proletariat is conceived as an anonymous mob with raised fists.

One of the original German intertitles in the Tower of Babel scene states that "*fremde Hände*" (foreign hands) were hired—a noteworthy detail (left out in the film's English-titled version) that could not be missed in the 1920s."Foreign hands" was an allusion to the massive influx of Polish laborers hired to work in German coal mines in the late nineteenth and early twentieth centuries. Laborers from the east were often stereotyped as drunkards prone to irrational violence, but they were also known for their ethnic class-consciousness. They founded a union of Polish workers and gained notoriety through numerous well-publicized strikes in which they (not unlike the masses in Lang's *Metropolis*) rebelled against exploitation.

For the Babel scene, so the legend goes, Lang hired more than one thousand extras and required that their heads be shaved—all for a few shots in which an anonymous mass suddenly turns into an uncontrollable mob that, in a single self-destructive moment, lays waste to all it had labored to build. The penultimate image of this scene is especially poignant: a sea of raised fists, filmed from a low angle to emphasize their force, obscures the tower that lies in ruins.

In Lang's film, writing itself becomes part of the visual design. The word Babel flashes three times on the screen in big letters that come alive, producing an effect that connotes the exploited workers' blood, sweat, and tears. Silent film can animate and anthropomorphize the dead letter: even the intertitles speak. The intensity of the shock appears to impact the writing and destroys it. Three times the letters of the word Babel appear in motion only to crumble as if exploded from within. This disintegration of writing is itself a sign of the breakdown of language and the final outcome of the Tower of Babel legend.

Because film images did not require words, they contributed to the belief in a universal human language, thus reversing post-Babel fragmentation.

Film, according to Béla Balázs, was capable of lifting the curse of the Tower of Babel. In a speech in September 1926 under the title "Ausblick auf morgen (Outlook for Tomorrow)," Lang followed Balázs almost verbatim, suggesting a postwar reconciliation among nations through the power of film:

> Through the silent speech of its moving images, in a language that is equally understood in all hemispheres, film can make an honest contribution to repairing the chaos that has prevented nations from seeing each other as they really are ever since the tower of Babel.[50]

The film's last scene, which takes place in front of a Gothic cathedral (a deliberate counterspace to the Tower of Babel), gestures toward reconciliation between classes and the rebirth of a wounded community. The two interwoven narratives come to a conclusion: while the private story of Freder and Maria is sealed with a kiss, the public one ends with a handshake between industrialist and workers. The very brevity of the reconciliation signifies that it is illusory and utopian, a film ending—open to criticism but necessary for the logic of the film. By allowing the idealistic rebellion against instrumental rationality and the domination of the machine to succeed, the film proposes that the end of class warfare (symbolized by the much-ridiculed handshake) will help rebuild the nation. The film also implies that technological modernity itself will continue to produce class division as well as the means of mass slaughter. The war goes on without the battles.

The Workers' Revolt

> *Film director Fritz Lang is grateful for every idea that allows him to show the masses.*
>
> —Theodor Heuss, "Metropolis," 1927

On July 14, 1927, something extraordinary happened in Vienna: an irate crowd set the Palace of Justice on fire to protest an unjust ruling. The court had acquitted three members of an extreme right-wing organization who were accused of having killed two innocent bystanders while shooting at socialist workers on strike. The news of this plainly partisan verdict mobilized the entire city within hours; thousands of incensed citizens poured into the streets and congregated in mounting numbers in front of the Palace of Justice. Caught unprepared and fearing unrest, the Social Democratic leadership decided against a protest march; instead it tried to calm and appease the infuriated masses, but to no avail. The workers organized their own spontaneous mass demonstrations. Elias Canetti, at the time a student in Vienna, remembers:

> From all districts of the city, the workers marched in tight formation to the Palace of Justice, whose sheer name embodied the unjust verdict for them. It was a totally spontaneous reaction: I could tell how spontaneous it was just by my own conduct. I quickly biked into the center of town and joined one of the processions. The workers, usually well disciplined, trusting their Social Democratic leaders, and satisfied that Vienna was administered by these leaders in an exemplary manner, were acting without their leaders on this day. When they set fire to the Palace of Justice, Mayor Seitz mounted a fire engine and raised his right hand high, trying to block their way. His gesture had no effect: the Palace of Justice was burning.[51]

When the huge amorphous mass turned into an unruly mob, the police president gave orders to shoot into the crowd, an action that brought the protest to a quick and bloody end. Eighty-four people were killed, and many more seriously wounded. The police, writes Heimito von Doderer in his novel *Die Dämonen* (*The Demons*), became "armed troops, advancing in step, firing and driving everything before them."[52] The masses dispersed, realizing they were fighting a hopeless battle against the firepower of the police. The violence was reminiscent of the war, but now workers and civilians were the enemy.

It fell, ironically, upon the Social Democratic Party to denounce the behavior of the outraged crowd as reckless, imprudent, and irrational, using a terminology that dates back to Gustave Le Bon's influential 1895 book on the psychology of the masses.[53] When the Social Democrats convened three months later to discuss the events of July, they reiterated their critique of the undisciplined and lawless masses, and emphasized the importance of transcending class differences for the sake of social harmony.

The "revolt of the masses" in the streets of Vienna in July 1927 bears an uncanny resemblance to the workers' rebellion depicted in *Metropolis*, which had opened in Vienna barely six months earlier. Both the historical event and Lang's film show revolutionary urban masses, both feature destruction out of blind rage, both make evident the futility of revolt, and both suggest closure by stressing (however vaguely) communitarian harmony over class struggle and political strife.

The very concept of "revolutionary masses" was hotly debated in the mid-1920s after the failed proletarian revolution in Germany at the end of the war. By 1932, Jünger claimed that the "old masses"—"those storming the Bastille, those involved in street uprisings and political gatherings, and those who cheered the outbreak of war in August 1914"—were a thing of the past. "The actions of the masses," Jünger declared confidently, as if referring to the events in Vienna, "lost their magic wherever they met resolute resistance, just as two or three old warriors behind an intact machine gun have no reason to be worried even when told that a whole battalion is approaching. Today, the masses are no longer able to attack, they can no longer even defend themselves."[54]

Jünger maintained that the concept of the mass needed to be reconfigured and even replaced. In his view, modernity itself had transformed the diffuse and potentially dangerous masses of the nineteenth century into a homogeneous mass of worker-soldiers. He writes in his 1932 philosophical treatise *Der Arbeiter* (*The Worker*): "Networks of traffic; the supply of the most elementary needs like fire, water and light; a developed credit system; and many other such things are like thin fibers, are like visible veins with which the amorphous body of the mass is forever bound together and interconnected."[55] The totality of industrial production has absorbed every aspect of personal and social life into an organic whole. Industrial life controls private and public matters in such an intricate way that any revolt against it seems to be not only self-defeating but even contrary to the natural order. The workers' revolt in *Metropolis* triggers apocalyptic floods and devastation.

The mass, according to Jünger, is continually constructed by bureaucratic and disciplinary institutions such as the school, the church, the military—and one might add, the technological medium of film. In the 1920s, the question arose of how to observe, supervise, discipline, and control the collective body and make it function ever more effectively for industrial labor. The military spirit, honed during the war years, persisted throughout the Weimar Republic. In a disconcerting (but logical) scene at the end of *Metropolis*, after the failed revolt, the worker-soldiers again march in formation, invoking once more a parallelism between factory and army.

In its evocation of the failed workers' revolution of 1918–19, *Metropolis* figures the workers' revolt in gendered terms. It is a woman, the evil machine-double of the saintly Maria, who unleashes the workers' passions. Since the female robot is "programmed" by the inventor Rotwang at the behest of the industrialist Fredersen, the very idea of a revolt is delegitimized. The viewer is aware of the deception from the beginning. We know that the revolt is artificial and engineered to fail, and our knowledge makes us feel superior to the workers who blindly follow the false leader. While the "real" Maria had preached class conciliation, her double incites the masses; while Maria had pleaded with the workers to be patient and wait for a mediator, her robot replica tells them they have waited long enough. Working women play no role in the film, only when the male workers riot do they join in the mayhem. The women, absent in the factory scenes, are now singled out from the mass with abrupt close-ups: stereotypically depicted as hysterical, they throw up their hands and behave erratically.

The figure of a female rabble-rouser carries echoes of Rosa Luxemburg, the Polish-born politician and antiwar activist. Disgusted by the Social Democrats' endorsement of what she called the "imperialist World War," in 1914 she founded the Spartacist League (named for the gladiator who led the slave revolt against the Romans). Along with Karl Liebknecht she was sentenced to prison in 1916 for organizing strikes against the war, but she kept publishing seditious pamphlets, including a criticism of the 1917 Russian revolution. When she was released at the end of the war, Luxemburg reorganized the Spartacist League and together with Liebknecht cofounded the Communist Party of Germany (KPD) on December 30, 1918. In the weeks of civil war following the armistice, she advocated resistance to the Social Democratic government and participated in the Spartacist uprising that lasted from January 5 to January 12, 1919. Although Luxemburg (unlike Liebknecht) opposed the violent overthrow of the government, she could not stop the striking workers from arming themselves and occupying the editorial offices of the liberal press. The uprising triggered severe reactions. To resolve the situation, Gustav Noske, the new Social Democratic minister of defense, called on the Freikorps. A paramilitary organization of soldiers who refused to put down their arms, the Freikorps hated the Left, which they believed had "stabbed them in the back." Eager to avenge defeat, they captured and killed both Liebknecht and Luxemburg and threw Luxemburg's corpse into Berlin's Landwehr Canal.

In *Metropolis,* a frenzied mob pursues the robot Maria and burns her at the stake—a monstrous scene in which she is tied up on top of a large heap of industrial junk. Marked as a "witch" and (as in Luxemburg's case) blamed for the destructive riots, she is accused of casting a spell over the working class to make them rebel against their oppressors. Following the biblical command "Thou shalt not suffer a witch to live" (Exodus 22:18), the mob murders the mechanical doppelgänger of the savior Maria. Already rich with allusions to the world of religion and magic, the film uses this scene to recast the battle against industrial modernity and its self-destructive potential as an irrational hunt for some supernatural agent that is responsible for modernity—a scapegoat that turns out to be a machine itself. As the flames reach the robot Maria, her movements become more mechanical and her grimaces more diabolical. Suddenly the underside of the false Maria is shown: a gleaming steel construction.

The atavistic murder of the robot Maria is preceded by scenes that highlight the primal forces unleashed by the revolution. After the destruction of the machine, the robot Maria and the workers dance around its ruins as if it were the biblical golden calf. Lang emphasizes the Dionysian element repressed by the West in its drive toward rationality, but also suggests that the return of the primitive and irrational is ultimately self-destructive. The primitive threatens to undermine both civilization and the patriarchal order. As Marianna Torgovnick puts it, "[t]he primitive was coded metaphorically as feminine, collective, and ecstatic, and civilization was coded as masculine, individualistic, and devoted to the quotidian business of the family, city, or state."[56] Even though the inventor Rotwang created the robot Maria as a machine, her/its flirtatiously cool demeanor and modern dress are modeled after the New Woman that had emerged in the early 1920s. Indicative of anxieties about the increased power of women as a result of the war, there was hardly a Weimar film after the mid-1920s that did not feature early versions of the femme fatale—sexual, independent, and pitiless. *Metropolis* was not alone in its strained, misogynistic view of the modern woman, as exemplified by Maria's splitting into Madonna and whore as well as by the fickleness and panic of working-class women.

The film takes a dim view of the proletarian revolution that happened only five years before the script was written. In 1924, the so-called stabilization phase of the Weimar Republic had just begun, and the economy was rapidly improving after the introduction of the Dawes Plan. There were constant rumblings on the far Right, but Hitler's putsch in 1923 was a complete failure for which he spent nine months in jail, from April to December 1924. (His five-year sentence was reduced due to an amnesty for political prisoners.) By the mid-1920s, little sympathy existed for Luxemburg's revolutionary fervor, and the film illustrates this postrevolutionary attitude. In 1925, it was widely reported that German union leaders paid a visit to Henry Ford to learn how to maintain social peace and still increase productivity. A brochure from that year with the self-explanatory title "Ford or Marx: The Practical Solution to the Social Question" makes an argument in favor of Ford.[57]

The alternative in *Metropolis* to the ill-fated rebellion is to hold out for a *Mittler*, a forceful mediator able to bring about social peace. Again, the film appropriates a major discourse of the 1920s—namely, the yearning for a savior or leader. Maria advocates neither revolt nor anything approaching self-rule; instead she tells the workers to wait passively for a messiah who will liberate them. Although Max Weber, in his celebrated 1919 lecture "Science as a Vocation," had admonished his young audience that "the prophet for whom so many of our younger generation yearn simply does not exist," the hope for a new charismatic leader was kept alive throughout the Weimar Republic.[58] After the Kaiser abandoned his "children" in 1918 by fleeing Germany, many in the republic considered themselves politically fatherless, without leadership and direction, especially because the parliament was for most a "pathetic comedy."[59] This awareness of a lost unity (the kind of enthusiastic unity that Germany experienced in August 1914) and the consequent hunger for a mediator or messiah may make Hitler's ascent easier to understand. (The renewed popularity of biographies of "great men" in the Weimar Republic is another symptom of this felt lack of charismatic leadership.) "When will the mediator come?" Lang's workers repeatedly pose the question and open themselves to be misled by a false messiah.

Although Lang invented the visual prototype of a long line of female cyborgs, the machine/human interface has its own long history, reaching back to Julien Offray de La Mettrie's 1748 book *L'Homme machine*. La Mettrie understood the human body and mind as products of mechanical laws. In the eighteenth century, the body was given over to materialist analysis and there were numerous experiments in using machines to do the mechanical work previously performed by humans. In the emerging industrial factories, human beings and machines seemed to become interchangeable: people became machines and machines in turn became humanoid automatons with moving hands. Since the romantics, mechanical figures have appeared as deadly doppelgänger and uncanny beings, uncontrollable and dangerous. Embodiments of the mechanization of life and the alienation produced by capitalist labor, they have both fascinated and terrified.

Villiers de L'Isle-Adam's 1886 science fiction novel *L'Eve future* (*The Future Eve*) presented Thomas Alva Edison as the Faustian creator of a female robot who not only personified the ideal woman and eternal female Hadaly ("the future Eve") but also substituted for his friend's beautiful young wife. Hanns Heinz Ewers, the popular German author of fantastic tales, published the German translation of this book in 1920, and the parallels between the female android and the robot Maria in *Metropolis* are striking.[60] Both Hadaly and the robot Maria are phantom machines, identical in appearance to their human models, but without consciousness or soul. Just like the future Eve, the female robot in *Metropolis* substitutes for a woman but takes on a life of its own. The process of creating a machine double also comments on the very nature of film: Are figures on-screen not already technical replicas of actors, brought to life by the filmmaker's will and the camera's technology?

Reviews in 1927 remarked on Lang and von Harbou's debt to H. G. Wells's science fiction novel *When the Sleeper Wakes* (1899; trans. *Wenn der Schläfer erwacht*, 1907); Wells himself wrote a long, scathing, and oft-cited review of *Metropolis* in *The New York Times Magazine* of April 17, 1927. Not only did he note the film's appropriation of motifs from his novel, he also disparaged Lang's allegorical style in general: "I have recently seen the silliest film. . . . It gives in one eddying concentration almost every possible foolishness, cliché, platitude, and muddlement about mechanical progress and progress in general, served up with a sauce of sentimentality that is all its own."[61]

Mechanization, alluded to in the robotic walk of the workers in the first scene of *Metropolis*, is shown as a product of labor. Rotwang's creation of a human machine is given ample film time and not surprisingly has become one of the film's most quoted scenes. It illustrates the symbiosis of modern science with the occult that fascinated Ernst Bloch in silent cinema, but also refers to the war-related trauma of mechanization.[62] Like Dr. Caligari who "programmed" Cesare to kill, Rotwang experiments with the mechanical Maria to program her for his destructive plan. The mechanization experienced in the war as machinery for efficient killing is revisited and narratively transformed into a "living" machine that can no longer be distinguished from a human. Are machine guns not simply extensions of the men using them? Rotwang himself wears a mechanical hand—a prosthesis in a black glove—that alludes to millions of veterans who lost limbs in the war and used machine parts to replace them. The boundaries between the mechanical and the human had broken down, not just in this science fiction movie, but in the daily reality of postwar Germany as well.[63]

Destruction and Regeneration

Chaos is here. . . . Minds are awakening, souls rising to responsibility, hands taking action. May the revolution bring rebirth.

—Gustav Landauer, *For Socialism*, 1919

Men have to destroy if they want to create anew.

—Joseph Goebbels, *Michael*, 1928

Following one of the most dazzling sequences in the film—the lascivious dance of Maria's mechanical double—Freder is shown reading a large-format book. A sudden and unmotivated close-up reveals the book's title: *Die Offenbarung Sankt Johannis* (*The Revelation of St. John*); it also states the book's publisher (Avalun) and the place of its publication (Hellerau). The precision of this information is noteworthy because such a book was indeed published by Avalun Press in Dresden-Hellerau in 1923. This documentary fragment in the middle of a highly stylized science fiction film anchors the futurist vision in its historical moment, when it was possible to buy a precious illustrated reprint of the Book of Revelation in a limited edition. The reference to the biblical book also authenticates Freder's hallucination and places his private crisis in a larger theological framework. Further, it illustrates the Book of Revelation's first paragraph: "Blessed is the one who reads aloud the words of the prophecy, and blessed are those who hear and who keep what is written in it; for the time is near." By intrusively pointing to the biblical Apocalypse as a source, Lang also provides a key to understanding the way his narrative is structured: as a palimpsest on the Book of Revelation. He reconfigures the Apocalypse for the modern period and interprets the futurist dystopian city through the lens of a biblical text.

The sequence in question begins when Freder mistakes the robot Maria for the woman with whom he has fallen in love. Unaware that it is Maria's double whom he discovers in the arms of his widowed father, Freder experiences a psychological shock that Lang illustrates through a burst of special effects—white circles going in and out of focus, stars exploding like bombs, and dizzyingly rotating images that depict in rapid succession a skull playing flute on a bone, a close-up of the mad inventor Rotwang, a picture of the stern father, and multiplied faces of Maria. The ground gives way under Freder's feet, and he begins a free fall through what seem to be several rings of hell, until the screen goes dark. As so many of the young protagonists in the cinema of the early 1920s, he ends up in a sickbed, recovering from his shock and in need of care.

Meanwhile, Rotwang presents the female robot as a dancer to a gathering of upper-class men. Her dance reduces them to nothing but leering eyes, to one voracious act of collective voyeurism. The film literalizes their being "all eyes" by cutting to a montage of a dozen eyes in extreme close-ups. The dance is Rotwang's proof that the machine double cannot be distinguished from its human original. Although Freder only knows about this dance through an invitation accidentally left on his bedside table, the film editing makes him part of the scene through crosscutting. In his feverish mind he envisions the Apocalypse the way he read about it in the Book of Revelation. The last canonical book of the New Testament and full of hallucinatory images of decadence and doom, the Book of Revelation describes the end of the world in terrifying detail. Peace is restored only after God's final victory over Satan at Armageddon and his violent judgment on nonbelievers. The controversial text was written by Saint John of Patmos in the first century after Christ, during the intensified persecution of Christians under Nero. The film refers indirectly to this biblical story when Maria and the workers meet for worship in catacombs deep under the city, like the early Christians.

Lang quotes biblical sources selectively, producing stylized set pieces not unlike the cinema of attractions in which visual pleasure trumped narrative economy. The depiction of the gyrating cyborg (Maria's machine double) rising up on a stone beast with seven heads triggers in Freder associations with the Whore of Babylon, who in the Apocalypse signified pre-Christian, pagan Rome. In *Metropolis*, the Whore of Babylon becomes a femme fatale stripper whose erotic dance causes men to lose their composure. A title card provides a biblical caption to this show of urban decadence and depravity: "Verily, I say unto you, the days spoken of in the Apocalypse are nigh!" The quote refers to the Book of Revelation, which elaborates:

> Fallen! Fallen is Babylon the Great! It has become a dwelling place of demons, a haunt of every foul spirit, a haunt of every foul and hateful bird; for all the nations have drunk the wine of her impure passions. . . . Alas, alas, for the great city that was clothed in fine linen,

purple and scarlet, bedecked with gold, with jewels, and with pearls! In one hour all this wealth has been laid waste.[64]

Punctuated by reaction shots of an increasingly agitated Freder, the frenzied montage also includes images of death as a skeleton and the seven deadly sins in the city's Gothic cathedral. The soundtrack changes from jazzy dance music to the thirteenth-century Latin hymn *Dies irae, dies illa, Solvet saeclum in favilla*, which describes the terror and despair of judgment day. Brought to life by Freder's hallucination, death and the seven deadly sins step down from their pedestal and jerkily move toward the camera. The scene illustrates the macabre dance of death that emerged in the late Middle Ages after the plague killed almost half the population.[65] Innumerable woodcuts, drawings, and other art forms gave expression to the dance. The scene is modeled after a relief of 1543, the so-called *Dresden Dance of Death*: a skeleton appears playing a flute and carrying a scythe, symbolizing the act of harvesting the soul from the body. The film cuts from the personification of death to an industrial cityscape of skyscrapers and smokestacks, and then back to a quick reaction shot of Freder, who holds his ears to keep out the siren blast that signals the beginning of the workers' shift.

As if in response to the doomed inhumanity of the city, the film juxtaposes the factory with the grim reaper, now alone, who approaches the camera (that is, Freder and us, the audience). He holds his scythe high, threatening to mow down everything in front of him. Cut back to Freder's terrified expression, his body and arms frantically reaching forward as if to warn us before the intertitle declares: "Death descends upon the city (*Der Tod ist über der Stadt*)!" The skeleton continues toward us, and in a third and final sweeping motion produces a huge scratch across the image that seems to erase Freder, and with him the film's material base, the very emulsion on the celluloid. An avant-garde technique that calls attention to the materiality of film, this radical abrasion also reinforces the apocalyptic nature of the scene; death threatens to annihilate not only the city but also the film and its viewer.

This sequence establishes on the formal level a nexus between the biblical Apocalypse, the medieval dance of death, and urban modernity. Soon after this scene, the workers attack the machines and the city breaks down. As in a myriad of subsequent science fiction films, an inordinate amount of film time is spent reveling in images of devastation: crumbling walls, exploding machines, bursting pipes, misfiring electricity, and rising water. As

Apocalypse as Spectacle:
Death scars the image
in *Metropolis*.

Susan Sontag points out in her essay "The Imagination of Disaster," there is a strange aesthetic pleasure to be derived from watching disaster and destruction. "In films it is by means of images and sounds, not words that have to be translated by the imagination, that one can participate in the fantasy of living through one's own death and more, the death of cities, the destruction of humanity itself."[66]

Metropolis ends with a scene that gestures toward the beginning of a new order *after* the destruction—a redemptive glimpse of a nation reborn. Von Harbou's novel is quite explicit about the dialectics of destruction and regeneration when Freder confronts his father:

> Father, don't you understand? Your city is being destroyed! Your machines have come to life, they're rampaging through the city! They're tearing Metropolis to pieces! . . . Why do you allow Death to lay his hand upon the city which is your own?[67]

The father answers: "The city must fall, Freder, so that you may build it up once more."[68] Had he planned all along for the workers to destroy their city in order to "force guilt upon the people" and enable his son to redeem them? This invocation of apocalypse, regeneration, and redemption highlights the inflationary use of these messianic concepts in the recent war: the world had to be destroyed in order to be rebuilt from the ground up.

In a high angle shot, the final scene shows an orderly mass of workers slowly filling the frame. The workers shuffle forward in formation. They come to a halt and stand in a triangle before the cathedral, silent witnesses to the publicly staged reconciliation between proletariat and management. Disillusioned and purged of revolutionary ardor, the mass of workers unknowingly form what later in the same year Kracauer would call a "mass ornament," possibly in reaction to *Metropolis*.[69] It is the technical apparatus of the camera that not only makes this formation visible but in fact produces it. The workers have become part of a giant spectacle created by the very act of filming. Benjamin once noted that the masses encounter themselves in these filmed events.[70]

The workers at the end of the film (just like the audience in the movie theater) watch the performance of a brief utopian moment: the display, just a few years after military defeat and crushed revolution, of a regenerated and reunified nation. The film's ambitious fusion of theater, architecture, film, and music also gestured toward the notion of a *Gesamtkunstwerk* for the masses—a project that Richard Wagner could only dream of in the 1880s. Lang's visionary film *Metropolis* pursued a regenerative agenda. It was a project of *re*-membering, after the war had dismembered the national body. The synthesis of the various arts articulated and enacted the wish for the unity of the body politic.

Aftershocks

Metropolis has become the archetypal film of the Weimar Republic. Iconic images from the film have been quoted, referenced, and spoofed in hundreds of films ever since it was re-edited with a disco sound track by Giorgio Moroder in 1984. It has become fair game for global postmodernist citation in every imaginable context. At the end of her music video "Express Yourself," Madonna, as a new incarnation of the lascivious robot Maria, even quotes the film's inscription: "Without the heart, there can be no understanding between the hand and the mind." *Metropolis*, which borrowed liberally from an unprecedented variety of sources, has itself become a giant image bank to be raided for music clip backgrounds and countless allusions in contemporary cinema.[71] Lang's dream of making a national film for the international market has come true, albeit belatedly. In 1927, the ambition to reconceive the aftershocks of a defeated Germany in world-historical terms seemed strained, and the grandiosity with which the film was promoted only underscored its problematic mythmaking.

The opening of *Metropolis* on January 10, 1927 was a carefully orchestrated event. An advertising campaign had run for several months; von Harbou's novel *Metropolis* appeared both in serialized form in the *Berliner Illustrirte Zeitung* and as a book with pictures from the film. Newspapers reported almost weekly about the film's progress, citing record-breaking statistics that were part of the promotion strategy. It was widely reported that *Metropolis* was the most expensive and ambitious European film production to date, with an unheard-of cost of 5.3 million Reichsmarks (almost four times its actual budget); a shooting ratio of 1:300 (with more than 1 million meters of film exposed); and thirty-six thousand extras, including seventy-five hundred children and one thousand unemployed whose heads had been shaved by one hundred hairdressers for a scene that in the final cut lasted less than a minute. Statistical hyperbole and such slogans as "a film of titanic dimensions," "the greatest film ever made," or "one of the most eternal artworks of all times," promised an epic that could compete with such large-scale American spectacles as the *The Thief of Bagdad* (1924) or *Ben Hur* (1925), which had all been shown in Berlin just before *Metropolis* went into production.

Twenty-five hundred guests attended opening night, among them the Reichskanzler, members of the diplomatic corps, leaders of finance and industry, and the entire Berlin intelligentsia. The newspapers commented on the unparalleled glamour of the gala, which resembled the festive opening of a new opera and certainly rivaled the glitter of a major Hollywood premiere. Fake currency for use in the imaginary city of Metropolis was distributed, along with other souvenirs. Copies of von Harbou's novel *Metropolis* were given away, and a record of the film's score was produced by Vox. When the first images of the film presented a vision of the prototypical cinematic city, spontaneous applause erupted. Director Lang and his team (scriptwriter von Harbou, cameraman Karl Freund, set designers Otto Hunte and Erich Kettelhut) even took bows, as they had at the premiere of the *Nibelungen* three years earlier.

The media event overshadowed the film. Expectations after a yearlong barrage of advertising, publicity, and hype were so high that probably no film could have fulfilled them. The papers on the following morning were almost unanimous in disparaging the film, pointing out the glaring contradiction between its strikingly innovative visual style and its seemingly reactionary ideology. The solution offered to the plight of the working class (namely, that they be suppressed by a kinder, more gentle management) seemed either too facile or too cynical; and the expressionist love story (oedipal son rebels against rich father to win the hand of a working-class girl) appeared to be incongruent with the technological fetishism characteristic of a science fiction film.

From the vantage point of a modern film audience of 1927, Lang's representation of seditious masses in *Metropolis* looked simplistic and passé. Workers who fanatically try to destroy the very system of which they are fully a part did not generate much sympathy from the new urban masses who had learned to be "realistic" (*sachlich*) in their aspirations. *Metropolis* shows the masses as misguided, unstable, and inclined to mindless violence. Lang was perpetuating and even magnifying these classical stereotypes and threats associated with unruly masses, but the audience he addressed was a new public that disdained social turmoil as an impediment to consumption.[72] Seen from this perspective, the workers appear to fill three roles:

first oppressed victims, then irrational revolutionaries, and, finally, passive spectators. At the end, they shuffle again in orderly formation until told to stand still and watch while those in power negotiate their fate. By 1927, the distressed working class, shown as primal and primitive, had itself become a movie spectacle for a new middle-class urban public.

"The many millions," wrote the film critic Eugen Tannenbaum already in 1923, "who sit every night in their movie theaters, mesmerized by the life that flickers across the screen in uncounted kilometers of celluloid, the many millions who were a minute ago businessmen, workers, handymen, academics, secretaries, snobs, and ladies of the night—they all have become, after just a few scenes, a *homogeneous mass*, their attention focused on a story or a star and hypnotized by the suggestiveness of passion."[73] Statistics confirm the movies' mass appeal: in 1927, Berlin alone had more than 300 movie theaters with 165,000 seats; about 30 of these "palaces of distraction" (Kracauer) seated more than 1,000 people, and several of them had up to 3,000 seats. In the Reich, about two million Germans went to the movies every day.

It seemed as if the German working masses, buoyed by the economic upswing after 1924 and entranced by images of modern life in the U.S. (widely disseminated by illustrated papers and movies), began to embrace consumerism at an unprecedented pace. The masses (now increasingly constituted by white-collar workers) were no longer portrayed as victims but as consumers. The movie industry catered to their desires: lavish cinema palaces were built in the mid-1920s, movies drastically increased their production values, and *Metropolis* outspent all others to show the failed rebellion of an obsolete nineteenth-century proletariat. The contradiction was glaring. And yet, the artificiality and hysterical idealism of the film had their own truth. The movie was symptomatic of the gargantuan efforts necessary to make sense of postwar Germany's ongoing battle with modernity: a bloody war had been fought against modernity and everything it stood for, but the war was lost. The film tries to embrace modernity in the spirit of the mid-1920s, but also critique it in order to reaffirm the reasons why Germany entered the war in the first place. In this negotiation of conflicting perspectives, the film replicates the dominant opinion in the 1920s that the entire Weimar Republic was one feeble compromise. Not socialist enough for the Left, and not nationalist enough for the Right, the republic was a construct that nobody fully supported, not in the least because it always carried the stigma of being born out of loss and defeat. It may be precisely this deep ideological paradox that has contributed to the longevity of *Metropolis*.

In 1927, this nearly three-hour-long German film, which ironically was made with at least one eye on the U.S. market, was considered simply "too much" for American audiences.[74] It was cut by a third and re-edited by a U.S. team headed by the playwright Channing Pollock. Not long afterwards, the shortened version was also shown in Germany. There was a consensus that no copy of the original version had survived until an almost complete print, though scratched and in bad condition, was found in the Museo del Cine in Buenos Aires in July 2008. Before that discovery, laborious efforts had been made to reconstruct the film from still pictures, censorship cards, and von Harbou's novel.[75] It seemed as if *Metropolis* itself had suffered the fate of Lang's overreaching Tower of Babel: it pushed the limits but failed. The missing thirty minutes are now being restored, but the film was a ruin for eighty years. Precisely because both the story line and the ideology it was to carry were not fully coherent, it was tempting to use the film as an image repertoire for allegorical representations of industrialization and modernization, of urban alienation and regimentation, of apocalypse and rebirth, of masses and machines, and of permanent mobilization. *Metropolis* has become a cult film known for its striking images, unmoored from story line and politics.

Like Lang's medieval epic *Nibelungen*, the science fiction fantasy of *Metropolis* places war and defeat into a larger narrative—Germany's mythical past in the one case, its futurist modernity in the other. The oversized productions (and the public relations campaigns accompanying them) signal a wish to win at least the cultural war against Germany's former enemies—and especially against Hollywood. The war is retrospectively justified as a war about German values. Whereas the *Nibelungen* ends in death and devastation, *Metropolis* suggests a different solution. When the cold industrialist father is told that workers will ask him "Where are our children?" he has a breakdown and seems to repent. Freed from the threat of unbridled sexuality and devious science (embodied by the robot Maria and the inventor Rotwang, respectively), the community is ready to reconstitute itself. The two films thus comment on their historical moments: the aftershocks of the war registered more strongly in 1924 than they would in 1927. *Metropolis* issued from an economically and politically far more stable postwar environment that even allowed for a brief utopian glimpse of social peace. Nonetheless, the film also intimated that the industrial war machine does not stop beneath the pacified surface.

In contrast, the last years of the Weimar Republic relived the anxieties of the immediate postwar years. The economic insecurity after the stock market crash of 1929 and the astounding gains by the National Socialists (from 12 to 107 seats) in the election of September 1930 radicalized the political scene, and the postwar paranoia returned. The aftershocks reverberated as World War I was revisited in countless war novels, autobiographies, photo collections, and films in 1929–30.

Lang's forced departure from Ufa in 1930 led him to make a low-budget film that dealt no longer with mythical or sci-fi environments, but with the gritty city of Berlin—a city populated by thousands of war cripples, including shell-shocked soldiers who had been released without being fully cured. In *M* (1931), Peter Lorre plays Beckert, a character who fits the profile of a shell-shocked veteran. We learn that he has spent time in a mental institution and that he, like thousands of other shell shock victims, does not have regular employment. Visibly disturbed and with a haunted look, he roams the streets in daylight in search of victims. Acting under a repetition compulsion, he cannot stop killing even though the war is over. At the end of the film, he pleads, "I can't help myself! How I am forced to act. . . . How I must . . . don't want to, must . . . don't want to, must." His is the plight that Freud in 1918 had analyzed as the conflict between "the old ego of peacetime and the war-ego of the soldier."[76] The peace ego does not want to kill, but the war ego must kill (or be killed). This traumatic double bind regularly led conscripted soldiers to mental and somatic breakdowns. We know from Lang's unpublished notebook that he had originally planned to add in Beckert's defense a flashback to the trenches to explain his unconscious compulsion to keep killing.[77] Lang decided against this direct reference to the war and war films proper, and therefore made the film doubly evocative: in *M* war trauma is present, yet invisible.

Lang's last film before fleeing Hitler's Germany once again connected shock-induced insanity with crime. *Das Testament des Dr. Mabuse* (*The Testament of Dr. Mabuse*), a sequel to the two-part *Dr. Mabuse, the Gambler* (1922), was completed in January 1933. It was immediately banned by Goebbels, allegedly out of fear that the power-hungry madman Dr. Mabuse might remind the audience of Hitler.[78] The film begins with a deafening sound montage that recreates what many soldiers described as *Trommelfeuer*, or the unceasing barrage of loud rumbling from artillery fire near and far. *The Testament* also features various instances of shell shock; even the criminal mastermind Dr. Mabuse himself is introduced as a catatonic patient in a mental clinic. We witness Mabuse's alter ego, the psychiatrist and professor Dr. Baum, deliver a lecture to medical students on mental disorders, which he claims are caused by "catastrophes like explosions, earthquakes, and railway crashes." The mind, so the doctor tells his students, reacts to "the impact of fear and terror" with a retreat into insanity. This chilling scene shows that by 1933 the causes and symptoms of shell shock had long since become a subject for academic lectures. At the same time, it demonstrates that Lang felt an urgent need to remind his audience of the unabated presence of trauma in German society. The warning came too late to be heard. *The Testament of Dr. Mabuse* was not shown in Germany until 1951, almost twenty years after its completion.

Conclusion

The next war is almost here, one feels, even without knowing who will start it.

—Thomas Mann, *Diary*, January 8, 1919

I thought the war would never end. And perhaps it never did.

—George Grosz, *An Autobiography*, 1955

Handwritten in white chalk, the word *Ende* concludes G. W. Pabst's 1930 film *Westfront 1918*, Germany's first motion picture explicitly about World War I. "The End" is followed by a large question mark and an even larger exclamation point—conflicting signals that make us uncertain about where things stand. The film is over, but what about the war? Indeed, the question mark makes one wonder whether any lessons were learned. Beyond that, it blurs the distinction between the world of the film and that of the film's audience. Will the traumatic events that we have just witnessed on-screen stay with us as we exit the cinema? Although the exclamation point urgently calls for an end to the violence, the sound of explosions and gunfire that accompanies The End suggests that the war is far from over.

Westfront 1918 opened on May 23, 1930 as one of the first sound films made in Germany. The new interest in realistic accounts of the front lines coincided with the historic shift from silent to sound film, resulting in an enduring synergy between war (or warlike) action movies and the latest sound technology. The addition of sound of course allowed a much more authentic representation of the front experience than any silent film could deliver. *Westfront 1918* not only gave voices to its actors but also reproduced battleground noise, from thundering explosions to howling sirens and screams for help, all with unprecedented faithfulness. Sound also expanded the visible frame; for instance, the piercing whistle of a grenade falling offscreen could not have been rendered in a silent film. Sound penetrated the space of the audience and heightened the narrative's psychological impact.[1]

This new verisimilitude rendered silent cinema's former emphasis on the hypnotic gaze and the symbolism of light and shadow, as well as its preference for allegorical characters anachronistic. Whereas the troubled figures of silent film had often blended into stylized sets and settings, actors in sound film regained the presence of individually inflected speaking voices. The new sound film was also less introspective and subjective; instead it described a soldier's "reality" in accurately staged battle scenes and psychologically credible stories of heroism, love, and loss. The friend-foe polemics based on national stereotypes (still fully evident in Rex Ingram's anti-German film of 1922, *The Four Horsemen of the Apocalypse*) gave way to universalized images of combatants from *all* nations as victims of war. In contrast to silent film heroes, characters in sound film seem less abstract and enigmatic because the voice humanizes them and creates melodramatic empathy. Combat action films rarely depict shell shock's silent suffering and unspeakable pain; they are not interested in the psychological consequences of war that are invisible.

The profusion of war literature in the final years of the Weimar Republic peaked in January 1929 with Erich Maria Remarque's novel *Im Westen nichts Neues* (*All Quiet on the Western Front*) and its movie version a year later. The book's remarkable commercial success—over a million copies were sold in one year—showed the popularity of fictional and autobiographical revisitations of the war, a full ten years after the shock of defeat.[2] Triggered by the economic crisis and unemployment in 1928–29, which demonstrated to most Germans the utter failure of the democratic system, memories of the lost war began to stir up the popular imagination. The Right became obsessed with rewriting the front experience as one of honor and heroism, while the Left tried to revise the failed proletarian revolutionary uprising of 1918–19.[3] Both used war and revolution to understand the present crisis as a reiteration of the misery of the immediate postwar years.

There were only scattered realistic depictions of the war during the Weimar Republic. In 1927, Ufa produced *Der Weltkrieg* (*The World War*), a two-part documentary that mixed original footage from the archive of the Reich's War Ministry with staged reenactments. Its director, Leo Lasko, had written the screenplay for one of the first Ufa propaganda films, *Toward the Light*, in 1918. The dramatic titles of the documentary's two parts, *Des Volkes Heldengang* (*The People's Heroic Call*) and *Des Volkes Not* (*The People's Distress*), alluded to the Nibelungen saga and announced the film's intent to serve as a memorial of a traumatized nation. The reviewers deplored the film's lack of compassion: "Nothing against this attempt to make a movie of this war. The film must be made. There is nothing that concerns us more. But the attempt has to be made by courageous men. One cannot see our destiny from 1914 to 1918 from a position of neutrality, as a good thing for everyone. The dead are still alive."[4]

Soon after, the living memory of the fallen soldiers became a highly contested subject for both sides of Germany's ideological split at the end of the Weimar Republic. For the Right, the war provided an opportunity to serve (and die for) the fatherland; the real essence of a man would manifest itself in the trenches. For the Left, the war was both a crime against the younger generation and a grim result of imperialist politics. The stage was thus set for the tumultuous reception of the first internationally acknowledged antiwar film, imported from a former enemy country but based on Remarque's 1929 novel. Directed by Lewis Milestone and produced by Carl Laemmle's Universal, *All Quiet on the Western Front* opened in Los Angeles in April 1930. In December of the same year, after major censorship battles and severe cuts, it made its Berlin debut and immediately gained notoriety among National Socialists for its supposed defamation of German soldiers. Its antimilitary ideology, Goebbels claimed, was part of a Jewish conspiracy to soil the memory of the war and sully German honor. After systematically interrupting performances, the Nazis organized a protest march of sixty thousand people. Their agitation proved successful; within a week of its first screening, the film was banned by the government as a disturbance to public order.[5]

Goebbels saw the campaign as a crucial victory, boasting that he could take down democracy by its own means—free speech and public protest. The campaign offered a test case in street terror, but more importantly, a poignant demonstration of the inordinate emotional power that inhered in the memory of the war. *All Quiet on the Western Front* confronted the German public with the repressed shame of its military and moral defeat more directly than any other film before, and it is not surprising that the Nazis could capitalize on the film's provocation. It was they who controlled the memory of the war.

This Hollywood version of the German war experience became the prototype for a new genre: the realistic big-budget antiwar film that often glorified combat, male camaraderie, and heroic action, only to end melodramatically with the tragic death of the protagonist. The narrative appeal and emotional impact of Hollywood's classical editing made it hard to comprehend war's deeper meaning beyond the fate of the protagonists.

In 1946, after another world war, Siegfried Kracauer noticed that the brutality and sadism typical of war pictures lived on in Hollywood's "terror films." In exile in New York since 1941, Kracauer noticed a shift in both the postwar American state of mind and the movies that emerged from it. Reviewing such disparate films as *Dark Corner, Shadow of a Doubt, The Stranger,* and *Spellbound*, he found they had one thing in common: a kind of fear and panic that touched "the very core of our existence."[6] With its fifty million casualties, World War II had again consequences far beyond the battlefield. "A civil war is being fought inside every soul," Kracauer writes, "and the movies reflect the uncertainties of that war in the form of general inner disintegration and mental disturbance."[7] Was he writing about American movies after World War II or rather about German cinema after World War I, the subject of his study *From Caligari to Hitler*, which would appear a year later? In 1947, Kracauer's views of Hollywood at the end of World War II echo his readings of post-World War I German films. The remedy for this shell-shocked state of mind might come, Kracauer speculates in 1946, in the form of psychoanalysis or religion. Although he never mentions Weimar cinema, its reverberations are unmistakable.

Film noirs of the 1940s share with shell shock cinema of the 1920s a focus on psychologically troubled characters who have experienced something deeply disturbing in their past. The lost souls of Weimar cinema reappear in film noir as American soldiers returning from the war—shell-shocked, amnesiac, and prone to violence. Gripped by the past, they no longer fit in the present. Repressed traumatic events return suddenly, intruding upon seemingly normal lives. In Fred Zinnemann's *Act of Violence* (1948), a traumatized veteran named Joe seeks revenge upon his former commanding officer Frank, who had betrayed his own men to the Nazis. The shadow of this act falls heavily on Frank's bright new middle-class life, and ultimately he cannot flee from that past. Using stark lighting effects and extreme angles, Zinnemann's noir classic expresses states of paranoia and mental breakdown in the tradition of Weimar's shell shock cinema.

Having killed on the front is one thing—killing someone at home is another. Or is it? Lang's film noir *Human Desire* (1953) addresses the porous border between killing in combat and in civilian life. Viki, the femme fatale in *Human Desire,* wants her lover Karl, a Korean War vet, to kill her husband, arguing that killing during the war should make it easy to do it again. Unable to reintegrate into a civil society that has little interest in them, and plagued by traumatic repetition compulsions, many veterans reenacted the war in the streets and living rooms of film noir.[8] It is no coincidence that some of the most poignant film noirs were made by Weimar filmmakers in exile.

Germany's first feature film after World War II, Wolfgang Staudte's *Die Mörder sind unter uns* (*The Murderers Are among Us*, 1946) picks up on the visual and narrative tradition of Weimar's shell shock cinema, a tradition that had been interrupted during the Third Reich. A traumatized veteran and former physician is unable to forget a mass execution of Polish civilians on Christmas Eve 1944. He attempts to kill his former superior, who was responsible for the crime. The repressed past haunts the present—the shock lives on and is acted out. Other post-traumatic films followed. In 1951, Peter Lorre returned to Germany from his Hollywood exile to direct *Der Verlorene* (*The Lost One*), an extremely dark German film noir in which he cast himself as a serial killer during World War II. He not only replayed his role in *M* as a pathological mass murderer, but also showed war trauma as the cause for his repeated killing. Shot in stark chiaroscuro style of early Weimar cinema, the film offers a narrative of unrelenting postwar melancholia.

The German cinema of the last half-century has been obsessed with characters who try come to grips with a traumatic history by compulsively revisiting and re-enacting it. Many films of the New German Cinema, from Werner Herzog's *Lebenszeichen* (*Signs of Life*, 1967) to Rainer Werner Fassbinder's epic *Berlin Alexanderplatz* (1980) feature protagonists who are haunted by their past. American and other national cinemas are at present similarly preoccupied with post-traumatic narratives that recall the shell shock cinema of the Weimar Republic.[9]

Although the diagnostic terms have changed from shell shock and war neurosis to combat stress reaction and post-traumatic stress disorder, the pain and suffering they stand for have stayed the same. The films that register the mental and emotional aftershocks of recent wars do not differ structurally from the post-traumatic German films that followed World War I. Like them, they show the invisible wounds that remain when war has ended.[10]

Notes

Introduction

1 Reitz's 1984 television mini-series was followed by sequels in 1992 and 2004. The trilogy encompasses a total of thirty episodes, lasting over fifty hours. *Heimat. Eine Chronik in elf Teilen* (*Heimat – A Chronicle of Germany*, 1984) covers the period between 1919 and 1969; *Die Zweite Heimat: Chronik einer Jugend in 13 Filmen* (*Heimat II: A Chonicle of a Generation*, 1992) ranges from the 1960s to 1989; the six-part *Heimat – Chronik einer Zeitwende* (*Heimat, Vol. 3: A Chronicle of Endings and Beginnings*, 2004) addresses events since the fall of the Berlin wall in 1989. On Reitz's *Heimat*, see Anton Kaes, *From Hitler to Heimat: The Return of History as Film* (Cambridge, MA: Harvard University Press, 1989), 161–92.

2 Walter Benjamin, "The Storyteller," in *Walter Benjamin: Selected Writings, Volume 3, 1935–1938*, Edmund Jephcott et al., trans., Michael W. Jennings, ed. (Cambridge, MA: Harvard University Press, 2002), 143–44.

3 "The historian of the future who wishes to report on this war," claimed Ernst Jünger in 1930, "will certainly be more perplexed by the excess than the lack of sources," in "War and Photography," *New German Critique* 59 (1993): 25. Originally published as "Krieg und Lichtbild," in *Das Antlitz des Weltkriegs: Fronterlebnisse deutscher Soldaten*, Ernst Jünger, ed. (Berlin: Neufeld and Henius, 1930), 9–11. The editor of a 1934 history of the war in pictures claims to have made his selection from sixty thousand photographs. See Wilhelm Retz, ed., *Eine ganze Welt gegen uns: Eine Geschichte des Weltkriegs in Bildern* (Berlin: Ullstein, 1934), 11.

4 See Wolfgang Schivelbusch, *The Culture of Defeat: On National Trauma, Mourning, and Recovery*, Jefferson Chase, trans. (New York: Henry Holt and Company, 2003).

5 See Wolfgang J. Mommsen, *Die Urkatastrophe Deutschlands. Der Erste Weltkrieg 1914–1918*, Handbuch der deutschen Geschichte, vol. 17, Jürgen Kocka, ed. (Stuttgart: Klett-Cotta, 2002). See also *Spiegel special* (2004): *Die Ur-Katastrophe des 20. Jahrhunderts.* The following studies de-emphasize the "catastrophe" model and embed the war in the larger framework of modernity: Belinda Davis, "Experience, Identity, and Memory: The Legacy of World War I," *Journal of Modern History* 75 (2003): 111–31; Bruno Thoss, "Die Zeit der Weltkriege—Epochen als Erfahrungseinheit?" in *Erster Weltkrieg—Zweiter Weltkrieg. Ein Vergleich*, Bruno Thoss and Hans-Erich Volkmann, eds. (Paderborn: Schöningh, 2002), 7–30. For the most comprehensive overview, see Gerhard Hirschfeld, Gerd Krumeich, and Irinia Renz, eds., *Enzyklopädie Erster Weltkrieg* (Paderborn: Schöningh, 2003). See also Eric D. Weitz, *Weimar Germany: Promise and Tragedy* (Princeton, NJ: Princeton University Press, 2007).

6 Quoted in Niall Ferguson, *The Pity of War: Explaining World War I* (New York: Basic Books, 2000), 313.

7 In her recent book, *This Republic of Suffering: Death and the American Civil War* (New York: Alfred A. Knopf, 2008), Drew Gilpin Faust speaks of the "work of death" (ix). As the United States "embarked on a new relationship with death" in the Civil War, so did Europe in World War I. Faust's study resonates strongly with the concerns of this book.

8 See Jay Winter, "Shell-shock and the Cultural History of the Great War," *Journal of Contemporary History* 35, no. 1 (January 2000): 11: "The history of shell-shock, properly configured, is not the history of the officer corps, but the history of the war itself." Winter's essay introduces the special issue of the *Journal of Contemporary History* on shell shock. See also Jay Winter, "Shell Shock, Memory, and Identity," in *Remembering War: the Great War between Memory and History in the Twentieth Century* (New Haven, CT: Yale University Press), 52-76.

9 Other films from the period that may be classified as shell shock cinema include Fritz Lang's *Der müde Tod* (*Destiny*, 1920), Leopold Jessner and Paul Leni's *Hintertreppe* (*Backstairs*, 1921), and Robert Wiene's *Orlacs Hände* (*Orlac's Hands*, 1924). Lang's *Dr. Mabuse, der Spieler* (*Dr. Mabuse, the Gambler*, 1922) and *Das Testament des Dr. Mabuse* (*The Testament of Dr. Mabuse*, 1933) are also shell shock films, as is Lang's protonoir thriller, *M* (1931).

10 Slavoj Žižek, *The Sublime Object of Ideology* (London: Verso, 1992), 169.

11 Siegfried Kracauer, *From Caligari to Hitler: A Psychological History of the German Film*, Leonardo Quaresima, rev. ed. (Princeton, NJ: Princeton University Press, 2004). This reprint of the original 1947 book also contains a list of Kracauer's factual errors and updates the bibliography. Kracauer's book appeared in a bowdlerized German translation in 1965 and was retranslated by Karsten Witte in 1979. On the book's reception history, see Christoph Brecht, "Strom

der Freiheit und Strudel des Chaos: Ausblicke auf Kracauers Caligari-buch," in *Im Reich der Schatten: Siegfried Kracauers "From Caligari to Hitler"* (Marbach am Neckar: Deutsche Schillergesellschaft, 2004), 5–52. For a discussion of Kracauer's argument and its consequences for our understanding of Weimar cinema, see Thomas Elsaesser, *Weimar Cinema and After: Germany's Historical Imaginary* (London: Routledge, 2000), 18–60

12 Kracauer, li

13 Ibid.

14 On the concept of back-shadowing, see Michael André Bernstein, *Foregone Conclusions: Against Apocalyptic History* (Berkeley: University of California Press, 1994).

15 See Jan-Christopher Horak, "Exilfilm, 1933–1945," in *Geschichte des deutschen Films*, Wolfgang Jacobsen, Anton Kaes, and Hans Helmut Prinzler, eds. 2nd ed. (Stuttgart: Metzler, 2004), 99–116.

16 See Anton Kaes, *Expressionismus in Amerika: Rezeption und Innovation* (Tübingen: Niemeyer, 1973).

17 These films were exported not only to London, Paris, and Moscow but all over the world. In summer 2008, a complete version of *Metropolis* (with an extra 30 minutes of long-lost footage) surfaced in Buenos Aires.

18 See Lotte H. Eisner, *The Haunted Screen: Expressionism in the German Cinema and the Influence of Max Reinhardt*, Roger Greaves, trans. (Berkeley: University of California Press, 1974). The first edition appeared in French as *L'écran demoniaque* in 1952.

19 On the concepts of "event" and "eventalization," see Michel Foucault, "Questions of Method," in *Power*, James D. Faubion, trans. Robert Hurley et al., eds. (New York: New Press, 1994), 226–28.

20 "To read what was never written" is a quote from Hugo von Hofmannsthal that appears as an epigraph for the chapter on the flâneur in Walter Benjamin, *The Arcades Project*, Howard Eiland and Kevin McLaughlin, trans. (Cambridge, MA: Harvard University Press, 1999), 416. On the concept of "the spoken and the unspoken" in literature, see Pierre Macherey, *Theory of Literary Production* (London: Routledge, 2006), 95–100.

1 The War at Home

1 On the founding of Ufa in 1917, see Klaus Kreimeier, *The Ufa Story: A History of Germany's Greatest Film Company, 1918–1945*, Robert Kimber and Rita Kimber, trans. (New York: Hill and Wang, 1996). The film was advertised as a Union Studio production of the company PAGU, which was one of the two major companies incorporated into the newly founded Ufa. In order to camouflage suspected propaganda, many films were produced by companies that retained their former names, although they were owned by Ufa. The filmmaker, Georg Jacoby, a prolific director who made more than two hundred films (many of them forgettable) in a career that lasted from 1913 to 1960, based his film on a story by Leo Lasko with dialogue by Hans Brennert.

Jacoby had made more than twenty films since the beginning of the war—among others, *Der feldgraue Groschen*, *Die Entdeckung Deutschlands*, and *Jan Vermeulen, der Müller aus Flandern*. These were films that cloaked a patriotic message in different genre conventions, ranging from comedy to science fiction to romance.

2 Charles S. Myers, "A Contribution to the Study of Shell Shock," *Lancet* 1 (1915): 320. See also his book, *Shell Shock in France, 1914–18* (Cambridge: Cambridge University Press, 1940).

3 His book *Die traumatischen Neurosen nach den in der Nervenklinik der Charité in den letzten 5 Jahren gesammelten Beobachtungen* (Berlin: Hirschwald, 1889) was published in a third edition in 1918. See also his book *Die Neurosen infolge von Kriegsverletzungen* (Berlin: Karger, 1916). For an excellent overview and analysis of the debates about war neurosis, see Paul Lerner, *Hysterical Men: War, Psychiatry, and the Politics of Trauma in Germany, 1890–1930* (Ithaca, NY: Cornell University Press, 2003).

4 Alois Alzheimer, *Der Krieg und die Nerven* (Breslau: Preuss and Jünger, 1915), 17. See also Wilhelm Weygandt, "Der Krieg und die Nerven," *Die Umschau* 19 (April 10, 1915), 281-84.

5 For accounts tracing the relationship of traumatic neurosis to war neurosis, see Peter Riedesser and Axel Verderber, *"Maschinengewehre hinter der Front": Zur Geschichte der deutschen Militärpsychiatrie* (Frankfurt am Main: Fischer, 1996); Peter Riedesser and Axel Verderber, *Aufrüstung der Seelen: Militärpsychologie in Deutschland und Amerika* (Freiburg: Dreisam, 1991); Esther Fischer-Homberger, *Die traumatische Neurose: Vom somatischen zum sozialen Leiden* (Bern: Huber, 1975); Günther Komo, *Für Volk und Vaterland: Die Militärpsychiatrie in den Weltkriegen* (Hamburg: Lit, 1992); Karl-Heinz Roth, "Die Modernisierung der Folter in den beiden Weltkriegen. Der Konflikt der Psychotherapeuten und Schulpsychiater um die deutschen 'Kriegsneurotiker' 1914–1945," *1999* 3 (1987): 8–75; Bernd Ulrich, "Nerven und Krieg. Skizzierung einer Beziehung," in *Geschichte und Psychologie*, Bedrich Loewenstein, ed. (Pfaffenweiler: Centaurus-Verlagsgesellschaft, 1992), 163–92; Paul Lerner, "'Ein Sieg deutschen Willens': Wille und Gemeinschaft in der deutschen Kriegspsychiatrie," in *Die Medizin und der Erste Weltkrieg*, Wolfgang Uwe Eckart and Christoph Gradmann, eds. (Pfaffenweiler: Centaurus-Verlagsgesellschaft, 1996), 85–107.

6 See Jay Winter, "Shell-shock and the Cultural History of the Great War," *Journal of Contemporary History* 35, no. 1 (2000): 7–11. On the medical, social, and cultural consequences of shell shock, see also Peter Leese, *Shell Shock: Traumatic Neurosis and the British Soldiers of the First World War* (New York: Palgrave, 2002).

7 Riedesser and Verderber, *Maschinengewehre*, 38.

8 For a detailed account of the discussions among German psychiatrists, see Lerner, *Hysterical Men*; Hans-Georg Hofer, *Nervenschwäche und Krieg: Modernitätskritik und Krisenbewältigung in der östereichischen Psychiatrie,*

1880–1920 (Vienna: Böhlau Verlag, 2004); Andreas Killen, *Berlin Electropolis: Shock, Nerves, and German Modernity* (Berkeley: University of California Press, 2006); Ben Shephard, *A War of Nerves: Soldiers and Psychiatrists in the Twentieth Century* (Cambridge, MA: Harvard University Press, 2001).

9 Marianne Weber, "The Special Cultural Mission of Women," in *The Weimar Republic Sourcebook*, Anton Kaes, Martin Jay, and Edward Dimendberg, eds. (Berkeley: University of California Press, 1994), 197.

10 Carl Zuckmayer, *A Part of Myself*, Richard Winston and Clara Winston, trans. (New York: Harcourt Brace Jovanovich, 1970), 148.

11 *Kriegs-Rundschau* 1 (1914): 43, quoted in Wolfdieter Bihl, ed., *Deutsche Quellen zur Geschichte des Ersten Weltkrieges* (Darmstadt: Wissenschaftliche Buchgesellschaft, 1991), 49.

12 The myth has been questioned because the enthusiasm did not extend to, for instance, the rural parts of Germany, where young men were needed for the harvest. On the "staging" of August 1914, see Jeffrey Verhey, *The Spirit of 1914: Militarism, Myth, and Mobilization in Germany* (Cambridge: Cambridge University Press, 2000).

13 Karl-Heinz Schöps, "Und als der Krieg im vierten Lenz: Brecht and the Two World Wars," in *1914/1939: German Reflections of the Two World Wars*, Reinhold Grimm and Jost Hermand, eds. (Madison: University of Wisconsin Press, 1992), 37–39.

14 Quoted in Hans Barkhausen, *Filmpropaganda für Deutschland im Ersten und Zweiten Weltkrieg* (Hildesheim: Olms, 1982), 21.

15 Hermann Häfker, "Kinematograph und Krieg," *Bild und Film* 4, no. 1 (1914–15): 1. See also Häfker, "Die Aufgaben der Kinematographie in diesem Kriege," in *Dürerbuch* 128, Flugschrift (October 1914): 1–21. In this pamphlet he discusses how the war enables a liberation from the morass of culture (*Kulturschlamm*).

16 Advertisements in *Licht-Bild-Bühne*, August 15, 1914, 3.

17 See *Der Kinematograph*, September 30, 1914.

18 On this distinction, see Friedrich Nietzsche, "Aus dem Nachlaß der 80er Jahre," in *Werke in drei Bänden*, Karl Schlechta, ed. (Munich: Hanser, 1966), 3:837. Thomas Mann elaborates on this chauvinistic opposition in his 1918 treatise *Reflections of a Nonpolitical Man*.

19 "Kriegszustand und Theaterpraxis," *Licht-Bild-Bühne*, August 22, 1914, 1–2.

20 Edgar Költsch, "Die Vorteile durch den Krieg für das Kinotheater," *Der Kinematograph*, October 14, 1914.

21 See Britta Lange, *Einen Krieg ausstellen* (Berlin: Verbrecher Verlag, 2003).

22 See Barkhausen, *Filmpropaganda für Deutschland*, 22.

23 See Wolfgang Mühl-Benninghaus, "Oskar Messters Beitrag zum Ersten Weltkrieg," *Kintop* 3 (1994): 103–15. See also Wolfgang Mühl-Benninghaus, *Vom Augusterlebnis zur Ufa-Gründung: Der deutsche Film im 1. Weltkrieg* (Berlin: Avinus, 2004).

24 Malwine Rennert, "Kriegslichtspiele," *Bild und Film* 4, no. 7–8 (1914–15): 139.

25 See Barkhausen, *Filmpropaganda für Deutschland*, 21–22.
26 "Kriegsabenteuer eines Kino-Operateurs," *Der Kinematograph*, May 12, 1915.
27 Robert Schwobthaler, "Mit der Kino-Kamera in der Schlachtfront! Darstellungen aus dem griechisch-bulgarischen Krieg." *Der Kinematograph*, October 1, 1913.
28 Ibid.
29 Advertisements in *Der Kinematograph*, December 17, 1913.
30 Ibid.
31 Paul Virilio, *War and Cinema: The Logistics of Perception*, Patrick Camiller, trans. (London: Verso, 1989), 39.
32 "Der Mangel an Aktualitäten," *Der Kinematograph*, August 26, 1914.
33 Ibid.
34 E. W., "Das Filmarchiv des Grossen Generalstabs. Was ein Kinooperateur erzählt," *Berliner Tageblatt*, April 1, 1915.
35 There has been much discussion—since 1922—about the status of the attack sequences. Were they authentic or fake? See Roger Smith, "'A Wonderful Idea of the Fighting': The Question of Fakes in 'The Battle of the Somme,'" *Historical Journal of Film, Radio, and Television* 13, no. 2 (1993): 149–68. See also S. D. Badsey, "Battle of the Somme: British War-Propaganda," *Historical Journal of Film, Radio, and Television* 3, no. 2 (1983): 99–115; Nicholas Reeves, "The Power of Film Propaganda: Myth or Reality?" *Historical Journal of Film, Radio, and Television* 13, no. 2 (1993): 181–201; David Culbert, "The Imperial War Museum: World War I Film Catalogue and the 'The Battle of the Somme' Video," *Historical Journal of Film, Radio, and Television* 14, no. 4 (1995): 575–80; Nicholas Reeves, "Cinema, Spectatorship, and Propaganda: 'Battle of the Somme' (1916) and Its Contemporary Audience," *Historical Journal of Film, Radio, and Television* 17, no. 1 (1997): 5–28. We also have the autobiographical account of the cameraman of *The Battle of the Somme*: Geoffrey H. Malins, *How I Filmed the War* (London: H. Jenkens, 1920).
36 Quoted in Rainer Rother, "'Bei unseren Helden an der Somme' (1917): The Creation of a 'Social Event,'" *Historical Journal of Film, Radio, and Television* 15, no. 4 (1995), 525–42. See also Martin Baumeister, "L'effet de réel": Zum Verhältnis von Krieg und Film 1914 bis 1918," in *Krieg und Militär im Film des 20. Jahrhunderts*, Bernhard Chiari et al., eds. (Munich: Oldenbourg, 2003), 239–69; Martin Loiperdinger, "World War I Propaganda and the Birth of the Documentary," in *Uncharted Territory: Essays on Early Non-fiction Film*, Daan Hertogs and Nico de Klerk, eds. (Amsterdam: Stichting Nederlands Filmmuseum, 1998), 25–31.
37 Oswald Spengler, *Der Untergang des Abendlandes*, vol. 2 (Munich: Beck, 1923), 2:122.
38 My., "Die Mobilmachung des Bildes," *Vossische Zeitung*, no. 214 (April 28, 1917): "Germany believes that the decision in this War will be made on the basis of the strength of the sword and the clarity of the cause. Only slowly one begins to recognize that in this life-and-death struggle all weapons, even the

spiritual and moral ones, are needed. Only after two years of war do we now have the first official attempts to make the most important of these weapons, photography and film, part of warfare."

39 Quoted in ibid., 537.

40 Hans Brennert, review of *Bei unseren Helden an der Somme, BZ am Mittag*, January 17, 1917.

41 See Rother, "Bei unseren Helden an der Somme"(note 36).

42 Ibid., 537. Less than twenty years later, Walter Benjamin made a similar observation with regard to photography. The camera, he writes in 1934, "is now incapable of photographing a tenement or a rubbish-heap without transfiguring it. Not to mention a river dam or an electric cable factory: in front of these, photography can only say: How beautiful. . . . It has succeeded in turning abject poverty itself, by handling it in a modish, technically perfect way, into an object of enjoyment." Walter Benjamin, "The Author as Producer," in *Thinking Photography*, Victor Burgin, ed. (London: Macmillan, 1982), 24.

43 Anonymous, "Der Kinematograph als Schießstand," *Die Umschau* 18 (1914): 648.

44 Ibid.

45 Quoted in Kreimeier, *The Ufa Story*, 8.

46 Quoted in Gerald D. Feldman, "Right-Wing Politics and the Film Industry: Emil Georg Stauß, Alfred Hugenberg, and Ufa, 1917–1933," in *Von der Aufgabe der Freiheit*, Festschrift für Hans Mommsen, Christian Jansen, ed. (Berlin: Akademie-Verlag, 1995), 222. On the emergence of the Ufa myth, see Kreimeier, *The Ufa Story*. See also David Welch, "A Medium for the Masses: Ufa and Imperial German Film Propaganda during the First World War," *Historical Journal of Film, Radio, and Television* 6, no. 1 (1986): 85–91.

47 Quoted in Bertolt Brecht, *Trommeln in der Nacht* (Augsburg version, 1922), Berliner Ensemble program 2007, 92.

48 Carl Sternheim, "Ulrike," in *Erzählungen: Auswahlband 3* (Darmstadt: Luchterhand, 1973), 153–54. The short story was originally published by the Kurt Wolff publishing house in 1918, after it had been banned for reasons of obscenity and antimilitarism.

49 Ibid.

50 Stefan Drössler of the Munich Film Museum reconstructed this film, which premiered at the 2008 Berlin Film Festival. Running now 110 minutes and with the original tints, this version incorporates copies from Gosfilmofond Moscow, the Library of Congress, and the Bundesarchiv-Filmarchiv. From censorship cards we know that about a third of the film is missing, due in large part to heavy censorship that cut most of the revolutionary street-fighting scenes. On *Nerves*, see David Bordwell, "Taking Things to Extremes: Hallucinations Courtesy of Robert Reinert," in *Poetics of Cinema* (New York: Routledge, 2008), 263–80.

51 In 1919, the conservative critic Wilhelm Stapel saw the medium itself as the cause for mental instability:

When a child goes one, two, three times a week to the movies, he becomes psychically damaged by the *form* of presentation alone, regardless of content. The cinema may be quite "decent," it may show a program that has no doubt been censored, but the sheer accustoming to the flashing, uttering, twitching images of the flickering screen slowly and surely destroys the psychic and, ultimately, the moral stability of the viewer. . . . Under the influence of cinema, a new psychic type is growing among the people. A human type, which only flutteringly "thinks" in rough, elementary ideas, which allows itself to be ceaselessly carried from impression to impression, which no longer has the capability to make clear and convincing judgments. A human type, which during the revolution has acted disastrously enough, and which, the more generations are shaped by the cinema and its soul-corrupting apparatus, will grow and make its mark on culture (as well as on political culture). *The cinema is constructing a new, spiritually and morally inferior human type*: homo cinematicus. (*Deutsches Volkstum*, 1919, 319–20)

52 *Deutsche Lichtspiel-Zeitung München*, no. 28, July 27, 1919, quoted in program notes for *Nerven*, 58th Internationale Filmfestspiele Berlin 2008.

2 Tales from the Asylum

1 Freud's handwritten text, titled "Memorandum on the Electrical Treatment of War Neurotics," was not published until 1955. See Sigmund Freud, *The Standard Edition of the Complete Psychological Works* (London: Hogarth Press, 1955), 17:211–15. The entire court case is exhaustively documented in K. R. Eissler, *Freud as an Expert Witness: The Discussion of War Neuroses between Freud and Wagner-Jauregg*, Christine Trollope, trans. (Madison, CT: International Universities Press, 1986).

2 The terms are notoriously hard to distinguish. According to Jean Laplanche and J.-B. Pontalis (*The Language of Psycho-Analysis*, Donald Nicholson-Smith, trans. [New York: W. W. Norton, 1973]), neurasthenia generally refers to symptoms of nervousness and fatigue (265); traumatic hysteria (as described by Jean-Martin Charcot) is characterized "by somatic symptoms, particularly paralysis, which appear following a physical trauma—though often after a phase of latency" (469). Laplanche and Pontalis define traumatic neurosis (which most closely resembles war neurosis) as follows: "Type of neurosis in which the appearance of symptoms follows upon an emotional shock generally associated with a situation where the subject has felt his life to be in danger. Such a neurosis manifests itself, at the moment of the shock, in the form of a paroxystic anxiety attack which may provoke states of agitation, stupor or mental confusion" (470). See also Laurence A. Rickels, *Nazi Psychoanalysis* (Minneapolis: University of Minnesota Press, 2002), 1:76–86.

3 See Max Nonne, "Therapeutische Erfahrungen an den Kriegsneurosen in den Jahren 1914 bis 1918," in *Handbuch der ärztlichen Erfahrungen im Weltkriege 1914/18* (Leipzig: J. A. Barth, 1922), 4:1:108–9.

4 Quoted in Eissler, *Freud as an Expert Witness*, 14.
5 Ibid., 15–16.
6 Freud, quoted in ibid., 25.
7 Ibid., 26.
8 Ibid.
9 Ibid., 28.
10 Ibid.
11 Ibid.
12 My analysis is based on the "restored authorized edition" of *The Cabinet of Dr. Caligari* (New York: Kino on Video, 2002). This version follows the German reconstruction by the Bundesarchiv-Filmarchiv.
13 Ernst Simmel, *Kriegs-Neurosen und "Psychisches Trauma": Ihre gegenseitigen Beziehungen dargestellt auf Grund psycho-analytischer, hypnotischer Studien* (Leipzig: Otto Nemnich Verlag, 1918), 25.
14 Freud, *Beyond the Pleasure Principle*, 18:29–30.
15 Ernst Simmel, "War Neuroses and 'Psychic Trauma,'" in *The Weimar Republic Sourcebook*, Anton Kaes, Martin Jay, and Edward Dimendberg, eds. (Berkeley: University of California Press, 1994), 8.
16 Freud, *Beyond the Pleasure Principle*, 18:32.
17 See Maureen Turim, *Flashbacks in Film: Memory and History* (New York: Routledge, 1989).
18 Violating numerous codes of narrative cinema that had become established by 1919, *The Cabinet of Dr. Caligari* has been called "the first self-reflexive filmic work." See Noël Burch and Jorge Dana, "Propositions," *Afterimage* 5 (1974): 44. The film's "archaic" tableau shots and frontality, rejection of verisimilitude in acting, ambiguous handling of "reality" through the mad narrator, and break-up of spatiotemporal continuity defied the conventions of classical Hollywood cinema.
19 Simmel, *Kriegs-Neurosen*, 43.
20 Terry Castle, *The Female Thermometer: Eighteenth-Century Culture and the Invention of the Uncanny* (New York: Oxford University Press, 1995), 144.
21 Sigmund Freud, *The Interpretation of Dreams*, in *The Standard Edition of the Complete Psychological Works* (London: Hogarth Press, 1953), 5:403–4.
22 See Thierry Lefebvre, "Georges Méliès und die Welt der Scharlatane," *Kintop* 2 (1993): 59–65.
23 See Tom Gunning, "The Cinema of Attraction," *Wide Angle* 8, no. 3–4 (1986): 63–70.
24 Tom Gunning, "An Aesthetic of Astonishment: Early Film and the (In)Credulous Spectator," *Art and Text* 34 (1989): 34.
25 Twenty-three years is a number that may self-reflexively refer to the history of film. The period from 1895, when the first film was shown, to 1918, when *Caligari* was written, is exactly twenty-three years.
26 It seems to me that the symbiosis, even synergy, between silent film and other public entertainments is still insufficiently known.

27 On this link, see Raymond Bellour, "Hypnose und Film," in . . . *kraft der Illusion*, Gertrud Koch and Christiane Voss, eds. (Munich: Fink, 2006), 18–38; Boaz Neumann, "Psychoanalyse und Hypnose in der Weimarer Republik," *Tel Aviver Jahrbuch für deutsche Geschichte* 32 (2004), 107–34.
28 See Simmel and Ferenczi on hypnosis as a treatment for shell shock in *Internationale Psychoanalytische Bibliothek*, no. 1 (Leipzig: Internationaler Psychoanalytischer Verlag, 1919).
29 Albert von Schrenck-Notzing, "Die Wachsuggestion auf der öffentlichen Schaubühne," *Archiv für Kriminologie* 72 (1920): 81–110. See also Albert von Schrenck-Notzing, *Materialisations-Phänomene: Ein Beitrag zur Erforschung der mediumistischen Teleplastie* (Munich: Reinhardt, 1914); and von Schrenck-Notzing, "Das Verbot hypnotischer Schaustellungen," *Berliner Klinische Wochenschrift* 47 (November 24, 1919): 1105–8. Wagner-Jauregg's published lecture *Telepathie und Hypnose im Verbrechen* spoke of "the hypnotic plague that has gripped Vienna at the moment." (Vienna: Verlag der Wiener Tagespresse, 1919), 6.
30 Schrenck-Notzing, "Die Wachsuggestion," 81.
31 See also Lang's 1922 film, *Dr. Mabuse, der Spieler* (*Dr. Mabuse, the Gambler*), where hypnosis and mass suggestion are used for criminal purposes. In the film's second part, Dr. Mabuse, in the disguise of psychoanalyst Sandor Weltmann, hypnotizes a lecture hall audience to give it the illusion of seeing a movie. The film shows this mass hallucination as a film within a film.
32 Schrenck-Notzing, "Die Wachsuggestion," 98.
33 Ibid., 99.
34 Sigmund Freud, letter to Martha Bernays, October 21, 1885, in *Letters of Sigmund Freud, 1873–1939*, Ernst L. Freud, ed., Tania Stern and James Stern, trans. (London: Hogarth Press, 1970), 187.
35 See Stefan Andriopoulos, *Possessed: Hypnotic Crimes, Corporate Fiction, and the Invention of Cinema* (Chicago: University of Chicago Press, 2008), 20–6. Jan Goldstein in *Console and Classify: The French Psychiatric Profession in the Nineteenth Century* (Cambridge: Cambridge University Press, 1987) speaks of "the transformation of charlatanism" in the treatment of insanity in the late eighteenth century.
36 See Hans Hennes, "Die Kinematographie der Bewegungsstörungen," *Die Umschau* 15, no. 29 (1911): 605-06; Georges Didi-Huberman, *Invention of Hysteria: Charcot and the Photographic Iconography of the Salpêtrière*, Alisa Hartz, trans. (Cambridge, MA: MIT Press, 2003); Friedrich A. Kittler, *Gramophone, Film, Typewriter*, Geoffrey Winthrop-Young and Michael Wutz, trans. (Stanford: Stanford University Press, 1999), 115-75.
37 See poems by Alfred Lichtenstein and Jakob van Hoddis, among others, who translated the "mad" disjointedness of primitive film into the fragmented and broken form of their poems.
38 E. E. Southard, *Shell-Shock and Other Neuropsychiatric Problems Presented in 589 Case Histories from the War Literature, 1914–1918*. (1919; repr., New York: Arno Press, 1973), 506.

39 R. V. Adkinson, trans., *The Cabinet of Dr. Caligari* (New York: Simon and Schuster, 1972), 90. The book-within-a-book is a classical literary device that foregrounds the act of reading. To use this device in a film may also indicate some underlying tension between reading and watching—a tension that was not foreign to Germany, where high culture has always been associated with reading.

40 Ibid., 91–92.

41 Quoted in Ruth Harris, *Murder and Madness: Medicine, Law, and Society in the Fin-de-siècle* (Oxford: Oxford University Press, 1989), 29; A. Presst, "Hypnotisme et la presse," *Revue de l'hypnotisme* 3 (1889–90): 227.

42 Harris discusses various aspects of this medico-legal debate in *Murder and Madness*.

43 Ernst Simmel, *Psycho-analysis and the War Neuroses*, introduction by Sigmund Freud; Sándor Ferenczi, Karl Abraham, Ernst Simmel, and Ernest Jones, eds. (London: International Psycho-Analytical Press, 1921), 33.

44 Freud, "Introduction" to Simmel, *Psycho-analysis*, 3.

45 Sigmund Freud, *On Aphasia* (New York: International Universities Press, 1953), 62.

46 Oskar Maria Graf, *Wir sind Gefangene* (Munich: List Verlag, 1994), 174–75.

47 Quoted in Matthias Eberle, *World War I and the Weimar Artists: Dix, Grosz, Beckmann, Schlemmer*, John Gabriel, trans. (New Haven, CT: Yale University Press, 1985), 56–57.

48 Ibid., 57.

49 Carl von Ossietzky, preface to Wilhelm Lamszus, *Das Irrenhaus. Visionen vom Krieg. II. Teil* (Hamburg: Pfadweiser-Verlag, 1919), 8–9. There were even autobiographies of malingerers: for instance, Artur Zickler, *Im Tollhause* (Berlin: Buchhandlung Vorwärts Paul Singer, 1919). Zickler, a social democrat and war resister, proudly recounted his time in a mental clinic.

50 Lamszus, *Das Irrenhaus*, 12.

51 Ernst Toller, *I Was a German: The Autobiography of a Revolutionary*, Edward Crankshaw, trans. (New York: Paragon House, 1991), 135–36.

52 Hugo Ball, *Flight out of Time*, Ann Raimes, trans. (Berkeley: University of California Press, 1996), 75. There was also general interest in art produced by the insane at this time. See Hans Prinzhorn, *Bildnerei der Geisteskranken: ein Beitrag zur Psychologie und Psychopathologie der Gestaltung* (Berlin: J. Springer, 1922).

53 John Heartfield and Rudolf Schlichter's assemblage was called "Prussian Archangel." It depicted a life-size puppet with a pig's head and dressed in a military officer's uniform. It was wrapped in a sarcastic poster that read, "I come from heaven, from heaven on high," which is the refrain of a German Chistmas carol. In addition, a sign dangling from the body declared: "In order to fully comprehend this work of art, you should drill daily for twelve hours with a heavily packed knapsack in marching order in the Tempelhof field." The authorities charged the artists with defaming the German army, but the court acquitted them.

54 Quoted in Adkinson, *The Cabinet of Dr. Caligari*, 116.

55 Kracauer, *From Caligari to Hitler*, 65.

56 Ibid., 66–67.

57 See Anton Kaes, "What to Do with Germany? American Debates about the Future of Germany, 1942–1947," *German Politics and Society* 36 (Fall 1995): 130–41.

58 Kracauer, *From Caligari to Hitler*, li.

59 See Theodor W. Adorno et al., *The Authoritarian Personality* (New York: Harper, 1950).

60 The script is now reprinted in *Das Cabinet des Dr. Caligari: Drehbuch von Carl Mayer und Hans Janowitz zu Robert Wienes Film von 1919/20* (Munich: edition text + kritik, 1995), 47–111.

61 See Rudolph Binion, *Hitler among the Germans* (New York: Elsevier, 1976), 5. Hitler's medical records of his four-week stay in Pasewalk from October to November 1918 were destroyed by the Gestapo. Forster, however, managed to give copies to Ernst Weiß, who wrote the novel *Der Augenzeuge* (1940) that is partly based on this material. The novel deals with a patient, "A.H.," who is diagnosed as "hysterically blind" due to shell shock (as opposed to physically blind), but is cured through psychotherapy—with echoes of *Toward the Light* and *The Cabinet of Dr. Caligari*. See also Norman Aechtler, "Hitler's Hysteria: War Neurosis and Mass Psychology in Ernst Weiß's *Der Augenzeuge*," *German Quarterly* 80, no. 3 (Summer 2007): 325–49; Bernhard Horstmann, *Hitler in Pasewalk: Die Hypnose und ihre Folgen* (Düsseldorf: Droste, 2004).

62 Quoted in Binion, *Hitler among the Germans*, 7.

63 Ibid.

64 Ibid., 138.

65 Adolf Hitler, *Mein Kampf. Complete and Unabridged*, Alvin Johnson, trans. (New York: Reynal and Hitchcock, 1939), 266.

66 Ibid., 267.

67 Quoted in Binion, *Hitler among the Germans*, 138.

68 Quoted in Rose-Carol Washton Long, ed., *German Expressionism: Documents from the End of the Wilhelmine Empire to the Rise of National Socialism* (Berkeley: University of California Press, 1993), 162.

69 The simulated trenches in London's Imperial War Museum give a strong sense of the constricted life "six feet under the ground."

70 Robert Wiene, "Expressionismus im Film," *Berliner Börsen-Courier*, July 30, 1922. Reprinted in *Das Cabinet des Dr. Caligari: Drehbuch von Carl Mayer und Hans Janowitz*, 149–52.

71 Gilles Deleuze, *Cinema 1: The Movement-Image*, Hugh Tomlinson and Barbara Habberjam, trans. (Minneapolis: University of Minnesota Press, 1986), 50–51.

72 See Herbert Jhering, an influential film critic who found fault with the motivation of the film: "It is telling that Carl Mayer and Hans Janowitz rendered their photoplay, *The Cabinet of Dr. Caligari*, expressionistically only because it is set in an insane asylum. It opposes the notion of a sick unreality to the notion of a healthy reality. In other words, impressionism concerns the arena in

which one remains accountable, expressionism the area in which one is unaccountable. In other words: insanity becomes the excuse for an artistic idea." Quoted in *The Weimar Republic Sourcebook*, 620.

73 Henri Lefebvre, *The Production of Space*, Donald Nicholson-Smith, trans. (Malden, MA: Blackwell, 1991), 25.

74 Quoted in Stephen Kern, "Cubism, Camouflage, Silence, and Democracy: A Phenomenological Approach," in *NowHere: Space, Time, and Modernity*, Roger Friedland and Deirdre Boden, eds. (Berkeley: University of California Press, 1994), 165.

3 The Return of the Undead

1 Robert Wohl, *The Generation of 1914* (Cambridge, MA: Harvard University Press, 1979), 1.

2 My analysis is based on Kino International's "ultimate DVD edition," which follows the so-called Bologna version, made available by Transit Film in 2007. It is ninety-four minutes long at the correct running speed for silent film (eighteen frames per second). The Bologna version was restored by Luciano Berriatúa for the F. W. Murnau Foundation in cooperation with the Bundesarchiv-Filmarchiv Berlin and the Cinémathèque Française in 2005–6 from a combination of various prints; L'immagine Ritrovata, Bologna, provided the lab work. Berndt Heller reconstructed the original music by Hans Erdmann. See Enno Patalas's report on the various earlier versions in *Filmblatt* 7, no. 18 (2002): 44–49.

3 The film speaks of "Nosferatu" whenever it alludes to vampire lore. The name Nosferatu comes from a legendary vampire figure according to Emily Gerard, *The Land beyond the Forest: Facts and Fancies from Transylvania* (New York: Harper, 1888).

4 Wohl, *Generation of 1914*, 1.

5 See the short story by Jim Shepard, "Flight Officer F.W. Murnau's Fifth Crash, Aircraft Unsalvageable, February 1917," *Southwest Review* 79 (Spring–Summer 1994): 457. Shepard uses a fictive diary to describe Murnau's thoughts and actions as he recovers from the crash.

6 Quoted in Daniela Sannwald, "Ein grosser Unbekannter," in *Friedrich Wilhelm Murnau: Ein Melancholiker des Films*, Hans Helmut Prinzler, ed. (Berlin: Bertz, 2003), 57.

7 The effect of this book was still profound in World War II. It sold 130,000 copies in 1917 and 682,000 in 1940. See Ulrike Brunotte, *Zwischen Eros und Krieg: Männerbund und Ritual in der Moderne* (Berlin: Wagenbach, 2004), 43.

8 See Walter Z. Laqueur, *Young Germany: A History of the German Youth Movement* (New York: Basic Books, 1962), 89: "They had not the slightest doubt of the rightness of the cause they were fighting for."

9 See Richard J. Evans, *Death in Hamburg: Society and Politics in the Cholera Years, 1830–1910* (Oxford: Clarendon Press, 1988).

10 William H. McNeill, *Plagues and Peoples* (New York: Doubleday, 1976), 231.

11 Alfred W. Crosby Jr., *Epidemic and Peace, 1918* (Westport, CT: Greenwood Press, 1976), 160. See also Fred R. Van Hartesveldt, ed., *The 1918–1919 Pandemic of Influenza: The Urban Impact in the Western World* (Lewiston, NY: Edwin Mellen Press, 1992).

12 Langemarck is the German name for the battle generally known as the First Battle of Ypres, also known as "The Massacre of the Innocents of Ypres," or in German "Kindermord von Ypern" (the child murders at Ypres). The most severe casualties were suffered by young volunteer students. On Langemarck and the myth of the heroic youth, see Bernd Hüppauf, "Schlachtenmythen und die Konstruktion des 'Neuen Menschen,'" in *"Keiner fühlt sich hier mehr als Mensch . . .": Erlebnis und Wirkung des Ersten Weltkriegs*, Gerhard Hirschfeld, Gerd Krumeich, and Irina Renz, eds. (Essen: Klartext, 1997), 43–84.

13 Quoted in Bernd Hüppauf, "War and Death: The Experience of the First World War," in *Essays on Mortality*, Mira Crouch and Bernd Hüppauf, eds. (Kensington: University of New South Wales, Faculty of Arts, 1985), 71.

14 See Gerhard Hirschfeld et al., *Die Deutschen an der Somme 1914–1918* (Essen: Klartext, 2006), 7–8.

15 Quoted in Jay Winter, ed., *The Great War and the Shaping of the 20th Century* (London: Studio, 1996), 202.

16 See Heeres-Sanitätsinspektion des Reichswehrministeriums, *Sanitätsbericht über das Deutsche Heer im Weltkriege 1914/18*, vol. 3 (Berlin: E.S. Mittler, 1934), 25.

17 Rainer Maria Rilke, *Wartime Letters of Rainer Maria Rilke, 1914–1921*, Mary Dows Herder Norton, trans. (New York: W. W. Norton, 1940), 18.

18 Sigmund Freud, "Thoughts for the Times on War and Death," in *The Standard Edition of the Complete Psychological Works* (London: Hogarth Press, 1957), 14:289.

19 Ibid., 299.

20 Ibid.

21 Ibid., 290.

22 Ibid., 291.

23 Ibid.

24 Ibid.

25 Quoted in Loy Arnold, Michael Farin, and Hans Schmid, eds., *Nosferatu, eine Symphonie des Grauens* (Munich: Belleville Verlag, 2000), 62.

26 David J. Skal offers a detailed anecdotal history of the legal dispute over the film rights to Stoker's *Dracula* in his *Hollywood Gothic: The Tangled Web of Dracula from Novel to Stage to Screen* (New York: W. W. Norton, 1990). Because Prana, the German production company, failed to obtain permission to use the novel as the basis for its film (although the film states that it is a free adaptation of *Dracula*), Stoker's widow, Florence, sued the company to stop the film's distribution. She had hoped for a more lucrative stage adaptation. Years of legal wrangling ensued, even after Prana had gone bankrupt and the film had been shown all over Europe. In 1924, the court decided in her favor

and ordered all extant prints destroyed. Luckily, two years after the film's premiere, sufficient prints were in circulation outside Germany to make the verdict meaningless.

27 Eric J. Leed, *No Man's Land: Combat and Identity in World War I* (Cambridge: Cambridge University Press, 1979). The high likelihood of death made soldiers desire it, as Siegfried Sassoon stated: "As for me, I had more or less made up my mind to die; the idea made things seem easier" (quoted in ibid., 22).

28 Paul Barber, *Vampires, Burial, Death: Folklore and Reality* (New Haven, CT: Yale University Press, 1988), 2.

29 Ibid., 3.

30 The location shooting took place in August 1921, while the indoor shots were filmed in Berlin in October and November 1921. It was presented to the censorship board in Berlin in December 1921 and approved (but not for children).

31 Sigmund Freud, "General Theory of the Neuroses," in *The Standard Edition of the Complete Psychological Works* (London: Hogarth Press, 1963), 16:294–95.

32 Victor Sjöström's 1921 Swedish film *Körkarlen* (*The Phantom Carriage*), released in 2007 in a restored version, pioneered the use of double exposure and in-camera visual effects, portraying the unseen reality of death as the coachman of a phantom carriage that collects the souls of the recently deceased. Murnau quotes the motif of the phantom carriage in his film *Phantom*, which opened at the end of 1922, approximately eight months after *Nosferatu*. Here a simpleminded clerk and amateur poet is hit by the carriage of a wealthy woman. He experiences a shock that results in hallucinations and flashbacks, seeing the world around him in a radically new way. The Danish filmmaker Carl Theodor Dreyer, who worked for Ufa in the 1920s, adapts the vampire motif in his *Vampyr—der Traum des Allan Gray* (*Vampyr—the Dream of Allan Gray*, 1931–32).

33 Train journeys and their rapid point-of-view shifts have also been linked to the experience of early movies. See Lynne Kirby, *Parallel Tracks: The Railroad and Silent Cinema* (Durham, NC: Duke University Press, 1997).

34 For instance, Klaus Kinski in Werner Herzog's remake of Murnau's film, titled *Nosferatu—Phantom der Nacht* (1979) and Willem Dafoe in E. Elias Merhige's *Shadow of the Vampire* (2000). The latter film's premise is that Murnau's Nosferatu was played by an actor named Max Schreck (*Schreck* means "terror" in German), who was not playing a vampire but actually was a vampire. Max Shreck [sic] is also the name of a villain (played by Christopher Walken) in *Batman Returns* (1992).

35 Dix, who volunteered in 1915, fought in the battle of the Somme in 1916 and was wounded. In 1917 he was sent to the eastern front, then back to the western front, where he was part of the spring offensive. In 1924 he finished a collection of fifty prints, etchings, and drawings, titled *Krieg* (*War*), that shows images of death and dying in the trenches, of battles and destruction. See Dietrich Schubert, *Otto Dix—Der Krieg. 50 Radierungen von 1924* (Marburg: Jonas Verlag, 2002).

36 Hermann Broch, *The Sleepwalkers*, Willa Muir and Edwin Muir, trans. (New York: Universal Library, 1947), 350. I thank Stefan Andriopoulos for the reference.

37 Johannes Haas, letter, November 27, 1915, reprinted in Philipp Witkop, ed., *German Students' War Letters*, A. F. Wedd, trans. (New York: E. P. Dutton, 1929), 205.

38 Peter Stallybrass and Allon White, *The Politics and Poetics of Transgression* (Ithaca, N.Y.: Cornell University Press, 1986).

39 Alfred Döblin, *Journey to Poland*, Joachim Neugroschel, trans. (New York: Paragon, 1991), 81.

40 Jürgen Müller speculates that *Nosferatu* responds to the nationalists' call in 1920 for a plebiscite on the question of whether Germany should stop Eastern Jews from immigrating. He shows that Galeen's script contained several anti-Semitic motifs that Murnau either dropped or attenuated. See Müller, "Der Vampir als Volksfeind: Friedrich Wilhelm Murnaus '*Nosferatu*': Ein Beitrag zur politischen Ikonografie der Weimarer Zeit," *Fotogeschichte* 19, no. 72 (1999): 51.

41 Walter Liek, *Der Anteil des Judentums am Zusammenbruche Deutschlands: Flugblatt aus Deutschlands Erneuerung* (Munich: Lehmann, 1919). For a summary and concise analysis, see George L. Mosse, *The Jews and the German War Experience, 1914–1918*, Leo Baeck Memorial Lecture 21 (New York: Leo Baeck Institute, 1977). See also "'Der Jude' als Todesmetapher des 'politischen Körpers' und der Kampf gegen die Zersetzung des nationalen 'Überlebens,'" in *Die Konstruktion der Nation gegen die Juden*, Peter Alter, Claus-Ekkehard Bärsch, and Peter Berghoff, eds. (Munich: Fink, 1999), 159–72.

42 Houston Stewart Chamberlain (1855–1939), a British-born Germanophile writer, who married Richard Wagner's daughter in 1908 and became a German citizen in 1916, was one of the most prolific evangelists of Aryan racial superiority. After several books on Wagner, he published his two-volume, twelve-hundred-page work, *Die Grundlagen des 19. Jahrhunderts (Foundations of the Nineteenth Century)* in 1899; by 1922 it was in its fourteenth edition. His perniciously anti-Semitic ideas about race and the German nation endeared him to Hitler, who visited him several times in Bayreuth.

43 Artur Dinter, *Die Sünde wider das Blut: ein Zeitroman*, 16th ed. (Leipzig: Matthes und Trost, 1920), 276–77.

44 Adolf Hitler, *Mein Kampf* (Boston: Houghton Mifflin, 1943), 1:358. For numerous further examples, see Alexander Bein, "Der jüdische Parasit," *Vierteljahrshefte für Zeitgeschichte* 13 (April 1965): 121–49.

45 Alexander Granach, *There Goes an Actor*, Willard Trask, trans. (Garden City, NY: Doubleday, 1945), 275. The autobiography ends in 1919. Granach died in 1949.

46 Ibid., 160.

47 On the system of stereotypical signifiers, see Sander Gilman, *Difference and Pathology: Stereotypes of Sexuality, Race, and Madness* (Ithaca, NY: Cornell University Press, 1985).

48 Mark S. Micale, *Approaching Hysteria: Disease and Its Interpretations* (Princeton, NJ: Princeton University Press, 1995), 286. See Elaine Showalter, *The Female Malady: Women, Madness, and English Culture, 1830–1980* (New York: Pantheon Books, 1985).
49 Josef Breuer and Sigmund Freud, *Studies on Hysteria*, in *The Standard Edition of the Complete Psychological Works* (London: Hogarth Press, 1955), 2:247.
50 Nina Auerbach, quoted in Micale, *Approaching Hysteria*, 294.
51 Elisabeth Bronfen, *Over Her Dead Body: Death, Femininity, and the Aesthetic* (New York: Routledge, 1992), 385.
52 Sigmund Freud, *The Interpretation of Dreams*, in *The Standard Edition of the Complete Psychological Works* (London: Hogarth Press, 1953), 4:149.
53 Sigmund Freud, "Formulations on the Two Principles of Mental Functioning," in *The Standard Edition of the Complete Psychological Works* (London: Hogarth Press, 1958), 12:225. In the "Preliminary Communication" of their joint *Studies on Hysteria* of 1895, Breuer and Freud suggest that "hysterics suffer mainly from reminiscences" (2:7), or as Freud claims in 1900, from "fantasies erected on the basis of memories" (5:491).
54 On the interrelationship between Caspar David Friedrich and Murnau, see Brigitte Peucker, *Incorporating Images: Film and the Rival Arts* (Princeton, NJ: Princeton University Press, 1995), 39–41. See also Kenneth S. Calhoon, "Leinwand: Zur Physiognomie des Raums in Murnau's *Nosferatu*," in *Raumkonstruktionen in der Moderne*, ed. Sigrid Lange (Bielefeld: Aeisthesis Verlag, 2001), 289–97.
55 S. An-ski, *Der Dybbuk: Dramatische Legende in vier Akten*, Arno Nagel, trans. (Berlin: Winz, Verlag Ost und West, 1921). Another edition is An-ski, *Zwischen zwei Welten (der Dybbuk)*, Rosa Nossig, trans. (Berlin: Harz, 1922). See also Michal Waszynski's Yiddish film *Der Dybbuk*, which is an adaptation of the popular play. The film was shot in Poland and released in the United States in 1938.
56 See Alfred Döblin, "Deutsches und Jüdisches Theater," in *Kleine Schriften*, Heinz Graber, ed. (Freiburg: Olten, 1985), 1:362–67. See also Peter Sprengel, *Scheunenviertel-Theater: Jüdische Schauspieltruppen und jiddische Dramatik in Berlin*, 1916–18 (Berlin: Gesellschaft für Theatergeschichte, 1995); Peter Sprengel, *Populäres jüdisches Theater in Berlin von 1877 bis 1933* (Berlin: Haude und Spener, 1997), 126–28.
57 See Nicolas Abraham, "Notes on the Phantom: A Complement to Freud's Metapsychology," in *The Shell and the Kernel: Renewals of Psychoanalysis*, Nicolas Abraham and Maria Torok, eds. (Chicago: University of Chicago Press, 1994), 171–76.
58 Wilhelm Stekel, *Impotence in the Male: The Psychic Disorders of Sexual Function in the Male*, Oswald H. Boltz, trans. (New York: Boni and Liveright, 1927), 175. See also Magnus Hirschfeld, *Sittengeschichte des Weltkrieges*, 2nd ed. (Leipzig: Verlag für Sexualwissenschaft Schneider, 1930); George L. Mosse, *Nationalism and Sexuality: Respectability and Abnormal Sexuality in Modern*

Europe (New York: Howard Fertig, 1985); Jason Crouthamel, "Male Sexuality and Psychological Trauma: Soldiers and Sexual Disorder in World War I and Weimar Germany," *Journal of the History of Sexuality* 17, no.1 (January 2008): 60–84.

59 Stekel, *Impotence in the Male*, 176.

60 Sigmund Freud, "The Uncanny," in *The Standard Edition of the Complete Psychological Works* (London: Hogarth Press, 1955), 17:241–42.

61 Ibid., 242.

62 Ernst Jünger, *Storm of Steel*, Michael Hofmann, trans. (London: Penguin Books, 1961), 1.

63 Hero Hellich, letter to his parents, December 1916, reprinted in Philipp Witkop, ed., *German Students' War Letters*, A.F. Wedd, trans. (New York: E. P. Dutton, 1929), 300. Hellich was killed that same month. He was twenty years old. See also Herbert Jahn, July 5, 1915: "It is strange that for a long time I have been constantly thinking of being killed, though I have really no belief in premonitions" (ibid., 178). Jahn was killed April 10, 1916. He was twenty-five. This collection in English translation is a shorter version of the German edition: Philipp Witkop, ed., *Kriegsbriefe gefallener Studenten* (Munich: G. Müller, 1928). Witkop made his selection from twenty thousand letters, "placed at his disposal by relatives and friends of the fallen, through the German Ministry of Education" (Wedd, introduction to *German Students' War Letters*, v).

64 Leed, *No Man's Land*: *Combat and Identity in World War I* (Cambridge: Cambridge University Press, 1979), 129.

65 On heightened suggestibility and hallucinations in the trenches, see Peter Berz, "The Angels," in *HardWar/SoftWar: Krieg und Medien 1914 bis 1945*, Martin Stingelin and Wolfgang Scherer, eds. (Munich: Fink, 1991), 13–29.

66 E. H. Gombrich, *Shadows: The Depiction of Cast Shadows in Western Art* (New Haven, CT: Yale University Press, 1995), 55.

67 See Marina Warner, *Phantasmagoria: Spirit Visions, Metaphors, and Media into the Twenty-first Century* (New York: Oxford University Press, 2006); Terry Castle, *The Female Thermometer: Eighteenth-Century Culture and the Invention of the Uncanny* (New York: Oxford University Press, 1995).

68 Maxim Gorky, "The Lumière Cinematograph," in *The Film Factory*, Richard Taylor, ed. (Cambridge, MA: Harvard University Press, 1988), 25. See also Tom Gunning, "Animated Pictures: Tales of Cinema's Forgotten Future," *Michigan Quarterly Review* 34 (Fall 1995): 465–85; Laura Mulvey, "Uncertainty: Natural Magic and the Art of Deception," in *Death 24x a Second: Stillness and the Moving Image* (London: Reaktion Books, 2006), 33–53.

69 See Victor I. Stoichita's *A Short History of the Shadow* (London: Reaktion Books, 1997) about the self-reflexive use of the shadow in *Nosferatu*: "The proof that this meta-aesthetical interpretation is formulated in the story is only given to the viewer at the end of the film, at the very moment when the first rays of light falling on Bremen annihilate Nosferatu, and the lights are turned on in the projection room and the screen is once again white" (152).

70 Tom Gunning, "Phantom Images and Modern Manifestations: Spirit Photography, Magic Theater, Trick Films, and Photography's Uncanny," in *Fugitive Images: From Photography to Video*, Patrice Petro, ed. (Bloomington: Indiana University Press, 1995), 42–43. See also Gunning's brilliant analysis of the status of ghosts in cinema, referencing *Nosferatu's* phantomic polyp scene, in his article "To Scan a Ghost: The Ontology of Mediated Vision," *Grey Room* 26 (Winter 2007): 94–127, esp. 94–100; and his earlier article "Ghosts, Photography, and the Modern Body," in *The Disembodied Spirit*, Alison Ferris, ed. exhibition catalog (Brunswick, ME: Bowdoin College, 2003), 8–19. On spirit photography, see Rolf H. Krauss, *Beyond Light and Shadow: The Role of Photography in Certain Paranormal Phenomena: An Historical Survey* (Tucson: Nazraeli Press, 1995); *The Perfect Medium: Photography and the Occult*, exhibition catalog (New Haven, CT: Yale University Press, 2005); Martyn Joly, *Faces of the Living Dead: The Belief in Spirit Photography* (London: British Library, 2005); Silke Arnold-de Simine, "Lichtspiel im Königreich der Schatten: Geisterphotographie und Vampirfilm," in *Dracula Unbound: Kulturwissenschaftliche Lektüren des Vampirs*, Christian Begemann, Britta Herrmann, and Harald Neumeyer, eds. (Freiburg: Rombach, 2008).

71 See Klaus Kreimeier, Antje Ehmann, and Jeanpaul Goergen, eds., *Geschichte des dokumentarischen Films in Deutschland*, vol. 2, *Die Weimarer Republik* (Stuttgart: Reclam, 2006), 95.

72 Paracelsus, also known as Theophrastus Bombastus von Hohenheim, was a sixteenth-century physician, alchemist, and astrologer. He was considered a heretic by the church because he argued that a life-giving spirit united the universe as one coherent organism—hence the difference between a plant and a human being was insignificant. The cosmos for him was a wealth of symbols that needed to be interpreted as God's "language." A human being was not an autonomous subject or ruler over nature but always already imbricated in, and subject to, nature. The goal for a Paracelsian doctor was to see the correspondences between human life and nature, and therefore to respect both human beings and nature. The violent acts of war ran against the grain of his worldview. Ellen's reprimand of Hutter (the first sentence she utters), "Why have you killed the beautiful flowers?" betrays a deeply Paracelsian sentiment. On Paracelsus as "semiotician," see Hartmut Böhme, *Natur und Subjekt* (Frankfurt am Main: Suhrkamp, 1988), 55–60. Paracelsus was made popular by Erwin Guido Kolbenheyer's widely read trilogy *Die Kindheit des Paracelsus* (Munich: Langen/Müller, 1917), followed by *Das Gestirn des Paracelsus* (Munich: Langen/Müller, 1921), and *Das Dritte Reich des Paracelsus* (Munich: Langen/Müller, 1930). Friedrich Gundolf also devoted a study to him: *Paracelsus* (Berlin: Bondi, 1927). In his essay "To Scan a Ghost," Gunning places Bulwer in the tradition of romantic scientists like J. W. Ritter, who wrote, "Where then is the difference between the parts of an animal, of a plant, of a metal, and of a stone—are they not all members of the cosmic-animal, of Nature?" (96).

73 Freud, The Uncanny, 247.
74 Ibid., 250–51.
75 Ibid., 244.
76 Sigmund Freud, "Mourning and Melancholia," in *The Standard Edition of the Complete Psychological Works* (London: Hogarth Press, 1957), 14:243.
77 Georg Simmel, "The Ruin," in *Georg Simmel, 1858–1918*, Kurt H. Wolff, ed. (Columbus: Ohio State University Press, 1959), 261.
78 Philippe Hamon, *Expositions: Literature and Architecture in Nineteenth-Century France*, Katia Sainson-Frank and Lisa Maguire, trans. (Berkeley: University of California Press, 1992), 62.
79 Aros, "Kunst oder Nichtkunst—das ist die Frage!" *Film-Echo* (supplement to *Berliner Lokal-Anzeiger*), no. 10 (March 6, 1922). See also Aros, "Das Fest des Nosferatu," *Deutsche Lichtspiel-Zeitung*, no. 10 (1922): 11: "But before the guests were allowed to enjoy 'Jazz' and 'Shimmy,' they had to endure the movie—the 'Symphony of Horror.' Whoever did not brace themselves with strong nerves, still felt shivers afterwards, in the chaos of the dance, run down their spines."
80 *Nosferatu* and the vampire film genre in general have acquired camp status in the last eight decades, as dozens of Dracula films testify, ranging from Tod Browning's 1931 *Dracula* with Bela Lugosi and Terence Fisher's 1966 *Dracula: Prince of Darkness* with Christoper Lee to Francis Ford Coppola's 1992 *Bram Stoker's Dracula* with Gary Oldman. Like good vampires, these films all feed on each other, despite historically significant variations. Horror films often quote from *Nosferatu* (for instance, *Scream 2*), while television tends to spoof it—for example, *The Simpsons*' "The Treehouse of Horror IV" or *Buffy the Vampire Slayer*. On *Nosferatu: Phantom der Nacht* (*Nosferatu: the Vampyre*), Werner Herzog's influential 1979 remake with Klaus Kinski as Nosferatu and the music of Popol Vuh, see S. S. Prawer, *Nosferatu: Phantom der Nacht* (London: BFI, 2004).

4 Myth, Murder, and Revenge

1 The sign, which survived the Allied bombing in World War II and still puzzles visitors to the Reichstag, is a multilayered historical document. The oversize letters were cast from the molten iron of two cannons seized during the Wars of Liberation in 1813–14. The Jewish owners of the S. A. Loevy foundry, which was commissioned to cast the letters, had to flee Hitler after 1933. See the catalog to the exhibition: *"Dem Deutschen Volke": Die Geschichte der Berliner Bronzegießer Loevy* (Berlin: Jüdisches Museum Berlin, 2003).
2 My analysis follows Kino on Video's restored two-disc version of *Die Nibelungen* (*Siegfried*, 143 minutes, and *Kriemhild's Revenge*, 148 minutes) from 2002. This version is based on the restoration by the Munich Film Museum and includes the original 1924 orchestral score. The Murnau Foundation is presently preparing a new, further improved restoration of the film.
3 On the reception history of the *Nibelungenlied* in the Weimar Republic, see Günter Hess, "Siegfrieds Wiederkehr: Zur Geschichte einer deutschen My-

thologie in der Weimarer Republik," *Internationales Archiv für Sozialgeschichte der deutschen Literatur* 6 (1981): 112–44; Frank G. Gentry, "Die Rezeption des Nibelungenliedes in der Weimarer Republik," in *Das Weiterleben des Mittelalters in der deutschen Literatur*, James F. Poag and Gerhild Scholz-Williams, eds. (Königsstein: Athenäum, 1983), 142–56; see also Herfried Münkler and Wolfgang Storch, *Siegfrieden: Politik mit einem deutschen Mythos* (Berlin: Rotbuch-Verlag, 1988). The film was also advertised by means of picture-cards placed in packs of cigarettes: each pack of cigarettes contained a card with a still from the film; the collector pasted them into a blank book supplied by the cigarette company. Constantin Cigaretten-Fabrik introduced its Nibelungen album of 1928 as follows:

> To us today the world turns with rapid speed. Daily, even hourly, the images change; we confront new facts, new experiences. Thus the wave of time rushes over us, pulls us along. Only short moments of breathing are given to us for self-reflection and concentration. Then we look back, examine, compare what generations before us have experienced. This educates, steels us and encourages us. We see history through the eyes of the poets. And there a word shoots up like a flame: Nibelungen Distress, Nibelungen Loyalty. German destiny centuries ago, German destiny still today. This is the reason why Fritz Lang's masterful film gripped our heart. We saw as if in a mirror our fortune and our misfortune and our—soul. The Constantin company wants to keep the memory of the artistic experience alive. It also wants to stimulate the old joy, the quiet enjoyment of devoted collecting. That is why it offers this album to the world with the most beautiful pictures from the Nibelungen film.

These albums were still being given away in the 1940s.

4 The most famous Middle High German epic, the *Nibelungenlied* was composed by an anonymous writer around 1200 in the region between Passau and Vienna. Combining several Germanic and Nordic sagas from oral tradition, the epic depicts the defeat of the Burgundians by the Huns in the fifth century. There is a large literature on the reception of the Nibelungen saga in Germany over the last two hundred and fifty years. See Christian Kiening and Cornelia Herberichs, "Fritz Lang: *Die Nibelungen* (1924)," in *Mittelalter im Film*, Christian Kiening and Heinrich Adolf, eds. (Berlin: de Gruyter, 2006), 189–225.

5 Czeschka, who like Lang was born in Vienna, was a graphic designer for the magazine *Jugend* and a scenarist for Reinhardt as well as a major representative of the Viennese Jugendstil. See also Heide Schönemann, *Fritz Lang: Filmbilder, Vorbilder* (Berlin: Edition Hentrich, 1992).

6 Thea von Harbou, *Das Nibelungenbuch* (Munich: Drei Masken Verlag, 1924). There are major differences between this novel and the film. The novel concentrates on Kriemhild and thus reverses the order of the film: it begins with Kriemhild's decision to marry Attila to avenge Siegfried's murder. The life and death of Siegfried are told in a long flashback. There are scenes in the book

(for instance, two appearances of Siegfried's ghost) that are missing from the film, whereas other, cinematically striking scenes (for example, the flowering tree morphing into a skeletal death head) are Lang's invention. See also Stanley R. Hauer, "The Sources of Fritz Lang's *Die Nibelungen*," *Literature/Film Quarterly* 18, no. 2 (1990): 103–10.

7 Fritz Lang, "Worauf es beim Nibelungen-Film ankam," in *Die Nibelungen: Programmheft* (Berlin: Ufa, February 14, 1924), 12.

8 The lineage was already established by Arzen von Cserépy's widely acclaimed and popular historical film, *Fridericus Rex*, whose four parts played between January 1921 and March 1923. One can safely assume that these nationalist costume films prepared the ground for Lang's *Nibelungen*.

9 Thea von Harbou, "Vom Epos zum Film," in *Reklame-Broschüre der Ufa-Decla*, 1924, 9.

10 Anonymous, *Paul Richter: Jung-Siegfried, der Held* (Vienna: "Mein Film" Buch- und Zeitungsverlag, 1925), 39–40.

11 See Iris Wigger, *Die "Schwarze Schmach am Rhein": Rassistische Diskriminierung zwischen Geschlecht, Klasse, Nation und Rasse* (Münster: Westfälisches Dampfboot, 2007); Margaret Pawle, *The Watch on the Rhine: The Military Occupation of the Rhineland, 1918–1930* (London: Palgrave Macmillan, 2007).

12 *Siegfried-Drehbuch*, Collection Adalbert von Schlettow. Quoted with permission from Filmmuseum-Deutsche Kinemathek.

13 Béla Balázs, *Der sichtbare Mensch oder die Kultur des Films* (Vienna: Deutsch-österreichischer Verlag, 1924), 32–33. Fritz Victor Meier argues in "Der nordische Mensch als das Kunstideal aller Zeiten" (*Schönheit: Familiensinn und Rassenpflege* 20, no. 12 [1924]: 541–42) that precisely because of their leadership role, blond Nordic types were decimated in the war.

14 See Richard Dyer, *White* (London: Routledge, 1997), 207.

15 In "Die Tarzan-Epidemie" (*Eckart* 1 [October 1924]: 21–22), Otto Koischwitz reports that the popularity of the translated novels was such that even a parody had appeared in German. After denigrating the reading public's bad taste, the author attempts to account for the phenomenal success of the Tarzan books in Germany (four volumes appeared in 1924 alone): "It is not only sensationalism that is satisfied but also, if only darkly unconscious and debased, the dreamlike longing of an epoch that is tired of culture (*kulturmüde*)." He speaks of "an epoch that seeks in fantasy liberation, denied in real life, from the pressures of a prison-like culture," an epoch that "lends the natural and unmediated life of animals and savages as its spiritual ideal."

16 Hans Surén, *Der Mensch und die Sonne* (Stuttgart: Dieck and Co., 1924). See also the telling titles of his subsequent, increasingly racist books: *Volkserziehung im dritten Reich: Manneszucht und Charakterbildung* (Stuttgart: Frankhsche Verlagshandlung, 1934); *Gymnastik der Deutschen: Rassenbewusste Selbsterziehung und Charakterbildung* (Stuttgart: Frankhsche Verlagshandlung, 1938).

17 See S. Goltermann, *Körper der Nation: Habitusformierung und die Politik des Turnens 1860–1890* (Göttingen: Vandenhoeck and Ruprecht, 1998).

18 Ben Brewster and Lea Jacobs, *Theatre to Cinema* (New York: Oxford University Press, 1997), 85–98.

19 See Sabine Hake, "Architectural Hi/Stories: Fritz Lang and *The Nibelungs*," *Wide Angle* 12, no. 3 (July 1990): 38–57; see also Schönemann, *Fritz Lang*.

20 Lang thanked Otto Hunte, the set designer, for having constructed the film's forest like a cathedral. See Lang, "Worauf es beim Nibelungen-Film ankam," 12.

21 Anonymous [Julius Langbehn], *Rembrandt als Erzieher. Von einem Deutschen* (Leipzig: C. L. Hirschfeld, 1890).

22 See Franz Servaes, "Der Wille zum Stil," *Die Neue Rundschau* 16 (1905): 105–11.

23 See Sebastian Weber, "Anonymer Expressionismus," afterword to Wilhelm Worringer, *Abstraktion und Einfühlung: ein Beitrag zur Stilpsychologie* (1908; repr., Amsterdam: Verlag der Kunst, 1996), 193–206.

24 Fritz Lang, "Stilwille im Film," in *Fritz Lang, die Stimme von Metropolis*, Fred Gehler and Ullrich Kasten, eds. (Berlin: Edition Hentrich, 1992), 163.

25 See also Walter Gropius's "Program for the State Bauhaus in Weimar," published in April 1919 as a four-page leaflet whose title page contained a woodcut (*Cathedral*) by Lyonel Feininger: "Let us then create a new guild of craftsmen without the class distinctions that raise an arrogant barrier between craftsman and artist! Together let us desire, conceive, and create the new structure of the future, which will embrace architecture and sculpture and painting in one unity and which will one day rise toward heaven from the hands of a million workers like the crystal symbol of a new faith." Quoted in Hans Wingler, *The Bauhaus: Weimar, Dessau, Berlin, Chicago* (Cambridge, MA: MIT Press, 1978), 31.

26 See Frieda Grafe, "Für Fritz Lang. Einen Platz, kein Denkmal," in *Fritz Lang*, Frieda Grafe, Enno Patalas, and Hans Helmut Prinzler, eds. (Munich: Hanser, 1976), 59: "When the Nibelungen film was created, the ornamental was fashionable. It stood for the interdependence and connections within the world of objects which were just beginning to be recognized. . . . For Lang the ornamental is a stage in the exploration of film as a medium, a possibility of fusing the interior with exterior space."

27 Quoted in Konrad Wünsche, *Bauhaus: Versuche, das Leben zu ändern* (Berlin: Wagenbach, 1989), 13.

28 Fritz Lang, "Arbeitsgemeinschaft im Film," *Der Kinematograph*, February 17, 1924. Reprinted in *Fritz Lang, die Stimme von Metropolis*, 166.

29 Quoted in Münckler and Storch, *Siegfrieden*, 86.

30 Ibid., 87.

31 For an image of the Hermannsschlacht monument and reflections on Hermann's pose, see Hinrich C. Seeba, "Raising the Sword: On the Construction of the Heroic Subject," *Daidalos* 49 (September 1993): 37–51. In the liberation wars of the early nineteenth century, fighting a dragon was associated with fighting Napoleon. The first Nibelungen edition was published in 1807, the first year of the Napoleonic occupation. The raised sword visualized the call to arms of the heroic subject.

32 Contemporary German television often presents the *Nibelungen* as a matinee on religious holidays like Easter or Christmas.

33 In 1931, a nineteenth-century guardhouse in Berlin (Neue Wache) was redesigned and rededicated to the memory of the fallen German soldier. In 1993, it was renamed the "Central Memorial of the Federal Republic of Germany for the Victims of War and Tyranny."

34 See Reinhart Koselleck, "Kriegerdenkmale als Identitätsstiftungen der Überlebenden," in *Identität*, Odo Marquard and Karlheinz Stierle, eds. (Munich: Fink, 1979), 255–76. Further work dealing with the question of memorials to the fallen soldiers includes Dietrich Schubert, "Das 'harte Mal' der Waffen oder Darstellung der Kriegsopfer. Aspekte der Visualisierung der Gefallenen nach 1918," in *Mo(nu)mente: Form und Funktion ephemerer Denkmäler*, Michael Diers, ed. (Berlin: Akademie-Verlag, 1993); Sabine Behrenbeck, "Zwischen Trauer und Heroisierung. Vom Umgang mit Kriegstod und Niederlage nach 1918," in *Kriegsende 1918: Ereignis, Wirkung, Nachwirkung*, Jörg Duppler and Gerhard P. Groß, eds. (Munich: Oldenbourg, 1999), 315–75. See also George L. Mosse, *Fallen Soldiers: Reshaping the Memory of the World Wars* (New York: Oxford University Press, 1990).

35 Oskar van der Pernt, "Bildhauer Professor Josef Müllner," *Der getreue Eckart* 4 (1927): 410. Quoted in Margarete Grandner, Gernot Heiß, and Elisabeth Klamper, "Im Kampf um das Haupt des deutschen Helden Siegfried," *Forum* (December 1990): n.p. See also the extensive documentation of the 1990 controversy over the proposal to replace the Siegfried bust with commemorative plaques, in Ulrike Davy and Thomas Vasek, *Der "Siegfried-Kopf": Eine Auseinandersetzung um ein Denkmal in der Universität Wien* (Vienna: Universitätsverlag, 1991).

36 Davy and Vasek, *Der "Siegfried-Kopf,"* 12.

37 Joseph Goebbels, *Siegfrieds Tod: Broschüre als Reklameanleitung* (Berlin, 1933), n.p. Significantly, the second part of the film, which shows Kriemhild's revenge ending in self-destruction, was kept locked away. The "will to form" and the emphasis on the mass ornament continues in Leni Riefenstahl's 1936 propaganda film *Triumph des Willens* (*Triumph of the Will)*, much as the myth of the beautiful, battle-ready body lives on in her 1938 two-part *Olympia*. Goebbels's Ufa sent out the following letter to school directors in Germany: "Dear Director: Ufa has always made it a task to contribute to the national education of the German youth in school. Therefore we bring back the first part of the wonderful and unforgettable film of the Nibelung saga, *Siegfried's Death*. This masterwork, which won over all of Germany already some years ago, is in its grandeur and beauty bound to deepen a yearning in German youth for German heroism" (ibid.).

38 Quoted in Rolf Aurich, Wolfgang Jacobsen, and Cornelius Schnauber, eds., *Fritz Lang: Leben und Werk, Bilder und Dokumente* (Berlin: Jovis, 2001), 23.

39 Ibid., 25.

40 Ibid.

41 Ibid., 26.
42 Ibid., 28.
43 Ingmar Bergman's *The Seventh Seal* alludes to Lang's pictorial representation of Death in *Destiny*.
44 R. Buchwald, afterword to *Der heilige Krieg: Gedichte aus dem Beginn des Kampfes* (Leipzig: Eugen Diederichs, 1914), n.p.
45 General Friedrich von Bernhardi, *Britain as Germany's Vassal*, J. Ellis Barker, trans. (London: W. M. Dawson, 1914).
46 Werner Jansen, *Das Buch Treue: Nibelungenroman* (Hamburg: Jansen, 1917). Significantly, new editions of this novel appeared in 1929, 1939, and 1940. In 1916, a collection of German legends and myths dealing with "German loyalty" was published: Anton Ohorn, ed., *Das goldene Buch von deutscher Treue: Erzählungen aus deutscher Sage und Geschichte* (Berlin: Phönix-Verlag, 1916).
47 Quoted in Münkler and Storch, *Siegfrieden*, 74.
48 Herbert Jhering, *Von Reinhardt bis Brecht* (Berlin: Aufbau, 1959), 2:477. His review first appeared on May 1, 1924.
49 In *The Cabinet of Dr. Caligari*, Cesare also predicts that Alan will die at dawn.
50 Quoted in Wolfgang Schivelbusch, *The Culture of Defeat: On National Trauma, Mourning, and Recovery*, Jefferson Chase, trans. (New York: Henry Holt and Company, 2003), 211.
51 Ibid., 212.
52 Ibid., 201.
53 See the detailed explanation for this nonevent in Michael Geyer, "Insurrectionary Warfare: The German Debate about a *Levée en Masse* in October 1918," *Journal of Modern History* 73 (September 2001): 459–527.
54 Of course, this difficulty did not keep the Nazis from instrumentalizing it in an hour of crisis. Immediately following the Battle of Stalingrad, as part of the final mobilization of all resources and in an attempt to preserve the authority of the Hitler regime, Hermann Göring invoked the images of the Burgundians in the burning hall. "We all know a powerful hero's tale of a battle without equal, it is called 'The Battle of the Nibelungen.' They too stood in a hall consumed by fire, quenched their thirst with their own blood, but they fought to the last man. Such a battle rages there today, and in a thousand years every German will still speak of this battle, shuddering with awe and recall that despite everything, Germany gained its victory there." Quoted in Münckler and Storch, *Siegfrieden*, 103.
55 On the ceremonial form of this downfall, see Jan-Dirk Müller, *Spielregeln für den Untergang: Die Welt des Nibelungenliedes* (Tübingen: Niemeyer, 1998).

5 The Industrial Battlefield

1 See Kurt Flasch, *Die geistige Mobilmachung: Die deutschen Intellektuellen und der Erste Weltkrieg: ein Versuch* (Berlin: Fest, 2000).
2 My analysis is based on the 2004 version of *Metropolis*, which was the result of decades of restoration work by Enno Patalas of the Munich Film Museum and

Martin Koerber of the Filmmuseum Berlin. The U.S. version is identical to the German except for translated intertitles. I quote from the intertitles of the Kino version except when they are imprecise or incomplete. I also consulted the "critical edition" of the film, produced by Patalas and his students at the Universität der Künste Berlin, which fills in the lost parts with quotes from the screenplay and available still photos. In summer 2008, large parts of the missing footage, believed lost for eighty years, were found in the Museo del Cine in Buenos Aires. This full-length version offers new scenes that flesh out subplots and minor characters. It also provides more footage of apocalyptic deluge and destruction. It appears that a forthcoming "Buenos Aires version" is likely to further illustrate my argument. On the sensational discovery of the lost footage, see the *Metropolis* issue of *Zeit-Magazin* 28 (July 3, 2008): 10–33.

3 Oswald Spengler, *The Decline of the West*, Charles Francis Atkinson, trans. (New York: Knopf, 1926), 2:503. The German title *Der Untergang des Abendlandes* means, more literally translated, "The Downfall of the Occident."

4 Ibid., 2:504.

5 Ibid.

6 See Albert Renger-Patzsch's photo books *Die Welt ist schön* (Munich: K. Wolff, 1928), and *Eisen und Stahl* (Berlin: H. Reckendorf, 1930).

7 Spengler, *The Decline of the West*, 2:505.

8 Ibid.

9 Ibid.

10 See, for instance, Michael Minden and Holger Bachmann, eds., *Fritz Lang's* Metropolis: *Cinematic Visions of Technology and Fear* (Rochester, NY: Camden House, 2000).

11 This is borne out by the sizable fictional and nonfictional oeuvre von Harbou produced before she met Lang. Between 1910 and 1920 she published more than a dozen novels, short stories, and essays, including *Der Krieg und die Frauen* (*The War and Women*, 1913) and *Die deutsche Frau im Weltkrieg* (*The German Woman in World War*, 1916). In her 1915 novel *Der unsterbliche Acker. Ein Kriegsroman* (*The Immortal Field. A War Novel*), written in the tradition of nineteenth-century "blood and soil" fiction, she points out that her book is appearing only a hundred days into the war between the peoples; thus it can only give a few chords of the "gargantuan melody" that will be heard in the future. "To rewrite the history of the Great War—to rewrite because it is its own best writer—and to place the experience of individuals into the story of the war as an uplifting and devastating event, is a task that is reserved for the chosen few (*die Auserwählten*)." She declares further: "An army can be beaten—a people (*Volk*) never. And whoever has experienced the first hundred days of this Great War of the German Reich, knows: It's the common people that go to war and it's the *Volk* that will bring home the victory. Therefore this book will be nothing more than a ballad of the German people." Thea von Harbou, *Der unsterbliche Acker* (Berlin: Cotta, 1915), 5–6. The book ends with the

farmer Hannes looking westward at an endless column of marching soldiers who sing "Lieb Vaterland, magst ruhig sein (Dear Fatherland, rest easy)!" This gives Hannes confidence: "They will make it—they or their brothers." The novel concludes with this sentence: "And over the earth, which the sword defends, goes the plow" (230). Von Harbou joined the Nazi party in 1932 and kept writing film scripts. On her career in the 1920s, see Reinhold Keiner, *Thea von Harbou und der deutsche Film bis 1933* (Hildesheim: Olms, 1984).

12 Quoted in Peter Bogdanovich, *Fritz Lang in America* (New York: Praeger, 1967), 124.

13 Filippo Tommaso Marinetti, *Let's Murder the Moonshine: Selected Writings*, R. W. Flint and Arthur A. Coppotelli, trans. (Los Angeles: Sun and Moon Classics, 1991), 63.

14 See Anson Rabinbach, *The Human Motor: Energy, Fatigue, and the Origins of Modernity* (Berkeley: University of California Press, 1992).

15 Ernst Jünger, "Der Kampf als inneres Erlebnis," in *Sämtliche Werke* (Stuttgart: Klett-Cotta, 1980), 7:102.

16 Ernst Jünger, "Die Technik in der Zukunftsschlacht," *Militär-Wochenblatt*, October 1, 1921, 288.

17 For a historical account from the nineteenth century to World War I, see Daniel Pick, *War Machine: The Rationalization of Slaughter in the Modern Age* (New Haven, CT: Yale University Press, 1993).

18 Ernst Jünger, "Feuer und Blut: Ein kleiner Ausschnitt aus der großen Schlacht," quoted in Jeffrey Herf, *Reactionary Modernism: Technology, Culture, and Politics in Weimar and the Third Reich* (Cambridge: Cambridge University Press, 1984), 79. See also Manfred Maengel, *Das Wissen des Kriegers oder Der Magische Operateur: Krieg und Technik im Frühwerk von Ernst Jünger* (Berlin: Xenomos, 2005).

19 Ernst Jünger, *Copse 125: A Chronicle from the Trench Warfare of 1918* (New York: Howard Fertig, 2003), 21. Originally published as *Das Wäldchen 125* in 1930.

20 Jünger, "Feuer und Blut," in *Sämtliche Werke*, I: 450.

21 Henry Ford, *My Life and Work* (New York: Doubleday, Page and Co., 1923); it appeared in German as *Mein Leben und Werk*, Curt Thesing and Marguerite Thesing, trans. (Leipzig: Paul List Verlag, 1923). The publisher advertised it with the following blurb: "Every thinking person, whether manager or worker, must read this book." This volume was followed by more German translations: Henry Ford, *Das grosse Heute und das grössere Morgen* (Leipzig: Paul List Verlag, 1926), and *Philosophie der Arbeit* (Dresden: Paul Aretz Verlag, 1929). The last chapter of the 1929 book is titled "The Machine—the New Messiah."

22 Ford, *My Life*, 105.

23 Ibid., 108.

24 Ibid., 209.

25 See also Friedrich von Gottl-Ottlilienfeld, *Fordismus: Über Industrie und technische Vernunft* (Jena: Gustav Fischer, 1926). This was the third edition. The

much-discussed second edition appeared in 1924, the year that Lang and von Harbou began working on the script for *Metropolis*. Von Gottl-Ottlilienfeld gives a historical overview from Frederick Winslow Taylor to Ford and claims that the entire world has fallen under the spell of "technical reason." See also Philipp Gassert, "'Without Concessions to Marxist or Communist Thought': Fordism in Germany, 1923–1939," in *Transatlantic Images and Perceptions: Germany and America since 1776*, David E. Barclay and Elisabeth Glaser-Schmidt, eds. (Washington, DC: German Historical Institute, 2003), 217–42.

26 For instance, in Reinhard Johannes Sorge's *Der Bettler* (1911) or Walter Hasenclever's *Der Sohn* (1913).

27 Karl Marx, *Capital: A Critique of Political Economy, Vol. 1*,. Ben Fowkes, trans. (1976; repr., New York: Penguin Classics, 1990), 552.

28 In his expressionist poem "Ophelia" (1911), Georg Heym evokes Moloch as an apocalyptic image of the modern city. Charlie Chaplin alludes to this motif in a more playful, fairy-tale-like way in his film *Modern Times*, made in 1935, when the machine he operates first devours him and then spits him out.

29 Fritz Kreisler, *Four Weeks in the Trenches* (New York: Houghton Mifflin, 1915), 54–55.

30 Walter Benjamin, "The Storyteller: Observations on the Works of Nikolai Leskov," in *Walter Benjamin, Selected Writings, Vol. 3 (1935–1938)*, Michael W. Jennings, ed. (Cambridge, MA: Harvard University Press, 2002), 144.

31 Jünger edited a coffee-table book in 1931, titled *Der gefährliche Augenblick* (The Dangerous Moment), which assembles pictures of accidents, crashes, and devastation. On the link between war and the senses, see Julia Encke, *Augenblicke der Gefahr: Der Krieg und die Sinne. 1914–1934* (Munich: Fink, 2006).

32 Mendelsohn published a book of photographs from this trip: *Amerika. Bilderbuch eines Architekten* (Berlin: Mosse, 1928).

33 Fritz Lang, "Was ich in Amerika sah: Neuyork [*sic*]–Los Angeles," *Film-Kurier* 292, December 11, 1924.

34 Bertolt Brecht, *Gesammelte Werke* (Frankfurt am Main: Suhrkamp, 1967), 17:10.

35 Gottfried Benn, "Inquiry," *Transition* 13 (1928): 251–52. Reprinted in Benn, *Gesammelte Werke* (Wiesbaden: Limes, 1968), 2218.

36 Adolf Halfeld, *Amerika und der Amerikanismus: Kritische Betrachtungen eines Deutschen und Europäers* (Jena: Eugen Diederichs Verlag, 1927).

37 See Stanley Corngold, "The Great War and Modern German Memory," in *The Cambridge Companion to the Literature of the First World War*, Vincent Sherry, ed. (Cambridge: Cambridge University Press, 2005), 191–217.

38 See the exhaustive documentation of this architectural contest: Florian Zimmermann, ed., *Der Schrei nach dem Turmhaus: Der Ideenwettbewerb Hochhaus am Bahnhof Friedrichstrasse Berlin 1921/22* (Berlin: Argon, 1988). See also Dietrich Neumann, *Die Wolkenkratzer kommen: Deutsche Hochhäuser der Zwanziger Jahre. Debatten, Projekte, Bauten* (Braunschweig: Vieweg, 1995). German architects, among them Walter Gropius, Bruno Taut, Brothers Luck-

hardt, and Hans Scharoun, also participated in the *Chicago Tribune*'s skyscraper contest of 1922.

39 See Ulrich Conrads and Hans G. Sperlich, *Phantastische Architektur* (Stuttgart: Gerd Hatje, 1960); Dietrich Neumann, ed., *Film Architecture: Set Designs from Metropolis to Blade Runner* (New York: Prestel, 1996).

40 Fritz Lang, "The Future of the Feature Film in Germany," in *The Weimar Republic Sourcebook*, 623.

41 Siegfried Kracauer, "Über den Expressionismus: Wesen und Sinn einer Zeitbewegung. Abhandlung," in *Werke. Frühe Schriften aus dem Nachlass*, Inka Mülder-Bach, ed. (Frankfurt am Main: Suhrkamp, 2004), 9.2:9.

42 In Lang's 1922 film *Dr. Mabuse, the Gambler,* a countess asks Mabuse at a cocktail party: "Tell me Doctor, what is Expressionism?" Mabuse replies: "It's a game."

43 See Harro Segeberg, "Simulierte Apokalypsen: Georg Kaisers 'Gas'-Dramen im Kontext expressionistischer Technik-Debatten," in *Literatur in einer industriellen Kultur*, Götz Großklaus and Eberhard Lämmert, eds. (Stuttgart: Cotta, 1989), 294–313.

44 Kracauer, "Über den Expressionismus," 74.

45 See http://architecture.about.com/library/bl-libeskind-statement.htm. On the Tower of Babel, see Ulrike B. Wegener, *Die Faszination des Maßlosen: Der Turmbau zu Babel von Pieter Bruegel bis Athanasius Kircher* (Hildesheim: Olms, 1995). See Hanna Strzoda, "Berlin—Babylon," in *Babylon: Mythos*, Moritz Wullen and Günter Schauerte, eds. (Berlin: Staatliche Museen, 2008), 215–24.

46 See Robert Koldewey, *Das wieder erstehende Babylon: Die bisherigen Ergebnisse der deutschen Ausgrabungen*, 4th ed. (Leipzig: J. C. Hinrichs, 1925). For context, see Joachim Marzahn, "Die deutschen Ausgrabungen in Babylon," in *Babylon: Wahrheit*, Joachim Marzahn and Günther Schauerte, eds. (Berlin: Staatliche Museen, 2008), 67–78.

47 "Was wir in Metropolis erlebten," *Film-Kurier* 263, November 7, 1925.

48 Walter Benjamin, "Theses on the Philosophy of History," in *Illuminations*, Hannah Arendt, ed., Harry Zohn, trans. (New York: Schocken Books, 1968), 261.

49 See Miriam Hansen, *Babel and Babylon: Spectatorship in American Silent Film* (Cambridge, MA: Harvard University Press, 1994).

50 Fritz Lang, "Ausblick auf Morgen. Zum Pariser Kongress," *Lichtbild-Bühne*, September 25, 1926, 1.

51 Elias Canetti, *The Torch in My Ear*, Joachim Neugroschel, trans. (New York: Farrar, Straus and Giroux, 1982), 245. The incident triggered Canetti's book-length meditation on the power of the masses in *Crowds and Power*, Carol Stewart, trans. (New York: Farrar, Straus and Giroux, 1984).

52 Heimito von Doderer, *The Demons*, Richard Winston and Clara Winston, trans. (New York: Knopf, 1961), 1261.

53 Le Bon's book of 1895 was translated into German in 1908 as *Psychologie der Massen*, Dr. Rudolf Eisler, trans. (Leipzig: W. Klinkhardt, 1908). On Le Bon and

his context, see Susanna Barrows, *Distorting Mirrors: Visions of the Crowd in Late Nineteenth-Century France* (New Haven, CT: Yale University Press, 1981). See also Serge Moscovici, *The Age of the Crowd: A Historical Treatise on Mass Psychology* (Cambridge: Cambridge University Press, 1985); Helmut König, *Zivilisation und Leidenschaften: Die Masse im bürgerlichen Zeitalter* (Hamburg: Rowohlt, 1992). It may not be a coincidence that 1895 marked the beginning of cinema and the publication of the first major book on mass psychology.

54 Ernst Jünger, *Der Arbeiter* (Hamburg: Hanseatische Verlagsanstalt, 1932), 115.

55 Ibid., 120.

56 Marianna Torgovnick, *Primitive Passions: Men, Women, and the Quest for Ecstasy* (New York: Alfred A. Knopf, 1997), 14.

57 Jakob Walcher, *Ford oder Marx: Die praktische Lösung der sozialen Frage* (Berlin: Neuer Deutscher Verlag, 1925).

58 Max Weber, "Science as a Vocation," in *From Max Weber: Essays in Sociology*, H. H. Gerth and C. Wright Mills, trans. and eds. (New York: Oxford University Press, 1946), 153.

59 Erich von Kahler, *Beruf der Wissenschaft* (1920), quoted in Klaus Schreiner, "'Wann kommt der Retter Deutschlands?': Formen und Funktionen von politischem Messianismus in der Weimarer Republik," *Saeculum* 49, no. 1 (1998): 127. See also Roger Dadoun, "*Metropolis*: Mother-City—'Mittler'—Hitler," Arthur Goldhammer, trans., *Camera Obscura: A Journal of Feminism, Culture, and Media Studies* 15 (1986): 137–63.

60 Auguste Villiers de L'Isle-Adam, *Die Eva der Zukunft*, Hanns Heinz Ewers, trans. (Munich: Thespis Verlag, 1920). See Annette Michelson, "On the Eve of the Future: The Reasonable Facsimile and the Philosophical Toy," *October* 29 (Summer 1984), 3–21; see also Raymond Bellour, "Ideal Hadaly," Stanley E. Gray, trans., *Camera Obscura* 15 (1986), 110–35.

61 Reprinted in Minden and Bachmann, *Fritz Lang's Metropolis*, 94.

62 See Ernst Bloch, "Occult Fantasticality and Paganism," in *Heritage of Our Times*, Neville and Stephen Plaice, trans. (Berkeley: University of California, 1990), 168–78. See also Ernst Bloch, "Die Angst des Ingenieurs," in *Gesamtausgabe* (Frankfurt am Main: Suhrkamp, 1965), 9:347–58.

63 See Peter Sloterdijk, "Artificial Limbs. Functionalist Cynicisms II: On the Spirit of Technology," in *Critique of Cynical Reason*, Michel Eldred, trans. (Minneapolis: University of Minnesota Press, 1987), 443–59. See also Klaus Theweleit, "The Soldierly Body, the Technological Machine, and the Fascist Aesthetic," in *Male Fantasies*, Erica Carter and Chris Turner, trans. (Minneapolis: University of Minnesota Press, 1989), 2:197–206; Mia Fineman, "Ecce Homo Prostheticus," *New German Critique* 76 (Winter 1999): 85–114. For a contemporary account of the importance of the hand for the industrial process (and a mechanical hand is the ultimate allegory for it), see Fritz Giese, *Die Psychologie der Arbeitshand* (Berlin: Urban und Schwarzenberg, 1928). Also note the motif of severed hands in the 1924 film *Orlacs Hände* (*Orlac's Hands*) by Robert Wiene. Orlac is a world-famous pianist whose hands were

amputated after a railway crash; because they are replaced with transplants from an executed murderer, his hands cannot stop killing. A further variation on the loss of limb, prothesis, and the decline into violent insanity, is *Mad Love* (Karl Freund, 1935) with Peter Lorre.

64 Revelation 18:2–3, 18:16–17, in *New Oxford Annotated Bible* (New York: Oxford University Press, 2007). In Alfred Döblin's city novel, *Berlin Alexanderplatz*, which he began writing in 1927, the Whore of Babylon is invoked six times.

65 The numbers vary between 30 and 60 percent. If Europe had approximately eighty million inhabitants in the mid-fourteenth century, the number killed by the plague would be around fifty million. See O. J. Benedictow, *The Black Death, 1346–1353: The Complete History* (Woodbridge, UK: Boydell Press, 2004).

66 Susan Sontag, "The Imagination of Disaster," in *Against Interpretation and Other Essays* (New York: Farrar, Straus and Giroux, 1986), 212.

67 Quoted in Minden and Bachmann, *Fritz Lang's* Metropolis, 67.

68 Ibid., 68.

69 See Siegfried Kracauer's essay "The Mass Ornament," which appeared in the *Frankfurter Zeitung* on June 9 and 10, 1927: "The structure of the mass ornament reflects that of the entire contemporary situation. Since the principle of the *capitalist production process* does not arise purely out of nature, it must destroy the natural organisms that it regards either as a means or as resistance. Community and personality perish when what is demanded is calculability." Siegfried Kracauer, *The Mass Ornament: Weimar Essays*, Thomas Y. Levin, ed. and trans. (Cambridge, MA: Harvard University Press, 1995), 78.

70 Walter Benjamin, "The Work of Art in the Age of Its Technological Reproducibility," in Walter Benjamin, *Selected Writings 1938-40*, Howard Eiland and Michael W. Jennings, eds., Edmund Jephcott et al., trans. (Cambridge, Mass.: Harvard University Press, 2003), 4:282: "In great ceremonial processions, giant rallies, and mass sporting events, and in war, all of which are now fed into the camera, the masses come face to face with themselves. . . . In general, mass movements are more clearly apprehended by the camera than by the eye. A bird-eye view best captures assemblies of hundreds of thousands. . . . This is to say that mass movements, including war, are a form of human behavior especially suited to the camera."

71 In 2008, the Internet Movie Database listed approximately a hundred films in which *Metropolis* is featured, referenced, or spoofed. In 2001, *Metropolis* was included as the first film in the UNESCO's Memory of the World Register. See also the animated version, titled *Meoroposiu* in the original Japanese, and *Metropolis* in its American release. *Terminator 3: Rise of the Machines* (2003) with Arnold Schwarzenegger may be seen as a contemporary riff on *Metropolis*.

72 See also Friedrich Zelnik's film *Die Weber*, based on the naturalist play by Gerhart Hauptmann. It opened in May 1927, just a few months after *Metropolis*.

73 Eugen Tannenbaum, "Der Großfilm," in *Der Film von Morgen*, Hugo Zehder, ed. (Berlin: Kämmerer, 1923), 63 (emphasis added).

74 R. E. Sherwood, "The Silent Drama: Metropolis," *Life* 89 (March 4, 1927): 24. See also Randolph Bartless, "German Film Revision Upheld as Needed Here," *New York Times*, March 13, 1927, reprinted in Minden and Bachmann, *Fritz Lang's* Metropolis, 89–90.

75 Her novel was published by August Scherl Verlag (owned by the nationalist media mogul Alfred Hugenberg) in 1926. In the same year, a shortened paperback version (194 instead of 274 pages) with eight images from the film also appeared. See also the English translation: Thea von Harbou, *Metropolis* (Norfolk, VA: Donning Company Publishers, 1988).

76 Sigmund Freud, introduction to Sandor Ferenczi, Karl Abraham, Ernst Simmel, and Ernest Jones, *Psycho-analysis and the War Neuroses*, (Vienna: International Psycho-analytical Press, 1921), 3.

77 Anton Kaes, *M* (London: BFI, 2001), 68.

78 *The Testament of Dr. Mabuse* opened in Budapest and Vienna in April and May 1933.

Conclusion

1 See Helmut Lethen "'Knall an sich': Das Ohr als Einbruchsstelle des Traumas," in *Modernität und Trauma*, Inka Mülder-Bach, ed. (Vienna: Edition Parabasen, 2000), 192–210; Julia Encke, *Augenblicke der Gefahr*, 111–93.

2 See Michael Gollbach, *Die Wiederkehr des Weltkrieges in der Literatur: Zu den Frontromanen der späten Zwanziger Jahre* (Kronberg: Scriptor Verlag, 1978); Hans-Harald Müller, *Der Krieg und die Schriftsteller: Der Kriegsroman der Weimarer Republik* (Stuttgart: Metzler, 1986).

3 Representative works from the Right include Franz Schauwecker's *Aufbruch der Nation* (1930), Werner Beumelburg's *Die Gruppe Bosemüller* (1930), Josef Magnus Wehner's *Sieben vor Verdun* (1930), and Hans Zöberlein's *Der Glaube an Deutschland* (1931). Influential antiwar novels include (besides Remarque's 1929 *All Quiet on the Western Front*) Ludwig Renn's *Krieg* (1928), Siegfried Kracauer's *Ginster: von ihm selbst geschrieben* (1928), and Edlef Köppen's *Heeresbericht* (1930).

4 Bernhard von Brentano, *Wo in Europa ist Berlin?* (Frankfurt am Main: Insel, 1928), 86. On *Der Weltkrieg*, see Ofer Ashkenazi, "The Incredible Transformation of Dr. Bessel: Alternative Memories of the Great War in German War Films of the Late 1920s," *History and Memory* 20–21 (Spring–Summer 2008): 121–52, especially 129–35.

5 See Bärbel Schrader, ed., *Der Fall Remarque: Im Westen nichts Neues: eine Dokumentation* (Leipzig, Reclam 1992). See also the autobiographical account by Hanns Brodnitz, the owner of the theater that showed *All Quiet on the Western Front*, in Brodnitz, *Kino Intim. Eine vergessene Biographie*. Jüdische Memoiren, vol. 14, Hermann Simon, ed. (Teetz, Germany: Hentrich und Hentrich, 2005). I thank Gero Gandert for this reference.

6 Siegfried Kracauer, "Hollywood's Terror Films: Do They Reflect an American State of Mind?" *New German Critique* 89 (Spring/Summer, 2003), 111. First published in *Commentary* 2 (1946), 132-36.

7 Ibid.

8 Postwar disillusionment that turned into antagonism toward American society itself can be found in, among many other film noirs, in *Cornered, The Blue Dahlia, Dead Reckoning,* and *Ride the Pink Horse.*

9 See, for instance, Thomas Elsaesser, *Melodrama and Trauma: Modes of Cultural Memory in the American Cinema* (New York: Routledge, forthcoming) or Nurith Gertz and George Khleifi, *Palestinian Cinema: Landscape, Trauma, and Memory* (Bloomington: Indiana University Press, 2008).

10 A recent study shows that currently about one in every five U.S. soldiers suffers from post-traumatic stress. Three hundred thousand out of the 1.6 million deployed in Iraq and Afghanistan have mental health problems. See Terri Tanielian and Lisa H. Jaycox, eds. *Invisible Wounds of War: Psychological and Cognitive Injuries, Their Consequences, and Services to Assist Recovery* (Santa Monica: Rand Corporation, 2008). See also Sue Halperin, "Virtual Iraq: Using Simulation to Treat a New Generation of Traumatized Veterans," *The New Yorker*, May 19, 2008, 32–37.

Weimar Cinema on DVD

The following list contains films made in Germany between 1919 and 1933 that are currently available on DVD. Film titles listed in both German and English indicate that the film is available with subtitles or intertitles in English. While the large majority of the DVDs are NTSC format, some are PAL (region 0 or 2). German DVD's in PAL are shown as "G," British as "UK." German editions are listed only when no U.S. or UK edition exists or if the German version differs significantly.

Die Abenteuer des Prinzen Achmed / The Adventures of Prince Achmed

Lotte Reiniger, 1926

DVD: Image Entertainment (2002), 67 min. Reconstructed version. German intertitles with English subtitles, optional English voice-over. Extras: 1921 animated advertising trailer for *The Secret of the Marquise*; documentary on Reiniger by Katja Raganelli (1999, 64 min.); stills gallery.

DVD (UK): BFI Video (2001), 66 min. PAL, region 2.

Anders als die Andern / Different from the Others

Richard Oswald, 1919

DVD: Kino on Video (2004), 50 min. English intertitles only.

DVD (G): Edition Filmmuseum (2007), 51 min. PAL, region 0. German intertitles with English subtitles. Includes short documentary on the history of the film, documents by Magnus Hirschfeld, and a letter exchange between directors Richard Oswald and Veit Harlan. Includes *Gesetze der Liebe: Schuldlos geächtet! / Laws of Love: Innocently Outlawed!* (see below).

Anna Boleyn/Anna Boleyn (aka _Deception_)
Ernst Lubitsch, 1920
DVD: Kino on Video (2006), 100 min. Restored version. English intertitles only. Features image gallery; Lubitsch filmography.

Asphalt/ Asphalt
Joe May, 1929
DVD: Kino on Video (2006), 93 min. Restored version. English intertitles only.
DVD (UK): Eureka Video (2005), 90 min. PAL, region 2. German intertitles with optional English subtitles. Essay by R. Dixon Smith.

Die Austernprinzessin / The Oyster Princess
Ernst Lubitsch, 1919
DVD: Kino on Video (2006), 60 min. Restored version. English intertitles only. Package includes Lubitsch filmography and Lubitsch's *Ich möchte kein Mann sein / I Don't Want to Be a Man* (see below).

Avant-Garde: Experimental Cinema of the 1920s and 1930s
DVD: Kino on Video (2005). Two-disc collection of early European and American experimental cinema. Includes Hans Richter's *Rhythmus 21* (1921, 3 min.), *Vormittagsspuk / Ghosts before Breakfast* (1928, 9 min.), and Ernö Metzner's *Überfall* (1928, 22 min.).

Berge in Flammen
Luis Trenker, 1931
DVD (G): VZ Handels GmbH (2004), 94 min. PAL, region 0. In German. Features: photo gallery; background information. Second disc contains the documentary *Sperrfort Rocca Alta* (28 min.) about Luis Trenker.

Die Bergkatze / The Wildcat
Ernst Lubitsch, 1921
DVD: Kino on Video (2006), 82 min. Restored version. English intertitles only. With Lubitsch filmography.

Berlin Alexanderplatz/ Berlin Alexanderplatz
Phil Jutzi, 1931
DVD: Criterion Collection (2007), 83 min. In German with English subtitles. Included on the supplements disc for Criterion's edition of Rainer Werner Fassbinder's *Berlin Alexanderplatz* (1980, 940 min.).

Berlin, die Sinfonie der Großstadt / Berlin: Symphony of a Great City
Walther Ruttmann, 1927
DVD: Image Entertainment (1999), 62 min. Includes Ruttmann's short *Opus I* (1922, 10 min.).
DVD (G): Edition Filmmuseum (2008), 65 min. PAL, region 0. Restored version with newly recorded original score by Edmund Meisel. This edition includes all of Ruttmann's surviving works from 1920–31: *Opus 1–4* (1920–25), *Der*

Sieger (1922), *Das Wunder* (1922), *Das wiedergefundene Paradies* (1925), *Der Aufstieg* (1926), *Spiel der Wellen* (1926), *"Dort wo der Rhein . . ."* (1926), and *In der Nacht* (1931); lobby cards, posters, programs, and text documents; paintings and drawings by Ruttmann; booklet with essays. Includes *Melodie der Welt / Melody of the World* (see below).

Der blaue Engel / The Blue Angel
Josef von Sternberg, 1930
DVD: Kino on Video (2001), 106 min. Restored version. In German with English subtitles. Audio commentary. Includes English-language version (94 min.); Marlene Dietrich's screen test; Dietrich interview footage; trailer; Dietrich concert footage; photo gallery; filmmaker and cast biographies; production history.
DVD (UK): Eureka Video (2002), 105 min. PAL, region 2.

Das blaue Licht / The Blue Light
Leni Riefenstahl, 1932
DVD (G): Archiv-DVD (2006), 70 min. In German with English subtitles.

Bomben auf Monte Carlo
Hanns Schwarz, 1931
DVD (G): Black Hill Pictures (2005), 101 min. PAL, region 2. In German. Features background information; photo gallery.

Die Büchse der Pandora / Pandora's Box
G. W. Pabst, 1929
DVD: Criterion Collection (2006), 133 min. German intertitles with optional English subtitles. Audio commentary by Thomas Elsaesser and Mary Ann Doane. Includes *Looking for Lulu*, documentary on Louise Brooks (1998, 60 min.); 1971 interview with Louise Brooks (48 min.) by Richard Leacock; interviews with Leacock and Michael Pabst, son of G. W. Pabst; stills gallery; book with essays.
DVD (UK): Second Sight Films (2002), 131 min. PAL, region 0.

Das Cabinet des Dr. Caligari / The Cabinet of Dr. Caligari
Robert Wiene, 1920
DVD: Image Entertainment (1996), 72 min. English intertitles only. Audio commentary by Mike Budd.
DVD: Kino on Video (2002), 75 min. English intertitles only. Tinted. Includes an excerpt of Wiene's subsequent film, *Genuine: Tale of a Vampire* (1920, 43 min.); footage of Wiene on the set of his film *I.N.R.I.*; gallery of photos, posters, and production sketches.
DVD (UK): Eureka Video (2000), 72 min. PAL, region 2.

Die vom Rummelplatz
Carl Lamac, 1930
DVD (G): absolut Medien (2008). PAL, region 0. In German. This film is included in the collection "Film im Herzen Europas."

Doktor Dolittle & andere Archivschätze
Lotte Reiniger, 1927
DVD (G): absolut Medien (2008), 153 min. PAL, region 0. Includes booklet. German intertitles.

Douaumont– Die Hölle von Verdun
Heinz Paul, 1931
DVD: International Historic Films, 84 min. In German.

Die Dreigroschenoper / The Threepenny Opera
G. W. Pabst, 1931
DVD: Criterion Collection (2007), 105 min. In German with English subtitles. Audio commentary by David Bathrick and Eric Rentschler. Includes archival introduction by stars Fritz Rasp and Ernst Busch; documentary on the play's history; Pabst's French-language version; presentation on different versions by Charles O'Brien; archival interview with Fritz Rasp; galleries of production photos and sketches; essay by Tony Rayns.
DVD (UK): BFI Video (2004), 203 min. PAL, region 2.

Die Drei von der Tankstelle
Wilhelm Thiele, 1930
DVD (G): Universum Film (2004), 95 min. PAL, region 2. In German.

Dr. Mabuse, der Spieler / Dr. Mabuse, the Gambler
Fritz Lang, 1922
DVD: Kino on Video (2006), 270 min. Restored version. English intertitles only. Supplements: "The Story behind Dr. Mabuse" (52 min., German with English subtitles); Lang biography and filmography; stills gallery; film notes.
DVD: Image Entertainment (2001), 230 min. English intertitles only. Audio commentary by David Kalat.
DVD (UK): Eureka Video (2004), 270 min. PAL, region 2. German intertitles with English subtitles. Extras: photo gallery; features on "Mabuse's Motives," "Mabuse's Music," and Norbert Jacques; biographies; facts and dates.

Einbrecher
Hanns Schwarz, 1930
DVD (G): Black Hill Pictures (2005), 103 min. In German. Includes background information; biographies.

Die elf Teufel / The Eleven Devils
Zoltan Korda, 1927
DVD (G): Edition Filmmuseum (2006), 98 min. PAL, region 0. German intertitles with English subtitles. Includes short documentary *Der Länderkampf Deutschland-Italien im Duisburger Stadion / International Competition Germany vs. Italy in the Duisburg Stadium* (9 min.) and *König der Mittelstürmer / King of the Centre Forwards* (see below).

Ella Bergmann-Michel: Dokumentarische Filme 1931-1933 / Documentary Films 1931-1933
Ella Bergmann-Michel, 1933
DVD (G): Edition Filmmuseum (2008), 143 min. PAL, region 0. German intertitles with English subtitles. Films on the DVD include: *Wo wohnen alte Leute / Where Old People Live* (1931), *Erwerbslose kochen für Erwerbslose / Unemployed are Cooking for the Unemployed* (1932), *Fliegende Händler in Frankfurt am Main / Travelling Hawkers in Frankfurt am Main* (1932), *Fischfang in der Rhön (an der Sinn) / Fishing in the Rhön (at the Sinn)* (1932), *Wahlkampf 1932 (Letzte Wahl) / Election Campaign 1932 (Last Election)* (1932/33), *Fragmente / Fragments*, *Mein Herz schlägt Blau - Ella Bergmann-Michel / Blue is the Beat of my Heart - Ella Bergmann-Michel* Jutta Hercher & Maria Hemmleb, (1989)

Emil und die Detektive
Gerhard Lamprecht, 1931
DVD (G): Universum Film (2003). PAL, region 2. In German. Includes the 1954 version directed by Robert A. Stemmle.

Faust / Faust
Friedrich Wilhelm Murnau, 1926
DVD: Kino on Video (2001), 116 min. Restored version. English intertitles only. Includes gallery of production stills; essay by Jan Christopher Horak.
DVD (UK): Eureka Video (2006), 100 min. PAL, region 2. German intertitles with optional English subtitles. Audio commentary by David Ehrenstein and Bill Krohn. Includes video feature with Tony Rayns; comparison of the different versions of *Faust* by R. Dixon Smith; production stills and promotional art gallery; booklet with essay by Peter Spooner and archive reprints.

Die Finanzen des Großherzogs / The Finances of the Grand Duke
Friedrich Wilhelm Murnau, 1924
DVD: Kino on Video (2009), 77 min. Restored edition, color tinted, English intertitles. Included on the *Murnau* Six-DVD Box Set (*The Haunted Castle, Nosferatu, The Last Laugh, The Finances of the Grand Duke, Tartuffe, and Faust*). Extra feature: audio commentary by film historian David Kalat.

F.P. 1 antwortet nicht
Karl Hartl, 1932
DVD (G): Black Hill Pictures (2005), 107 min. PAL, region 2. In German. Includes background information; photo gallery.

Frau im Mond / Woman in the Moon
Fritz Lang, 1929
DVD: Kino on Video (2004), 169 min. Restored version. English intertitles only. With photo gallery.
DVD (UK): Eureka Video (2008), 163 min. PAL, region 2. German intertitles with optional English subtitles. Includes documentary *The First Science-Fiction Film* (Gabriele Jacobi, 15 min.); booklet with analysis by Michael E. Grost.

Die freudlose Gasse / The Joyless Street
G. W. Pabst, 1925
DVD: Synergy Entertainment (2007), 60 min. Region 0. Truncated version with English intertitles; the reconstructed version (forthcoming in Edition Filmmuseum) is 180 min.

Friedrich Schiller—eine Dichterjugend / The Poet as a Young Man
Curt Goetz, 1923
DVD (G): Edition Filmmuseum (2006), 102 min. PAL, region 0. German intertitles with English subtitles. Includes deleted and missing scenes from the original screenplay.

Geheimnisse einer Seele / Secrets of a Soul
G. W. Pabst, 1926
DVD: Kino on Video (2008), 73 min. Restored version. English intertitles only. With illustrated film notes.

Genuine/ Genuine
Robert Wiene, 1920
DVD: Kino on Video (2002), 43 min. English intertitles only. The fragment is included on Kino's edition of *Das Cabinet des Dr. Caligari / The Cabinet of Dr. Caligari* (see above).

Geschlecht in Fesseln—Die Sexualnot der Gefangenen / Sex in Chains
Wilhelm Dieterle, 1928
DVD: Kino on Video (2004), 86 min. Restored version. English intertitles.

Gesetze der Liebe: Schuldlos geächtet! / Laws of Love: Innocently Outlawed!
Magnus Hirschfeld, 1927
DVD (G): Edition Filmmuseum (2007), 40 min. PAL, region 0. German intertitles with English subtitles. Included in *Anders als die Andern / Different from the Others* (see above).

Der Golem—wie er in die Welt kam / The Golem: How He Came into the World
Paul Wegener, 1920
DVD: Kino on Video (2002), 86 min. Restored version. English intertitles only. Includes excerpt from *Le Golem* (Julien Duvivier, 1936); scene comparison with excerpts of Friedrich Wilhelm Murnau's *Faust* (1926) and Chayim Bloch's book *The Golem* (1925); photo and art gallery.
DVD (UK): Eureka Video (2003), 84 min. PAL, region 2. German and English intertitles. With documentary by R. Dixon Smith; photo gallery.

Der heilige Berg / The Holy Mountain
Arnold Fanck, 1926
DVD: Kino on Video (2003), 105 min. Reconstructed version. English intertitles only. Features interview footage of Leni Riefenstahl and Luis Trenker.

DVD (UK): Eureka Video (2004), 106 min. PAL, region 2. German intertitles with English subtitles. Inludes Ray Mueller's 1993 documentary *The Wonderful, Horrible Life of Leni Riefenstahl* (180 min.); booklet with essay by David Cummings.

Herrin von Atlantis / Mistress of Atlantis

G. W. Pabst, 1932

DVD: Sinister Cinema, 79 min. In English.

Ich küsse Ihre Hand, Madame

Robert Land, 1928

DVD (G): Salzgeber and Co. Medien (2003), 83 min. PAL, region 2. Restored version. German intertitles with sound sequence in German.

Ich möchte kein Mann sein / I Don't Want to Be a Man

Ernst Lubitsch, 1920

DVD: Kino on Video (2007), 45 min. Restored version. English intertitles only. With Lubitsch filmography. Includes Lubitsch's *Die Austernprinzessin / The Oyster Princess* (see above).

Das indische Grabmal / The Indian Tomb

Joe May, 1921

DVD: Image Entertainment (2000), 212 min. English intertitles only.

Kameradschaft

G. W. Pabst, 1931

DVD (G): Universum Film (2006), 86 min. PAL, region 2. In German.

Karl Valentin & Liesl Karlstadt—Die Kurzfilme, 1912-1941

DVD (G): VZ-Handelsgesellschaft (2002), 480 min. PAL, region 2. Films made between 1919-1933 included in the three-disc set: *Die lustigen Vagabunden* (1912, 4 min.), *Der neue Schreibtisch* (1914, 8 min.), *Mysterien eines Frisiersalons* (1922/23, 25 min., dir. Erich Engels and Bert Brecht), *Auf dem Oktoberfest* (1923, 11 min.), *Der Antennendraht* (1932, 19 min. dir. Joe Stöckl), *Im Photoatelier* (1932, 27 min., dir. Karl Ritter), *Orchesterprobe* (1933, 22 min., dir. Carl Lamac). In German.

Karl Valentin, der Sonderling

Walter Jerven, 1929

DVD (G): VZ Handels GmbH (2004), 88 min. PAL, region 0. German intertitles. This film appears on the three-disc set "*Karl Valentin—Die Spielfilme*," which also includes *Donner, Blitz und Sonnenschein* (1936), *Kirschen in Nachbars Garten* (1935), and four early silents.

Der Kongress tanzt

Erik Charell, 1931

DVD (G): Universum Film (2005), 94 min. PAL, region 2. In German.

König der Mittelstürmer / King of the Center Forwards

Fritz Kreisler, 1927

DVD (G): Edition Filmmuseum (2006), 95 min. PAL, region 0. German intertitles with English subtitles. With short documentary *Der Länderkampf Deutschland-Italien im Duisburger Stadion / International Competition Germany vs. Italy in the Duisburg Stadium* (9 min.). Includes *Die elf Teufel / The Eleven Devils* (see above).

Kuhle Wampe, oder wem gehört die Welt? / Kuhle Wampe, or Who Owns the World?

Slatan Dudow, 1932

DVD: DEFA Film Library / Icestorm, 69 min. DVD features include: Improved English subtitles, supervised Marc Silberman; *How the Worker Lives* (1930); *Slatan Dudow – A Film About a Marxist Artist* (1974, Volker Koepp); *Original Film Prologue with Herbert Jhering* (1958); *Before & After: Restoring Kuhle Wampe* (2008, Marta Carlson); "At the Hairdresser's with Brecht and Dudow" from a 1981 interview by Ralf Schenk; "On Kuhle Wampe" an essay by Marc Silberman; "The Second Life of *Kuhle Wampe*" by Wolfgang Klaue; Biographies & Filmographies

DVD (G): Filmedition Suhrkamp (2008), 80 min. In German.

Lachende Erben

Max Ophüls, 1933

DVD (G): Black Hill Pictures (2005), 72 min. In German. With background information; photo gallery.

Der letzte Mann / The Last Laugh

Friedrich Wilhelm Murnau, 1924

DVD: Kino on Video (2008), 91 min. Restored version. English intertitles only. Includes excerpts from alternate version; photo gallery.

DVD (UK): Eureka Video (2008), 91 min. PAL, region 2. German intertitles with optional English subtitles. Includes documentary *Der letzte Mann: The Making of* (Luciano Berriatúa, 41 min.); liner notes by R. Dixon Smith, Tony Rayns, and Lotte Eisner.

Die Liebe der Jeanne Ney / The Love of Jeanne Ney

G. W. Pabst, 1927

DVD: Kino on Video (2001), 113 min. English intertitles only.

Liebe muss verstanden sein

Hans Steinhoff, 1933

DVD: Warner Home Video (2004), 80 min. PAL, region 2. In German. Digitally remastered, with image gallery.

M: eine Stadt sucht einen Mörder / M

Fritz Lang, 1931

DVD: Criterion Collection (2004), 110 min. Restored version. In German with English subtitles. Audio commentary by Anton Kaes and Eric Rentschler. Disc

2 includes interview with Lang by director William Friedkin (50 min.); Claude Chabrol's short film *M le maudit*; classroom tapes of editor Paul Falkenburg; interview with Harold Nebenzahl; the documentary *A Physical History of M*; stills gallery with photos and production sketches. Booklet includes an essay by Stanley Kaufmann; 1963 interview with Lang; script for a missing scene; contemporaneous newspaper articles.

DVD (UK): Eureka Video (2003), 105 min. PAL, region 2. Restored version. In German with English subtitles. Audio commentary by Thorsten Kaiser. Includes audio interview of Lang by Peter Bogdanovich; Lang documentary; essay by R. Dixon Smith; film restoration and comparison with Martin Koerber and Torsten Kaiser; photo gallery; animated slide show; set designs; final screen comparisons; animated biographies; historical backgrounds.

Mädchen in Uniform

Leontine Sagan, 1931

DVD (G): Arthaus (2008), 83 min. PAL, region 2. In German. With photo gallery; director biography; press material.

Der Mann, der seinen Mörder sucht

Robert Siodmak, 1930

DVD (G): Black Hill Pictures (2005), 50 min. PAL, region 2. In German. Includes background information with film scenes.

Melodie der Welt / Melody of the World

Walther Ruttmann, 1929

DVD (G): Edition Filmmuseum (2008), 40 min. PAL, region 0. Included in *Berlin: die Sinfonie der Großstadt / Berlin: Symphony of a Great City.*

Menschen am Sonntag / People on Sunday

Robert Siodmak, Edgar G. Ulmer, Billy Wilder, 1929

DVD (UK): BFI Video (2005), 73 min. PAL, region 2. Restored version. With filmmaker biographies; booklet.

Metropolis/ Metropolis

Fritz Lang, 1927

DVD: Kino on Video (2002), 124 min. Restored version. English intertitles only. Newly recorded original score. Audio commentary by Enno Patalas. Includes a documentary by Enno Patalas on the making of the film (43 min.); featurette on the digital restoration; photo galleries; cast and crew biographies.

DVD (UK): Eureka Video (2005), 118 min. PAL, region 2. Restored version. German intertitles with optional subtitles in English. Audio commentary by Enno Patalas in English and German. Extras: documentary *The Metropolis Case* by Patalas (2002, 44 min.); documentary on the restoration with Martin Koerber; production stills, posters, costume designs, stills of missing scenes, and architectural designs; booklet with restoration notes, contemporary writing, and an essay by Jonathan Rosenbaum.

Mikaël / Michael
Carl Theodor Dreyer, 1924
DVD: Kino on Video (2004), 86 min. English intertitles only. Audio commentary by Caspar Tybjerg. With Dreyer filmography.
DVD (UK): Eureka Video (2004), 90 min. PAL, region 0. German and English intertitles. Audio commentary by Tybjerg. Includes audio interview with Dreyer from 1965 (26 min.); booklet; reprint of Tom Milne's *The World Inside* (1971); reprint of Jean Renoir's tribute, *Dreyer's Sin* (1968); translation of original Danish program; essay by Nick Wrigley.

Der müde Tod / Destiny
Fritz Lang, 1921
DVD: Image Entertainment (2000), 99 min. English intertitles only.

Die Mysterien eines Frisiersalons
Erich Engel and Bertolt Brecht, 1923
DVD (G): VZ Handels GmbH (2002), 25 min. PAL, region 2. In German. Included on the 3-disc set "Karl Valentin and Liesl Karlstadt: Die Kurzfilme." Includes documentary on Valentin; photo galleries; chronologies; biographies of Valentin and Karlstadt.

Nathan der Weise / Nathan the Wise
Manfred Noa, 1922
DVD: Edition Filmmuseum (2007), 123 min. PAL, region 0. German intertitles with English subtitles. Includes 1923 lobby cards; booklet with essay by Stefan Drössler.

Nerven / Nerves
Robert Reinert, 1919
DVD: Edition Filmmuseum (2008), 110 min. PAL, region 0. Reconstructed and newly tinted version. German intertitles with French and English subtitles. Supplements: fragment comparisons; documentary shorts on the proletarian revolution in Munich 1919; posters, stills, and lobby cards; essays by Jan-Christopher Horak, Stefan Drössler, and David Bordwell.

Die Nibelungen / The Nibelungen
Fritz Lang, 1924
DVD (2 discs): Kino on Video (2002), 291 min. *Part 1: Siegfried* (143 min.); *Part 2: Kriemhild's Revenge* (144 min.) Restored version. English intertitles only. Newly recorded original score. Includes footage of Lang on the set; design sketches by Erich Kettelhut; comparison of dragon-slaying scenes from *Siegfried* and *The Thief of Bagdad* (1924); essay by Jan-Christopher Horak; photo gallery.

Nosferatu, eine Symphonie des Grauens / Nosferatu
Friedrich Wilhelm Murnau, 1922
DVD: Kino on Video (2007), 94 min. 2007 restoration. German and English intertitles, optional English subtitles. Original score. Supplements:

documentary by Luciano Berriatúa on the film's production (52 min.); feature on the restoration; excerpts from other Murnau films; photo gallery; scene comparison.

DVD (UK): Eureka Video (2007), 93 min. PAL, region 2. Audio commentary by R. Dixon Smith and Brad Stevens. Additional book with articles by Thomas Elsaesser, Gilberto Perez, and Enno Patalas; archival pieces by producer Albin Grau; notes on restoration; archival imagery.

Orlacs Hände / The Hands of Orlac

Robert Wiene, 1924

DVD: Kino on Video (2008), 110 min. Restored version. English intertitles only. Supplements: scene comparison; information on the restoration; film notes by John T. Soister; image gallery; trailer for *Mad Love* (Karl Freund, 1935).

Othello/ Othello

Dimitri Buchowetzki, 1922

DVD: Kino on Video (2001), 80 min. English intertitles only. Features four silent Shakespearean shorts; essay by Douglas Brode.

Phantom/ Phantom

Friedrich Wilhelm Murnau, 1922

DVD: Flicker Alley (2006), 120 min. Restored version. Tinted. English intertitles only. Supplements: "Invitation to *Phantom*" (Janet Bergstrom, 15 min.); cast and crew biographies; documents gallery; essay on the restoration ("The Colors of Phantom," by Luciano Berriatúa and Camille Blot-Wellens).

Die Puppe / The Doll

Ernst Lubitsch, 1919

DVD: Kino on Video (2006), 64 min. Restored version. English intertitles only. Includes a documentary on Lubitsch, *Lubitsch in Berlin* (Robert Fischer, 109 min).

Der Rebell

Luis Trenker and Kurt Bernhard, 1932

DVD (G): EMS (2004), 83 min. PAL, region 2. In German. Includes biographies and filmographies of Trenker and Luise Ullrich; image gallery; Trenker's 1957 film *Unser Freund, der Haflinger*.

Ruf des Nordens

Nunzio Malasomma, 1929

DVD (G): EMS (2004), 62 min. PAL, region 2. In German. Introduction and commentary by Luis Trenker. Supplements: biography and filmography of Trenker; photo gallery; Trenker's film *S.O.S. Zinnennordwand* (1955, 19 min.).

Schatten: eine nächtliche Halluzination / Warning Shadows: A Nocturnal Hallucination

Arthur Robison, 1923

DVD: Kino on Video (2006), 85 min. Restored version. Color tinted. English intertitles only.

Der Schatz

G. W. Pabst, 1923

DVD (G): Arthaus (2007), 80 min. PAL, region 2. Restored version. German intertitles. Audio commentary by Hermann Kappelhoff and Marek Bringezu. Extras: documentary on the reconstruction; interviews with conductor Frank Strobel and Michael Pabst; booklet with text by Klaus Kreimeier; director and cast biographies; photo gallery.

Schicksalswürfel / A Throw of Dice

Franz Osten, 1930

DVD: Kino on Video (2008), 74 min. Restored version. English intertitles.

DVD (UK): BFI Video (2007), 74 min. PAL, region 2. Restored version. English intertitles. Features interview with Nitin Sawhney; booklet with essay by Amrit Gangar; essay by filmmaker Asif Kapadia.

Schloss Vogelöd / The Haunted Castle

F.W. Murnau, 1921

DVD: Kino on Video (2009), 81 min. Restored edition, color tinted, English intertiles. Included on the *Murnau* Six-DVD Box Set (*The Haunted Castle, Nosferatu, The Last Laugh, The Finances of the Grand Duke, Tartuffe, and Faust*). Extra features include gallery of set design paintings by Robert Herlth and excerpts of Rudolf Stratz's novel.

Der Sohn der weißen Berge

Mario Bonnard and Luis Trenker, 1930

DVD (G): EMS (2004), 64 min. PAL, region 2. In German. Features biographies and filmographies of stars Luis Trenker and Renate Müller; image gallery; Trenker's 1952 film *Die Sphinx von Zermatt*; interview with son Florian Trenker.

S.O.S. Eisberg

Arnold Fanck, 1933

DVD (G): Universum Film (2005), 101 min. PAL, region 2. In German.

Die Spinnen / Spiders

Fritz Lang, 1919

DVD: Image Entertainment (1999), 137 min. German intertitles with English subtitles. Includes both parts: *Der goldene See / The Golden Sea* (1919) and *Das Brillantenschiff / The Diamond Ship* (1920).

Spione / Spies

Fritz Lang, 1928

DVD: Kino on Video (2004), 143 min. Restored version. English intertitles only. Includes photo gallery.

DVD (UK): Eureka Video (2005), 145 min. PAL, region 2. German intertitles with optional English subtitles. Supplements: gallery with promotional material; booklet with essay by Jonathan Rosenbaum.

Der Stolz der 3. Kompanie
Fred Sauer, 1931
DVD (G): Power Station (2008), 85 min. PAL, region 2. In German.

Der Student von Prag / The Student of Prague
Henrik Galeen, 1926
DVD: Alpha Video (2004), 90 min. Region 0. English intertitles only.

Stürme über dem Mont Blanc / Storm over Mont Blanc
Arnold Fanck, 1930
DVD: Kino on Video (2005), 95 min. In German with English subtitles. Includes short film by Fanck *Das Wolkenphänomen in Maloja / Cloud Phenomena of Maloja*, 1924; photo gallery.

Sumurun / One Arabian Night
Ernst Lubitsch, 1920
DVD: Kino on Video (2006), 103 min. Restored version. English intertitles only.

Tabu/ Tabu
Friedrich Wilhelm Murnau, 1931
DVD: Image Entertainment (2002), 81 min. Restored version. English intertitles. Audio commentary by Janet Bergstrom. Includes photo gallery; outtake footage; short film *Reri in New York*; theatrical trailer; PDF's of telegrams and script pages.
DVD (UK): Eureka Video (2007), 83 min. PAL, region 2. Restored version. English intertitles. Audio commentary by R. Dixon Smith and Brad Stevens. Includes documentary by Luciano Berriatúa (15 min.). Additional book includes articles by Scott Eyman, Richard Griffiths, and David Flaherty; interview with cinematographer Floyd Crosby; original story treatments by Murnau and Flaherty for *Tabu* and its aborted predecessor "Turia."

Das Tagebuch einer Verlorenen / Diary of a Lost Girl
G. W. Pabst, 1929
DVD: Kino on Video (2001), 116 min. Restored version. English intertitles only. Includes the short Roscoe "Fatty" Arbuckle film *Windy Riley Goes Hollywood* (18 min.).
DVD (UK): Eureka Video (2007), 107 min. PAL, region 2. German intertitles with optional English subtitles. Features liner notes with writing by Louise Brooks, Lotte Eisner, Louella Interim, Craig Keller, and R. Dixon Smith.

Tartüff / Tartuffe
Friedrich Wilhelm Murnau, 1926
DVD: Kino on Video (2003), 63 min. Restored version. Color tinted. English intertitles only. Includes documentary on Murnau (*The Way to Murnau*, 35 min.); essay by Jan-Christopher Horak.
DVD (UK): Eureka Video (2005), 64 min. PAL, region 2. German intertitles with optional English subtitles. Features gallery with production stills; booklet with essay by R. Dixon Smith.

Das Testament des Dr. Mabuse / The Testament of Dr. Mabuse
Fritz Lang, 1933
DVD: Criterion Collection (2004), 121 min. In German with optional English subtitles. Audio commentary by David Kalat. Includes excerpts from 1964 interview with Lang; *Mabuse in Mind* (Thomas Honickel, 1984); comparison between German- and French-language versions as well as the U.S. edit of the film; interview with Michael Farin about *Mabuse* and writer Norbert Jacques; production drawings; memorabilia, press books, stills, and posters; essay by Tom Gunning. Disc 2 includes the simultaneously filmed French-language version of the film.
DVD (UK): Eureka Video (2004), 115 min. PAL, region 2. In German with English subtitles. With documentary by R. Dixon Smith; photo gallery.

Theodor Herzl, der Bannerträger des jüdischen Volkes
Otto Kreisler, 1921
DVD: International Historic Films, 2006, 65 min. In German.

Vampyr/ Vampyr
Carl Theodor Dreyer, 1932
DVD: Criterion (2008), 75 min. German intertitles with English subtitles. DVD features include: The original German version in a new high-definition digital transfer from the 1998 restoration by Martin Koerber and the Cineteca di Bologna. Newly credited alternate version with English text. Audio commentary by Tony Rayns. *Carl Th. Dreyer* (1966), a documentary by Jørgen Roos chronicling Dreyer's career. Visual essay by scholar Casper Tybjerg on Dreyer's influences in creating *Vampyr*. Radio broadcast from 1958 of Dreyer reading an essay about filmmaking. New and improved English subtitle translation. A booklet featuring new essays by Mark Le Fanu and Kim Newman, Koerber on the restoration, and a 1964 interview with producer and star Nicolas de Gunzburg, as well as a book featuring Dreyer and Christen Jul's original screenplay and Sheridan Le Fanu 1872 story "Carmilla," a source for the film.

Viktor und Viktoria
Reinhold Schünzel, 1933
DVD (G): Black Hill Pictures (2005), 94 min. PAL, region 2. In German. Includes background information; biographies.

Vom Reiche der sechs Punkte
Hugo Rütters, 1927
DVD (G): Edition Filmmuseum (2007), 100 min. PAL, region 0. German intertitles with English subtitles. Features audio description for blind viewers (German only); booklet with texts about the film; contemporary press reviews and documents (German only).

Das Wachsfigurenkabinett / Waxworks
Paul Leni, 1924
DVD: Kino on Video (2002), 83 min. Restored version. English intertitles only.

Die Weiße Hölle vom Piz Palü / The White Hell of Piz Palu
Arnold Fanck and G. W. Pabst, 1929.
DVD: Kino on Video (2005), 133 min. Restored version. English intertitles only. Includes 2002 interview with Leni Riefenstahl (59 min.); excerpt from the 1935 sound reissue of the film; photo gallery.

Der weisse Rausch
Arnold Fanck, 1931
DVD (G): VZ Handels GmbH, 75 min. PAL, region 0. In German. Includes background information.

Westfront 1918
G. W. Pabst, 1930
DVD: International Historic Films, 89 min. In German.
DVD (G): Universum Film (2006), 88 min. PAL, region 2. In German.

Bibliography

Shell Shock and Trauma Theory

Acton, Carol. *Grief in Wartime: Private Pain, Public Discourse*. New York: Palgrave Macmillan, 2007.
Alexander, Jeffrey C., et al., eds. *Cultural Trauma and Collective Identity*. Berkeley: University of California Press, 2004.
Alzheimer, Alois. *Der Krieg und die Nerven*. Breslau: Preuss and Jünger, 1915.
Antze, Paul, and Michael Lambek. *Tense Past: Cultural Essays in Trauma and Memory*. New York: Routledge, 1996.
Arthurs, Jane, and Iain Grants, eds. *Crash Cultures: Modernity, Mediation, and the Material*. London: Intellect Ltd., 2000.
Babington, Anthony. *Shell-shock: A History of the Changing Attitudes to War Neurosis*. London: Leo Cooper, 1997.
Baer, Ulrich. *Spectral Evidence: The Photography of Trauma*. Cambridge, MA: MIT Press, 2002.
Ball, Karyn. *Traumatizing Theory: The Cultural Politics of Affect in and beyond Psychoanalysis*. New York: Other Press, 2007.
Barham, Peter. *Forgotten Lunatics of the Great War*. New Haven, CT: Yale University Press, 2004.
Barker, Pat. *Regeneration*. London: Viking, 1991.
Bennett, Jill. *Empathic Vision: Affect, Trauma, and Contemporary Art*. Stanford, CA: Stanford University Press, 2005.
Binnefeld, J.M.W. *From Shell Shock to Combat Stress: A Comparative History of Military Psychiatry*. Amsterdam: Amsterdam University Press, 1997.
Bourke, Joanna. *Dismembering the Male: Men's Bodies, Britain, and the Great War*. Chicago: University of Chicago Press, 1996.

Bronfen, Elisabeth. *Over Her Dead Body: Death, Femininity, and the Aesthetic*. New York: Routledge, 1992.

Bronfen, Elisabeth, Birgit Erdle, and Sigrid Weigel, eds. *Trauma zwischen Psychoanalyse und kulturellem Deutungsmuster*. Cologne: Böhlau, 1999.

Bynym, F.W., Roy Porter, and Michael Shepherd. *The Anatomy of Madness: Essays in the History of Psychiatry*. 3 vols. Cambridge: Cambridge University Press, 1988.

Call, Annie Payson. *Nerves and the War*. Boston: Little Brown, 1918.

Carpentier, Nico, ed. *Culture, Trauma, and Conflict: Cultural Studies, Perspectives on War*. Newcastle, UK: Cambridge Scholars Publishing, 2007.

Caruth, Cathy. *Trauma: Explorations in Memory*. Baltimore: Johns Hopkins University Press, 1995.

———. *Unclaimed Experience: Trauma, Narrative, and History*. Baltimore: Johns Hopkins University Press, 1996.

Coleman, Penny, ed. *Flashback: Posttraumatic Stress Disorder, Suicide, and the Lessons of War*. Boston: Beacon Press, 2006.

Davoine, Françoise. *History beyond Trauma: Whereof One Cannot Speak, Thereof One Cannot Stay Silent*. New York: Other Press, 2004.

Dean, Eric T. *Shook over Hell: Post-traumatic Stress, Vietnam, and the Civil War*. Cambridge, MA: Harvard University Press, 1997.

Denham, Scott D. *Visions of War: Ideologies and Images of War in German Literature before and after the Great War*. Frankfurt am Main: Peter Lang, 1992.

Didi-Huberman, Georges. *Invention of Hysteria: Charcot and the Photographic Iconography of the Salpêtrière*. Cambridge, MA: MIT Press, 2003.

Eckart, Wolfgang U., and Christoph Gradmann, eds. *Die Medizin und der Erste Weltkrieg*. Pfaffenweiler: Centaurus-Verlagsgesellschaft, 1996.

Eder, Montague David. *War-Shock: The Psycho-Neuroses in War Psychology and Treatment*. London: W. Heinemann, 1917.

Edkins, Jenny. *Trauma and the Memory of Politics*. Cambridge, UK: Cambridge University Press, 2003.

Eissler, K. R. *Freud as an Expert Witness: The Discussion of War Neuroses between Freud and Wagner-Jauregg*. Translated by Christine Trollope. New York: International Universities Press, 1986.

Faust, Drew Gilpin. *This Republic of Suffering: Death and the American Civil War*. New York: Alfred A. Knopf, 2008.

Felman, Shoshana, and Dori Laub. *Testimony: Crises of Witnessing in Literature, Psychoanalysis, and History*. New York: Routledge, 1992.

Fenton, Norman. *Shell Shock and Its Aftermath*. London: Henry Kimpton, 1926.

Ferenczi, Sándor, et al. *Zur Psychoanalyse der Kriegsneurosen*. Leipzig: Internationaler Psychoanalytischer Verlag, 1919.

Finckh, Johannes. *Die Nerven: Ihre Gefährdung und Pflege in Krieg und Frieden*. Munich: Gmelin, 1918.

Fischer-Homberger, Esther. *Die traumatische Neurose: Vom somatischen zum sozialen Leiden*. Bern: Huber, 1975.

Freud, Sigmund. "Introduction" to *Psycho-analysis and the War Neuroses*, by Sándor Ferenczi, Karl Abraham, Ernst Simmel, and Ernest Jones, 1–4. Vienna: International Psycho-analytical Press, 1921.

———. "Memorandum on the Electrical Treatment of War Neurotics." In *The Standard Edition of the Complete Psychological Works*, 17:211–15. London: Hogarth Press, 1955.

———. *On War, Sex, and Neurosis*. New York: Arts and Science Press, 1947.

———. *The Standard Edition of the Complete Psychological Works*. London: Hogarth Press, 1953–1974.

Fricke, Hannes. *Das hört nicht auf: Trauma, Literatur und Empathie*. Göttingen: Wallstein, 2004.

Friedrich, Ernst. *Krieg dem Kriege! Guerre à la guerre! War against War! Oorlog aan den Oorlog!* Berlin: Freie Jugend, 1924.

Gabriel, Richard. *No More Heroes: Madness and Psychiatry in War*. New York: Hill and Wang, 1988.

Goodwin, Sarah Webster, and Elisabeth Bronfen, eds. *Death and Representation*. Baltimore: Johns Hopkins University Press, 1993.

Green, Bonnie L. *Trauma Interventions in War and Peace: Prevention, Practice, and Policy*. New York: Kluwer Academic and Plenum Publishers, 2003.

Greenberg, Judith, ed. *Trauma at Home: After 9/11*. Lincoln: University of Nebraska Press, 2003.

Harris, Ruth. *Murder and Madness: Medicine, Law, and Society in the Fin-de-siècle*. Oxford: Oxford University Press, 1989.

Heinl, Peter. *Splintered Innocence: An Intuitive Approach to Treating War Trauma*. New York: Routledge, 2001.

Higonnet, Margaret R., et al., eds. *Behind the Lines: Gender and the Two World Wars*. New Haven, CT: Yale University Press, 1987.

Hipp, Daniel W. *The Poetry of Shell Shock: Wartime Trauma and Healing in Wilfred Owen, Ivor Gurney, and Siegfried Sassoon*. Jefferson, NC: McFarland and Co., 2005.

Hirsch, Joshua Francis. *Afterimage: Film, Trauma, and the Holocaust*. Philadelphia: Temple University Press, 2004.

Hoche, Alfred. *Krieg und Seelenleben*. Freiburg im Breisgau: Speyer und Koerner, 1915.

Hofer, Hans-Georg. *Nervenschwäche und Krieg: Modernitätskritik und Krisenbewältigung in der österreichischen Psychiatrie, 1880–1920*. Vienna: Böhlau, 2004.

Holden, Wendy. *Shell Shock*. London: Channel 4 Books, 1998.

Horstmann, Bernhard. *Hitler in Pasewalk: Die Hypnose und ihre Folgen*. Düsseldorf: Droste, 2004.

Howlett, Jana, and Rod Mengham, eds. *The Violent Muse: Violence and the Artistic Imagination in Europe, 1910–1939*. Manchester: Manchester University Press, 1994.

Hüppauf, Bernd, ed. *War, Violence, and the Modern Condition*. Berlin: De Gruyter, 1997.

Jones, Edgar, and Simon Wessely. *Shell Shock to PTSD: Military Psychiatry from 1900 to the Gulf War*. Hove, UK: Psychology Press, 2005.

Jong, Joop T.V.M. de. *Trauma, War, and Violence: Public Mental Health in Socio-Cultural Context*. New York: Kluwer Academic Plenum Publishers, 2002.

Kaplan, E. Ann. *Trauma Culture: The Politics of Terror and Loss in Media and Literature*. New Brunswick, NJ: Rutgers University Press, 2005.

Kaplan, E. Ann, and Ban Wang, eds. *Trauma and Cinema: Cross-Cultural Explorations*. Hong Kong: Hong Kong University Press, 2004.

Killen, Andreas. *Berlin Electropolis: Shock, Nerves, and German Modernity*. Berkeley: University of California Press, 2006.

Kingsbury, Celia Malone. *The Peculiar Sanity of War: Hysteria in the Literature of World War I*. Lubbock: Texas Tech University Press, 2002.

Komo, Günther. *Für Volk und Vaterland: Die Militärpsychiatrie in den Weltkriegen*. Hamburg: Lit, 1992.

Kramer, Alan. *Dynamic of Destruction: Culture and Mass Killing in the First World War*. Oxford: Oxford University Press, 2007.

Krippner, Stanley, and Teresa M. McIntyre. *The Psychological Impact of War Trauma on Civilians: An International Perspective. Psychological Dimensions to War and Peace*. Westport, CT: Praeger, 2003.

Leese, Peter. *Shell Shock: Traumatic Neurosis and the British Soldiers of the First World War*. New York: Palgrave, 2002.

Lerner, Paul. *Hysterical Men: War, Psychiatry, and the Politics of Trauma in Germany, 1890–1930*. Ithaca, NY: Cornell University Press, 2003.

Leys, Ruth. *Trauma: A Genealogy*. Chicago: University of Chicago Press, 2000.

Lowenstein, Adam. *Shocking Representation: Historical Trauma, National Cinema, and the Modern Horror Film*. New York: Columbia University Press, 2005.

McNally, Richard J. *Remembering Trauma*. Cambridge, MA: Harvard University Press, 2003.

Micale, Mark S. *Approaching Hysteria: Disease and Its Interpretations*. Princeton, NJ: Princeton University Press, 1995.

———. *The Mind of Modernism: Medicine, Psychology, and the Cultural Arts in Europe and America, 1880–1940*. Stanford, CA: Stanford University Press, 2004.

Micale, Mark S., and Paul Lerner, eds. *Traumatic Pasts: History, Psychiatry, and Trauma in the Modern Age, 1870–1930*. Cambridge: Cambridge University Press, 2001.

Miller, Emanuel, and Hugh Crichton-Miller. *The Neuroses in War*. New York: Macmillan Company, 1944.

Milne, Joseph S. *Neurasthenia, Shell-Shock, and a New Life*. Newcastle upon Tyne: R. Robinson and Co. Ltd., 1918.

Mixa, Elisabeth, ed. *Körper–Geschlecht–Geschichte: Historische und aktuelle Debatten in der Medizin*. Innsbruck: Studien-Verlag, 1996.

Moran, Patricia. *Virginia Woolf, Jean Rhys, and the Aesthetics of Trauma*. New York: Palgrave Macmillan, 2007.

Mott, Frederick W. *War Neuroses and Shell Shock*. London: Frowde/Hodder and Stoughton, 1919.

Mülder-Bach, Inka, ed. *Modernität und Trauma: Beiträge zum Zeitenbruch des Ersten Weltkrieges*. Vienna: Edition Parabasen, 2000.

Myers, Charles Samuel. *Shell Shock in France, 1914–18*. Cambridge: Cambridge University Press, 1940.

Naythons, Matthew. *The Face of Mercy: A Photographic History of Medicine at War*. New York: Random House, 1993.

Puusepp, Louis. *Traumatische Kriegsneurose*. Tartu: Mällo, 1925.

Radkau, Joachim. *Das Zeitalter der Nervosität: Deutschland zwischen Bismarck und Hitler*. Munich: Carl Hanser, 1998.

Richter, Hans-Günther. *Imagination und Trauma: Bilder und Träume von traumatisierten Menschen*. Frankfurt am Main: Lang, 2006.

Rickels, Laurence R. *Nazi Psychoanalysis*. Vol. 1. Minneapolis: University of Minnesota Press, 2002.

Riedesser, Peter, and Axel Verderber. Aufrüstung der Seelen: Militärpsychologie in Deutschland und Amerika. Freiburg im Breisgau: Dreisam, 1991.

———. *"Maschinengewehre hinter der Front": Zur Geschichte der deutschen Militärpsychiatrie*. Frankfurt am Main: Fischer, 1996.

Ross, Gina. *Beyond the Trauma Vortex: The Media's Role in Healing Fear, Terror, and Violence*. Berkeley: North Atlantic Books, 2003.

Ryan, James M., et al., eds. *Ballistic Trauma: Clinical Relevance in Peace and War*. London: Hodder Arnold, 1997.

Salmon, Thomas W. *The Care and Treatment of Mental Diseases and War Neuroses ("Shell Shock") in the British Army*. New York: War Work Committee of the National Committee for Mental Hygiene Inc., 1917.

Schaffellner, Barbara. *Unvernunft und Kriegsmoral: Am Beispiel der Kriegsneurose im Ersten Weltkrieg*. Vienna: Lit, 2005.

Schäffner, Wolfgang. *Die Ordnung des Wahns: Zur Poetologie psychiatrischen Wissens bei Alfred Döblin*. Munich: Fink, 1995.

Shay, Jonathan. *Achilles in Vietnam: Combat Trauma and the Undoing of Character*. New York: Atheneum, 1994.

———. *Odysseus in America: Combat Trauma and the Trials of Homecoming*. New York: Scribner, 2002.

Shephard, Ben. *A War of Nerves: Soldiers and Psychiatrists in the Twentieth Century*. Cambridge, MA: Harvard University Press, 2001.

Shorter, Edward, and David Healy. *Shock Therapy: The History of Electroconvulsive Treatment in Mental Illness*. New Brunswick, NJ: Rutgers University Press, 2007.

Showalter, Elaine. *The Female Malady: Women, Madness, and English Culture, 1830–1980*. New York: Pantheon Books, 1985.

———. *Hystories: Hysterical Epidemics and Modern Culture*. New York: Columbia University Press, 1997.

Silverman, Kaja. *Male Subjectivity at the Margins.* New York: Routledge, 1992.
Simmel, Ernst. *Kriegs-Neurosen und "Psychisches Trauma": Ihre gegenseitigen Beziehungen dargestellt auf Grund psycho-analytischer, hypnotischer Studien.* Leipzig: Otto Nemnich Verlag, 1918.
Smith, Grafton Elliot, and Tom Hatherley Pear. *Shell Shock and Its Lessons.* 2nd ed. Manchester: University Press, 1971.
Sommer, Robert. *Krieg und Seelenleben.* Giessen: Kindt, 1915.
Sontag, Susan. *Regarding the Pain of Others.* New York: Farrar, Strauss and Giroux, 2003.
Southard, Elmer Ernest. *Shell-Shock and Other Neuropsychiatric Problems Presented in Five Hundred and Eighty-Nine Case Histories from the War Literature, 1914–1918. Mental Illness and Social Policy: The American Experience.* New York: Arno Press, 1973. First published 1919.
Stewart, Victoria. *Women's Autobiography: War and Trauma.* New York: Palgrave Macmillan, 2003.
Stingelin, Martin, and Wolfgang Scherer, eds. *HardWar/SoftWar: Krieg und Medien 1914 bis 1945.* Munich: Fink, 1991.
Stout, Janis P. *Coming out of War: Poetry, Grieving, and the Culture of the World Wars.* Tuscaloosa: University of Alabama Press, 2005.
Strümpell, Adolf. *Die Schädigungen der Nerven und des geistigen Lebens durch den Krieg.* Leipzig: Vogel, 1917.
Veer, Guus van der. *Counselling and Therapy with Refugees: Psychological Problems of Victims of War, Torture, and Repression.* 2nd ed. New York: John Wiley, 1998.
Wagner-Jauregg, Julius von. *Telepathie und Hypnose im Verbrechen.* Vienna: Verlag der Wiener Tagespresse, 1919.
Walker, Janet. *Trauma Cinema: Documenting Incest and the Holocaust.* Berkeley: University of California Press, 2005.
Wietfeldt, Heinrich. *Kriegsneurose als psychisch-soziale Mangelkrankheit.* Leipzig: Thieme, 1936.
Winter, Jay, ed. "Shell Shock." Special issue, *Journal of Contemporary History* 35 (2000).
Yealland, Lewis Ralph. *Hysterical Disorders of Warfare.* London: Macmillan, 1918.
Young, Alan. *The Harmony of Illusions: Inventing Post-traumatic Stress Disorder.* Princeton, NJ: Princeton University Press, 1995.

World War I and the Weimar Republic

Adams, Michael C. *The Great Adventure: Male Desire and the Coming of World War I.* Bloomington: Indiana University Press, 1990.
Anz, Thomas, and Joseph Vogl, eds. *Die Dichter und der Krieg: Deutsche Lyrik 1914–1918.* Munich: C. Hanser, 1982.
Audoin-Rouzeau, Stéphane, and Annette Becker. *14–18: Understanding the Great War.* New York: Hill and Wang, 2002.

Aurich, Rolf, Wolfgang Jacobsen, and Cornelius Schnauber, eds. *Fritz Lang: Leben und Werk, Bilder und Dokumente/Fritz Lang: His Life and Work, Photographs and Documents*. Berlin: Jovis, 2001.
Barth, Boris. *Dolchstoßlegenden und politische Desintegration: Das Trauma der deutschen Niederlage im Ersten Weltkrieg 1914–1933*. Düsseldorf: Droste, 2003.
Baumgartner, Alois. *Sehnsucht nach Gemeinschaft: Ideen und Strömungen im Sozialkatholizismus der Weimarer Republik*. Munich: Schöningh, 1977.
Berghahn, Volker R. *Der Erste Weltkrieg*. Munich: C. H. Beck, 2003.
Bessel, Richard. *Germany after the First World War*. Oxford: Oxford University Press, 1993.
Booth, Allyson. *Postcards from the Trenches: Negotiating the Space between Modernism and the First World War*. Oxford: Oxford University Press, 1996.
Brandt, Susanne. *Vom Kriegsschauplatz zum Gedächtnisraum: Die Westfront 1914–1940*. Baden-Baden: Nomos, 2000.
Bredow, Wilfried von, and Rolf Zurek, eds. *Film und Gesellschaft in Deutschland. Dokumente und Materialien*. Hamburg: Hoffmann und Campe, 1975.
Brenner, Michael, and Derek Jonathan Penslar. *In Search of Jewish Community: Jewish Identities in Germany and Austria, 1918–1933*. Bloomington: Indiana University Press, 1998.
Brokoff, Jürgen. *Die Apokalypse in der Weimarer Republik*. Munich: Fink, 2001.
Busche, Jürgen. *Heldenprüfung: Das verweigerte Erbe des Ersten Weltkriegs*. Munich: DVA, 2004.
Chickering, Roger, and Stig Förster, eds. *Great War, Total War: Combat and Mobilization on the Western Front, 1914–1918*. Cambridge: Cambridge University Press, 2000.
Cohen, Deborah. *The War Comes Home: Disabled Veterans in Britain and Germany, 1914–39*. Berkeley: University of California Press, 2001.
Davis, Belinda. *Home Fires Burning: Food, Politics, and Everyday Life in World War I Berlin*. Chapel Hill: University of North Carolina Press, 2000.
Denham, Scott D. *Visions of War: Ideologies and Images of War in German Literature before and after the Great War*. Frankfurt am Main: Lang, 1992.
Dinter, Artur. *Die Sünde wider das Blut: ein Zeitroman*. 16th ed. Leipzig: Matthes und Thost, 1921.
Dülffer, Jost, and Gerd Krumeich, eds. *Der verlorene Frieden: Politik und Kriegskultur nach 1918*. Essen: Klartext, 2002.
Duppler, Jörg, and Gerhard Paul Gross. *Kriegsende 1918: Ereignis, Wirkung, Nachwirkung*. Munich: Oldenbourg, 1999.
Durst, David. *Weimar Modernism: Philosophy, Politics, and Culture in Germany, 1918–1933*. Lanham, MD: Lexington Books, 2004.
Eberle, Matthias. *World War I and the Weimar Artists: Dix, Grosz, Beckmann, Schlemmer*. Translated by John Gabriel. New Haven, CT: Yale University Press, 1985.
Ekstein, Modris. *Rites of Spring: The Great War and the Birth of the Modern Age*. New York: Houghton Mifflin Company, 1989.

Encke, Julia. *Augenblicke der Gefahr: Der Krieg und die Sinne, 1914–1934*. Munich: Fink, 2006.

Ernst, Petra, Sabine A. Haring, and Werner Suppanz, eds. *Aggression und Katharsis: Der Erste Weltkrieg im Diskurs der Moderne*. Vienna: Passagen, 2004.

Ferguson, Niall. *The Pity of War: Explaining World War I*. New York: Basic Books, 2000.

Fisher, Peter S. *Fantasy and Politics. Visions of the Future in the Weimar Republic*. Madison: University of Wisconsin Press, 1991.

Flasch, Kurt. *Die geistige Mobilmachung: Die deutschen Intellektuellen und der Erste Weltkrieg: Ein Versuch*. Berlin: A. Fest, 2000.

Frantzen, Allen J. *Bloody Good: Chivalry, Sacrifice, and the Great War*. Chicago: University of Chicago Press, 2004.

Fussell, Paul. *The Great War and Modern Memory*. Oxford: Oxford University Press, 1975.

Gangl, Manfred, ed. *Intellektuellendiskurse in der Weimarer Republik: Zur politischen Kultur einer Gemengelage*. Darmstadt: Wissenschaftliche Buchgesellschaft, 1994.

Gordon, Mel. *Voluptuous Panic: The Erotic World of Weimar Berlin*. Los Angeles: Feral House, 2000.

Hagemann, Karen, and Stefanie Schüler-Springorum. *Heimat-Front: Militär und Geschlechterverhältnisse im Zeitalter der Weltkriege*. Frankfurt: Campus, 2002.

Halfeld, Adolf. *Amerika und der Amerikanismus: Kritische Betrachtungen eines Deutschen und Europäers*. Jena: Eugen Diederichs Verlag, 1927.

Hamann, Brigitte. *Der Erste Weltkrieg. Wahrheit und Lüge in Bildern und Texten*. Munich: Piper, 2004.

Hecht, Cornelia. *Deutsche Juden und Antisemitismus in der Weimarer Republik*. Bonn: Dietz, 2003.

Heinemann, Ulrich. *Die verdrängte Niederlage: Politische Öffentlichkeit und Kriegsschuldfrage in der Weimarer Republik*. Göttingen: Vandenhoeck und Ruprecht, 1983.

Hentig, Hans. *Psychologische Strategie des Grossen Krieges*. Heidelberg: C. Winter, 1927.

Herf, Jeffrey. *Reactionary Modernism: Technology, Culture, and Politics in Weimar and the Third Reich*. Cambridge: Cambridge University Press, 1984.

Hermand, Jost. *Old Dreams of a New Reich: Volkish Utopias and National Socialism*. Bloomington: Indiana University Press, 1992.

Hermand, Jost, and Frank Trommler. *Die Kultur in der Weimarer Republik*. Munich: Nymphenburger, 1978.

Hirschfeld, Gerhard, Gerd Krumeich, and Irina Renz, eds. *Die Deutschen an der Somme 1914–1919: Krieg, Besatzung, Verbrannte Erde*. Essen: Klartext, 2006.

———, eds. *Enzyklopädie Erster Weltkrieg*. Paderborn: Schöningh, 2003.

———, eds. *"Keiner fühlt sich hier mehr als Mensch . . . ": Erlebnis und Wirkung des Ersten Weltkriegs*. Essen: Klartext, 1993.

Howard, Michael. *The First World War: A Very Short Introduction*. Oxford: Oxford University Press, 2003.

Hüppauf, Bernd, ed. *Ansichten vom Krieg: Vergleichende Studien zum Ersten Weltkrieg in Literatur und Gesellschaft*. Königstein: Forum Academicum, 1984.

———, ed. *War, Violence, and the Modern Condition*. Berlin: De Gruyter, 1997.

Isenberg, Noah. *Between Redemption and Doom: The Strains of German-Jewish Modernism*. Lincoln: University of Nebraska Press, 1999.

Jeismann, Michael, and Reinhart Koselleck, eds. *Der politische Totenkult: Kriegerdenkmäler in der Moderne*. Munich: C. H. Beck 1994.

Jünger, Ernst. *Copse 125: A Chronicle from the Trench War of 1918*. New York: Howard Fertig, 2003.

———. *Sämtliche Werke*. Stuttgart: Klett, 1978–2003.

———. *Storm of Steel: From the Diary of a German Storm-troop Officer on the Western Front*. New York: Howard Fertig, 1996.

Kaes, Anton, Martin Jay, and Edward Dimendberg, eds. *The Weimar Republic Sourcebook*. Berkeley: University of California Press, 1994.

Kniesche, Thomas W., and Stephen Brockmann, eds. *Dancing on the Volcano: Essays on the Culture of the Weimar Republic*. Columbia, SC: Camden House, 1994.

Koch-Hillebrecht, Manfred. *Hitler: Ein Sohn des Krieges—Fronterlebnis und Weltbild*. Munich: Herbig, 2003.

Korte, Barbara, Sylvia Paletschek, and Wolfgang Hochbruch, eds. *Der Erste Weltkrieg in der populären Erinnerungskultur*. Essen: Klartext, 2008.

Krumeich, Gerd, ed. *Versailles 1919: Ziele–Wirkung–Wahrnehmung*. Essen: Klartext, 2001.

Kruse, Wolfgang, ed. *Eine Welt von Feinden. Der Große Krieg 1914–1918*. Frankfurt am Main: Fischer, 1997.

Lange, Britta. *Einen Krieg ausstellen*. Berlin: Verbrecher Verlag, 2003.

Leed, Eric J. *No Man's Land: Combat and Identity in World War I*. Cambridge: Cambridge University Press, 1979.

Lethen, Helmut. *Cool Conduct: The Culture of Distance*. Berkeley: University of California Press, 2002.

Lipp, Anne. *Meinungslenkung im Krieg. Kriegserfahrungen deutscher Soldaten und ihre Deutung 1914–1918*. Göttingen: Vandenhoeck and Ruprecht, 2003.

Long, Rose-Carol Washton, ed. *German Expressionism: Documents from the End of the Wilhelmine Empire to the Rise of National Socialism*. Berkeley: University of California Press, 1993.

Maengel, Manfred. *Das Wissen des Kriegers oder Der Magische Operateur: Krieg und Technik im Frühwerk von Ernst Jünger*. Berlin: Xenomos, 2005.

Martus, Steffen, Marina Münkler, and Werner Röcke, eds. *Schlachtfelder. Codierung von Gewalt im medialen Wandel*. Berlin: Akademie Verlag, 2003.

Michalka, Wolfgang. *Der Erste Weltkrieg: Wirkung, Wahrnehmung, Analyse*. Munich: Piper, 1994.

Mommsen, Wolfgang J. *Der Erste Weltkrieg: Anfang vom Ende des bürgerlichen Zeitalters.* Frankfurt am Main: Fischer, 2004.

Mommsen, Wolfgang J., and Elisabeth Müller-Luckner, eds. *Kultur und Krieg: Die Rolle der Intellektuellen, Künstler und Schriftsteller im Ersten Weltkrieg.* Munich: Oldenbourg, 1996.

Mosse, George L. *Fallen Soldiers: Reshaping the Memory of the World Wars.* Oxford: Oxford University Press, 1991.

———. *The Jews and the German War Experience, 1914–1918.* Leo Baeck Memorial Lecture 21. New York: Leo Baeck Institute, 1977.

Müller, Hans-Harald. *Der Krieg und die Schriftsteller: der Kriegsroman der Weimarer Republik.* Stuttgart: Metzler, 1986.

Münkler, Herfried, and Wolfgang Storch. *Siegfrieden: Politik mit einem deutschen Mythos.* Berlin: Rotbuch-Verlag, 1988.

Peukert, Detlev. *The Weimar Republic.* New York: Hill and Wang, 1993.

Rohkrämer, Thomas. *Eine andere Moderne? Zivilisationskritik, Natur und Technik in Deutschland, 1880–1933.* Munich: Schöningh, 1999.

Roshwald, Aviel, and Richard Stites, eds. *European Culture in the Great War.* Cambridge: Cambridge University Press, 1999.

Rother, Rainer, ed. *Die letzten Tage der Menschheit. Bilder des Ersten Weltkrieges.* Berlin: Deutsches Historisches Museum, 1994.

———, ed. *Der Weltkrieg 1914–1918: Ereignis und Erinnerung.* Wolfratshausen: Edition Minerva, 2004.

Rühle, Günther, ed. *Theater für die Republik 1917–1933: Im Spiegel der Kritik.* Frankfurt am Main: Fischer, 1967.

Saehrendt, Christian. *Der Stellungskrieg der Denkmäler. Kriegerdenkmäler im Berlin der Zwischenkriegszeit (1919–1939).* Bonn: J.H.W. Dietz Nachfolger, 2004.

Schickedanz, Margareta. *Deutsche Frau und deutsche Not im Weltkrieg.* Leipzig: B. G. Teubner, 1938.

Schivelbusch, Wolfgang. *The Culture of Defeat: On National Trauma, Mourning, and Recovery.* Translated by Jefferson Chase. New York: Henry Holt and Company, 2003.

Schneider, Uwe, and Andreas Schumann. *Krieg der Geister: Erster Weltkrieg und Literarische Moderne.* Würzburg: Königshausen and Neumann, 2000.

Schulze, Hagen. *Weimar: Deutschland 1917–1933.* Berlin: Siedler, 1994.

Sieg, Ulrich. *Jüdische Intellektuelle im Ersten Weltkrieg: Kriegserfahrungen, weltanschauliche Debatten und kulturelle Neuentwürfe.* Berlin: Akademie- Verlag, 2001.

Sloterdijk, Peter. *Critique of Cynical Reason.* Translated by Michael Eldred. Minneapolis: University of Minnesota Press, 1987.

Spilker, Rolf, and Bernd Ulrich, eds. *Der Tod als Maschinist.* Bramsche: Rasch, 1998.

Strachan, Hew, ed. *The Oxford Illustrated History of the First World War.* Oxford: Oxford University Press, 2000.

Theweleit, Klaus. *Male Fantasies*. Translated by Stephen Conway, Erica Carter, and Chris Turner. 2 vols. Minneapolis: University of Minnesota Press, 1987-89.
Todman, Daniel. *The Great War: Myth and Memory*. London: Hambledon and London, 2005.
Toepfer, Karl. *Empire of Ecstasy: Nudity and Movement in German Body Culture, 1910–1935*. Berkeley: University of California Press, 1997.
Ulrich, Bernd, and Benjamin Ziemann, eds. *Frontalltag im Ersten Weltkrieg: Wahn und Wirklichkeit. Quellen und Dokumente*. Frankfurt am Main: Fischer, 1994.
Von Ankum, Katharina, ed. *Women in the Metropolis: Gender and Modernity in Weimar Culture*. Berkeley: University of California Press, 1997.
Vondung, Klaus, ed. *The Apocalypse in Germany*. Translated by Stephen D. Ricks. Columbia: University of Missouri Press, 2000.
———. *Kriegserlebnis: Der Erste Weltkrieg in der literarischen Gestaltung und symbolischen Deutung der Nationen*. Göttingen: Vandenhoeck and Ruprecht, 1980.
Weitz, Eric D. *Weimar Germany: Promise and Tragedy*. Princeton, NJ: Princeton University Press, 2007.
Welch, David. *Germany, Propaganda, and Total War, 1914–1918: The Sins of Omission*. London: Athlone Press, 2000.
Whalen, Robert Weldon. *Bitter Wounds: German Victims of the Great War, 1914–1939*. Ithaca, NY: Cornell University Press, 1984.
Widdig, Bernd. *Culture and Inflation in Weimar Germany*. Berkeley: University of California Press, 2001.
Willett, John. *The Weimar Years: A Culture Cut Short*. New York: Abbeville Press, 1984.
Winkler, Heinrich August. *Weimar 1918–1933: Die Geschichte der ersten deutschen Demokratie*. Munich: C. H. Beck, 1993.
———, ed. *Weimar im Widerstreit: Deutungen der ersten deutschen Republik im geteilten Deutschland*. Munich: Oldenbourg, 2002.
Winter, Jay. *The Experience of World War I*. Oxford: Oxford University Press, 1989.
———. *Remembering War: The Great War between Memory and History in the Twentieth Century*. New Haven, CT: Yale University Press, 2006.
———. *Sites of Memory, Sites of Mourning: The Great War in European Cultural History*. Cambridge: Cambridge University Press, 1995.
Winter, Jay, and Leo Baeck Institute, eds. *Fighting for the Fatherland: The Patriotism of Jews in World War I—An Exhibition of the Leo Baeck Institute, New York*. New York: Leo Baeck Institute, 1999.
Winter, Jay, and Blaine Baggett. *1914–18: The Great War and the Shaping of the 20th Century*. London: BBC Books, 1996.
Winter, Jay, and Antoine Prost, eds. *The Great War in History: Debates and Controversies, 1914 to the Present*. Cambridge: Cambridge University Press, 2005.
Winter, Jay, and Jean-Louis Robert, eds. *Capital Cities at War: Paris, London, Berlin, 1914–1919*. Cambridge: Cambridge University Press, 1997.

Witkop, Philipp, A. F. Wedd, and Jay Winter, eds. *German Students' War Letters.* Philadelphia: Pine Street Books, 2002.

Wohl, Robert. *The Generation of 1914*. Cambridge, MA: Harvard University Press, 1979.

Zuckmayer, Carl. *A Part of Myself.* Translated by Richard Winston and Clara Winston. New York: Harcourt Brace Jovanovich, 1970.

Weimar Film History

Andriopoulos, Stefan. *Possessed: Hypnotic Crimes, Corporate Fiction, and the Invention of Cinema.* Chicago: University of Chicago Press, 2008.

Arnheim, Rudolf. *Film Essays and Criticism.* Madison: University of Wisconsin Press, 1997.

Aurich, Rolf, and Wolfgang Jacobsen, eds. *Werkstatt Film. Selbstverständnis und Visionen von Filmleuten der zwanziger Jahre.* Munich: edition text + kritik, 1998.

Balázs, Béla. *Schriften zum Film.* Helmut H. Diederichs, Wolfgang Gersch, and Magda Nagy, eds. 2 vols. Berlin: Henschel, 1982.

Bär, Gerald. *Das Motiv des Doppelgängers als Spaltungsphantasie in der Literatur und im deutschen Stummfilm.* Amsterdam: Rodopi, 2005.

Barkhausen, Hans. *Filmpropaganda für Deutschland im Ersten und Zweiten Weltkrieg.* Hildesheim: Olms Presse, 1982.

Barlow, John D. *German Expressionist Film.* Boston: Twayne, 1982.

Bartov, Omer. *The "Jew" in Cinema: From the "Golem" to "Don't Touch My Holocaust."* Bloomington: Indiana University Press, 2005.

Berg-Ganschow, Uta, and Wolfgang Jacobsen, eds. *Film . . . Stadt . . . Kino . . . Berlin.* Berlin: Argon, 1987.

Bock, Hans-Michael, and Michael Töteberg, eds. *Das Ufa-Buch: Kunst und Krisen. Stars und Regisseure, Wirtschaft und Politik: die internationale Geschichte von Deutschlands grösstem Film-Konzern.* Frankfurt am Main: Zweitausendeins, 1992.

Bogdanovich, Peter. *Fritz Lang in America.* New York: Praeger, 1967.

Bongartz, Barbara. *Von Caligari zu Hitler—von Hitler zu Dr. Mabuse? Eine "psychologische" Geschichte des deutschen Films von 1946 bis 1960.* Münster: MAKS Publikationen, 1992.

Brecht, Christoph, and Ines Steiner. *Im Reich der Schatten: Siegfried Kracauers "From Caligari to Hitler."* Marbacher Magazin 105. Marbach am Neckar: Deutsche Schillergesellschaft, 2004.

Brennicke, Ilona, and Joe Hembus. *Klassiker des deutschen Stummfilms 1910–1930.* Munich: Wilhelm Goldmann, 1983.

Bruns, Karin. *Kinomythen 1920–1945. Die Filmentwürfe der Thea von Harbou.* Stuttgart: Metzler, 1995.

Bub, Gertraude. *Der deutsche Film im Weltkrieg und sein publizistischer Einsatz.* Berlin: C. Trute, 1938.

Calhoon, Kenneth S., ed. *Peripheral Visions: The Hidden Stages of Weimar Cinema.* Detroit: Wayne State University Press, 2001.

Chiari, Bernhard, Matthias Rogg, and Wolfgang Schmidt, eds. *Krieg und Militär im Film des 20. Jahrhunderts.* Beiträge zur Militärgeschichte. Munich: Oldenbourg, 2003.
Coates, Paul. *The Gorgon's Gaze: German Cinema, Expressionism, and the Image of Horror.* Cambridge: Cambridge University Press, 1991.
Cobley, Evelyn. *Representing War: Form and Ideology in First World War Narratives.* Toronto: University of Toronto Press, 1993.
Collier, Jo Leslie. *From Wagner to Murnau: The Transposition of Romanticism from Stage to Screen.* Ann Arbor, MI: UMI Research Press, 1988.
DeBauche, Leslie. *Reel Patriotism: The Movies and World War I.* Madison: University of Wisconsin Press, 1997.
Deleuze, Gilles. *Cinema 1: The Movement-Image.* Translated by Hugh Tomlinson and Barbara Habberjam. Minneapolis: University of Minnesota Press, 1986.
Dibbets, Karel, and Bert Hogenkamp, eds. *Film and the First World War.* Amsterdam: Amsterdam University Press, 1995.
Duppler, Jörg, and Gerhard Paul Gross. *Kriegsende 1918: Ereignis, Wirkung, Nachwirkung.* Munich: Oldenbourg, 1999.
Eisner, Lotte H. *Fritz Lang.* London: Seeker and Warburg, 1976.
———. *The Haunted Screen: Expressionism in the German Cinema and the Influence of Max Reinhardt.* Translated by Roger Greaves. Berkeley: University of California Press, 1974.
———. *Murnau.* Revised and enlarged edition. Berkeley: University of California Press, 1973.
———. *Murnau.* Frankfurt a. M.: Kommunales Kino, 1979.
Elsaesser, Thomas, ed. *Companion to German Cinema.* London: BFI, 1999.
———, ed. *Early Cinema: Space, Frame, Narrative.* London: BFI, 1997.
———. *Weimar Cinema and After: Germany's Historical Imaginary.* London: Routledge, 2000.
Ernst, Petra, Sabine Haring, and Werner Suppanz, eds. *Aggression und Katharsis: Der Erste Weltkrieg im Diskurs der Moderne.* Vienna: Passagen, 2004.
Frankfurter, Bernhard, ed. *Carl Mayer: Im Spiegelkabinett des Dr. Caligari.* Frankfurt am Main: Promedia, 1997.
Gehler, Fred, and Ullrich Kasten. *Fritz Lang, Die Stimme von Metropolis.* Berlin: Henschel, 1990.
———. *F. W. Murnau.* Berlin: Henschel, 1990.
Ginsberg, Terri, and Kirsten Moana Thompson, eds. *Perspectives on German Cinema.* New York: G. K. Hall, 1996.
Grafe, Frieda. *Licht aus Berlin: Lang, Lubitsch, Murnau und weiteres zum Kino der Weimarer Republik.* Berlin: Brinkmann and Bose, 2003.
Grafe, Frieda, Enno Patalas, and Hans Helmut Prinzler. *Fritz Lang.* Munich: Hanser, 1976.
Guerin, Frances. *A Culture of Light: Cinema and Technology in 1920s Germany.* Minneapolis: University of Minnesota Press, 2005.
Gunning, Tom. *The Films of Fritz Lang: Allegories of Vision and Modernity.* London: BFI, 2000.

Güttinger, Fritz, ed. *Kein Tag ohne Kino. Schriftsteller über den Stummfilm*. Frankfurt am Main: Deutsches Filmmuseum Frankfurt, 1984.
———, ed. *Köpfen Sie mal ein Ei in Zeitlupe! Streifzüge durch die Welt des Stummfilms*. Munich: Wilhelm Fink, 1992.
Hake, Sabine. *The Cinema's Third Machine: Writing on Film in Germany, 1907–1933*. Lincoln: University of Nebraska Press, 1993.
Hantke, Steffen, ed. *Caligari's Heirs: The German Cinema of Fear after 1945*. Lanham, MD: Scarecrow, 2005.
Hoormann, Anne. *Lichtspiele: Zur Medienreflexion der Avantgarde in der Weimarer Republik*. Munich: Fink, 2003.
Jacobsen, Wolfgang, Anton Kaes, and Hans Helmut Prinzler, eds. *Geschichte des deutschen Films*. 2nd ed. Stuttgart: Metzler, 2004.
Jacobsen, Wolfgang, Hans Helmut Prinzler, and Werner Sudendorf, eds. *Filmmuseum Berlin*. Berlin: Nicolai, 2000.
Jenkins, Stephen. *Fritz Lang: The Image and the Look*. London: BFI, 1981.
Jung, Uli, and Walter Schatzberg. *Beyond Caligari: The Films of Robert Wiene*. New York: Berghahn, 1999.
———, eds. *Filmkultur zur Zeit der Weimarer Republik*. Munich: Saur, 1992.
Kabatek, Wolfgang. *Imagerie des Anderen im Weimarer Kino*. Bielefeld: Transcript, 2003.
Kaes, Anton, ed. *Kino-Debatte. Texte zum Verhältnis von Literatur und Film 1909–1929*. Munich: Deutscher Taschenbuch Verlag, 1978.
———. *M*. London: British Film Institute, 2001.
Kaplan, E. Ann. *Fritz Lang: A Guide to References and Resources*. Boston: G. K. Hall, 1981.
Kappelhoff, Hermann. *Der möblierte Mensch: G.W. Pabst und die Utopie der Sachlichkeit. Ein poetologischer Versuch zum Weimarer Autorenkino*. Berlin: vorwerk 8, 1995.
Kasten, Jürgen. *Carl Mayer: Filmpoet. Ein Drehbuchautor schreibt Filmgeschichte*. Berlin: Vistas, 1994.
———. *Der expressionistische Film. Abgefilmtes Theater oder avantgardistisches Erzählkino? Eine stil-, produktions- und rezeptionsgeschichtliche Untersuchung*. Münster: MAKS Publikations, 1990.
Keiner, Reinhold. *Thea von Harbou und der deutsche Film bis 1933*. Hildesheim: Olms, 1984.
Kelly, Andrew. *Cinema and the Great War*. London: Routledge, 1997.
Kessler, Michael, and Thomas Y. Levin, eds. *Siegfried Kracauer: Neue Interpretationen*. Tübingen: Stauffenburg, 1990.
Kester, Bernadette. *Film Front Weimar: Representations of the First World War in German Films of the Weimar Period, 1919–1933*. Amsterdam: Amsterdam University Press, 2003.
Kittler, Friedrich. *Draculas Vermächtnis: Technische Schriften*. Leipzig: Reclam Verlag, 1993.

———. *Gramophone, Film, Typewriter*. Translated by Geoffrey Winthrop-Young and Michael Wutz. Stanford, CA: Stanford University Press, 1999.

Knieper, Thomas, and Marion G. Muller, eds. *War Visions: Bildkommunikation und Krieg*. Cologne: Herbert von Halem Verlag, 2005.

Koch, Gertrud. *Siegfried Kracauer: An Introduction*. Princeton, NJ: Princeton University Press, 2000.

Koebner, Thomas, ed. *Diesseits der "Dämonischen Leinwand." Neue Perspektiven auf das späte Weimarer Kino*. Munich: edition text + kritik, 2003.

———, ed. *Idole des deutschen Films: Eine Galerie von Schlüsselfiguren*. Munich: edition text + kritik, 1997.

Köppen, Manuel. *Das Entsetzen des Beobachters: Krieg und Medien im 19. und 20. Jahrhundert*. Probleme der Dichtung 35. Heidelberg: Universitätsverlag Winter, 2005.

Korte, Helmut, ed. *Film und Realität in der Weimarer Republik*. Frankfurt am Main: Fischer, 1980.

Kracauer, Siegfried. *From Caligari to Hitler: A Psychological History of the German Film*. Leonardo Quaresima, ed. rev. ed. Princeton, NJ: Princeton University Press, 2004. First published 1947.

———. *Kleine Schriften zum Film*. Inka Mülder-Bach, ed. 3 vols. Frankfurt am Main: Suhrkamp, 2005.

———. *The Mass Ornament: Weimar Essays*. Edited and translated by Thomas Y. Levin. Cambridge, MA: Harvard University Press, 1995.

Krause, Ulrike. *Realität der Weimarer Republik: Gewalt und Kriminalität in deutschen Filmen der "Goldenen Zwanziger."* Saarbrücken: VDM Müller, 2007.

Kreimeier, Klaus. *The Ufa Story: A History of Germany's Greatest Film Company, 1918–1945*. Translated by Robert Kimber and Rita Kimber. New York: Hill and Wang, 1996.

Kühn, Gertraude, Karl Tümmler, and Walter Wimmer, eds. *Film und revolutionäre Arbeiterbewegung in Deutschland 1918–1932: Dokumente und Materialien zur Entwicklung der Filmpolitik der revolutionären Arbeiterbewegung und zu den Anfängen einer sozialistischen Filmkunst in Deutschland*. 2 vols. Berlin: Henschel, 1975.

Kurtz, Rudolf. *Expressionismus und Film*. Berlin: Verlag der Lichtbildbühne, 1926. Reprint edition with an afterword by Christian Kiening and Ulrich Johannes Bell. Zurich: Chronos, 2007.

Lang, Fritz. *Interviews*. Barry Keith Grant, ed. Jackson: University Press of Mississippi, 2003.

Levin, David. *Richard Wagner, Fritz Lang, and the Nibelungen: The Dramaturgy of Disavowal*. Princeton, NJ: Princeton University Press, 1998.

McCormick, Richard W. *Gender and Sexuality in Weimar Modernity: Film, Literature, and "New Objectivity."* New York: Palgrave, 2001.

McGilligan, Patrick. *Fritz Lang: The Nature of the Beast*. New York: St. Martin's Press, 1997.

Monaco, Paul. *Cinema and Society: France and Germany during the Twenties*. New York: Elsevier, 1976.

Mühl-Benninghaus, Wolfgang. *Vom Augusterlebnis zur Ufa-Gründung: Der deutsche Film im 1. Weltkrieg*. Berlin: Avinus, 2004.

Müller, Jürgen. *Filme der 20er.* Cologne: Taschen, 2007.

Murphy, Richard. *Theorizing the Avant-Garde: Modernism, Expressionism, and the Problem of Postmodernity*. Cambridge: Cambridge University Press, 1999.

Murray, Bruce. *Film and the German Left in the Weimar Republic: From Caligari to Kuhle Wampe*. Austin: University of Texas Press, 1990.

Neumann, Dietrich, ed. *Film Architecture: Set Designs from Metropolis to Blade Runner*. New York: Prestel, 1996.

Oppelt, Ulrike. *Film und Propaganda im Ersten Weltkrieg: Propaganda als Medienrealität im Aktualitäten- und Dokumentarfilm*. Stuttgart: Franz Steiner, 2002.

Ott, Frederick W. *The Films of Fritz Lang*. Secaucus, NJ: Citadel Press, 1979.

Palmier, Jean-Michel. *Weimar in Exile: The Antifascist Emigration in Europe and America*. Translated by David Fernbach. London: Verso, 2006.

Paris, Michael. *The First World War and Popular Cinema: 1914 to the Present*. Edinburgh: Edinburgh University Press, 1999.

Paul, Gerhard. *Bilder des Krieges, Krieg der Bilder: Die Visualisierung des modernen Krieges*. Paderborn: Schöningh, 2004.

Petro, Patrice. *Joyless Streets: Women and Melodramatic Representation in Weimar Germany*. Princeton, NJ: Princeton University Press, 1989.

Peucker, Brigitte. *Incorporating Images: Film and the Rival Arts*. Princeton, NJ: Princeton University Press, 1995.

Pomerance, Murray, ed. *Cinema and Modernity*. New Brunswick, NJ: Rutgers University Press, 2006.

Powell, Anna. *Deleuze and Horror Film*. Edinburgh: Edinburgh University Press, 2006.

Prawer, S. S. *Between Two Worlds: The Jewish Presence in German and Austrian Film, 1910–1933*. New York: Berghahn Books, 2005.

Prinzler, Hans Helmut, ed. *Friedrich Wilhelm Murnau: ein Melancholiker des Films*. Berlin: Bertz, 2003.

Rother, Rainer, ed. *Die Ufa 1917–1945: Das deutsche Bilderimperium*. Berlin: Deutsches Historisches Museum und Stiftung Deutsche Kinemathek, 1992.

Saunders, Thomas J. *Hollywood in Berlin: American Cinema and Weimar Germany*. Berkeley: University of California Press, 1994.

Scheunemann, Dietrich, ed. *Expressionist Film: New Perspectives*. Rochester, NY: Camden House, 2003.

Schilling, René. *"Kriegshelden": Deutungsmuster heroischer Männlichkeit in Deutschland 1813–1945*. Paderborn: Schöningh, 2002.

Schivelbusch, Wolfgang. *The Culture of Defeat: On National Trauma, Mourning, and Recovery*. Translated by Jefferson Chase. New York: Henry Holt and Company, 2003.

Schlüpmann, Heide. *Ein Detektiv des Kinos: Studien zu Siegfried Kracauers Filmtheorie*. Basel: Stroemfeld, 1998.
Schönemann, Heide. *Fritz Lang: Filmbilder, Vorbilder*. Berlin: Edition Hentrich, 1992.
———. *Paul Wegener: Frühe Moderne im Film*. Stuttgart: Axel Menges, 2003.
Schrader, Bärbel, ed. *Der Fall Remarque: Im Westen nichts Neues: eine Dokumentation*. Leipzig: Reclam, 1992.
Segeberg, Harro, ed. *Die Perfektionierung des Scheins: Das Kino der Weimarer Republik im Kontext der Künste*. Munich: Fink, 2000.
Thompson, Kristin. *Herr Lubitsch Goes to Hollywood: German and American Film after World War I*. Amsterdam: Amsterdam University Press, 2005.
Virilio, Paul. *War and Cinema: The Logistics of Perception*. London: Verso, 1989.
Waller, Gregory A. *The Living and the Undead: From Stoker's "Dracula" to Romero's "Dawn of the Dead."* Urbana: University of Illinois Press, 1986.
Ward, Janet. *Weimar Surfaces: Urban Visual Culture in 1920's Germany*. Berkeley: University of California Press, 2001.
Webber, Andrew. *The Doppelgänger: Double Visions in German Literature*. Oxford: Oxford University Press, 1996.
Zimmermann, Peter, ed. *Geschichte des dokumentarischen Films in Deutschland*. Vol. 2, *Die Weimarer Republik*. Ditzingen: Reclam, 2005.

Films Discussed

Das Cabinet des Dr. Caligari /The Cabinet of Dr. Caligari

Credits

Director: Robert Wiene; Production: Decla-Bioscop; Producers: Erich Pommer and Rudolph Meinert; Script: Carl Mayer and Hans Janowitz (based on a story by Hans Janowitz); Cinematography: Willy Hameister; Design: Walter Reimann, Hermann Warm, and Walter Röhrig; Original Music: Giuseppe Becce. Cast: Werner Krauss as Dr. Caligari; Conrad Veidt as Cesare; Lil Dagover as Jane; Friedrich Fehér as Francis; Hans Heinz von Twardowski as Alan; Rudolf Letinger as Dr. Olson; Rudolf Klein-Rogge as Captured Murderer. —First Screening at the Marmorhaus in Berlin on February 26, 1920

Sources

The Cabinet of Dr. Caligari. Translated by R. V. Adkinson. Classic Film Scripts. New York: Simon and Schuster, 1972.
Das Cabinet des Dr. Caligari. Robert Fischer and Klaus-Peter Hess, eds. Stuttgart: Verlagsgemeinschaft Robert Fischer et al., 1985.
Das Cabinet des Dr. Caligari. Drehbuch von Carl Mayer und Hans Janowitz zu Robert Wienes Film von 1919/1920. Helga Belach and H. M. Bock, eds. Munich: text + kritik, 1995.

Remakes/Adaptations

The Cabinet of Dr. Caligari. Directed by Roger Kay. Twentieth Century Fox, 1962.

Horror Vacui. Directed by Rosa von Praunheim. WDR, 1984.

The Cabinet of Dr. Ramirez. Directed by Peter Sellars. BBC, 1991.

Das Cabinet des Dr. Caligari, photo story. Karl Lagerfeld. 1995.

Doktor Caligari, play. Robert Wilson. Berlin, 2002.

The Cabinet of Dr. Caligari. Directed by David Lee Fisher. Highlander Films, 2006.

Secondary Literature

Allen, Jerry C. *Conrad Veidt: From "Caligari" to "Casablanca."* Pacific Grove, CA: Boxwood Press, 1987.

Andriopoulos, Stefan. "Spellbound in Darkness: Hypnosis as an Allegory of Early Cinema." *Germanic Review* 77, no.2 (Spring 2002): 102–16.

Aurich, Rolf, and Wolfgang Jacobsen. "Hypnose und Krieg, Mord und Kokain." In *Filmmuseum Berlin*, Wolfgang Jacobsen and Hans Helmut Prinzler, eds., 35–52. Berlin: Nicolai, 2000.

Barsacq, Leon. *Caligari's Cabinet and Other Great Illusions: A History of Film Design*. New York: New American Library, 1978.

Beicken, Peter. "Faust in Film: The Case of Dr. Caligari." In *Doctor Faustus: Archetypal Subtext at the Millennium*. Armand E. Singer and Jürgen Schlunk, eds., 43–67. Morgantown: West Virginia University Press, 1999.

Budd, Mike. *The Cabinet of Dr. Caligari: Texts, Contexts, Histories*. New Brunswick, NJ: Rutgers University Press, 1990.

———. "Modernism and the Representation of Fantasy: Cubism and Expressionism in *The Cabinet of Dr. Caligari*." In *Forms of the Fantastic*, Jan Hokenson and Howard D. Pearce, eds., 15–21. Westport, CT: Greenwood, 1986.

Burch, Noël, and Jorge Dana. "Propositions." *Afterimage* 5 (1974): 41–45.

Cardullo, Bert. "Expressionism and the Real *Cabinet of Dr. Caligari*." *Film Criticism* 6, no. 2 (Winter 1982): 28–34.

Carroll, Noël. "The Cabinet of Dr. Kracauer." *Millennium* 2 (Spring–Summer 1978): 77–85.

Donahue, Neil H. "Unjustly Framed: Politics and Art in *Das Cabinet des Dr. Caligari*." *German Politics and Society* 32 (July 1994): 76–88.

Fleishman, Avrom. "Dramatized Narration: *The Cabinet of Dr. Caligari* and *Hiroshima Mon Amour*." In *Narrated Films: Storytelling Situations in Cinema History*, Avrom Fleishman, ed., 99–127. Baltimore: Johns Hopkins University Press, 1992.

Frank, Steven. "On 'the Verge' of a New Form: *The Cabinet of Dr. Caligari* and Susan Glaspell's Experiments in the Verge." In *Experimenters, Rebels, and Disparate Voices: The Theatre of the 1920s Celebrates American Diversity*, Arthur Gewirtz and James J. Kolb, eds., 119–29. Westport, CT: Praeger, 2003.

Friedman, Regine-Mihal. "*Das Cabinet des Dr. Caligari*: Jüdische Mythen oder Mythen des Juden?" In *Carl Mayer, Scenar[t]ist*, Brigitte Mayr, ed., 89–96. Vienna: Synema, 2003.

Gay, Peter. "The Weimar Resemblance." *Horizon* 12, no. 1 (1970): 4–15.
Genova, J. A. "Wittgenstein and Caligari." *Philosophical Forum* 4, no. 2 (Winter 1972–73): 186–95.
Gerdes, Peter. "*Das Kabinett des Dr. Caligari*: Unlösbarer Konflikt?" In *Expressionismus und Kulturkrise*, Bernd Hüppauf, ed., 245–62. Heidelberg: Winter, 1983.
Grace, Sherrill E. "'Dans le cristallin de nos yeux': Neige noire, Caligari, and the Postmodern Film Frame-up." *New Comparison: A Journal of Comparative and General Literary Studies* 5 (July 1988): 89–103.
Gray, Richard T. "From Caligari to Kafka: Expressionist Film and the Teaching of Kafka's Short Fiction." In *Approaches to Teaching Kafka's Short Fiction*, Richard T. Gray, ed., 53–63. New York: Modern Language Association, 1995.
Gruber, Bettina. "Hoffmann, Chamisso, Caligari: *Der Student von Prag* und *Das Cabinet des Doktor Caligari*: Zu den romantischen Prämissen zweier deutscher Stummfilme." *E.T.A. Hoffmann-Jahrbuch* 13 (2005): 117–32.
Hall, Sara F. "Pursuits across the Threshold of Modernity: Projecting the Primitive against the Backdrop of Emergent Urban Culture in *The Cabinet of Dr. Caligari*." In *Die Grossstadt und das Primitive: Text–Politik–Repräsentation*, Kristin Kopp and Klaus Müller-Richter, eds.,177–200. Stuttgart: Metzler, 2004.
Hankins, Leslie K. "The Doctor and the Woolf: Reel Challenges—*The Cabinet of Dr. Caligari* and Mrs. Dalloway." In *Virginia Woolf: Themes and Variations*, Vara Neverow-Turk and Mark Hussey, eds., 40–51. New York: Pace University Press, 1993.
Hubbert, Julie. "Modernism at the Movies: *The Cabinet of Dr. Caligari* and a Film Score Revisited." *Musical Quarterly* 88, no 1 (2005): 53–94.
Jung, Uli. "The Invisible Man behind Caligari. The Life of Robert Wiene." *Film History* 5, no. 1 (March 1993): 22–23.
Jung, Uli, and Walter Schatzberg. "Caligari: Das Kabinett des Dr. Wiene." In *Filmkultur zur Zeit der Weimarer Republik*, Uli Jung and Walter Schatzberg, eds., 71–89. Munich: Saur, 1992.
———. *Beyond Caligari: The Films of Robert Wiene*. New York: Berghahn Books, 1999.
Kaes, Anton. "April 1921. A German Film Introduces Americans to a New Aesthetic: Cinema and Expressionism." In *A New History of German Literature*, David Wellbery, Judith Ryan, Hans Ulrich Gumbrecht, Anton Kaes, Joseph Leo Koerner, and Dorothea von Mücke, eds., 718–23. Cambridge, MA: Harvard University Press, 2004.
———. "*The Cabinet of Dr. Caligari*: Expressionism and Cinema." In *Masterpieces of Modernist Cinema*, Ted Perry, ed., 41–59. Bloomington: Indiana University Press, 2006.
———. "Modernity and Its Discontents: Notes on Alterity in Weimar Cinema." Translated by David Levin. *Qui Parle* 5, no. 2 (Spring–Summer 1992): 135–42.
———."War—Film—Trauma." In *Modernität und Trauma*, Inka Mülder-Bach, ed., 121–30. Vienna: Edition Parabasen, 2000.
Kaul, Walter, ed. *Caligari und Caligarismus*. Berlin: Deutsche Kinemathek, 1979.

Ketchiff, Nancy. "Dr. Caligari's Cabinet: A Cubist Perspective." *Comparatist: Journal of the Southern Comparative Literature Association* 8 (May 1984): 7–13.

Kiening, Christian. "Blick und Schrift: *Das Cabinet des Dr. Caligari* und die Medialität des frühen Spielfilms." *Poetica: Zeitschrift für Sprach- und Literaturwissenschaft* 37, no. 1–2 (2005): 119–45.

Mahoney, Dennis, F. "From Caligari to Strangelove: The German as (Mad) Scientist in Film and Literature." In *Analogon rationis*, Marianne Henn and Christoph Lorey, eds., 419–32. Edmonton: University of Alberta Press, 1994.

McCormick, Richard W. "From Caligari to Dietrich: Sexual, Social, and Cinematic Discourses in Weimar Film." *Signs* 18, no. 3 (April 1993): 640–68.

Meyers, Jeffrey. "Caligari and Cipolla: Mann's 'Mario and the Magician.'" *MFS: Modern Fiction Studies* 32, no. 2 (July 1986): 235–39.

Minden, Michael. "Politics and the Silent Cinema: *The Cabinet of Dr. Caligari* and *Battleship Potemkin*." In *Visions and Blueprints: Avant-garde Culture and Radical Politics in Early Twentieth-Century Europe*, Edward Timms, Peter Collier, and Raymond Williams, eds., 287–306. Manchester: Manchester University Press, 1988.

Murphy, Richard J. "Carnival Desire and the Sideshow of Fantasy: Dream, Duplicity, and Representational Instability in *The Cabinet of Dr. Caligari*." *Germanic Review* 66 (1991): 48–56.

Murray, Bruce. *Film and the German Left in the Weimar Republic: From Caligari to Kuhle Wampe*. Austin: University of Texas Press, 1990.

Pegge, C. Dennis. "Caligari: Its Innovations in Editing." *Quarterly of Film, Radio, and Television* 11 (Winter 1956): 136–48.

Petro, Patrice. "The Woman, the Monster, and *The Cabinet of Dr. Caligari*." In *The Cabinet of Dr. Caligari: Texts, Contexts, Histories*, Mike Budd, ed., 205–17. New Brunswick, NJ: Rutgers University Press, 1990.

Prawer, S. S. *Caligari's Children: The Film as Tale of Terror*. Oxford: Oxford University Press, 1980.

Quaresima, Leonardo. "Die 'Geburtsurkunde' des *Caligari*." *Filmdienst*, no. 5 (March 3, 1992): 16–7.

———. "Wer war Alland? Die Texte des Caligari." In *Carl Mayer: Im Spiegelkabinett des Dr. Caligari*, Bernhard Frankfurter, ed., 99–118. Vienna: Promedia, 1997.

Riess, Rolf. "Im Schatten von Dr. Caligari: Hans Janowitz im Exil." *Filmexil* 7 (December 1995): 20–27.

Roberts, Ian. "Caligari Revisited: Circles, Cycles, and Counter-revolution in Robert Wiene's *Das Cabinet des Dr. Caligari*." *German Life and Letters* 57, no. 2 (April 2004): 175–87.

Robinson, David. *Das Cabinet des Dr. Caligari*. London: BFI, 1997.

Rubenstein, Lenny. "Caligari and the Rise of Expressionist Film." In *Passion and Rebellion: The Expressionist Heritage*, Stephen Eric Bronner and Douglas Kellner, eds., 363–73. South Hadley, MA: Bergin, 1983.

Salt, Barry. "From Caligari to Who?" *Sight and Sound* 48, no. 2 (Spring 1979): 119–23.

Sandford, John. "Caligari's Children." *German Life and Letters* 34, no. 3 (April 1981): 337–43.
———. "Chaos and Control in the Weimar Film." *German Life and Letters* 48, no.3 (July 1994): 311–23.
Schaal, Hans Dieter. "*Intolerance–Caligari–Potemkin*: Zur ästhetischen Funktion der Zwischentitel im Frühen Film." In *Text und Ton im Film*, Paul Goetsch and Dietrich Scheunemann, eds., 11–43. Tübingen: Narr, 1997.
———. "Spaces of the Psyche in German Expressionist Film." *Architectural Design* 70, no. 1 (January 2000): 12–15.
Scheunemann, Dietrich. "The Double, the Decor, and the Framing Device: Once More on Robert Wiene's *The Cabinet of Dr. Caligari*. In *Expressionist Film: New Perspectives*, Dietrich Scheunemann, ed., 125–56. Rochester, NY: Camden, 2003.
Schönfeld, Christiane. "Modern Identities in Early German Film: *The Cabinet of Dr. Caligari*." In *Engaging Film: Geographies of Mobility and Identity*, Tim Cresswell and Deborah Dixon. eds., 174-89. Lanham, MD: Rowman and Littlefield, 2002.
Sudendorf, Werner. "Expressionism and Film: The Testament of Dr. Caligari." In *Expressionism Reassessed*, Shulamith Behr, David Fanning, and Douglas Jarman, eds., 91-100. Manchester: Manchester University Press, 1993.
Thiele, Jens. "Die dunklen Seiten der Seele: *Das Cabinet des Dr. Caligari*." In *Fischer Filmgeschichte*, Werner Faulstich and Helmut Korte, eds., 1:344–60. Frankfurt am Main: Fischer, 1994.
Thompson, Kristin. "Dr. Caligari at the Folies-Bergère: Or, the Successes of an Early Avant-Garde Film." In *The Cabinet of Dr. Caligari: Texts, Contexts, Histories*, Mike Budd, ed., 121–69. New Brunswick, NJ: Rutgers University Press, 1990.
Tiessen, Paul. "The Shadow in Caligari: Virginia Woolf and the 'Materialists' Responses to Film." *Film Criticism* 11, no. 1–2 (October 1987): 75–83.
Vidler, Anthony. *The Architectural Uncanny: Essays in the Modern Unhomely*. Cambridge, MA: MIT Press, 1992.
Walker, Julia A. "'In the Grip of an Obsession': Delsarte and the Quest for Self-possession in *The Cabinet of Dr. Caligari*." *Theatre Journal* 58, no. 4 (December 2006): 617–31.
Wiene, Robert. "Expressionismus im Film." *Berliner Börsen-Curier*, no. 353, July 30, 1922.
Woolf, Virginia. "The Cinema" (1926). In *Collected Essays*, 2:268–72. London: Chatto and Windus, 1966.

Nosferatu, eine Symphonie des Grauens / Nosferatu

Credits

Director: Friedrich Wilhelm Murnau; Production: Prana-Film; Script: Henrik Galeen based on Bram Stoker's *Dracula*; Cinematography: Fritz Arno Wagner;

Design: Albin Grau; Original Music: Hans Erdmann; Cast: Max Schreck as Count Orlok/Nosferatu; Gustav von Wangenheim as Hutter; Greta Schröder as Ellen; Alexander Granach as Knock; John Gottowt as Prof. Bulwer. — First Screening at the Primus-Palast in Berlin on March 15, 1922.

Sources

Nosferatu. Translated by G. Mander et al., in Lotte M. Eisner, *Murnau*. London: Seecker and Warburg, 1976. (This is the English translation of Henrik Galeen's film script for *Nosferatu*).

Nosferatu, in Lotte M. Eisner, *Murnau*. Frankfurt: Kommunales Kino, 1979, 389-615. (This is the facsimile of the original script by Henrik Galeen with hand-written notes by F.W. Murnau).

Nosferatu. Edited by Michel Bouvier and Jean-Luc Leutrat. Paris: Gallimard, 1981. (A sourcebook containing the script, reviews, and historical documents in French translation)

Nosferatu, eine Symphonie des Grauens. Edited by Arnold, Loy, Michael Farin, and Hans Schmid. Munich: Belleville Verlag, 2000. (This book includes frame enlargements of the tinted copy of *Nosferatu* as restored by Enno Patalas.)

Remakes/Adaptations

Nosferatu: Phantom der Nacht. Directed by Werner Herzog. Werner Herzog Filmproduktion, 1979.

Nosferatu. A Novel. Jim Shepard. New York: Alfred A. Knopf, 1998.

Shadow of the Vampire. Directed by E. Elias Merhige. BBC, 2000.

Nosferatu. Music track composed by Del Rey and the Sun Kings. 2007.

Secondary Literature

Abbott, Stacey. *Celluloid Vampires: Life after Death in the Modern World*. Austin: University of Texas Press, 2007.

———. "Spectral Vampires: *Nosferatu* in the Light of New Technology." In *Horror Film: Creating and Marketing Fear*, Steffen Hantke, ed., 3–20. Jackson: University Press of Mississippi, 2004.

Ashbury, Roy. *F. W. Murnau's "Nosferatu."* London: York Press, 2001.

Auerbach, Nina. *Our Vampires, Ourselves*. Chicago: University of Chicago Press, 1995.

Brennan, Matthew C. "Repression, Knowledge, and Saving Souls: The Role of the 'New Woman' in Stoker's *Dracula* and Murnau's *Nosferatu*." *Studies in the Humanities* 19, no. 1 (June 1992): 1–10.

Bronfen, Elisabeth. "The Vampire: Sexualizing or Pathologizing Death." In *Disease and Medicine in Modern German Cultures*, Rudolf Käser and Vera Pohland, eds., 71–90. Ithaca, NY: Center for International Studies, Cornell University, 1990.

Calhoon, Kenneth S. "Leinwand: Zur Physiognomie des Raums in Murnaus *Nosferatu*." In *Raumkonstruktionen in der Moderne*, Sigrid Lange, ed., 289–97. Bielefeld: Aisthesis Verlag, 2001.

———. "F. W. Murnau, C. D. Friedrich, and the Conceit of the Absent Spectator." *Modern Language Notes* 120, no. 3 (April 2005): 633–53.

Callens, Johan. "Shadow of the Vampire: Double Takes on *Nosferatu*." In *Intermediality in Theatre and Performance*, Freda Chapple and Chiel Kattenbelt, eds., 195–205. Amsterdam: Rodopi, 2006.

Cardullo, Bert. "Expressionism and *Nosferatu*." *San Jose Studies* 11, no. 3 (October 1985): 25–33.

Catania, Saviour. "Absent Presences in Liminal Spaces: Murnau's 'Nosferatu' and the Otherworld of Stoker's 'Dracula.'" *Literature/Film Quarterly* 32 (2004): 229–36.

Combes, André. "Un cliché et sa destruction: Le *Nosferatu* de Murnau." *Germanica* 3 (1988): 9–29.

Dalle Vacche, Angela. "Murnau's *Nosferatu*: Romantic Painting as Horror and Desire in Expressionist Cinema." *Post Script: Essays in Film and the Humanities* 14, no. 3 (July 1995): 25–36.

Eisner, Lotte M. *Murnau*. London: Seecker and Warburg, 1976.

———. *Murnau*. Frankfurt a.M.: Kommunales Kino, 1979

Elsaesser, Thomas. "Six Degrees of *Nosferatu*." *Sight and Sound* 11, no. 2 (February 2001): 12–15.

Exertier, S. "La lettre oubliée de *Nosferatu*." *Positif* 228 (March 1980): 47–51.

Franklin, James C. "Metamorphosis of a Metaphor: The Shadow in Early German Cinema." *German Quarterly* 53, no. 2 (March 1980): 176–88.

Gelder, Ken. *Reading the Vampire*. London: Routledge, 1994.

Göttler, Fritz. *F. W. Murnau: Nosferatu*. Munich: Kulturreferat der Landeshauptstadt München, 1987.

Gunning, Tom. "To Scan a Ghost: The Ontology of Mediated Vision." *Grey Room* 26 (Winter 2007): 95–127.

Hensley, Wayne E. "The Contribution of F.W. Murnau's *Nosferatu* to the Evolution of Dracula." *Literature/Film Quarterly* 30, no. 1 (2002): 59–64.

Hogan, Patrick Colm. "Narrative Universals, Nationalism, and Sacrificial Terror: From *Nosferatu* to Nazism." *Film Studies: An International Review* 8 (July 2006): 93–105.

Hurka, Herbert M. *Filmdämonen: Nosferatu, das Alien, der Terminator und die anderen*. Marburg: Tectum Verlag, 2004.

———. "*Nosferatu*: Ein Immigrant aus Rumänien." *Journal Film* 32 (Winter 1998): 36–47.

King, Claire Sisco. "Imaging the Abject: The Ideological Use of the Dissolve." In *Horror Film: Creating and Marketing Fear*, Steffen Hantke, ed., 21–34. Jackson: University Press of Mississippi, 2004.

Koller, Michael. "*Nosferatu (eine Symphonie des Grauens)*." *Senses of Cinema* 8 (July–August 2000), http://www.sensesofcinema.com/contents/cteq/00/8/nosferatu.html.

Lefebvre, Thierry. "Les metamorphoses de *Nosferatu*." *1895* 29 (December 1999): 61–77.

Luhr, William. "*Nosferatu* and Postwar German Film." *Michigan Academician* 14, no. 4 (April 1982): 453–58.
Mayne, Judith. "Dracula in the Twilight: Murnau's *Nosferatu* (1922)." In *German Film and Literature: Adaptations and Transformations*, Eric Rentschler, ed., 25–39. New York: Methuen, 1986.
Michaels, Lloyd. "*Nosferatu*, or the Phantom of the Cinema." In *Play It Again, Sam: Retakes on Remakes*, Andrew Horton, Stuart Y. McDougal, and Leo Braudy, eds., 239–49. Berkeley: University of California Press, 1998.
Mittermayr, Florian, and Stefan Barth. "Grauenvolle Symphonie + Nächtlicher Phantomfilm? Ein Medialaugenschein." *Maske und Kothurn: Internationale Beiträge zur Theaterwissenschaft* 43, no. 4 (1997): 49–56.
Müller, Jürgen. "Der Vampir als Volksfeind: Friedrich Wilhelm Murnaus '*Nosferatu*': Ein Beitrag zur politischen Ikonografie der Weimarer Zeit." *Fotogeschichte* 19, no. 72 (1999): 39–58.
Nosferatu Issue. *Avant-Scene du Cinéma* (Paris), no. 228, 1979.
Papapetros, S. "Malicious Houses: Animation, Animism, Animosity in German Architecture and Film—From Mies to Murnau." *Grey Room* 20 (Fall 2005): 6–37.
Patalas, Enno. "On the Way to *Nosferatu*." *Film History: An International Journal* 14, no. 1 (2002): 25–31.
Perez, Gilberto. *The Material Ghost: Films and Their Medium*. Baltimore: Johns Hopkins University Press, 1989.
———. "*Nosferatu*." *Raritan: A Quarterly Review* 13, no. 1 (July 1993): 1–29.
Prawer, S. S. *Nosferatu—Phantom der Nacht*. London: British Film Institute, 2004.
Prodolliet, Ernest. *Nosferatu: Die Entwicklung des Vampirfilms von Friedrich Wilhelm Murnau bis Werner Herzog*. Freiburg: Universitätsverlag, 1980.
Rickels, Laurence A. *The Vampire Lectures*. Minneapolis: University of Minnesota Press, 1999.
Roth, Lane. "Dracula Meets the 'Zeitgeist': *Nosferatu* as Film Adaptation." *Literature/Film Quarterly*, no. 4 (1979): 309-13.
———. "Film, Society and Ideas: *Nosferatu* and the Horror of Dracula." In *Planks of Reason: Essays on the Horror Film*, Barry Keith Grant, ed., 245–54. Metuchen, NJ: Scarecrow Press, 1984.
Ruttner, Clemens. "Vampirische Schattenspiele: Friedrich Wilhelm Murnaus *Nosferatu—Eine Symphonie des Grauens*" (1922). In *Der Vampirfilm*, Stefan Keppler and Michael Will, eds., 29–54. Würzburg: Königshausen and Neumann, 2006.
Schlüpmann, Heide. "Der Spiegel des Grauens: Murnau's *Nosferatu*." *Frauen und Film* 49 (December 1990): 38–51.
Silver, Alain, and James Ursini. *The Vampire Film: From* Nosferatu *to* Interview with the Vampire. New York: Limelight Editions, 1997.
Skal, David J. *Hollywood Gothic: The Tangled Web of* Dracula *from Novel to Stage to Screen*. New York: W. W. Norton, 1990.

Smith, Evans Lansing. "Framing the Underworld: Threshold Imagery in Murnau, Cocteau, and Bergman." *Literature/Film Quarterly* 24, no. 3 (July 1996): 241–54.

Tulloch, John. "Narrative/Structure/Ideology in Murnau's *Nosferatu*." *Australian Journal of Screen Theory* 5–6 (January–July 1979): 138–62.

Unrau, Rona. "Eine Symphonie des Grauens or the Terror of Music: Murnau's *Nosferatu*." *Literature/Film Quarterly* 24, no. 3 (July 1996): 234–40.

Waller, Gregory A. *The Living and the Undead: From Stoker's Dracula to Romero's Dawn of the Dead*. Urbana: University of Illinois Press, 1986.

Webber, Andrew J. "On the Threshold to/of Alterity: *Nosferatu* in Text und Bild." In *Schwellen: Germanistische Erkundungen einer Metapher*, Nicholas Saul et al., eds., 333–48. Würzburg: Königshausen and Neumann, 1999.

Williams, Andrew P. 1996. "The Silent Threat: A (Re)viewing of the 'Sexual Other' in *The Phantom of the Opera* and *Nosferatu*." *Midwest Quarterly: A Journal of Contemporary Thought* 38, no. 1 (October 1996): 90–101.

Wood, Robin. "Burying the Undead: The Use and Obsolescence of Count Dracula." *Mosaic: A Journal for the Interdisciplinary Study of Literature* 16, no. 1–2 (Winter–Spring 1983): 175–87.

Die Nibelungen

Credits

Director: Fritz Lang; Production: Decla-Bioscop/Universum-Film AG (Ufa); Script: Thea von Harbou; Design: Otto Hunte, Erich Kettelhut, Karl Vollbrecht; Cinematography: Carl Hoffmann, Günther Rittau; Animation: Walther Ruttmann; Original Music: Gottfried Huppertz; Cast: Paul Richter as Siegfried; Margarethe Schön as Kriemhild; Hanna Ralph as Brunhild; Theodor Loos as King Gunther; Hans Adalbert Schlettow as Hagen Tronje; Bernhard Goetzke as Volker von Alzey. — First Screening at the Ufa-Palast am Zoo in Berlin on February 14, 1924 (First part: *Siegfried*); April 26, 1924 (Second part: *Kriemhilds Rache/Kriemhild's Revenge*).

Sources

Thea von Harbou. *Das Nibelungenbuch*. Munich: Drei Masken Verlag, 1924.

Die Nibelungen. (First part: *Siegfried*; second part: *Kriemhilds Rache*) 1924 screenplay in typescript at the Stiftung Deutsche Kinemathek, Berlin.

Remakes/Adaptations

Die Nibelungen. Directed by Harald Reinl. CCC Filmkunst, 1966–67.

Die Nibelungen, television miniseries. Directed by Uli Edel. Broadcast in the U.S. under the title *Dark Kingdom: The Dragon King*. Tandem Communications, 2004.

Siegfried. Directed by Sven Unterwaldt. Constantin Film Produktion, 2005.

Secondary Literature

Bratton, Susan Power. "From Iron Age Myth to Idealized National Landscape: Human-Nature Relationships and Environmental Racism in Fritz Lang's *Die Nibelungen*." *Worldviews: Environment, Culture, Religion* 4, no. 3 (2000): 195–212.

Breitmoser-Bock, Angelika. *Bild, Filmbild, Schlüsselbild: Zu einer kunstwissenschaftlichen Methodik der Filmanalyse am Beispiel von Fritz Langs* Siegfried. Munich: Schaudig/Bauer/Ledig, 1992.

Göttler, Fritz. *Fritz Lang: Die Nibelungen*. Munich: Kulturreferat der Landeshauptstadt München, 1986.

Hake, Sabine. "Architectural Hi/Stories: Fritz Lang and *The Nibelungs*." *Wide Angle* 12, no. 3 (1990): 38–57.

Hauer, Stanley R. "The Sources of Fritz Lang's *Die Nibelungen*." *Literature/Film Quarterly* 18, no. 2 (1990): 103–10.

Heller, Heinz-B. "'Man stellt Denkmäler nicht auf den flachen Asphalt': Fritz Langs *Nibelungen*-Film." In *Die Nibelungen. Ein deutscher Wahn, ein deutscher Alptraum: Studien und Dokumente zur Rezeption des Nibelungenstoffs im 19. und 20. Jahrhundert*, Joachim Heinzle and Anneliese Waldschmidt, eds., 351–69. Frankfurt am Main: Suhrkamp, 1991.

Kaes, Anton. "Der Mythos des Deutschen in Fritz Langs Nibelungen-Film." In *Deutsche Meister—böse Geister? Nationale Selbstfindung in der Musik*, Hermann Danuser and Herfried Münckler, eds., 326–43. Schliengen: Edition Argus, 2001.

———. "Siegfried: A German Film Star Performing the Nation in Lang's *Nibelungen* Film." In *The German Cinema Book*, Tim Bergfelder, Erica Carter, and Deniz Göktürk, eds., 63–70. London: British Film Institute, 2002.

Kiening, Christian, and Cornelia Herberichs, eds. "Fritz Lang: *Die Nibelungen* (1924)." In *Mittelalter im Film*, Christian Kiening and Heinrich Adolf, eds., 189–225. Berlin: de Gruyter, 2006.

Levin, David J. *Richard Wagner, Fritz Lang, and the* Nibelungen*: The Dramaturgy of Disavowal*. Princeton, NJ: Princeton University Press, 1998.

Renz, Tilo. "Remaking Is Regendering: Notions of Loyalty in the Nibelungen Films by Fritz Lang, Harald Reinl, and Uli Edel." In *Gendered Memories: Transgressions in German and Israeli Film and Theater*, Julia B. Köhne and Vera Apfelthaler, eds., 160–78. Vienna: Turia + Kant, 2007.

Stiles, Victoria M. "Fritz Lang's Definitive *Siegfried* and Its Versions." *Literature/Film Quarterly* 13, no. 4 (1985): 258–74.

———. "The Siegfried Legend and the Silent Screen: Fritz Lang's Interpretation of a Hero Saga." *Literature/Film Quarterly* 8, no. 4 (1980): 232–36.

Winkler, Martin M. "Fritz Lang's Mediaevalism: From *Die Nibelungen* to the American West." *Mosaic: A Journal for the Interdisciplinary Study of Literature* 36, no. 1 (2003): 135–46.

Wirwalski, Andreas. *Wie macht man einen Regenbogen? Fritz Langs Nibelungenfilm: Fragen zur Bildhaftigkeit des Films und seiner Rezeption*. Frankfurt am Main: Lang, 1994.

Metropolis

Credits

Director: Fritz Lang; Production: Universum-Film AG (Ufa); Script: Thea von Harbou; Design: Otto Hunte, Erich Kettelhut, Karl Vollbrecht; Cinematography: Karl Freund, Günther Rittau; Original Music: Gottfried Huppertz; Cast: Brigitte Helm as Maria; Alfred Abel as Joh Fredersen; Gustav Fröhlich as Freder Fredersen; Rudolf Klein-Rogge as Rotwang; Fritz Rasp as the Thin Man; Theodor Loos as Josaphat. — First Screening at the Ufa-Palast am Zoo in Berlin on January 10, 1927.

Sources

Fröhlich, Gustav. *Waren das Zeiten: Mein Film-Heldenleben*. Munich: Herbig, 1983.

Harbou, Thea von. *Metropolis*. Berlin: August Scherl, 1927. Reprint, with afterword by Herbert W. Franke, Frankfurt am Main: Ullstein, 1984.

———. *Metropolis*. Anonymous English translation. London: Hutchison, 1927. Reprinted, Norfolk: Donning Company Publishers, 1988.

Lang, Fritz. *Metropolis. Classic Film Scripts*. London: Lorrimer Publishing, 1973. Reprinted, London: Faber and Faber, 1989.

Remakes/Adaptations

Metropolis. Re-edited "Moroder version" (80 min.) with modern soundtrack by Giorgio Moroder, featuring Pat Benetar, Freddie Mercury, Bonnie Tyler, et al. 1984.

Madonna. "Express Yourself," music video. Directed by David Fincher. 1989.

Metropolis, musical. Directed by Jerome Savary. Music by Joe Brooks and Dusty Hughes. London, 1989.

Metropolis. Directed by Osamu Tezuka. Sony, 2001.

Secondary Literature

Ackeren, Robert van. "Wie ein Klassiker zum Video-Clip getrimmt wird." In *Der alte Film war tot*, Hans Helmut Prinzler and Eric Rentschler, eds., 272–75. Frankfurt am Main: Verlag der Autoren, 2001.

Benesch, Klaus. "Technology, Art, and the Cybernetic Body: The Cyborg as Cultural Other in Fritz Lang's *Metropolis* and Philip K. Dick's *Do Androids Dream of Electric Sheep?*" *Amerikastudien/American Studies* 44, no. 3 (1999): 379–92.

Bertellini, Giorgio. "Restoration, Genealogy, and Palimpsests: On Some Historiographical Questions." In *Fritz Lang's* Metropolis: *Cinematic Visions of Technology and Fear*, Michael Minden and Holger Bachmann, eds., 140–57. Rochester, NY: Camden House, 2000.

Biro, Matthew. "The New Man as Cyborg: Figures of Technology in Weimar Visual Culture." *New German Critique* 62 (1994): 71–110.

Brodnax, Mary. "Man a Machine: The Shift from Soul to Identity in Lang's *Metropolis* and Ruttmann's *Berlin*." In *Peripheral Visions: The Hidden Stages of Weimar Cinema*, Kenneth S. Calhoon, ed., 73–93. Detroit: Wayne State University Press, 2001.

Byrne, Deirdre C. "The Top, the Bottom, and the Middle: Space, Class, and Gender in *Metropolis*." *Literator: Tydskrif vir Besondere en Vergelykende Taal- en Literatuurstudie/Journal of Literary Criticism, Comparative Linguistics, and Literary Studies* 24, no. 3 (2003): 1–14.

Clark, Jill. "Scientific Gazing and the Cinematic Body Politic: The Demonized Cyborg of *Metropolis*." *Intertexts* 3, no. 2 (1999): 168–79.

Cornils, Ingo. "Problems of Visualisation: The Image of the Unknown in German Science Fiction." In *Text into Image: Image into Text*, Jeff Morrison and Florian Krobb, eds., 287–95. Amsterdam: Rodopi, 1997.

Cowan, Michael. "The Heart Machine: 'Rhythm' and Body in Weimar Film and Fritz Lang's *Metropolis*." *Modernism/Modernity* 14, no. 2 (2007): 225–48.

Dadoun, Roger. "*Metropolis*: Mother-City—'Mittler'—Hitler." Translated by Arthur Goldhammer. *Camera Obscura: A Journal of Feminism, Culture, and Media Studies* 15 (1986): 137–63.

Desser, David. "Race, Space, and Class: The Politics of Cityscapes in Science-Fiction Films." In *Alien Zone II: The Spaces of Science-Fiction Cinema*, Annette Kuhn, ed., 80–96. London: Verso, 1999.

Dolgenos, Peter. "The Star on C. A. Rotwang's Door: Turning Kracauer on Its Head." *Journal of Popular Film and Television* 25, no. 2 (Summer 1997): 68–75.

Dover, Julia. "The Imitation Game: Paralysis and Response in Fritz Lang's *Metropolis* and Contemporary Critiques of Technology." In *Fritz Lang's* Metropolis*: Cinematic Visions of Technology and Fear*, Michael Minden and Holger Bachmann, eds., 272–85. Rochester, NY: Camden House, 2000.

Eisner, Lotte H. *Fritz Lang*. Translated by Gertrud Mander, David Robinson, ed. Oxford: Oxford University Press, 1977.

Elsaesser, Thomas. "Innocence Restored? Reading and Rereading a 'Classic.'" In *Fritz Lang's* Metropolis*: Cinematic Visions of Technology and Fear*, Michael Minden and Holger Bachmann, eds. 123–39. Rochester, NY: Camden House, 2000.

———. *Metropolis*. London: British Film Institute, 2000.

Feldberg, Sonia, and Erika Engstrom. "Societal Relationships in the Film *Metropolis*: Portrayal of Tönnies' *Gemeinschaft and Gesellschaft*." *Popular Culture Review* 10, no. 1 (1999): 157–65.

Fliethmann, Axel. "Die Ähnlichkeit der Theorie des Bildes. Anmerkungen zu Fritz Langs und Rintaros *Metropolis*." In *Schriftlichkeit und Bildlichkeit: Visuelle Kulturen in Europa und Japan*, Ryozo Maeda, Teruaki Takahashi, and Wilhelm Vosskamp, eds., 149–66. Munich: Fink, 2007.

Frank, Gustav. "Turm Babel-Kathedrale-Andreïde: poetologische Denk-Gebäude/-Figuren im *Metropolis*-Komplex von Thea von Harbou und Fritz Lang." In *Abweichende Lebensläufe, poetische Ordnungen*, Thomas Betz and Volker Hoffmann, eds., 445–78. Munich: Kieser, 2005.

Gehler, Fred, and Ullrich Kasten. *Fritz Lang, die Stimme von Metropolis*. Berlin: Henschel, 1990.

Geser, Guntram. *Fritz Lang:* Metropolis *und* Die Frau im Mond*: Zukunftsfilm und Zukunftstechnik in der Stabilisierungszeit der Weimarer Republik.* Meitingen: Corian-Verlag H. Wimmer, 1996.

———. "Innovation und Anachronismus: Fritz Lang und die Kluft zwischen Filmtechnik und Stummfilmschauspiel gegen Ende der zwanziger Jahre." *TheaterZeitSchrift: Beiträge zu Theater, Medien, Kulturpolitik* 35 (1993): 109–17.

Gösta, Werner. "Fritz Lang und Goebbels: Myths and Facts." *Film Quarterly* 43 (Summer 1990): 24–27.

Hales, Barbara. "Fritz Lang's *Metropolis* and Reactionary Modernism." *New German Review: A Journal of Germanic Studies* 8 (1992): 18–30.

Higley, Sarah L. "A Taste for Shrinking: Movie Miniatures and the Unreal City." *Camera Obscura* 16 (2001): 1–35.

Huyssen, Andreas. "The Vamp and the Machine: Technology and Sexuality in Fritz Lang's *Metropolis*." *New German Critique* 24–25 (1981): 221–37.

Jacobsen, Wolfgang, and Werner Sudendorf, eds. *Metropolis: Ein filmisches Laboratorium der modernen Architektur/Metropolis: A Cinematic Laboratory for Modern Architecture*. Stuttgart: Menges, 2000.

Jelinek, Elfriede. "Ritterin des gefährlichen Platzes." *Meteor* 11 (1997): 3–16.

Jordanova, Ludmilla. "Science, Machines, and Gender." In *Fritz Lang's* Metropolis*: Cinematic Visions of Technology and Fear*, Michael Minden and Holger Bachmann, eds., 173–97. Rochester, NY: Camden House, 2000.

Kaes, Anton. "Cinema and Modernity: On Fritz Lang's *Metropolis*." In *High and Low Cultures: German Attempts at Mediation*, Reinhold Grimm and Jost Hermand, eds., 19–35. Madison: University of Wisconsin Press, 1994.

———. "Metropolis: City, Cinema, Modernity." In *Expressionist Utopias*, Timothy O. Benson, ed., 146–65. Los Angeles: LACMA, 1993.

———. "Movies and Masses." In *Crowds*, Jeffrey T. Schnapp and Matthew Tiews, eds., 149–57. Stanford, CA: Stanford University Press, 2006.

Lang, Fritz, Hans von Harbou, et al. *Metropolis: Un Film de Fritz Lang: Images d'un Tournage*. Paris: Cinémathèque, 1985.

Leblans, Anne. "Inventing Male Wombs: The Fairy-Tale Logic of *Metropolis*." In *Peripheral Visions: The Hidden Stages of Weimar Cinema*, Kenneth S. Calhoon, ed., 95–119. Detroit: Wayne State University Press, 2001.

Lungstrum, Janet. "*Metropolis* and the Technosexual Woman of German Modernity." In *Women in the Metropolis: Gender and Modernity in Weimar Culture*, Katharina von Ankum, ed., 128–44. Berkeley: University of California Press, 1997.

Mahoney, Dennis F. "From *Caligari* to *Strangelove*: The German as (Mad) Scientist in Film and Literature." In *Analogon Rationis*, Marianne Henn and Christoph Lorey, eds., 419–32. Edmonton: University of Alberta Press, 1994.

Mellencamp, Patricia. "Oedipus and the Robot in *Metropolis*." *Enclitic* 5, no. 1 (1981): 20–42.

"*Metropolis*." In *Deutschlandstudien international 2: Dokumentation des Symposiums "Interkulturelle Deutschstudien. Methoden, Möglichkeiten und Modelle"*

Takayama/Japan 1990, Kenichi Mishima and Hikaru Tsuji, eds., 81–103. Munich: iudicium, 1992.

Milner, Andrew. "Darker Cities: Urban Dystopia and Science Fiction Cinema." *International Journal of Cultural Studies* 7, no. 3 (2004): 259–79.

Minden, Michael. "The City in Early Cinema: *Metropolis, Berlin*, and *October*." In *Unreal City: Urban Experience in Modern European Literature and Art*, Edward Timms and David Kelley, eds., 193–213. New York: St. Martin's, 1985.

———. "Fritz Lang's *Metropolis* and the United States." *German Life and Letters* 53, no. 3 (2000): 340–50.

Minden, Michael, and Holger Bachmann, eds. *Fritz Lang's* Metropolis*: Cinematic Visions of Technology and Fear*. Rochester, NY: Camden House, 2000.

Möbius, Hanno. "Symbolische Massendarstellungen in Fritz Langs *Metropolis*." In *Das Volk: Abbild, Konstruktion, Phantasma*, Annette Grczyk, ed., 31–45. Berlin: Akademie Verlag, 1996.

Morgan, Ben. "*Metropolis*—The Archetypal Version: Sentimentality and Self-Control in the Reception of the Film." In *Fritz Lang's* Metropolis*: Cinematic Visions of Technology and Fear*, Michael Minden and Holger Bachmann, eds., 288–309. Rochester, NY: Camden House, 2000.

Morris, Nigel. "*Metropolis* and the Modernist Gothic." In *Gothic Modernisms*, Andrew Smith and Jeff Wallace, eds., 188–206. Basingstoke, UK: Palgrave, 2001.

Neumann, Dietrich. "The Urbanistic Vision in Fritz Lang's *Metropolis*." In *Dancing on the Volcano: Essays on the Culture of the Weimar Republic*, Thomas W. Kniesche and Stephen Brockmann, eds., 143–62. Rochester, NY: Camden House, 1994.

Patalas, Enno. "The City of the Future—A Film of Ruins: On the Work of the Munich Film Museum." In *Fritz Lang's* Metropolis*: Cinematic Visions of Technology and Fear*, Michael Minden and Holger Bachmann, eds., 111–22. Rochester, NY: Camden House, 2000.

———. "*Metropolis*, Scene 103." Translated by Miriam Hansen. *Camera Obscura: A Journal of Feminism, Culture, and Media Studies* 15 (1986): 164–73.

Patalas, Enno, and Rainer Fabich. *Metropolis in/aus Trümmern: Eine Filmgeschichte*. Berlin: Bertz, 2001.

Pike, David L. "'Kaliko-Welt': The Großstädte of Lang's *Metropolis* and Brecht's *Dreigroschenoper*." *Modern Language Notes* 119, no. 3 (2004): 474–505.

Roth, Lane. "Metropolis, the Lights Fantastic: Semiotic Analysis of Lighting Codes in Relation to Character and Theme." *Literature/Film Quarterly* 6, no. 4 (Fall 1978): 342–46.

Ruppert, Peter. "Fritz Lang's *Metropolis* and the Imperatives of the Science Fiction Film." *Seminar: A Journal of Germanic Studies* 37, no. 1 (2001): 21–32.

Rutsky, R. L. "The Mediation of Technology and Gender: *Metropolis*, Nazism, Modernism." *New German Critique* 60 (1993): 3–32.

Sawyer, Andy. "More Than Metaphor: Double Vision in Lang's *Metropolis*." *Foundation: The Review of Science Fiction* 64 (1995): 70–81.

Segeberg, Harro. "Utopischer Funktionalismus: Zum Bild der Stadt in Fritz Langs Film *Metropolis*." In *Utopie und Krise*, Johannes Krogoll and Ivo Runtic, eds., 83–94. Zagreb: Abteilung für Germanistik der Philosophischen Fakultät der Universität Zagreb, 1993.
Shikina, Akiyoshi. "Schrift und Bild: Literarische Zukunftsentwürfe am Beispiel von *Metropolis*." In *Deutschlandstudien international* 2, Kenichi Mishima and Hikaru Tsuji, eds., 81–103. Munich: iudicium, 1992.
Smith, Susan. "*Metropolis*: Restoration, Reevaluation." *Cineaction* 66 (April 2005): 12–23.
Stoicea, Gabriela. "Re-Producing the Class and Gender Divide: Fritz Lang's *Metropolis*." *Women in German Yearbook: Feminist Studies in German Literature and Culture* 22 (2006): 21–42.
Strzelczyk, Florentine. "Maschinenfrauen-Sci-Fi Filme: Reflektionen über *Metropolis* (1926) und *Star Trek: First Contact* (1996)." In *Textmaschinenkörper: Genderorientierte Lektüren des Androiden*, Eva Kormann, Anke Gilleir, and Angelika Schlimmer, eds., 243–53. Amsterdam: Rodopi, 2006.
Telotte, J. P. "Just Imagine-ing the *Metropolis* of Modern America." *Science-Fiction Studies* 23, no. 2 (1996): 161–70.
———. "The Seductive Text of *Metropolis*." *South Atlantic Review* 55, no. 4 (1990): 49–60.
Thomson, Michael. "Reproductivity, the Workplace, and the Gendering of the Body." *Law and Literature* 14, no. 3 (2002): 565–94.
Trutnau, John-Paul. *Fritz Lang's Metropolis and Its Influence on the American Science Fiction Film: Blade Runner, Terminator I + II*. Essen: Blaue Eule, 2005.
Tulloch, John. "Genetic Structuralism and the Cinema: A Look at Fritz Lang's *Metropolis*." *Australian Journal of Screen Theory* 1 (1976): 3–50.
Vana, Gerhard. *Metropolis: Modell und Mimesis*. Berlin: Gebrüder Mann, 2001.
Webber, Andrew. "Canning the Uncanny: The Construction of Visual Desire in *Metropolis*." In *Fritz Lang's* Metropolis*: Cinematic Visions of Technology and Fear*, Michael Minden and Holger Bachmann, eds., 251–69. Rochester, NY: Camden House, 2000.
Wilczek, Reinhard. "Fritz Langs *Metropolis* und Ernst Jüngers *Der Arbeiter*: Aspekte des intermedialen Technik-Diskurses in der Weimarer Zeit." In *Ernst Jünger*, Lutz Hagestedt, ed., 445–57. Berlin: de Gruyter, 2004.
Williams, Alan. "Structures of Narrativity in Fritz Lang's *Metropolis*." In *Fritz Lang's* Metropolis*: Cinematic Visions of Technology and Fear*, Michael Minden and Holger Bachmann, eds., 161–71. Rochester, NY: Camden House, 2000.
Williams, Keith. "'Seeing the Future': Urban Dystopia in Wells and Lang." In *Urban Mindscapes of Europe*, Godela Weiss-Sussex and Franco Bianchini, eds., 127–45. Amsterdam: Rodopi, 2006.
Wollen, Peter. "Cinema/Americanism/The Robot." *New Formations* 8 (Summer 1989): 7–34.

Index